ANTICLO

The Psychedelic World of Tara King:
The Avengers on film: Volume 3

edited by Rodney Marshall

© Copyright 2014 Rodney Marshall
(Essays are individually owned by specific writers as indicated in the text)

About the editor

The son of *Avengers* script-writer Roger Marshall, Rodney Marshall has produced six books about this iconic 1960s television drama: *Subversive Champagne*, a study of the Emma Peel era; *Adventure & Comic Strip: Exploring Tara King's The Avengers*; *Making It New? A reappraisal of The New Avengers*; *Bright Horizons* (editor), a critical exploration of the monochrome Emma Peel season; *Mrs. Peel, We're Needed* (editor), an exploration of the colour Emma Peel season; and *Anticlockwise* (editor), examining the Tara King era. He lives in Suffolk and South West France.

The Avengers on film collection:
Bright Horizons (Volume 1: Emma Peel monochrome)
Mrs. Peel, We're Needed (Volume 2: Emma Peel colour)
Anticlockwise (Volume 3: Tara King)
Avengerland Regained (Volume 4: *The New Avengers*)
Avengerland Revisited (Volume 5: a thematic guide)

My thanks to Jaz Wiseman for designing the striking, psychedelic cover and for his (and *Optimum/Studio Canal*'s) enormous contribution to preserving *The Avengers*' history: restoring the magical images and capturing the artists' thoughts before they disappeared irretrievably.

My thanks to JZ Ferguson for once again offering advice, suggestions and sharing the proof-reading responsibilities.

"*The Avengers* is a wonderful example of avoiding the tyranny of common sense." (Robert Fuest, *Avenging the Avengers*, 1992)

"*The Avengers* weaved a tapestry of the everyday and the far away into a picture-postcard portrait of a Britain where there was always honey still for tea, where men wore bowlers and carried umbrellas, women were English roses and dressed to kill, where scientists and diabolical masterminds fiendishly plotted domination (of one form or another), and where the Churchillian war-time spirit was always, always pushed that bit further". (Matthew Lee)

"Evolution or extinction. It doesn't just refer to the animal kingdom. It is also vital in the ever-changing world of television drama...Stand still and you stagnate; innovate and you re-energise. The Tara King era offers living or visual proof that *The Avengers* was still capable of changing its structure, style and content as it entered what would prove to be the final stretch." (Rodney Marshall)

"We were in our own time and space, almost as if *The Avengers* took place on an island. It was marvellously unpredictable, full of serendipity and madness." (Linda Thorson, cited in *The Avengers: A Celebration*)

"Set designs became increasingly psychedelic, helping to lend the sixth series a unique identity. More than ever, Steed and his partner's missions resembled a surreal game". (Marcus Hearn, *The Avengers: A Celebration*)

"He likes his tea stirred anticlockwise." (Emma Peel to Tara King, *The Forget-Me-Knot*)

"Anticlockwise, James – always anticlockwise." (Charles Lather, *Super Secret Cypher Snatch*)

FOREWORD

Lew Grade's relentless juggernaut of productions under the ITC mantle had fed audiences in the 1960s a healthy banquet of glamour, danger and international locations, adding colour to a decade which boasted some of the most fertile creative soil British television and theatre was ever likely to witness. Enthusiasts of *Danger Man* to *Gideon's Way*, *Randall and Hopkirk (Deceased)* to *The Persuaders* have all cited the virtues of "putting money on screen" as being the critical credentials of ITC's hit rate, offering what amounts to popcorn television – readily consumable, basically inoffensive and likely to be a comfortable time spent after work for Joe and Jane Everyman.

Like Ian Fleming's 007, Grade's ITC productions tapped into a Cool Britannia zeitgeist, offering audiences a reaffirming glimpse of an indefatigable part of the Empire on which the sun hadn't set: cool spies and private eyes, international detectives and their glamorous companions, keeping the British end up and usually showing their American friends a thing or two along the way. Successful as these productions may well have been, however, their capacity to keep in tune with the shifting cultural sands of that zeitgeist were almost always thwarted. One-series-wonders fleshed out a healthy and inviting catalogue of programmes with high production values, potently good musical scores and a raft of international faces in leading and guest roles. Nevertheless, ITC was a vehicle constantly changing gear, drivers, bodywork and engine without getting to the end of the lane.

Meanwhile, *The Avengers* weaved a far more consistent tapestry of the everyday and the far away into a picture-postcard portrait of a

Britain where there was always honey still for tea, where men wore bowlers and carried umbrellas, women were English roses and dressed to kill, where scientists and diabolical masterminds fiendishly plotted domination (of one form or another), and where the Churchillian war-time spirit was always, always pushed that bit further.

The Avengers was (and remains) a masterpiece of how to do television well. Crafted from a basic formula (good versus bad), tweaked slightly to tap into changing times (women aren't always meek and feeble), and then infused with a quirkiness which takes a view askew to the everyday (a handy tool for the housewife is a warm gun; leather, slightly oiled, is essential attire for the woman on the go; bowler hats are quite a knock-out; umbrellas are handy weapons to seek-hate-kill; never play poker with a Joker; and never meet business rivals in Little Storping-in-the-Swuff), the series became a permanent fixed point in popular culture.

Constantly challenging and reinventing itself, *The Avengers* never sat still. Gritty realism one week could give way to delicious comedy the next; hard-edged villains in one episode could be a lunatic on the verge of a lethal encounter on the next visit to what was becoming a palpably unique landscape: *Avengerland*. Not a car in sight, seldom a bird in flight, the main players flit across the stage in a world of their own, mixing it up with national and international nasties and doing it with British flair and style. Across almost a decade, the programme told some of the most memorable – albeit offbeat and quirky – tales which have lived long and large in the memory and continue to do so. The relative constant was John Steed (Patrick Macnee), the ubiquitous debonair Man from the Ministry who always arrived after the event, ready to act and preparing to avenge. Accompanied initially by men of a professional connection (doctors), the series later tapped into the ever-changing world of the 1960s woman (emerging from a subservient role and becoming equal to, and occasionally better than, her male counterparts).

Honor Blackman blasted away the cobwebs and the kitchen sink as Cathy Gale. Steed's arrival and intrusion in her own life was always portrayed as something of an irritant, occasionally a diversion but more often than not an inconvenience. Diana Rigg's deliciously alluring Emma Peel became the iconic British beauty of the moment – an all-action woman who could fell a villain with a karate chop and still manage not to lose a drop from her glass of champagne. As *The Avengers* unfolded across their tenure, the storylines drifted away from the more commonplace intrigue settings which were standard ITV and BBC fare and moved further into the recesses of the *Avengerland* landscape and world their writers had steadily crafted.

By 1968, Canadian actress Linda Thorson had joined a series which was very firmly established as 'out there'. For some critics, the programme was becoming tired and formulaic and offering little that had not already been seen before. Problems behind the scenes weren't helping to keep the series on an even keel, and in re-inventing itself one final time (under the able and capable stewardship of legendary creative forces Brian Clemens and Albert Fennell), some could accuse the programme of preparing to cater for jumping sharks.

However, the sixth and final season of the original run of *The Avengers* was, if anything, a beautifully abstract denouement for a programme which challenged audiences to enjoy art beyond the ordinary. Pushing the envelope that little bit further will always render some episodes as more successful than others, but the style and tone of the show itself remained constant, there was always a familiar "Ah, that's definitely *The Avengers*" feel to what was being presented and, on a few occasions, even a variation on a predictable theme could still produce a damnably entertaining hour in the coolest of company.

As the 1960s drew to a close, the diabolical masterminds of commercial television were still able to seduce viewers to the dark side of the dial with the simple promise of guaranteed escapism with *The Avengers*, a series which always prided itself on being far away from the everyday.

© Matthew Lee

CONTENTS

Preface (pages 16-23)
Introduction (24-30)

The Forget-Me-Knot by Dan O'Shea (31-40)

The Invasion of the Earthmen by Piers Johnson (41-48)

The Curious Case of the Countless Clues by Darren Burch (49-59)

Split! by Mark Saunders (60-69)

Get- A-Way! by Mark Saunders (70-80)

Have Guns – Will Haggle by Dan O'Shea (81-89)

Look – (stop me if you've heard this one) But There Were These Two Fellers... by Frank Hui (90-101)

My Wildest Dream by Darren Burch (102-113)

Whoever Shot Poor George Oblique Stroke XR40? by Matthew Lee (114-125)

All Done With Mirrors by Frank Shailes (126-138)

You'll Catch Your Death by Sam Denham (139-147)

Super Secret Cypher Snatch by Rodney Marshall (148-158)

Game by Richard Cogzell (159-167)

False Witness by Rodney Marshall & Sam Denham (168-181)

Noon Doomsday by Rodney Marshall (182-191)

Legacy of Death by Margaret J Gordon & Matthew Lee (192-219)

They Keep Killing Steed by JZ Ferguson (220-229)

Wish You Were Here by Piers Johnson (230-239)

Killer by Rodney Marshall (240-248)

The Rotters by Matthew Lee (249-265)

The Interrogators by Matthew Lee (266-281)

The Morning After by Frank Hui (282-288)

Love All by Rodney Marshall (289-298)

Take Me To Your Leader by Frank Hui (299-305)

Stay Tuned by Richard Cogzell (306-313)

Fog by Sunday Swift (314-323)

Who Was That Man I Saw You With? by JZ Ferguson (324-333)

Pandora by Rodney Marshall (334-342)

Thingumajig by Frank Shailes (343-355)

Homicide and Old Lace by Darren Burch & Bernard Ginez (356-372)

Requiem by Piers Johnson (373-382)

Take-Over by Margaret J Gordon (383-394)

Bizarre by Matthew Lee (395-413)

'Words of One Syllable: The Failures of the Tara King Era' by Lauren Humphries-Brooks (414-422)

Afterword by JZ Ferguson (423-430)
Contributors (431-434)
Quotations Glossary (435-483)
Season 6 Production Order (484-485)
Bibliography (486-487)

PREFACE

My 2013 book *Adventure & Comic Strip* covered every single episode of the Tara King season, but the chapters offered brief, fleeting guides. This third volume of *The Avengers on film* celebrates the variety of creative approaches taken in Season 6 while exploring and examining each hour in far greater depth. The title *Anticlockwise* is lifted from the crossover episode *The Forget-Me-Knot* as Rigg/Peel and Thorson/King pass each other for the only time in the story. Originally, it was intended that they would say nothing to each other, but Brian Clemens changed his mind. Emma advises Tara that Steed likes his tea stirred "anticlockwise". We rarely see Steed drinking tea in the series, but *The Avengers* usually takes a leftfield, anticlockwise approach to television drama and this final season was, arguably, the most experimental of them all: psychedelic, surreal and — in the words of Linda Thorson — "marvellously unpredictable, full of serendipity and madness."

As was the case in *Bright Horizons* and *Mrs. Peel, We're Needed*, I have assembled a group of expert *Avengers* fans/critics in order to offer as wide a range of ideas and approaches as possible. Critical commentary or non-linear analysis, each chapter tackles a single episode. In *Anticlockwise* we welcome back most of the people who contributed to the earlier volumes; in addition, we have two 'new' writers on board: Mark Saunders and Matthew Lee. Mark wrote to me as an enthusiastic reader of the first volume; he found himself being asked to join the team and write a couple of chapters. His writing reveals both expertise and humour. Matthew has provided the Foreword, as well as chapters on five specific episodes. His passion for and knowledge of British television and film is remarkable. Matthew's 'all-inclusive' commentaries brim with wit and intelligence, even if they continually break my 3,000 word rule!

Piers Johnson's review of *Invasion of the Earthmen* highlights the lack of avengerish touches in some of the early season episodes made in the brief John Bryce era. He isn't alone in thinking that some of these lack the high writing and production quality we associate with *The Avengers*. His chapter on *Wish You Were Here* reflects on what is, arguably, both a *Prisoner*-esque spoof but also an opportunity missed, in terms of what the episode could have offered. Piers' essay on *Requiem* celebrates this fascinating, darker episode and its clever self-referentiality. He draws parallels with Clemens' Season 5 classic *Epic* and argues that *Requiem* is a significant film in this final season.

Darren Burch's study of *The Curious Case of the Countless Clues* explores the episode in the light of the early season production changes and conflicts. He examines the extent to which Clemens and Levene manage to fulfil the criteria of 'thicker cardboard' characters. Intriguingly, he suggests that Tara plays Mother for much of the episode. His exploration of *My Wildest Dream* examines Robert Fuest's debut as an *Avengers* director as well as offering a glowing tribute to Philip Levene as he left the show after writing nineteen of the filmed episodes. Volunteering for the (thankless?) task of analysing *Homicide and Old Lace*, Darren explores how the original Bryce-produced episode and Clemens' added framework simply don't gel. Would it have worked better to simply stick with the original script? "As charming as the framework can be at times, it never lets us into the proper story. The real Great Great Britain Crime is that we'll probably never be able to see the original footage and make up our own minds about the episode."
Bernard Ginez – one of the French webmasters – offers a positive mini-review of this maligned episode, arguing that it represents a humourously satirical swipe at the Bryce era and a fitting homage to Mother. A shortened version of his essay has already created a

storm on the French *Avengers* website! His controversial review appears here both in translation and in its original form.

JZ Ferguson's chapter on *Who Was That Man I Saw You With?* centres its attention on Tara's character and the ways in which it has developed and 'thickened' since the early season episodes. She also examines how writer Jeremy Burnham twisted the over-used scenario of Steed as a potential traitor, this time allowing the female Avenger to be exposed and investigated as a possible double agent. Her chapter on *They Keep Killing Steed* sees this witty episode as, in some respects, a fore-echo of *The New Avengers*, a topic also covered in her Afterword.

Margaret J Gordon's chapter on *Take-Over* offers a daring, psychoanalytical reading of this disturbing episode, in which she reads Circe as a female Jack the Ripper who 'rapes' her victims by placing implants into their necks. She also explores the ways in which the content mirrors American network ABC's killing off of the series and EMI's takeover of the rights of *The Avengers*, two acts which took place around the time the shooting-script was being completed. Her exploration of *Legacy of Death* examines the episode both as *film noir* parody and tootsie lollipop: "The colour episodes sugar-coated and disguised the many deeper messages that the monochrome era more clearly exposed."

Matthew Lee's chapter on *Whoever Shot Poor George Oblique Stroke XR40?* explores the ways in which even 'standard' episodes can offer us a 'superior' product. He demonstrates how writer and director are able to "take something ordinary and make it extraordinary." His exploration of *The Rotters* both highlights and celebrates the importance of the darkly comic mastermind and/or his henchmen in *The Avengers*. Matthew sees it as one of the final season's highlights: "Comedy and surrealism are fused into a priceless work of art". His exploration of *The Interrogators* examines how scriptwriters Brian Clemens and Richard Harris combine to present "a tale not too far from *The Professionals* and *The New Avengers*. As the world emerged from the 1960s into the grittier and harsher brown light of the 1970s, this sort of content would become the order of the day." Matthew's chapter on *Legacy of Death* shares common ground with Margaret J Gordon's but their different approaches and styles make it a fascinating comparison. Matthew sees this episode as "a rare attempt to imitate a product of the ordinary world beyond the extraordinary which was *Avengerland*. As with *The Winged Avenger* before it, this truly was the real world knocking on the door for a guest appearance in a world populated by dashing heroes, beautiful heroines and the most diabolically upper-crust villains." *Bizarre* is placed within the context of the season and the series as a whole. Lee suggests that in common with *Doctor Who*, *The Avengers* represents a "perfect" work of art which has become "interwoven in the cultural fabric of the period; scarcely can one be mentioned without the other."

Frank Hui's chapter on *Look – (stop me if you've heard this one) But There Were These Two Fellers...*explores this opinion-dividing episode within the context of the Tara King era as a whole. He highlights the irony that it "represented the turning point where the show would diverge radically away from the format laid out during the Emma Peel period" yet is, arguably, "the Tara King episode that most closely resembles the structure of an Emma Peel adventure." His chapter on *Take Me to Your Leader* explores how this episode engages with both *Mission: Impossible* and the seven deadly sins. *The Morning After* is examined through the one-off partnership of Steed and Merlin. Hui suggests that "in a way the two are very much alike, but having taken different paths. Steed's agitation with

Merlin may partly stem from looking into a dark mirror he would prefer not to gaze at."

Sunday Swift's chapter on *Fog* examines the episode's critical reception, places it within the series' context, examines the problematic, changed role of Steed in Season 6 and explores *Fog*'s rich intertextuality, looking at how it connects with both the Ripper murders and other fictional re-workings of the serial killings.

The Forget-Me-Knot was covered in *Mrs. Peel, We're Needed* by two contrasting essays written by myself and Sunday Swift. Wisely deciding not to read these before writing his own chapter, **Dan O'Shea** has written a balanced essay in which he explores the departing and arriving characters in an episode which is not a classic, except for its historical significance. Dan's chapter on *Have Guns-Will Haggle* explores the successful use of a black actor in a main *Avengers* role. He wonders how bad the original 90 minute episode must have been if it really was worse than the (deemed acceptable) *Invasion of the Earthmen*. He also assesses the success of both Linda Thorson and Tara King in this early episode.

Mark Saunders' chapter on *Split!* explores some of the plot holes in Brian Clemens's script, as well as suggesting ways in which the writer and director could have added the necessary subtlety and mystery to raise it above the mediocre. At the same time, employing lyrics from the *Human League* – "...you know your worst is better than their best" – he states that "even the less-than-popular episodes are still head and shoulders over most other series, then and now." His chapter on *Get-A-Way!* explores our 'timeless' fascination with invisibility, and examines both the 'fantastic' plot and the powerful performance of guest actor Peter Bowles.

Richard Cogzell's chapter on *Game* explores the visual appeal of an episode in which both the locations and the sets sparkle. It is these, allied to Linda Thorson's growing confidence in her role, which are seen as the episode's key ingredients. His exploration of *Stay Tuned* examines its fascinating *déjà vu* structure; he sees the story as illustrating the dazzling diversity of the Tara King season.

Frank Shailes' chapter on *Thingumajig* places the episode within the context of science fiction writer Terry Nation's body of work and explores both the strengths and weakness of this much-maligned story. His chapter on *All Done With Mirrors* celebrates this iconic episode's ability to liberate Tara King/Linda Thorson and offer a visually memorably hour with stunning locations and innovative direction.

Sam Denham's exploration of *You'll Catch Your Death* explores Jeremy Burnham's conversion from *Avengers* guest actor to writer, in addition to the effective use of central London location filming. Sam's chapter on another Burnham episode, *False Witness*, draws on his private correspondence with the writer. It celebrates the inverted, psychedelic *Avengerland* which Burnham creates.

My own chapters explore six contrasting episodes. *Noon Doomsday* engages with the Western genre and combines disturbing drama with parody and surrealism. I see this Nation/Clemens hybrid as revolutionary, one of the highlights of the season. *Killer* resurrects an Emma Peel-like character, mischievously tempting us to make a choice between two contrasting types of Avenger: "The contrast between the two women couldn't be greater and the producers are clearly asking us to draw comparisons and possibly even make a choice of preferred female lead." *Super Secret Cypher Snatch* is an episode which often slips under the critic or fan's radar, yet "in many ways epitomises Season 6 at its best: witty, fast-paced action adventure offering viewers a thrilling ride." My chapter explores precisely what it is that makes this story stand out. *Love All* is explored as a typically witty Jeremy Burnham script. "Burnham's vision of *Avengerland* fits the psychedelic Tara King era perfectly...It is, arguably, his episodes which best capture the new spirit of the show, with affluent London street footage and witty drug-related plots in which the real and surreal playfully merge." This certainly applies to Burnham's *False Witness* which offers us a visual feast, not least the master-stroke of Mother's Routemaster bus, an *Avengers* version of *Doctor Who*'s Tardis. *Pandora*, in some respects, is an unavengerish film which contains a strangely hypnotic and sinister subtlety, an episode which offers us a genuinely disturbing psychological thriller. The six episodes illustrate the plurality of vision let loose in the final season.

Once again, each chapter is prefaced by a 'factual' double page covering fictional locations/sets and characters. Neither list is exhaustive; they are simply meant to provide rough guides. Some minor characters have been left out and I have no doubt that a number of the locations were actually studio sets and vice versa.

I invited **Lauren Humphries-Brooks** to write an essay on the 'failures' of the Tara King season in order to offer us a vital balancing act. Most of the episode chapters in *Anticlockwise* are written by fans of the Tara era. While no one paints a 'perfect picture' of this uneven season, this volume also requires the thoughts of critics – such as Sunday and Lauren – who are not fans of Season 6. After all, this is a 33 episode run which divides opinion to an unprecedented extent. Lauren poses powerful questions which need to be considered and digested as we reassess the season. As a reader, I'd be tempted – in true anticlockwise fashion –

to start with Lauren's essay and JZ Ferguson's Afterword before reading the episode chapters. They offer a fascinating contrast.

The endnotes which appear after each chapter are my own as editor. In each case contributors were able to read these and respond before going to press. Individual episode titles appear in italics – rather than in inverted commas – to highlight the one-off filmic nature of each one and its treatment in these four volumes.

There has been some questioning by readers of my use of 'season' rather than 'series' to define each era or run of The Avengers. After all, in the UK each vintage was originally called a 'series'. However, given that the show, in its entirety, is a television *series*, I prefer to use the more clearcut or unambiguous term 'season', and it seems to naturally fit the idea of a programme which was constantly changing.

"Until the boom of the home video market in the 1980s, television tended to be regarded as an ephemeral medium, like theatre, rather than a more lasting art form, such as cinema." (Richard McGinlay, *The Strange Case of the Missing Episodes*)

Thankfully this is no longer the case and this series of books dedicated to *The Avengers* on film celebrates each episode's film-like qualities, its glorious art form. With 2014 representing the 50th anniversary of *The Avengers* on film there is no better moment to celebrate the show.

© Rodney Marshall
Suffolk, UK
10th December 2014

INTRODUCTION

Evolution or extinction. It doesn't just refer to the animal kingdom. It is also vital in the ever-changing world of television drama. Evolution does not necessarily mean progress or improvement; it merely indicates change. One of the secrets to *The Avengers*' longevity was 'making it new'. Elements of this constant change were forced on the show, with the departure of lead actors, directors, etc. However, the production team also needs to be given some credit for this. The decision to replace Dr. Keel with a woman – initially inheriting a man's lines – instantly added a revolutionary twist to the evolution. The emergence of Emma Peel and the freedom of 35mm monochrome film represented further evolutionary steps, along with the film era's new vision of what Sam Denham terms 'elegant escapism'. 'Glorious Technicolor' added a further ingredient, encouraging a more cartoonish, wilder, bizarre *Avengerland* to become firmly established. However, with Diana Rigg having departed and definite signs of 'formula fatigue' *The Avengers* needed another creative rethink.

Stand still and you stagnate; innovate and you re-energise. The Tara King era offers living or visual proof that *The Avengers* was still capable of changing its structure, style and content as it entered what would prove to be the final stretch. [1]

"I think it's time to go back to femininity. We've had all the leather business – the new girl will essentially be a woman. She will be soft with all the female weaknesses – and attributes." (John Bryce, *The Daily Mail*, October 1967)

John Bryce's comments are controversial, raising all manner of questions. Wasn't Emma Peel 'feminine'? Do 'soft' and 'weak' represent positive aspects of a female Avenger? The reference to 'leather business' suggests that Bryce hadn't seen much of Season 5 as Rigg/Peel only wore a leather cat-suit once in the entire 24 episode run. Tara King is self-evidently a very different character to Emma Peel. Despite the two production teams – Bryce/Clemens [2] – undermining young actress Linda Thorson's confidence with a bewildering range of character traits, fashion styles, wigs etc., what slowly emerges is a character who offers a fresh angle to the Steed/female partner dynamic. [3] She is naïve and doting – lacking Emma Peel's intellectually cynical, 'canted' eye – but she is also brave and physical, a genuine action girl. As her performance in *All Done With Mirrors* demonstrates, Thorson has a tomboyishly sexy energy which she brings to the series. Steed now takes on a new, almost paternal role as protector/instructor. He soon drops the formal 'Miss King' for 'Tara', informality unthinkable in either the Cathy Gale or Emma Peel eras. However, it suits their more tactile working relationship. Some fans and critics bemoan King's lack of 'cool independence' when compared to Gale or Peel. Others respond positively to her natural warmth and hands-on fighting style. She lacks Emma Peel's cerebral elegance but offers a new energy, allowing *The Avengers* to evolve yet again, after fifty episodes of the Steed/Peel partnership.

The creation/emergence of Mother as a boss arguably takes away some of the show's element of mystery but it adds a revolutionary aspect to the tired formulaic structure. He breaks up the familiar dual lead pattern, creating a triptych structure in the episodes he appears in, as well as providing a dry British male humour. The ever-changing headquarters sets also create a new element to the structure, one which is constantly shifting. In many ways these one-off locations take the place of the 'Mrs. Peel, we're needed' post-teaser scenes which were dropped (during the mid-season break in the colour Peel era) at the request of the US ABC network. Part of the pleasure of the Tara era is waiting to discover the latest 'impossibly innovative' HQ location: down a manhole, through a telephone box, under water or on a London Routemaster bus. Sometimes these are cleverly thematically-linked to the episode, such as the plastic furniture in *The Rotters*. The silent Rhonda is also an effective addition. She adds a surreal humour and is a fascinatingly playful non-speaking character.

There would still be a number of 'well-made but formulaic' episodes in Season 6; once again an enjoyable episode such as *The Rotters* springs immediately to mind. Nevertheless, the writers began to experiment far more with other genres as *The Avengers* playfully engages with hardboiled fiction, Western films, rival television shows and Victorian Gothic horror among others. Just as *The Hour That Never Was* and *Epic* had threatened to deconstruct the series' formula in the previous filmed seasons, groundbreaking episodes such as *Stay Tuned* and *Requiem* offer innovative, revolutionary highlights in this final season. Amidst the 'candy-coloured' *Avengerland*, there are also some genuinely disturbing psychological thrillers such as *Pandora* and *Take-Over*. Indeed, the 'thicker cardboard' of some of the guest characters allows *The Avengers* to provide depth to relationships where the Peel colour era had simply drawn quick cartoons. In Season 6, once again victims are often friends of Steed but now their relationships are firmly established, as is the case in the memorable all-night party at Steed's mews apartment in *Get-A-Way!*

The use of a dozen writers and even more directors helped to provide a variety of spectacle arguably lacking in the previous season. There is even experimentation with the lead characters, Jennifer Croxton (Lady Diana Forbes-Blakeney) replacing Thorson/King in *Killer*, a reluctant/handcuffed Peter Barkworth (Jimmy Merlin) teaming up with Steed in *The Morning After*, while Ian

Ogilvy (Baron Von Curt) shows what a younger male partner might offer in the delightful *They Keep Killing Steed*.

The sets are ever more innovative and daring: the board games in *Game*, the mannequin factory bus in *Killer*, the book-lined entrance to Rosemary Glade's romantic fiction 'factory', the mastermind's quarry headquarters in *They Keep Killing Steed* and the giant nose in *You'll Catch Your Death* are all glorious highlights. The location filming – in *All Done With Mirrors* and *Noon Doomsday* for example – offers more visual delights away from the studio. A Home Counties ranch under attack, Tara's coastal cliff edge fall, a woodland hunt for multiple Steeds, an atmospherically deserted 'ghost' town; we even get car chases in central London.

If Steed and Mrs. Peel's apartments were almost characters in their own rights in Seasons 4 and 5, Tara King's takes this a giant step further. In *Adventure & Comic Strip* I described her apartment in the following terms:

"Our first glimpse of Tara King's apartment reveals a set designed for action, from its two separate entrances, its 'frilly' white twisting staircase with room to hide underneath, to a fireman's pole one just knows will be employed on a regular basis. It resembles an **indoor adventure playground**. In addition, there is an eclectic collection of aesthetic objects: a pair of spectacle-shaped mirrors, a penny farthing attached to the wall, a post box (drinks cabinet), some bizarre telephones, loud floral curtains with matching sofa, psychedelic stag heads mounted on a pink background, and a collection of daggers. We can already guess that some of these will become 'active' props in future episodes. (These accessories would be playfully altered as the season went on, as is the case in *Have Guns – Will Haggle* with the bizarre, ugly, porcelain heads bearing Tara's wigs.) Its owner will be less cool and refined than Emma Peel, but younger and funkier, perhaps." (*Adventure & Comic Strip*, p. 17)

Michael Richardson's *Bowler Hats and Kinky Boots* informs us that it was Brian Clemens who asked production designer Robert Jones to create a set which would offer a mirror-image of its owner's personality. Tara's Primrose Hill pad reflects her dynamic, all-action urban character and forces us to scan the space each time we visit, looking for subtle changes, wondering which prop will 'come alive' and become an active participant in the storyline. I would go as far as to describe this set as a key element in the overall success of Season 6. Clemens' initial idea and Jones' vibrant execution were both faultless. Steed's Stable Mews also becomes a key location in the season, atmospherically filmed in episodes such as *The Forget-Me-Knot* and *Get-A-Way!* The exterior scenes, shot at both locations, add a three-dimensional feel to our Avengers' homes.

The revamped title music and new opening credits also reflect the series' latest evolution:

"The Suits of Armour opening credits warn us to expect a strange, playful *Avengerland* in which rational explanations will not always be possible. The first thing we see is a group of still life objects on the ground, including the obligatory bowler hat. However, the subsequent images are oddly surreal. A field of mannequin knights, their colourful plumes moving in the breeze, appear to represent the enemy. Steed defends himself with a shield against an unseen attack, before knocking a knight down simply by pointing his umbrella. Meanwhile, Tara King runs through a doorway prop in the field. If this seems alien to us, then the red carnations and the familiar, iconic Tykes Water Lake Bridge which Tara runs across offer familiar connections with the Peel era." (*Adventure & Comic Strip*, p. 14) [4]

As I suggested in my own Tara King book, Season 6 is anything but a dull endgame from a terminally-ill patient. It is spectacularly uneven as a collective body of thirty-three episodes, but it certainly reignited *The Avengers* formula in the final moments of this original – in both senses of the word – drama series.

Some fans of the show cannot abide this sixth season, dismissing it out of hand because they see Tara King as a weak character and Linda Thorson as a poor replacement for the (irreplaceable) Diana Rigg. As I've stated before, there is no doubt that Rigg was the best actor/actress in the show's 161 episode run. However, she had decided to move on, and so did *The Avengers*. The following chapters celebrate the bewildering variety of the Tara era, warts and all.

© Rodney Marshall

1. Whether we should count *The New Avengers* as a new series or an extension of an existing one is debatable. Nevertheless, this five volume series of books considers it to be a legitimate part of the show's history. Personally, I feel very strongly that it *should* be included as an important final 'chapter' in *The Avengers* legacy.
2. An executive decision was taken to replace both Brian Clemens and Albert Fennell with video-tape era producer John Bryce. We will never know the exact nature of what went on – or wrong – under Bryce's brief command. Amidst production chaos, a pressing US episode deadline to meet and rumours that Patrick Macnee was considering quitting the show, Clemens was soon asked back to take charge. Season 6 sees a constant conflict between a desire to continue taking *The Avengers* to artistic extremes and an interest in returning the show to a more realistic Gale-era world. This was not simply a John Bryce/Brian Clemens ideological polarity as the artistic tension remains in place throughout the season. Ironically, sometimes this conflict produced exciting, radical episodes which playfully move between the two extremes.

3. It is not just Thorson/King who suffers from the end-of-decade's dubious fashions. John Steed/Patrick Macnee's former monochrome elegance is sometimes undermined in Season 6 with a number of loud, floral and patterned shirts which – like the late-Sixties sideburns – simply don't suit him. The French website *Le Monde des Avengers* suggests that Steed's former good taste suffers from these "garish" and sometimes "psychedelic" shirts, describing them as one of the most "irritating features" of the show. In the Peel era Emma had been 'unfashionably fashionable' while Steed's wardrobe reflected his anachronistic character; here there is an attempt to make him look 'trendy' too. In my opinion, Steed looks better in black and white, in more 'timeless' attire.
4. In the United States the initial seven episodes were seen with the 'shooting gallery' opening and closing titles; in the UK, where all 33 Tara King episodes were aired as a single season, with the exception of *The Forget-Me-Knot* and *Split!* it was the field of armour opening credits which were used. (*The Forget-Me-Knot* had modified Emma Peel opening credits while *Split!* used the shooting gallery ones.) *The New Avengers* titles would suffer from a similar crisis of identity a few years later.

THE FORGET-ME-KNOT

Filmed: January 1968

Exterior Locations:
Stable Mews
Mother's headquarters: entrance gate, grounds
Glasshouse works exterior
Country lanes
Tara King's street

Sets:
Glasshouse factory
Steed's mews apartment
Mother's headquarters: corridors, waiting room, office
Worpleton cottage hospital: bedroom
Tara King's apartment

THE FORGET-ME-KNOT

Main Character List:
Sean Mortimer: agent
Karl: biker henchman
Taxi driver
John Steed
Emma Peel
Brad: biker henchman
Giles: gardener at Mother's headquarters
George Burton: agent trainer, double agent
Tara King: Agent 69
Jenkins: works for Mother at headquarters
Simon Filson: works for Mother
Mother: Organisation's boss
Dr. Soames: at the cottage hospital
Nurse: at the cottage hospital

Ah...there they are in Steed's apartment. Steed's mixing some drinks while Mrs. Peel's working a crossword puzzle. Could there be a more typical beginning to a Peel era *Avengers* episode? *The Forget-Me-Knot*, of course, turns out to be anything but typical. It's the only episode in the series that bridges two eras and it contains the series' most emotional scene. The pure entertainment value of this Brian Clemens episode, with its hackneyed plot and forgettable guest characters, is almost non-existent. *The Forget-Me-Knot*, filmed concurrently with another Season 6 episode, *The Curious Case of the Countless Clues*, is primarily a vehicle both for explaining the departure of Mrs. Peel *and* introducing Tara, Mother and, perhaps slightly less importantly, Steed's sideburns.

The Departure of Mrs. Peel. Diana Rigg was contractually obligated to do two more episodes after the final Season Five episode, *Mission...Highly Improbable*, but came back for just this one and actually spent only four days on it. Prior to the tag scene, her role in this episode is a thankless one involving amnesia-inducing darts, captivity, and being paired scene after scene with arguably the most tedious character the series has ever seen, Sean Mortimer. She spends the episode in a holding pattern, waiting for the tag scene.

Even so *The Forget-Me-Knot* manages to be a treasure trove of scenes that might be telling us about the true nature of the relationship between Steed and Mrs. Peel. I use the word 'might' because there is always the recurring dilemma about what the real intentions are of the *Avengers* writers (particularly Clemens) when they create certain scenes. The viewer can't help but wonder sometimes whether he or she is reading too much into them. This dilemma crops up here and there throughout the series but really comes to a head in this episode. [1]

Take for example the scene in which Mrs. Peel, while suffering the effects of amnesia, is breaking bottles and chanting "he loves me…he loves me not…he loves me…" and suddenly starts seeing fleeting visions of Steed. Is Clemens saying in this scene that Mrs. Peel is able to recall Steed through word association – that the words "he loves me" trigger her memory of Steed? It's impossible to say with certainty but it does seem reasonable to think that is what he might be doing here. The scene where Steed, also suffering from amnesia, sees visions of a smiling Mrs. Peel when he looks at the nurse and at Tara could be saying that for Steed Mrs. Peel is the embodiment of the fairer sex. Is Clemens consciously and deliberately revealing to us (albeit indirectly) that Steed and Mrs. Peel are lovers? Or is he just trying to fill up the allotted fifty minutes with some interesting looking but not particularly well thought out or meaningful scenes? It is hard to say. The recollections of the people involved with the show are so contradictory – these folks not only contradict each other, they often contradict even themselves – that we unfortunately aren't able to get a definitive answer to the 'are they lovers?' question from any of them. We are, instead, left to decide for ourselves what we want to believe and this just adds to our fascination with these two characters. It is another example of how *The Avengers* defies any attempt to be put into a nice neat box.

A less ambiguous scene is the one where Mrs. Peel whispers something in Steed's ear and he smiles and responds "I'm afraid so". It's hard to tell what she whispers but it is obviously something sexually suggestive. "Are you the man who dallies with me?" seems to be the best guess. [2] This scene, their final one together before the tag scene, is a wonderful example of the Steed/Mrs. Peel chemistry: witty, elegant, and sexy, but with an undertone of genuine feeling for each other.

There is also a small moment in the tag scene that is a completely unambiguous indication that they are lovers. Steed's line "He's picking you up here?" and the way he delivers it, with a questioning tone in his voice as to the wisdom of it, would make no sense if they are just good friends. If their relationship is strictly platonic then it would be perfectly natural that Peter Peel would come to Steed's place to pick up his wife. Mrs. Peel would have introduced them to each other and Steed would have offered Peel a drink. Instead, Mrs. Peel just nods her head anxiously in answer to his question. It could also be surmised that Mrs. Peel, always a straight shooter, has Peter pick her up at Steed's for a reason — to prepare him for what she must tell him about the relationship she has had with Steed while he was away.

This dilemma of whether we read too much into *The Avengers* is also very much present when we look at a couple of other things in the tag scene. Why did they portray Peter Peel as a clone of Steed? Is Clemens (or the director James Hill) saying that Steed and Peter Peel are basically interchangeable? That Steed was a mere stand-in for Mrs. Peel's dear departed husband? If so, the slap in the face to Steed (and those of us who cherish him) is inexcusable. The only alternative explanation is that they are making a little throw-away joke to lighten the atmosphere after the heart-breaking goodbye scene. Shame on them either way! And speaking of shame, what were they thinking when they dressed up Tara for her part in the tag scene to look like a hooker?

As to the goodbye scene — if you've led a full life you've at some point in it been there yourself, on both sides of the coin — the leaver and the leavee. You know that it is an excruciating painful experience for both. She (Mrs. Peel or Diana Rigg, take your pick) clearly feels terrible. The sorrow in her eyes is genuine. It makes it all the harder that they both know that in reality she does have a choice; she could leave Peter Peel for Steed but chooses not to. As I've discussed in my chapter on *Return of the Cybernauts* in the previous book in this series (*Mrs. Peel, We're Needed*) my theory is that Mrs. Peel, although caring deeply for Steed, had been getting restless and was looking for a graceful way to leave both him and the crime fighting game. She knows full well how badly she is hurting Steed but she also knows that she would be doing him no favour if she stayed for the sole reason of not wanting to hurt him.

Mrs. Peel is fortunate that the leavee is someone like Steed. The man has to be devastated but he is so proud and gallant that she is in no danger of facing any long, drawn-out guilt inducing conversations. Steed didn't invent the stiff upper lip but he does show how it should be utilised. His matter-of-fact call to Mother about getting him a replacement ("You know my taste") would be incredibly callous if it weren't merely an attempt to paper over this tragedy with false bravado. I'm sure it didn't fool Mother.

So Mrs. Peel leaves with her husband – what would the rest of her life be like? We care because of the unforgettable character that Diana Rigg has created and that we have had the privilege of viewing for fifty episodes. [3] Once again we are running the risk of reading too much into something in *The Avengers*, but what Rigg did with this character is truly remarkable. She plays this beautiful, intelligent, regal yet warm hearted and fun loving woman so effortlessly and she is at the same time able to suggest a depth to this character that went well beyond the scripts. [4]

We do know, thanks to *The New Avengers* episode *K is for Kill: The Tiger Awakes*, that she doesn't stay married to Peter Peel. That's not too surprising; she didn't seem all that happy about his return and the look she turns to give Steed while they're driving away is like that which a naughty teenage girl would give to a disreputable boy her dad had caught her with as her dad is angrily driving her home. It didn't bode well for Mr. Peel. Like Tara King, he has a very tough act to follow.

The most likely scenario for the rest of Mrs. Peel's life is that she spends it living alone, fiercely independent, pursuing her varied and diverse interests one after another until each one bores her, at which time she moves on to the next one. She never runs out of new interests and this quicksilver woman never belongs to anyone but herself.

The Introduction of Tara King and Mother. It is fitting that it took two people to fill the void created by the departure of the iconic Mrs. Peel. There simply isn't any one person who could have been anything but a disappointment, particularly in the chemistry department. This is a bit of an oversimplification, but it could be said that Tara and Mother split Mrs. Peel's duties, Tara providing the 'eye candy' and Mother providing the banter.

Tara's first scene is somewhat prophetic. In it she enthusiastically and athletically takes a man down who, unfortunately, proves to be the wrong one. Enthusiasm, athleticism and goofiness – just what one would expect from a twenty year old girl thrown into the situation Linda Thorson (as Tara King) found herself in as the replacement for the irreplaceable Mrs. Peel. We learn right from the start that Tara is no Mrs. Peel. That's actually not a bad thing. It was wise on the part of the *Avengers* decision makers to make no attempt to go with some kind of Mrs. Peel clone. [5] There is no such thing. The character Tara King is a complete departure not only from the Mrs. Peel mould but also from the mould of all of Steed's previous partners. Dr. Keel, Mrs. Gale, and Mrs. Peel are all formidable, fully-formed adults. Tara is not. She's very much a novice in every way. [6]

What does Linda Thorson bring to the role? To start with she certainly carries on the *Avengers* female tradition by being another stunning beauty. Her buxom figure has already been extoled by many but her beautiful face is not as well appreciated as it should be, perhaps due to the silly wigs she sometimes wears. The scene where her head is wrapped in a bath towel showcases just how beautiful Linda Thorson's face actually is. Miss Thorson also brings to the role some considerable comedic talent. Her self-depreciating wit, so different from her predecessors' 'acid Chelsea' wit, makes her very likeable, if not exactly iconic. Her reaction when she realises that the "single-handed death grip" she has on Steed is going to fail is a wonderful example of the type of humour we see from her throughout her tenure.

As to Mother, the idea that Steed and partner have a boss and operate within the constraints of a visible organisation is a big and unwelcome step backwards from the breeziness of the Peel era in which our heroes, in their hazily defined partnership, just seem to show up at the crime scene and go from there. This really added to the charm of the series. [7] The audience got it – there was never any need to explain the organisational structure. There was still no need to in Season 6 but there was a need to add a character that Steed could interact with as an equal, someone to exchange some of that 'witty banter' with. Macnee has said that at first he wasn't happy with the idea of adding this character but the fact that Patrick Newell was selected for the role made it easier to accept. I think we can agree with him. Newell is a big guy with a big personality and he does prove to be entertaining as he adeptly matches wits with Steed.

We are also introduced to the Season 6 version of John Steed in *The Forget-Me-Knot*. John Steed is now a firmly established legend. The agents at Mother's place salute him. He's come a long way from his rascally days in Season 1 to this point. And Macnee himself needs to shoulder a bigger load now. He has always been an unselfish actor who made everyone around him look better but he is now working with a much younger and much less accomplished actress. He has to make his bumbling new partner seem to be a credible agent and he has to play his flirtation scenes with this girl – young enough to be his daughter – in such a way that he doesn't come across as a dirty old man. As always, this under-rated actor comes through this minefield with flying colours. As to those who would laugh at Steed's new sideburns, I would caution you (if you were around in those days) to ponder the biblical admonition, "Judge not lest ye be judged!" [8]

The Forget-Me-Not, although banal and just plain boring for long stretches, is certainly in no danger of being forgotten. It introduces the Tara King era that, if judged on its own merits (and not as a comparison to the previous era), successfully provides plenty of entertaining television. It also brings to a close the magical Peel era. The bleakness on Steed's face as he turns away from the window after watching Mrs. Peel drive away is truly unforgettable. It mirrors the dismay that the fans feel as they realise that they will never see this wonderful woman again.

© Dan O'Shea

1. As in a novel, play, painting etc., I think the viewer is perfectly entitled to 'read against the grain', adding his/her own interpretation, regardless of the artist's original intentions.
2. This is certainly the line suggested on David K Smith's wonderful *The Avengers Forever!* website by experts who used audio analysis equipment to sample the sound during Emma's whisper.
3. 51 if we include this one!

4. Dan's comment mirrors my suggestion in a previous volume that it was Diana Rigg's acting ability which made the character of Emma Peel outstanding, not vice versa.
5. It also fits in with *The Avengers*' constant evolution: Dr. Keel to independent female co-lead Cathy Gale; the often frosty Gale to the 'cooler warmth' of Emma Peel; surreal monochrome to candy colour; 'canted eye', almost cynical Emma to naïve, doting action girl Tara.
6. Of course, unlike all the previous partners – 'talented amateurs' – she is a professional agent.
7. I agree with Dan. It added a magical mystery to the Peel era.
8. Sorry, Dan, but like the webmasters on *Le Monde des Avengers*, I think that the sideburns are truly awful and a disservice to Steed's sartorial elegance.

INVASION OF THE EARTHMEN

Filmed: November 1967

Exterior Locations:
Country hotel
Country lanes
Alpha Academy: front gate, driveway, courtyard, main building, grounds

Sets:
Alpha Academy: boundary fence, quarry (survivor area), corridors, Commander's office, cryo-biology room, cellar, tunnel, ventilator shaft
Tara King's apartment
Country hotel: guest bedroom
John Steed's mews apartment

INVASION OF THE EARTHMEN

Main Character List:
Grant: agent
Trump: AA student
Emily: AA student
Sarah: AA student
Tara King
John Steed
Huxton: AA student
Bassin: AA student
Brigadier Brett: AA commander

A Tale of Two Taras

Invasion of the Earthmen starts well enough: a spy cuts through a fence and spies on some oddly fascist youth but it quickly goes downhill when he is then attacked by a very unconvincing boa constrictor. The youths laugh nastily at his unlikely predicament as we freeze for the opening titles.

Steed drops in on Tara, who is practising her judo. In a touch of long-winded humour, he advises her to always try to throw her opponent through a plate glass window. [1] Sadly, our first sight of Tara in close-up is out of focus. The script too, has a jarring note; we are clearly being introduced to the Tara King character, despite this being screened mid-season as Clemens cast about for anything he could use to get them back on track for the extremely tight production schedule. Strangely, the scene where mid-season Tara goes to 'put on her disguise' to become Bryce-era Tara, with blonde hair, maintains the tyro spy angle, possibly because the rest of the script had too much of it to ignore.

They investigate the disappearance of Steed's colleague, Grant, and discover the prospectus for a nearby elite school, The Alpha Academy, hidden in his luggage. Tara recalls that the Land Rover outside bears the school's logo: they are being watched. They drive to the Academy, escorted by a posse of officious youths and are admitted to the office of the 'headmaster', Brigadier Brett, which they soon discover is electrocuted to prevent snooping.

They tell Brett that they want their son to remain in England while they're posted abroad (Tara claims to be John's second wife when the commander raises his eyebrows). This ruse is wholly unconvincing, both to us as an audience and to the characters. The dialogue has them deliberately make slip-ups. Is it deliberate? Are they out of character? It's hard to judge.

On their way out, Steed tries to investigate the school by pretending to take a wrong turn. While he's doing that, Tara stumbles into a classroom and sees an inflated astronaut floating around a chamber full of stars. One of the students knocks her out before she can investigate further.

Brigadier Brett demands that they be followed and Steed, driving a modern sports car later handed over to Tara, manages to lose them in an uncharacteristic car chase. This is another opportunity for Clemens to explain Tara's blonde hair, as she removes the wig in the car.

Brett instructs two of his leading students to go out on 'survival' – they are to hunt each other down; only one is to return alive. Steed and Tara return under cover of darkness but the fence is monitored so they're detected straight away. They find the grounds filled with traps and deadly animals and split up, Tara searching the grounds while Steed breaks into the house. Steed certainly gets the best of it!

Steed searches the house, finding a cryogenically frozen student, hilariously named Felicity Hardwood. The scene is ruined as Don Sharp gets the camera angle wrong to make the most of the false perspective in the set. Steed then locates 'The Tunnel', another training facility where students are forced to face their deepest fears, and he steals a map of it. There is a terrible shot where the camera jerkily pans and zooms in on the sign on the door: another example of either slipshod production or overly tight deadlines.

Meanwhile, Tara is trapped when the astronaut appears, using a metal detector to find her. She flings the wire cutters away just in the nick of time; barely able to move due to the scorpion perched on her hand. She flings that away as well once the astronaut has gone and flees. She then happens across the two survival students and prevents the murder of one of them, but the boy she has rescued fires an arrow at her for her effort. She escapes them but is captured when she returns to the car for her *rendez-vous* with Steed.

Back at the house, Brett interrogates her in finest megalomaniac style – he tells her all of his plans for galactic domination with an army of cryogenically frozen astronaut warriors, while learning little from her. (This is one of the original scenes as it's very clear that Linda Thorson's hair is bleached rather than it being a wig).The script is marvellously optimistic here, with Tara declaring it won't happen for at least fifty years – that would be 2015 and we're nowhere near space travel like that yet!

This is a Terry Nation script, so you can expect the usual obsession with neo-Nazis, world domination, psychological warfare and space; in fact, parts of it remind me of the *Blake's Seven* episode *Duel*.

Brett, as over-confident as any Bond villain, gives Tara a 60 second head start over his students and she manages to escape into The Tunnel. The Tunnel is a weak plot device, subsequently put to much better use by George Lucas. It is supposed to be a chamber full of horrors to try the mettle of the student, but the execution of the concept is amateurish. It has rats running in shallow water, a metal tube that seals at both ends into which spiders descend, a slippery ramp, and a long pool of acid. I don't think I've missed anything except an empty cavern with an opportunity for escape.

Now, I daresay I would be greatly disturbed if I were made to crawl through a metal tube in the dark and spiders started dropping into it, but it does not make for good television. There is no real attempt to heighten the tension, bar the in-joke of reusing music from *The Fear Merchants*. The spiders are dreadfully fake – you can see them being pushed over the edge to drop, and you can see the square edge of the supposedly round tube seal when Tara heaves it open.

Steed has also entered The Tunnel from the other end, poking ahead with a stick. He sets off a man trap which chops the stick in two, giving him the opportunity for trademark humour. "Might as well have it all", he jokes, and tosses away the remains. He and Tara meet in the middle, trapped by two squads of students. Steed produces the map and they escape through a ventilation shaft then proceed to seal the students inside. Brett is then easily taken care of and *The Avengers* return to Steed's flat for some more judo practice, Tara now back in mid-season garb but still acting the tyro. In all, a disappointing episode that is an example of wasted opportunity.

A major problem with this episode are the props and general set design; it's as though we're watching a different show, as the production values are so low compared to the previous season. Unfortunately, with a script as tenuous as this one, you need every chance to suspend disbelief and the utterly unconvincing terrors within 'The Tunnel' do nothing to achieve this. There are a few nice sets such as the stone spike trap and the cryogenic chamber but the quarry and tunnel sets are horribly false. [2]

John Bryce had returned as producer of *The Avengers* for this season and this is one of three episodes he managed to make before he was replaced by the previous producers, late in 1967. This episode resembles one of the cheaper production-line ITC series like *The Champions*, as do the other remnants of Bryce's tenure. Producing television on film in 1967 bears little relation to doing so on videotape in 1962!

Terry Nation's plot is weak: an elite public school run along quasi-military lines is training its students to be astronaut warriors for an epic galactic battle far in the future, cryogenically freezing them so they'll be at their peak when needed. Perhaps it's only weak in retrospect as fifty years later we are no nearer extended space exploration. Certainly, little is made of the subject matter and the set pieces are like a school play. [3]

On top of these two failings, the "That'll do" approach to filming is unforgiveable. Poor camera angles, over-use of zoom, badly panned or framed shots, out of focus sequences. All of these ought to have been picked up by the director when reviewing the rushes, or by the editor who would have either sent the crew out for pick-up shots or re-edited the footage to cut them out. Upon reflection, much of this may be due to this being an abandoned episode, resurrected out of necessity. Unforgiveable lapses such as seeing the unfinished edge of a prop should never occur.

I will declare that I am a biased reviewer; I love *The Avengers* and can usually find something good about every episode. This, however, embarrasses me and while I can see some merit to it, I would never make anyone else watch it.

© Piers Johnson

1. I wonder whether this was meant to echo the fencing duel which introduced Emma Peel in *The Town of No Return*. If so, the scene – like the episode – is far less stylish.
2. Unlike in Season 5, where a number of sets/locations are deliberately artificial-looking in order to highlight the show's move towards self-conscious art, here they simply look badly made.

3. The episode simply isn't avengerish enough in terms of atmosphere, wit or theme. *Have Guns – Will Haggle* is a far better Bryce/Clemens salvage operation.

THE CURIOUS CASE OF THE COUNTLESS CLUES

Filmed: January 1968

Exterior Locations:
Burgess' house: drive, grounds
Tara King's street and apartment
Country lanes
Scott's cottage: drive, grounds
Flanders' house: gated entrance
Earle's cottage and grounds

Sets:
Dawson's apartment
Tara King's apartment
Burgess' house: billiard room
Gardiner's car
Flanders Finance Corporation: lobby, lift, underground car park
Flanders' house: study, stable, hall
Garage
Earle's cottage: hall, living room
Steed's car
Telephone box

THE CURIOUS CASE OF THE COUNTLESS CLUES

Main Character List:
Earle: blackmailer
Gardiner: Earle's assistant
Reginald Hubert Dawson: 'a man of no importance'
Tara King: wheelchair-bound
John Steed
Sir Arthur Doyle: detective
Sir William Burgess: cabinet minister and industrialist
Robert Flanders: financier
Stanley: fake mechanic
Scott: ex-employee of Flanders
Janice Flanders: sister of Robert, ex-flame of Steed

The Curious Case of the Countless Clues
...or *A Murderous Connection*

With this episode, it was all change behind the scenes. One man's crumbling vision was rejected and replaced by the previous vision. With the ousting of Brian Clemens and Albert Fennell, John Bryce, a 'whizzkid' from the early videotape days of the show, was given the Season 6 producer's job. Bryce's hiring would indicate that the executives at ABC (or Thames as it was becoming) had a desire to take the series back to its supposed roots. As a script editor and then producer, Bryce saw through the ground-breaking development of Cathy Gale and her kinky accessories. It's not unreasonable to think that he would be the man to restore a more grounded approach to *The Avengers*, especially following episodes like *Mission...Highly Improbable* that saw both Steed and Emma reduced in size, like something from the U.S. series *Land of the Giants*. *Mission* was an episode with quite a long gestation period. ABC boss Brian Tesler was very concerned over its fantasy elements. It seems that it was probably passed over for too long. When it finally did appear in Season 5B, the show had started to settle down from the wilder, more stylised, frivolous excesses of the first sixteen episodes of 5A. Episodes like *You Have Just Been Murdered* and *Murdersville* show a programme getting back to its more dramatic roots, quite literally in the case of *The £50,000 Breakfast*, a minimal rewrite of a season 2 episode, *Death of a Great Dane*. [1]

As history shows, Bryce was sacked and Clemens and Fennell were reinstated. The Clemens/Fennell regime joined work on *A Murderous Connection* written by prolific *Avengers* scribe, Philip Levene. Out of the four writers instigated by Bryce, Levene was the only one who'd worked on the most recent season. He clearly had no shortage of new ideas and this one was a beauty. The teaser at first seems rather ordinary, the kind so familiar from many a police drama. Two characters survey the scene of a crime and deduce the sequence of events from the evidence left. It's natural at this point to assume that they are policemen. They are interrupted by the owner of the apartment. He is bemused to find the two men in his home. On discovering that there has been a murder, he is swiftly told that he is the victim. With a shot from the murder weapon, he conveniently falls into the pre-prepared chalk outline and provides a wonderfully composed image for the title caption and credits. [2] As Earle later explains to one of his blackmail victims: "Crime, these days, rarely pays. The scientific evidence soon seeks out the criminal. So I have turned a drawback into a virtue. I have made you a murderer."

When Steed arrives on the murder scene, he and Ministry Sleuth, Sir Arthur Doyle (perfectly cast with Peter Jones), go through the patter of the real investigation but not before some playful character interaction around the concept of deduction:

Sir Arthur: I see you walked through the park this morning. Your shoes carry a film of pale blue dust peculiar to that area...Deduction, Steed. Deduction.
Steed: I see you've changed your secretary [pulling a blonde hair from Doyle's coat]. The last one was brunette. Seduction, Sir Arthur?

They re-enact almost word for word the villains' spiel. As an audience we have heard it all before. As an accompaniment to the recap, Steed plays a violin that he finds on the sofa which adds an extra, fun Sherlock touch to the routine. He points out how convenient the incriminating clues are, which is just as well as it's something the law fails to notice. Steed's playful distraction with the violin shows that he recognises that he shouldn't be involved with the situation as presented. It's routine, there's nothing special about it; he's not fully engaged. So why has he been called into this new mundane world?

Considering the emphasis on changing the show, *A Murderous Connection* is quite similar in style to Levene's *You Have Just Been Murdered* in that it shows a blackmailer with a cruel, threatening hold over his victims. But the tone is much darker for this newer episode and, to use Clemens' phrase, 'the cardboard is thicker'. *You Have Just been Murdered* is about bankers and wealthy businessmen who have created their own worlds. The conversations they have are – to quote Steed – "money, how to make it...how to hold on to it." The victims in *A Murderous Connection* are wealthy but they also have lives: they have families, they have reputations, they have friends, they play snooker, and they go riding. Their lives are made of thicker cardboard and they engage our sympathy and compassion. Since we feel for the victims in their distress, our loathing of the cool, calm and collected villains, in this case Earle and Gardiner, is heightened. [3]

Steed's connection to the victims had long been entirely on a professional basis. They were government officials, scientists, eccentrics, people whose sole existence and identity was what they did. These people rarely had lives; they were just fodder for the purpose of the plot. But now when dealing with thicker cardboard, these victims are actually his friends, people he knows and respects. Steed has a personal, intimate investment in their lives. [4] The idea that these people have committed murder matters to him. He's called in as he's a friend and the matter is delicate. Sir Arthur directly suggests that Steed question William Burgess' alibi "as a casual enquiry from an old friend". The cavalier attitude of the old Steed isn't appropriate here. This time it's personal. It sees Steed involved personally, just as Mrs. Peel had been in *Murdersville*.

This new, more personally involved Steed (who would be on the verge of a tear in the next episode in production – *The Forget-Me-Knot*) – has a new associate for Levene to write about: Mother...no that's not right, sorry, Tara King, a character who spends the episode in a wheelchair, is often on the phone, who Steed reports back to and who feeds him information. It's Mother an episode early, actually played by a woman.

Bryce made statements of intent regarding Tara King in early Season 6 publicity:

"I think it's time to go back to femininity. We've had all the leather business - the new girl will be essentially a woman. She will be soft with all the female weaknesses and attributes."

ABC bosses resented the fact that sometimes Emma Peel didn't need rescuing, or even rescued Steed, making him look 'unmasculine' (citing *The Superlative Seven*). With this in mind, they must have been thrilled with Bryce's intentions. Words like 'vulnerable' have been used for Tara. When you're in an action adventure thriller series, you can't get more vulnerable than being invalided and confined to a wheelchair. But Levene is a clever writer and, even in that state, she's no damsel in distress.

It's easy to forget, due to the Clemens reformatting of Season 6, that at this stage in the production, Tara wasn't yet the trainee agent given to us in *The Forget-Me-Knot*. She was the "daughter of a prosperous farmer, and had all the skill associated with the outdoors life". She'd been to an expensive finishing school and acquired skills like skiing, gliding and flying. With talk in the episode of her skiing accident and all her anxious friends phoning up, it implies an international lifestyle; all very sophisticated. Without the attachment of colleagues, it does leave the rather awkward question of why Steed and this very young lady are hanging out together. But we needn't worry about that as the episode was 'retconned' an episode later with Tara being a fellow member of department "MI5½". [5]

Production on Levene's script was already in motion when Clemens and Fennell returned. Several scenes had been shot on *A Murderous Connection* when a rewrite was issued, with the alliterated title *The Curious Case of the Countless Clues*. It's probable that Clemens performed the rewrites himself. [6] Director Don Sharp remembered that it wasn't just changes to scenes yet to be filmed but also sequences already shot. The episode had been moved back into the special Clemens world of *The Avengers*.

Looking at the episode, it seems clear to me who added a few playful names and characters. There are three characters who take on the role of the bad guys called Earle, Gardiner and Stanley. Brian Clemens would later contribute episodes to the Perry Mason TV series and the Mason books were written by Earl Stanley Gardner. The new title itself is very much in the vein of the Mason books. We also get the character of 'ministry sleuth' Sir Arthur Doyle who walks around wearing a deerstalker hat and Inverness cloak, a clear reference to Conan Doyle and his famous sleuth (though he could have been in the original script anyway). In Dave Rogers' story synopsis in *The Complete Avengers* book, it seems an earlier draft of the script had Doyle with a female assistant called Watson (US TV show *Elementary* didn't get there first then). I imagine Watson became a victim of the economising of speaking roles to keep the Clemens *Avengers* feel.

New to the show, director Don Sharp's work is solid but there's a disappointing lack of visual style which the show prided itself in. Patrick Macnee recalls Bryce labouring on how great the show would look yet, judging from the remnants of the Bryce episodes, they seem to lack any artistic aesthetic qualities. Despite this lack of visual artistry, Sharp makes up for it through the casting. Anthony Bate is sickeningly cold and calculating; he's a villain you truly hate as he plays with his victims and extorts yet more wealth and treasures from them through his 'dastardly' plans. The impersonal manner in which his death is handled by Sharp is truly justified. The focus of the shot is Tara being brave and heroic and all we see of him is his back. For a man who kills people described as "of no real importance" and uses them as pawns to obtain wealth, it's fitting that he doesn't get his moment of glory in death. Kenneth Cope as Gardiner adds a touch of personality to the role of a basic leg man. The ever dependable Edward de Souza and George A. Cooper make Flanders and Burgess highly sympathetic. Tracey Reed plays Flanders' sister, Janice, a former fling of Steed's. Macnee always has great chemistry with the ladies. The whole Janice set-up is amusingly played as both Sir Arthur and Tara playfully nudge Steed for more information on the relationship. At this time it was rare for Steed to ever have a romantic partner aside from his flirting with the female lead. Was Janice another attempt to add some depth and reality to the show? She even calls him John!

As well as the great casting, Sharp shines in other ways. There are some excellent transitions to new scenes; for example, Flanders' painting is taken away by the blackmailers leaving a blank wall and the next shot is a blank wall at Burgess' home showing their earlier victim. There is also a nice moment that plays with our expectations. Burgess wishes to confess to Steed before the police are sent by the blackmailers. Steed drives to Burgess' home and a light version of *The Avengers* theme plays. The doorbell rings and the visitor is admitted. The pace and music have lulled us into a false sense of security as it's not Steed but Arthur Doyle and the police who enter.

Sharp does a good job at communicating the drama. One of the most effective moments comes when Tara, alone and with the vulnerability of a badly "bumped, bruised and dislocated" ankle, has to prevent the bad guys from entering her apartment. There's an excellent sense of tension as Tara pulls herself up her stairs to lock the front door. For a show that had for a long time glibly handled the threats, the tension is all the more impressive, ably assisted by Laurie Johnson's effective incidental music. Sharp manages to show Tara's unease as the blackmailers vandalise her eccentric apartment and construct her death scene. [7] Whilst this is happening, Steed is racing in the stolen mechanics' vehicle. With any other show, you would expect Steed to arrive just in time to prevent the murder of his colleague. But no, this is *The Avengers*; even with her impairment she is quite capable of taking care of herself. Tara, 'the girl with a brick in her handbag', deals with the villains through the use of whatever comes to hand, like the contents from a hot water bottle, Steed's steel lined bowler, a ski pole, a paint pallet, an umbrella, a basket of apples and finally a gun.

One of the most impressive aspects to Season 6 is a new dynamism to the fights. They'd always been enjoyable but Joe Dunne's work is so excitingly choreographed and well shot. The fight has to end with our leading man getting a look in though, so he gets to dispatch Gardiner with an off-screen punch that sends him flying down the stairs, resulting in the breakage of the banisters (a common occurrence).

After the bad guys are dealt with Steed rushes into Tara's apartment to find a display of destruction and there, sitting casually in the centre with her foot up, is Tara reading a magazine. Neither character mentions the obvious; they're far too sophisticated for that. Even with all the life-threatening danger they can't forget the pleasantries. Steed slides down the fireman pole and squashes his bowler on landing.

The original script deviated at this point. It was Steed's turn to be the invalid and Tara would be his ministering angel; and they would of course share some therapeutic champagne. However, the final version of the tag scene sees Tara performing surgery on Steed's battered bowler, only to demonstrate her own mended battered ankle by performing a gymnastic cartwheel across the room.

The Curious Case of the Countless Clues shows us that *The Avengers* could still provide interesting concepts and play with viewers' expectations. In addition, we have a new leading lady who – even when an invalid – is more than capable.

© Darren Burch

1. As Season 5B was more 'grounded', generally speaking, than the earlier episodes, it begs the question as to why the company felt the need for a change of producer. In reply to this note, Darren offered the following: "It does seem rather strange. Maybe the reason given was just a smoke screen. Maybe they wanted someone behind the show who they could control."
2. As with so many *Avengers* teasers, the promise of realism is almost immediately undercut; here, through surrealism and parody of formulaic detective shows.
3. It is a (minor) weakness of *You Have Just Been Murdered* that – as I observed in *Mrs. Peel, We're Needed* – the victims are unlikeable characters/caricatures who we don't care about.
4. The death of his two friends in *Get-A-Way!* is another example of this, with time spent building up their rapport and relationships at Steed's all-night party. *Take-Over* also contains an emotive layer, with Steed's close friends (the Bassetts) held hostage.

5. If, like me, you needed a definition of this word...Retcon: revise (an aspect of a fictional work) retrospectively, typically by introducing a piece of new information that imposes a different interpretation on previously described events.
6. This suggestion is backed up by Michael Richardson in *Bowler Hats and Kinky Boots*.
7. There is no doubt that the darker, subversive drama which is – generally speaking – dropped in Season 5, is re-established in a number of Season 6 episodes such as *Requiem, Stay Tuned, Pandora, Take-Over* and this episode.

SPLIT!

Filmed: January-February 1968

Exterior Locations:
Ministry of Top Secret Information: gated front entrance
Open countryside and helicopter
Country roads
Barnes' house
Nullington Private Hospital: car park, front entrance

Sets:
Ministry of Top Secret Information: corridor, executive rest room, lift
Tara's car
Steed's mews apartment
Handwriting expert office
Nullington Hospital: reception, operating theatre, lift
Barnes' house: hall, study

SPLIT!

Main Character List:
Harry Mercer: Ministry of TSI
Frank Compton: Ministry of TSI
Dr. Constantine: Nullington Hospital
Tara King
Lord Barnes: Ministry of TSI
Major Peter Rooke: Ministry of TSI
John Steed
Swindin: handwriting expert
Petra: nurse at Nullington
Hinnell: foreign mastermind
Miller: Barnes' butler
Morrell: henchman
Vitch: henchman
Boris Kartovski: foreign agent, kept artificially alive

As the *Human League* said in their song 'Open Your Heart', "...you know your worst is better than their best." That's how I feel about *The Avengers*. Even the less-than-popular episodes are still head and shoulders over most other series, then and now. *Split!* is an example of this. On paper, it should be up there with the best of the series: it's directed by Roy Ward Baker, written by Brian Clemens, and has a great cast, including regulars Nigel Davenport, Bernard Archard, Maurice Good, John G Heller, Julian Glover, and a memorable 'comedy expert' cameo from Christopher Benjamin, and yet something's missing. It contains some elements that are good, some that are bad, and others that I'm in two minds about (sorry!). The 'mind swap'/loss of identity scenario has been done before and, arguably, better in the series. Two examples are *Who's Who???* and, later, in *The New Avengers*' *The Three-Handed Game*.

The teaser starts things off intriguingly enough, with the viewer as the eyes of Frank Compton, an agent returning to the hysterically-named Ministry of Top Secret Information (TSI) after a mission, demonstrating what a high security establishment this is by having to constantly show his ID (every few feet in one case, which is gloriously tongue-in-cheek). This hyper-security is definitely the way to keep things secret, particularly when the establishment has already spelled out what it does so clearly in its name on all the signs! We get a feeling there's going to be trouble when - after a friendly exchange of words - Compton leaves his silenced pistol on the desk of buddy Harry Mercer, who's engaged in writing up a report, and goes into another room (why would an agent leave his gun like that?). A phone call to Mercer with the message, "May I speak to Boris, please?" abruptly changes things as Mercer transforms from affable Harry to a snarlingly-aggressive Hyde-like personality, with a strangely clenched left hand. As this is occurring, his handwriting changes from small, subdued lettering to large, expressive words. Somehow, Mercer has been turned from friend to enemy. When Compton returns, he's shot down almost immediately by Mercer, who, having completed this task, changes back to himself and, unaware of what he's done, returns to his paperwork. (As Mercer wiped his fingerprints from the gun, how did Compton's prints manage to remain on it?). So far so strange. At this point, it's not clear at all what has happened to Mercer. We realise that the phone call was the catalyst for the murder, but how was it done? How could a phone call turn someone briefly from friend to foe? If this could happen to *anyone* at the TSI that received a phone call, then there would be no security at all in this 'secure' establishment. Could it even happen to Steed or Tara?

As Tara and Lord Barnes join Steed to investigate, an odd thing happens: Tara seems to see the significance of appropriating the report Mercer had been working on, finds it immediately with scarcely a look, and slips it unseen into her coat before leaving! Why would she do that? There's no indication at this stage that Mercer has any connection whatsoever with the murder – his conscious self thinks that Compton must have already been lying dead behind the desk when he arrived in the room. The reason why is simply one of plotting. Without this sample of Mercer's dual writing, there would be nothing for later comparison with the handwriting of Boris Kartovski, the solid evidence that forms a starting point for uncovering what's actually happening at the TSI in *Split!*

As Steed leaves, Mercer mentions remembering "October 1963" which is a massive slip of a detail that presumably has accidentally leaked into Mercer's mind. This starts Steed thinking. He knows Mercer wasn't there, but he also knows that a certain Agent Kartovski was! This leads us to a lovely cameo scene with Christopher Benjamin's "remarkable" handwriting expert, Swindin, in which we learn, as Tara sums it up, that the handwriting shows a "strong, weak, happy, sad, anxious, carefree man".

There's a misstep once Kartovski's name starts being referenced. In storytelling, it's better to 'show, not tell', but here we're just 'told' about Steed and Kartovski in East Berlin five years earlier. From that we have to take Steed's word for it that he was one of the enemy's best agents and a serious threat. Far better would have been to show a brief flashback of Steed crossing swords with Kartovski. While Steed's word is perhaps good enough for regular viewers, it's nonetheless not as strong as actually showing Kartovski in his prime, maybe also showing his clenched fist injury to tie the character to the current situation. [1]

We're then shown the 'Kartovski problem' through the behaviour of the agents who are embodying it, but at first we don't understand exactly how it's being done, which is intriguing and makes us want to continue to watch, in order to learn what the magic trick is. Possibly to make it absolutely clear to the viewer, the 'symptoms' associated with the process are largely the same for each person, which makes these scenes slightly repetitive, but that does follow the pattern of other episodes in which repetition is a strength (e.g., showing a death and the cause of it, then putting another character in the same position so that the viewer fears for their safety). Here it doesn't work as well as it's not very subtle: each character sneers menacingly, his left fist clenches, his accent changes, and we see various other behaviours leak out. This is typified in one early example: Mercer's brief burst of Cossack dancing, which is so sudden and unexpected that it verges on the comic (was this the intention?). As well as the invading attribute, a character also *loses* an attribute of their own, such as Lord Barnes's sudden switch from accomplished pianist to ham-fisted tune-wrecker while playing the piano. This also symbolises the character's gradual loss of identity.

All the afflicted characters behave like this: at first they're unaware of their behaviour switches, yet they gradually realise they're literally 'not themselves' any more in a frighteningly irreversible way. This is a powerful reflection of 1960s concerns about loss of identity, largely to a communist antagonist for whom group duty is more important than individual choice. As with someone who knows they're seriously ill, it affects behaviour and rearranges priorities which conflict with the agent's sense of loyalty to the Service. The scene in which Lord Barnes drives to Nullington Hospital to get help (as mostly-Kartovski), then, after a brief pause, drives away again (as mostly-Barnes) reflects this mental battle.

How exactly did Nullington Private Hospital get taken over by foreign agents? It's hard to imagine how a relatively small group of people (as far as can be seen: Dr. Constantine, Hinnel, Petra and a few henchmen) could occupy a private hospital and run it for several years without anyone noticing anything strange about it. There would have been periodic Ministry of Health visits. Where are the former staff and patients? Or was the venue bought first and set up as a fake hospital? That would have taken even longer. Any current patients must either be genuinely ill people (i.e., a real hospital is run alongside the Kartovski activity as cover) or the other patients (we never actually see any) are also agents? Was it developed solely for this project, or just as a convenient base for spying? [2] All of this (and a scene in which Dr. Constantine explains the whole plot to Petra) gives us the clue that what the communist agents are trying to achieve is to find a suitable 'donor' enemy mind to replace with Kartovski's, to both keep their agent alive/make use of him again, and to simultaneously wreak havoc at the TSI. We're shown how they capture the agents when they do this to Tara: she stops to investigate a faked car accident, is chloroformed and driven away in an ambulance. You wonder why the other agents wouldn't remember being abducted in this way, or perhaps the completed 'process' (which doesn't happen to Tara) removes that memory of the abduction as well.

When we actually see Kartovski, Petra the 'nurse' is uneasy at being asked to stand near him. This is extremely effective, and is (deliberately) reminiscent of a horror film scene where a character is only shown the 'monster' at close quarters because they're about to fall foul of it! Given that he's lying in an ice-filled metal and glass trolley, wired to some indeterminate medical equipment, that's perhaps understandable, but no – she says she's actually uneasy because she's repelled by him *as a person* first, which just reinforces what we know of him. "He's not a monster", says Dr. Constantine. A wonderfully ironic comment! [3]

As they're still perfecting the transfer process, it makes you wonder why they didn't use hospital patients or abductees as 'safe' guinea-pigs for the experiments. But no, they seem to have aimed straight for the ministry infiltration from the off, and have built up a 'back catalogue' of TSI agents on the off-chance that one of them, when activated, will be successful. The mind replacement method turns out to be less intriguing than the story had earlier hinted at: it's simply a 'mad scientist' using a magical electronic *MacGuffin* to copy Kartovski's mind into the brain of the TSI agents. However, during Tara's transformation where the doctor suggests to Tara that she should "give in" to Boris, we can see that the process is a form of mental rape, which adds a distasteful angle to the whole thing. [4]

One missed opportunity is to have had Tara (or Steed) as the successful example of the Kartovski personality takeover (at least for a time) so that it was Steed/Tara effectively travelling round with Kartovski in Tara/Steed's body investigating his own case.

Perhaps that was too obvious (or confusing?) a plot. Having Major Rooke as the sole successful (or was it?) embodiment of the mind transplant is less effective as we know his character much less well than we know Tara; it is less of a concern to us as viewers. At least it does give Julian Glover the chance to show the changing personalities in Rooke's mind before the scene is ended with some haste by a punch from Steed – removing much in the way of a dramatic conclusion for the enemies' plot – with his memorable line "Kill you, old chap? I'd rather cure you!"

Mention must be made of the incidental music in this episode. While it's generally used imaginatively and appropriately throughout the whole series, here the repetitive 'Kartovski theme' (on piano, flute and bassoon) that plays every time a mental transformation has occurred to a character becomes very irritating. It's the equivalent of having the character wear a hat that says "I'm Boris now" on it: too obvious and unnecessary.

This is not a strong episode for either Steed or Tara, neither of whom is actually given much of interest to do, other than drive around or be attacked. Tara behaves as very much the 'junior' agent, with Steed front and centre as driving force/mentor. The *Pygmalion* idea was perhaps understandable as an attempt to both drop and challenge the Steed/Mrs. Peel dynamic of the previous two seasons, but it wasn't projected much further into this final run. As the best Tara episodes feature her in a more girlfriend type relationship with Steed, this is perhaps as well. Tara and Steed barely get a scene together (until the epilogue teaser), and when they do the scenes are all brief, which to me is why it feels less avengerish than most other episodes.

Kartovski is revealed to have been in a state of paralysis – presumably for the five years since Steed shot him – when we see him wired up to the machine that's keeping him alive. But what kind of life is this? From the semi-successful transfers it would appear that his mind is still reasonably viable, but all he can physically do is move his eyes (spot the continuity error when he clenches his left hand at the end!). Boris is actually imprisoned within himself, presumably unable to communicate for the last five years. His physical presence echoes Frankenstein's monster on the slab, and the parallel is strong: he's being kept alive not for his own sake, but in order that he can be used by an evil scientist. Has anyone asked Kartovski what he wants? Can they? After five years of being sentient but unable to communicate, though, would he not have gradually gone insane? Perhaps that's why the transfers fail. Kartovski should have died in 1963. When he becomes disconnected from the life-support machine during Steed's fight with the villains, is it just me that thinks there's a hint of gratitude in Kartovski's eyes – and perhaps a tear – as he passes? [5] Actually, now that I've re-watched it several times, this episode's not that bad after all. I've changed my mind (so shoot me).

© Mark Saunders

1. Apart from employing previously used footage, *The Avengers* doesn't tend to use flashbacks. Maybe, rather than 'telling', the script writer and director could have held more back, adding a layer of mystery and subtlety.
2. I guess that one of the idiosyncrasies of *The Avengers* in the filmed seasons is that, on the whole, plots don't bear too much scrutiny!
3. On another level, when Petra questions whether Kartovski's current vegetative state constitutes being alive, is this a critique of medical science keeping people artificially alive at all costs? (This would fit in with Mark's comments at the end of the chapter.)

4. I agree with Mark that there is something deeply unpleasant about this element of the storyline. I feel particularly uneasy when the doctor tells Tara: "Relax, Miss King, and let his mind flood into yours."
5. Like the nurse, our feelings towards Kartovski are, perhaps, a strange mixture of revulsion and sympathy.

GET-A-WAY!

Filmed: February 1968

Exterior Locations:
Monastery: grounds, turrets, gated entrance
Stable Mews
London street
Bryant's Natural History magazine office: street entrance
Magnus Importing Company warehouse: parking and entrance

Sets:
Monastery: passageway, corridors, James' office, cells,
Steed's mews apartment and outer corridor
Tara King's apartment
Ryder's apartment: living room, bathroom, outside corridor
Peters' office
Bryant's Natural History magazine: office
Magnus Importing Company warehouse

GET-A-WAY!

Main Character List:
Colonel James: in charge of monastery prison
Price: guard
Baxter: guard
Martin Ezdorf: foreign agent prisoner
Lubin: foreign agent prisoner
Rostov: foreign agent prisoner
Edwards: guard
Tara King
John Steed
Paul Ryder: agent friend of Steed
George Neville: agent friend of Steed
Professor Percival Dodge: 'scientific Houdini'
Peters: ministry employee, lizard enthusiast
Cedric Bryant: natural history magazine editor
Magnus: importing company

I'm the invisible man,
I'm the invisible man.
Incredible how you can
See right through me!
(Queen, *The Invisible Man*, 1989).

An invisible man has been a regular character type in literature, film and television since H G Wells' original novella of 1897 (and before that in mythology and legend). Wells' scientist Griffin made a particular impact in the memorable 1933 film starring Claude Rains. Here Griffin explains to reluctant doomed confederate Dr. Kemp some of the problems he encounters:

"I must always remain in hiding after meals. The food is visible inside me until it is digested. I can only work on fine, clear days. If I work in the rain, the water can be seen on my head and shoulders. In a fog, you can see me, like a bubble. In smoky cities the soot settles on me until you can see a dark outline. You must always be near at hand to wipe off my feet. Even dirt between my fingernails would give me away."

Wells' story is a morality tale of a person who finds himself in a situation unfettered by any behavioural limits and is tempted to transgress moral and social convention to the extreme (the fact that the chemical – 'monocaine' in the film – also turns him insane and megalomaniacal adds nothing positive to the situation). Several 'invisible agents' followed, including a film of that title in 1942, and in television series such as *The Invisible Man* ITC series (1958), the 1975 series with David McCallum, and the *Gemini Man* with Ben Murphy (1976).

The Peel/Steed Avengers team had already encountered an invisible agent (of sorts) in the episode *The See-Through Man*. This is a better take on invisibility in *The Avengers*, being 'real' in story terms for one thing, though it is not without its flaws in practical and scientific terms. I'll take a moment to explore this a little. There are two main problems with the logic of the camouflage method used: firstly, there is how it is applied to the body and how it could work in terms of fooling the observer. As we see when Ezdorf finally demonstrates as much of the technique as Philip Levene/Don Sharp will allow us to see, he takes the hidden liquid and pours most of it into a very shallow bath of water that could only possibly cover the back of him (head to toe) when immersed. It is hard to see how this would then work as a concealment: the rear side of him (as it were) is completely covered with the liquid. In some strange way this means that when the agent turns to face the wall and presents his back to the room, no one standing anywhere in the vicinity can then see him *from any angle.* At 90 degrees to him it is just about plausible, but not *anywhere in the room.* From certain angles people would be able to see where on his body he was not covered by the liquid. Amusingly, Ezdorf revels in the invisibility and is seen to turn to the wall and back, disappearing and reappearing – but how would he know it was working as there is no mirror and he can't very well see himself vanishing?

Secondly, even if the 'science' of this worked in some clever light-refracting way, there is then a flaw in logic that possibly didn't occur to Levene when writing the script. In order for the technique to succeed, the person folds his arms across his chest (we must assume this has significance as all three agents appear to do it) and turns to face the wall he's next to, at which point he vanishes. So far so good, except that while facing the wall how is he then supposed to see what the other people in the room are doing, in order to work out when to strike at them or to make his escape? The moment he turns into the room to see where they are, he reveals himself, as we see Ezdorf demonstrate prior to escaping his cell. He even tells Tara near the end of the episode, "If I turn my back now I am at my most invulnerable". A large dollop of suspension of disbelief in the camouflage is therefore required. [1]

The episode begins strongly and very avengerishly: a castle under a dark sky. Sinister hooded figures on the battlements. A distant bell tolls. Is this going to be a supernatural episode? No. We quickly realise the monks are a subterfuge and the castle (Oldhill Monastery) is for incarcerating foreign agents. Not just any agents: three of the top opposition agents. One of the monks (Baxter) is making a regular visual check of the prisoners. He checks Ezdorf, Lubin, but the third prisoner – Rostov – doesn't seem to be in his cell. The door is opened, and...no-one is there. Except he *is* still there, but concealed. Baxter is quickly subdued, his gun taken, and Rostov is on the run. He heads to a corridor that clearly has no exit. As the alarm sounds, a number of gun-wielding monks are hot on his trail to the dead end, but when they turn the corner, he's gone. How? The viewer is left as stunned as the bewildered guards.

However, the episode isn't just about the foreign agents disappearing. They weren't over here randomly engaged in espionage. As we discover after the first killing, it appears that they had been sent over to take part in the 'G.A.P.' (Great Assassination Plot), their targets established as three top British agents. Two are known, but the third target (that of the deadliest agent of the three - Ezdorf) is a mystery (to Steed at least, but I imagine most viewers would have realised it had to be him!).

We first encounter Steed having a drink in his mews flat with two of his old friends and fellow agents, who happen to be the two named on the hit list, even though we don't know this yet. Coincidence? Or does this possibly point to a specific incident involving all three agents that the three captive foreign agents are now to avenge? (if I may use that word!). Steed says the other two saved his life – might that have happened during the same operation? Could this be the 'E.B.A.' (Exploding Bootlace Affair) that is mentioned? (a satirical reference to the story title style of *The Man From U.N.C.L.E*, perhaps.) The party winds up and Neville refuses an offer of a lift from Steed. [2] A pity as he might have lived longer. As it is, within a minute of leaving on foot, Neville is haunted by the echoing voice of Rostov, taunting him unseen (how did he achieve the ethereal voice?) and gunned down. Steed hears the shot and looks from the window to see a dying Neville, but no sign of a gunman. Neville survives long enough to say "Rostov" to Steed before passing. Steed now has a clue about what's happening, but not how. Tara is also in the flat with the men, just hanging around while they reminisce, looking notably relaxed. This is not the junior agent of *Split!* who we might imagine would have been rather ill at ease in her superior's residence, but more like a fixture and joint host, almost as if it is her home as well.

Steed is walked through Rostov's inexplicable escape by Colonel James (a beleaguered Andrew Keir). This is where we discover what the captured agents were in England for. The Colonel explains that Rostov was to kill Neville – which he has – and Lubin's target was Steed's other friend, Ryder. When Ryder is killed, Tara inevitably arrives just after the nick of time, to find him literally falling to the floor in death, but no one else in the room to have done it. Lubin has toyed with Ryder longer than Rostov had with Neville, taunting him and 'showing off' his invisibility (if that's not an oxymoron), before shooting him down. In a nice directorial touch, when Tara arrives at Ryder's she sees what appears to be blood spilled under his door, only to find that it is from a tumbled tin of red paint. This nicely plays with the usual 'no blood' rule without breaking it. Aside from the red paint and some footprints left in it leading away from the scene, Tara finds nothing of use and tells Steed that the whole thing is impossible. Does he believe in invisible men? "Only when I can't see them," says Steed.

There are several strong, tense scenes between Steed and Ezdorf in *Get-A-Way!* They are like two wary tigers observing each other and probing for weaknesses before engaging in battle, and all the scenes contain great dialogue. "I've been expecting you," says Ezdorf on their first meeting (he doesn't add "Mr Steed" at the end of that to make it a Bond reference, but it's almost there!). They share a drink (*not* vodka) to "freedom", and Steed asks Ezdorf what he's doing. "I plan," is his enigmatic reply. "First Rostov, then Lubin, then me," and not an idle boast. "You're bluffing", Steed counters. The alarm bell then rings because Lubin's escaping, and Ezdorf responds, "Perhaps not." On another visit, Ezdorf announces, "I will escape." Steed wants to know who his target is (all together now viewers – shout it at the screen so Steed can hear!). "We are evenly matched, aren't we? That's why they chose me," he hints. Steed's still not picking up on these clues, but fortunately Ezdorf then decides to reveal all: "It is *you*, Steed!" Later, as Ezdorf prepares to kill Steed we get the lovely detail that he asks Magnus for a Smith & Wesson rather than his usual Beretta because Steed had earlier said he preferred that as his weapon of choice. At the conclusion to the Ezdorf saga, he is brought his comeuppance, suitably hoist by his own petard by Steed out-lizarding him, thus demonstrating that they are not evenly matched: whatever Ezdorf can do, Steed can do better. Steed leaves the unconscious, invisible Ezdorf with a nice pun as he turns him over to break the invisibility effect: "Glad to see you back." As Ezdorf survives, it may be that Levene considered him a strong enough character to leave a rematch with Steed a possibility had the series continued (or when Steed returned in *The New Avengers*).

Peter Bowles is superb as Ezdorf in every scene he's in, despite having to wear a red tracksuit throughout. All sinister looks and controlled threatening voice as he portrays Ezdorf's (over) confidence and his love/hate feelings towards Steed: an enemy, but one to be admired and even respected. "I do admire you," he specifically tells Steed during one of his visits. He claims he and Steed are "identical". Steed counters that the difference is that Ezdorf enjoys killing. It is a pity that most new viewers would probably be more likely to recognise Bowles as regular character Richard DeVere from the comedy series *To The Manor Born* rather than for the superb dramatic characters – often villains at which he excelled – he played in many 1960s and 1970s series including his *Avengers* appearances in *Second Sight*, *Dial A Deadly Number* and *Escape in Time* and in the likes of *The Prisoner, Danger Man, The Saint, The Baron* and *Department S*. He is an excellent actor, equally adept at playing serious roles and comedy.

With all the escaping going on from his prison, you might wonder why Colonel James doesn't have the prisoners put in chains and manacles. Fortunately, the Colonel answers this very question for us: "If we did that we'd be no better than the enemy," he tells Steed. Hmm...Given the killings that have resulted, the manacles seem like they really would have been a good idea!

Peter Bayliss (earlier in *The Murder Market* with Patrick Cargill) is Professor Dodge, a specialist in breaking in and out of places, brought in by Steed for a short comedy cameo to state categorically that no one could have escaped through the walls, floor, or windows in the cells. Amusingly, he's shown to be unable to open a box he takes out of his pocket, somewhat undermining his credentials. We already know this is a red herring, but for Steed, having also found the magazine with a page missing, this convinces him that some clever trick is definitely the answer. Can he piece it all together in time, before Ezdorf escapes and kills him?

The foreign agencies – specifically those planning the escapes – clearly have little respect for the British secret service, as they present the three agents with their 'escape kit' in exactly the same way, allowing Steed to put two and two together much faster than he otherwise would have. You take a bottle of vodka with a hidden compartment (Colonel James clearly drank too much of the vodka he sampled and didn't try simply unscrewing the bottle, part way up, as Steed does), add a page of a wildlife magazine (24/25) that includes an article *Lizards and Their Habits* and is followed by a reference to Lizard Vodka helping "Runaway People Escape", mix well, serve in a large bath and you have your answer, as Steed discovers when he tries some on his bowler, which then disappears.

To get the viewer on track in piecing together what is going on, there are plenty of clues scattered around as to how the whole invisibility trick is enacted. Levene ensures that these are liberally spread between Steed and Tara as they investigate separately. Steed picks up on the fact that Lubin doesn't drink, so why did he order Lizard Vodka? A very good question! All three prisoners apparently share an unlikely preference for Lizard Vodka.

When Tara visits Peters, the archivist, to collect the three prisoners' files, she finds that he has an interest in lizards and a very helpful conversation about chameleons crops up. In one of these visits there's a mention of "chromaphores", which sounds like a *Doctor Who* monster, but is in fact referring to the cells in a chameleon's skin that enable the colour changes. (Magnus later briefly expands on this by describing to Ezdorf that it's done with a concentration of "pigmented plastoid"). The archivist says that the same Roman numerals were written on the bottom of each prisoner's shoes.

Finding the amusingly-named *Code Breaking For Beginners* book no help, she then sees that the numerals match the *Bryant's Natural History Magazine – Special Reptile Issue* (CXVIIIVI), and finds the same page number torn out that Steed had. A phone call to Bryant for an intact copy of the magazine ends with Lubin cutting off Bryant's call - permanently. Once again arriving after the nick of time – she is good at that in this episode – Tara at least ends up with the last intact copy of the magazine. But, after Lubin takes a fatal tumble through the window, she also sees the 'Magnus Importing Company' van drive away; it is not difficult – being *Avengerland*, there are no other moving vehicles around. She remembers this clue when she and Steed pool information that they have discovered.

Steed finds an ill-prepared Mr. Magnus who states that he no longer imports Lizard Vodka, even though it seems likely that all the wrapped bottles we see there are bottles of it. [3] (A desperate lie to play for time?). Steed ends up delivering a bottle of 'Lizard' that we'd seen at Magnus's, helpfully labelled "Express Delivery – Martin Ezdorf" (Martin? Not very spy-like!) to his cell in the prison. "Would you like to try it?" says a very confident Ezdorf. After Steed tries to get him to discuss his apparent interests in lizards and vodka, Ezdorf says "You're getting very close, Steed". He teases Steed and attempts a misdirection by tipping out some of the vodka near the cell entrance and suggesting he might pour himself under the door. During the same scene, Ezdorf is seen to almost deliver the 'arms across the chest' move we associate with the vanishing trick (chance, or a planned subtle misdirection to the viewer that he's about to disappear?).

This is a very enjoyable episode: lots of satisfying avengerish sleuthing and piecing together of clues and facts, a memorable performance from Peter Bowles, and a clever, imaginative story make this one well worth repeated visits. [4] There is even a fun tag scene which sees Tara believing Steed is invisible in the flat, only to find that Steed is simply on his hands and knees mending his tuba. In a nice rounding off of the invisibility theme, Steed and Tara then both literally 'disappear' behind the sofa.

There is one final mystery in this episode: what happened to Rostov? We last see him killing Neville early in the episode. If he had been recaptured we would have seen him being interrogated as to how he'd escaped, or returned to the monastery. We also didn't see him killed. Would he not therefore have gone to Magnus and been involved in helping Magnus and Lubin in completing the mission and tying up the various loose ends? But no, he seems to have just vanished into thin air...

© Mark Saunders

1. Isn't this nearly always the case with *Avengers* plots?!
2. This 'party until dawn' is very well written/filmed, establishing their friendship and adding 'thicker cardboard' to the victims.
3. The Magnus Importing Company offers us another of those delightfully atmospheric deserted warehouse locations which work so well in *Avengerland*.
4. I would add that there are some lovely sets: the monastery prison, the vodka warehouse and the magazine office.

HAVE GUNS – WILL HAGGLE

Filmed: began October 1967; reworked February 1968

Exterior Locations:
State Ordnance Depot: perimeter fence, warehouse
Stokely House: ornamental gardens, lawns, terrace, driveway, greenery/undergrowth, hut
Reservoir
Cadogan Towers Hotel forecourt
Ballistics Research Centre building
Country lanes
London street
Hut (armoury)

Sets:
Ordnance Depot: warehouse, Crayford's office, parking area
Tara King's apartment
Hotel: room, lobby, corridor, lift, phone booth
Ballistics Research Centre
Stokely House: drawing room
Hut (armoury)
Steed's mews apartment

HAVE GUNS – WILL HAGGLE

Main Character List:
Crayford: villains' inside man
Tara King
John Steed
Conrad: assassin, Adriana's brother
Smith
Lady Adriana Beardsley: mastermind
Colonel Martin Nsonga: planning a military coup
Giles: Nsonga's henchman
Lift attendant
Professor Spencer: ballistics expert
Jackson: henchman
Bart: henchman

This early Season 6 episode has one of the more interesting production histories and is fairly entertaining from several standpoints. It all started with a 90 minute episode called *Invitation to a Killing* written by Donald James, directed by Robert Asher, and filmed in October and November 1967 during the ill-fated John Bryce regime. Shortly thereafter Bryce was dismissed and Brian Clemens and Albert Fennell were re-installed as co-producers of *The Avengers*. They didn't like this episode but thought some of it could be salvaged. Clemens revised the episode, eliminating many of the original scenes, filming new ones and integrating them among the remaining original ones. The new scenes were filmed in February and March 1968. Ray Austin, just one of several directors who worked on this episode, received director credit.

The teaser scene gets the episode off to a promising start. The precision with which the four man team works as they use a trampoline to scale a security fence is a joy to watch. The viewer is pretty sure that they're bad guys, yet can't help but admire their crisp performance. Sure enough, they're breaking into a government armoury to steal state-of-the-art assault rifles. The gratuitous kinkiness of their inside man's desire to be hurt is a little off-putting, but it's a good start for *Have Guns-Will Haggle* nevertheless. There are echoes of the Season Four episode *The Master Minds* here. That one also opens with a group of bad guys stealing from the government. The use of a trampoline to enter a high security government installation also takes place later in the Season Four episode. The parallels continue in the next scene in *Have Guns-Will Haggle* when Steed discusses the case with Tara while she is jumping on the trampoline. Steed did the same thing with Mrs. Peel in *The Master Minds*. This recycling is typical of *The Avengers,* who deserve some kind of an award from the environmentalists for their fine work in this area. Clemens also earns recycling bonus points for the music in this episode. It is 100% recycled from previous episodes. This isn't a negative - there certainly isn't anything wrong with evoking echoes of the immensely popular Peel era as the series transitions to a new era. A personal favourite is the scene where Colonel Nsonga is listening to music that originated in another underrated Season Four episode, *Small Game for Big Hunters*; Steed enters the room and says with a smile, "I see you're playing our tune". [1]

In contrast to the silky smoothness of the dialogue in previous seasons, there is a fascinating awkwardness to some of the conversations in *Have Guns-Will Haggle*. For instance, after Steed drags the body of a murdered mercenary (using his umbrella of course) out of the water, he is discussing whether or not there is a link with the missing rifles and says to Tara, "We'll know as soon as the doctors have, a, well, as soon as they've done what they have to do." Tara replies "You mean after the autopsy, after they've dug the bullet out." Steed then gives Tara a look that seems to say, "Hmm, she knows what an autopsy is. Maybe she isn't an eight year old child. Maybe she is a real secret agent!" It's hard to imagine how they came up with that blatantly silly exchange. It seems to point to the difficulty they were having in trying to figure out how to make Tara King a credible partner for Steed.

Another howler is when, after Nsonga tries to induce Steed to abandon the president and work for him instead, Steed says, "No, I don't think so. Loyalty, amongst other virtues, was something they impressed upon me at Eton." It would be nice to think that whoever actually wrote that line was being ironic but this is doubtful. Steed's mentioning Eton, a symbol of the British upper class, in his smug, holier-than-thou rejection is unintentionally ironic. He is attempting to put this Third World upstart in his place by implying that Eton alumni and by extension the British upper class are superiorly loyal and virtuous. Steed seems to be oblivious to how ridiculous this snobbish remark is, given the fact that the conversation takes place at the palatial estate of Lady Beardsley, a fully-fledged member of the British aristocracy who steals from her own government and sells arms to the highest bidder, who in this particular case is an enemy of her country.

This brings us to a discussion of some of the more serious elements that are touched upon in *Have Guns-Will Haggle*. Let's start with the *Realpolitik* aspect. We are treated to some of John Steed's back story in this episode. We learn that at some time in his past he has intervened in the internal affairs of a newly independent African country. We don't know exactly when but if the country is newly independent it would probably have been after his 'adventurer' days and during the time he was operating as a British agent. Why would a British secret agent help the friendly leader of a resources-rich Third World nation fight off an attempted *coup d'état*? The answer is obvious – it is in Britain's economic and/or political interest to keep this ruler (and possible puppet) in power. Whether or not this leader is a good one for the people who live in that country is usually considered irrelevant. This type of covert meddling by First World nations was and still is very common. This practice is a very cynical one and has caused many Third World people to suffer under brutal regimes, the repercussions of which we are still seeing. Britain certainly doesn't come across as virtuous here. The episode on the whole paints a fairly sordid picture of the nation. Except for our heroes, the British characters in it are, to put it mildly, not a very wholesome lot. We have the masochistic, thieving warehouseman Crayford, the corrupt lift attendant, the clueless bureaucrat Spencer, the psychopathic Conrad and his gang of mercenaries, and last but not least the cynical, thieving, traitorous Lady Beardsley. Steed and partners don't as a general rule encounter choir boys and girls in their line of work but this particular cast of characters is a bit more unsavoury than usual. [2]

Lady Beardsley stands out as being particularly despicable. However, it's a bit hard for the viewer to grasp this, thanks to the chipper portrayal by the 22 year old Nicola Pagett. It was really genius casting. This actress is very, very cute and the twinkle in her eyes as she goes about her business makes one think of her as more rascally than despicable. The untold suffering and death that is a direct result of unscrupulous arms dealing seems to be just an abstraction. [3]

Another aspect to *Have Guns-Will Haggle* is its approach to racial characterisations. We have to go all the way back to Season Three to find the only other major role portrayed in *The Avengers* by a black actor, when Edric Connor played the affable leader of a gang bent on a heist at a gold vault in *The Gilded Cage*. Johnny Sekka's Colonel Nsonga is one of the bright spots in *Have Guns-Will Haggle*. He has many Steed-like qualities – he's charming, impeccably dressed, and has thoroughly mastered the art of hiding his steel fist in a velvet glove. Sekka has a great screen presence and verbally spars very ably with Macnee in their scenes together. Nsonga keeps his malevolence well hidden until he reveals it by insisting on Tara's duel with Conrad. There is no real need for the duel – he has already purchased the rifles – and he doesn't even know who Tara is. However, he does know that her almost certain death would be a blow to Steed. The charming yet thoroughly villainous Nsonga is not a stereotypical black character. Instead he is a stereotypical *Avengers* villain, and for that I think we should give the show some credit in the race department. Blacks in movies and on television in the 60's tended to be either negative stereotypes or more often (and more condescendingly) portrayed as some sort of Sidney Poitier–like saints. Colonel Nsonga is neither. The role (with a change in the country he's from) could actually have been portrayed by an actor of any race. This is also true of Edric Connor's role in *The Gilded Cage*.

But enough of this pseudo-serious palaver. *The Avengers* is much more (yet not entirely) about entertainment. We are certainly entertained by the performances of the above mentioned guest actors, Johnny Sekka and Nicola Pagett. Also, this episode is brimming with action-lots of fights, car chases, duels, and an explosion. (Speaking of the explosion, you could not blame the viewer for wondering why Steed would choose to blow up 3000 of Her Majesty's new rifles instead of finding the nearest telephone and informing Mother where they could be picked up.) There is also a certain amount of humour in this one, most of it coming from the exchanges between Steed and Nsonga.

The highest entertainment value that *Have Guns-Will Haggle* provides is the opportunity for *Avengers* fans to view the new *Avenger* and see how she meshes with her partner. This episode contains the first Tara King scenes ever filmed. How does the character Tara King come across in her initial outing? She is supposed to be a trained but inexperienced agent, a replacement for the departed icon Mrs. Peel. The various producers knew full well that the vast *Avengers* fan base adored Mrs. Peel and were devastated to see her go. They realised the futility in trying to find a Mrs. Peel-like replacement and wisely attempted to create a new character with a different identity and a different way of relating to John Steed. It is a bit of a rocky start for this character. They definitely struggle with finding the right outfits for her. The blonde wig doesn't flatter the actress and the pink outfits she wears in her investigations are jarringly out of place. It gets worse when she changes into what seems to be a prep high school girl's uniform for the scenes at Lady Beardsley's estate. [4] They do better in the tag scene where her outfit of purple blouse and gold pants is very chic indeed. As to her relationship with her partner, the 'autopsy' conversation is a definite misstep but overall it seems about right for one between a mentor and a pupil. They both seem to be trying to figure each other out. Concerning her competence as an agent, Tara King probably deserves a solid B+. She gets the better of Conrad in the car chase, she defeats a couple of beefy mercenaries in hand-to-hand combat in the warehouse, and she shows some quick wits as she in (a very Steed-like manner) defies the rules of the game and defeats the murderous Conrad in their duel. She does get captured, not once but twice. Steed tries but fails to save her the first time, hence her duel with Conrad in which she has to save herself. He does manage to save her the second time but the accolades coming his way for doing so are limited, since he is saving her from getting blown up by an explosion he himself caused.

What about the actress Linda Thorson? What grade should we give her performance in *Have Guns-Will Haggle*? Given the circumstances, an 'A' would not be inappropriate in my opinion. Considering the turmoil with multiple writers, directors, and producers involved, and considering that this was not only her first *Avengers* appearance, it was her first **screen** appearance; this young actress looks remarkably comfortable in her role in this one. She certainly doesn't make the mistake of trying to imitate the mannerisms of her predecessor. Mrs. Peel's legendary *sang froid* would have been completely out of place in a young agent on her first assignment. In scenes where one would expect her to look anxious and a bit scared, Thorson does indeed look anxious and a bit scared. The character Tara King is young, plucky, and a bit naïve and that is how Thorson plays her. She manages to keep her hero worship under wraps fairly well in her scenes with Steed in this episode, something she doesn't always do in other episodes.

It would be fascinating to be able to view the original episode *Invitation to a Killing*. It must have been a catastrophe of epic proportions. If Clemens thought the other Bryce produced episode, *Invasion of the Earthmen* was good enough to broadcast and *Invitation* wasn't, it boggles the mind to imagine just how bad the predecessor of *Have Guns-Will Haggle* must be. David K Smith, on his incomparable *The Avengers Forever!* website, summed it up perfectly about *Invasion of the Earthmen*; "*Plan Nine from Outer Space* meets classic *Star Trek*." It is by far the worst *Avengers* episode ever seen. [5] And *Invitation to a Killing* is actually worse? Brian Clemens justifiably has his critics but it is to his immense credit that he was able to rework it into the very watchable *Have Guns-Will Haggle*.

© Dan O'Shea

1. I think that in this case it is an intelligently playful example of recycling, adding an intertextual richness, as opposed to the more lazy recycling of Peel-era music.
2. The series' critique of British colonialism and its civil servants offers an interesting darker layer.
3. As a female mastermind she is a rarity, and her moral darkness clashes wonderfully with her beauty.
4. Frank Hui reckons that Tara is wearing a Mod sportswear interpretation of a dress-kilt ensemble.
5. Worse than *Homicide and Old Lace*? Or *Thingumajig*? Or the Peel-era *The Living Dead*? It's very difficult to choose between them!

LOOK – (STOP ME IF YOU'VE HEARD THIS ONE) BUT THERE WERE THESE TWO FELLERS...

Filmed: February 1968

Exterior Locations:
Caritol Land and Development Corporation office block, car park
Lake
Country lanes
Vauda Villa: entrance, drive

Sets:
Caritol Land and Development offices: boardroom, office, lobby
Tara's car
Steed's mews apartment
Rugman's make-up registration office
Marler's gag office
Vauda Villa: artistes' lounge/stage/reading room, store

LOOK – (STOP ME IF YOU'VE HEARD THIS ONE) BUT THERE WERE THESE TWO FELLERS...

Main Character List:
Miss Charles: secretary
Sir Jeremy Broadfoot: director
Merry Maxie Martin: vaudevillian clown
Jennings: vaudevillian clown
Tara King
John Steed
Thomas Cleghorn: director
Marcus Rugman: make-up registration artist
Brigadier Wiltshire: director
Bradley Marler: comedy writer
Lord Dessington: director
Seagrave: director, mastermind
Fiery Frederick: vaudeville artiste
Merlin: principal of Vauda Villa for 'resting artistes'
Tenor: artiste
Escapologist: artiste
Ventriloquist: artiste

A countdown followed by the rapid beat of furious percussions:
8..7..6..5..4..3..2..1
A gun site tracks a roving male target to an all familiar tune. The target transforms into a dapper master spy.
A sensuous brass accompanies a more feminine silhouette that flashes to bright lips attached to an *ingénue* with gorgeous eyes.
This opponent is persistent, determined to gun down our heroes. Despite the furore, the assassin's efforts are skillfully blocked by a trusty bowler. [1]

The Avengers was a show that constantly evolved throughout the duration of its run. It was originally presented with the underlying premise of vengeance over the death of an innocent. It was reconceived as a more straightforward counter-espionage thriller with a ground-breaking feminist bent. It expanded to become a whimsical spoof of the genre that was both satirical and yet surreal and made a pop culture icon out of Diana Rigg. The final period featuring Linda Thorson would struggle to further that evolution. The early conflict parallels the instability and changes in the production staff. This resulted in an extensive period of transition, requiring well over a dozen episodes before settling down to a consistent tone and dynamic.

The early adventures were produced by John Bryce, with a weak attempt to remain in sync with the tone and dynamic of the Rigg episodes. This is apparent when watching the episodes in production order. Such a strategy is not surprising when one takes into account that in the US the first seven stories from the Tara King era formed a block that was originally transmitted in conjunction with the final eight episodes featuring Mrs. Peel. Six of those seven episodes would air in the United States several months before they were shown in the United Kingdom. Under this scheduling one can observe a partial through-line with the prior era.

With the return of the previous producers Brian Clemens and Albert Fennell, many of the characteristics associated with the Rigg period would, oddly enough, be phased out and eventually replaced with a divergent style and a different interaction between the leads. *Look, (Stop Me if You've Heard This One) But There Were These Two Fellers...* is a polarizing episode that bears quite a distinction. It would be the final episode of the aforementioned US specific block and represented the turning point where the show would diverge radically away from the format laid out during the Emma Peel period. Ironically *Two Fellers* is the Tara King episode that most closely resembles the structure of an Emma Peel adventure. It is the formulaic murder spree wrapped up in elements that typically would be labelled by fans as subversive and placed in an arch, fantasy setting. It is arguably the most extreme example of its type: pushing the boundaries to the limit and challenging the audience's suspension of disbelief more so than any other episode. The artificiality is pervasive, playing up different aspects of the same themes. Some would claim 'relentlessly so' and 'without any subtlety'. That in itself may be a root cause for its polarising effect. It is one of those works that viewers either whole heartedly embrace or abhor. [2]

The theme being played at is something considered 'obsolete' going up against something 'progressive'. In this case it takes the form of pranks and practical jokes. Cream pies to the face, banana peels, prop guns, fake hands and the like are part of a bygone art form. They are instruments of a type of humour that ceased to draw admirers and are amusing mainly to a more juvenile mindset. A shadow of another era, they are as outmoded as their owners: Merrie Maxie Martin and his partner Jennings, once great stars of the Gladchester Palladium.

Their motive for murder is based on desperation. They and their fellow obsolete Vaudevillians have been (sadly) duped into thinking that killing off the board members of the Carrollton Land and Development Corporation (the company that has taken possession of their performance venues) will allow them to return to their former lives and regain some measure of happiness. For them, blocking urban renewal via such extreme measures will lead to regaining paradise lost. The degree of denial and delusion is so massive that it evokes sympathy. It's particularly pitiful since they genuinely believe that this is all it will take for them to return to their former lives. They refuse to accept that they are not just out of step, but also perhaps just plain lousy. An inept escape artist, a singer with a limited range, a ventriloquist whose lips move, a magician who's a one-trick pony and a pony that has no tricks all make for a rather pathetic bunch. It's a group who are led by fallen idols: a pair of comedians who have remained obstinately stagnant and cannot accept that the world no longer has any need for what made them celebrated. Compounding all of this is how deeply they are all defined by performing. For them to be denied the opportunity to enact their art is likened to a homicidal attack. Striking back is just self-defence. [3]

It is perversely ironic that the archaic shtick of Merry Maxie Martin would prove to be quite effective as a means for murder. Ironic but not surprising since practical jokes awkwardly straddle a thin line between *Schadenfreude* humour and fatal consequences. Only minimal effort is required to cross it. But Maxie, ever craving the spotlight, does far more than the minimum. Every murderous act is committed as a full blown variation of his comedy routine, complete with cakewalks and jazz hands. The man needs to perform. The venue is irrelevant. The *modus operandi* of our killers is undoubtedly bizarre – some might say downright silly – making each death progressively more absurd. Simultaneously, they become more brutal and horrifying. The accumulation of which comes full force with the final murder, that of Lord Dessington. The manner of the attack is utterly ridiculous, with the rug literally being pulled out from under him. Yet director James Hill sets it up with a Hitchcockian structure and pacing. The audience can clearly see what Martin and Jennings intend to do, but there is a suspenseful fascination as their machinations steadily play out in time with the banter unfolding between Tara and Lord Dessington. It is during that dialogue that their victim is presented at his most sympathetic: a warm human being who is being unfairly targeted. That we know how the scene will end does not diminish the impact of his death. Once the deed is done, all silliness ceases. Satire is tossed out the window along with this poor man's body in what is arguably one of the most shocking deaths ever aired on the show. When the villains take their final bow, the feeling that remains is no longer one of absurdity but gruesomeness, even repulsion.

This is all in keeping with the satiric mix of violent surrealism and low comedic theatricality that writer Dennis Spooner and director James Hill have infused throughout the episode.

1) Steed and Tara deal with a polymorphic clue;
2) They play magic tricks with each other during their investigation;
3) The writer Bradley Marler works in an office over three feet deep in discarded jokes;
4) Marcus Rugman is a register who uses eggs that he doesn't bother to blow out the internal contents of or even hard-boil;
5) The merry Vaudevillains are defeated with the blackjacks of silent film, each attack reflecting their individual craft (and Steed getting to enact the funnier assaults);
6) Our heroes take a bow and dance off at the end of the episode;
7) In the tag, Steed shows off his mastery of Maxie Martin's quick change skills.

The capper to all this is that our mastermind, Seagraves, presents himself as Punch and Judy. His performance is done in true Punchinello form with the crocodile practically stealing the show when he utters the line, "Yes! Give her to Fiery Frederick!" Furthermore, this particular disguise raises an interesting question. Appearing as these descendants from the *Commedia Dell'arte* is consistent with the episode's motif, as well as being the most effective way of winning over our desperate performers. But the choice perhaps was not solely a Machiavellian one. Seagraves is shown to be remarkably adept at playing the most famous puppets in history. It brings up the possibility that he also might have been a failed performer. If this was the case, his decision to make use of these "resting artistes" to execute his plan may also indicate an act of empathy on his part to give them some purpose. Not to mention that it would explain how he knew where to find them to begin with.

As stated earlier, *Two Fellers* represents a turning point in the direction *The Avengers* would take during the Tara King era. This story and the ones previously produced are much more in line with the structure of the Peel era, granted with variable quality. It is with the stories that came afterwards where the series would undergo substantial and uneven changes before finally settling down into a feasible style. Within *Two Fellers* there were many aspects similar to the Emma Peel formula, yet there were already a number that deviated from the structure and foreshadowed the more radical upcoming changes. Some of which did not always sit well with the fans. Those aspects can be characterised accordingly:

Credits: the earlier described opening credits and the corresponding closing credits that were attached to the US transmission of those early adventures are clearly in the same vein of those designed for the colour Peel series. We have our two leads, interacting against a stark white studio space, playing out a surreal narrative. The closing credits differ a bit in continuing that narrative with the imagery that was more Freudian: Tara erotically assessing the hole to Steed's bowler with her finger. Later, her hand caresses the lapel of his jacket in close-up. The tone is also more whimsical as the mysterious assassin from the opener comes back, mischievously trying to finish the job. That same irreverence is observed with Tara using her gun as a mirror, immediately followed by her shooting it at their unknown opponent. The moment is consistent with the attitude of *The Avengers* while characterising her as different from her predecessor. This partner is a more feminine, playful entity.

These end credits would subtly reflect the instability that the show was under at the time. When comparing this block of seven, one can see that the end credits slightly differ for almost all of them. Come the autumn of 1968, the opening credits would be completely overhauled. It would still be true to the spirit of the show with Steed very much being Steed. But Tara would be presented in a new way as she instantly changes from a beautiful but impractical gown to a colourful, combat-ready pantsuit.

Plot Structure: We have a script that predictably follows the patented Peel formula:

1) A group of people is targeted for murder;
2) The crimes are organised by a mysterious boss who turns out to one of the characters we met early on;
3) In between killings, Steed and his partner investigate and engage in banter and/or activities that may or may not relate to their case;
4) We encounter eccentric characters performing jobs in a surreal manner;
5) The heroes team up for a final fight against a pair of adversaries with stylized choreography;
6) Right after the fight is over they engage in more witty banter.

Check. Check. Check. Check. Check. And Check.

It is noteworthy that this story – that is so close in format to an Emma Peel script – was written by someone who never had a story produced during that era. It's the only King story that Dennis Spooner and James Hill worked on. The successive episodes would go on to greatly break away from the above recipe. Yes, we would still see stories with a serial hit list or quirky characters or the occasional tongue-in-cheek humour, but we would never again see one that so closely adhered to this blueprint.

The Dynamic Between the Leads: One of the complaints levelled against the King era is the more obvious manner in which the romantic relationship between Steed and Tara is shown. It should be pointed out that while these early King episodes presented their relationship as less ambiguous than Steed's situation with Mrs. Peel or Mrs. Gale, it was still fairly low key. The only exception being *The Forget-Me-Knot* which was written by Clemens. For example, when Steed rescues Tara from being burned in half by Fiery Frederick, her reaction to his arrival is rather nonchalant and she merely lets loose a quick quip. There are no tears or blatant fawning. That kind of response would appear in succeeding episodes like *Game* and *Noon Doomsday*. Such overstated emotions would occur for several stories before the show runners would wisely downplay such displays by the final third of the series.

During the epilogue, Steed for the first time directly addresses Tara by her first name. In earlier episodes he uses Miss King. It is important to note this happened after Clemens and Fennell returned as producers. It is key to something more critical. Once he starts referring to her as Tara instead of Miss King, that familiarity allows the writers to portray them much more openly as lovers. If he had continued referring to Tara by her surname, it is doubtful we would have got such frequent displays of open histrionics, if at all. [4]

Amateur Status: Another key change was Tara's professional ranking. Her first two episodes had her initially as another amateur that Steed recruits to help with his investigations. That was altered by Clemens and Fennell, a prudent decision since her original conception came off as 'weak'. In those initial scripts she was more akin to a glorified Venus Smith. The audience is left wondering why Steed would recruit her since she doesn't seem to possess any unusual skills, compared to Cathy Gale or Emma Peel. Shifting her to official spy status justifies her presence and gives her a new dimension. Unfortunately, she is a novice agent at this point in the series. A charming novice, but still a novice nonetheless. This character detail would contribute to the dynamic of Steed taking on an overprotective attitude. Fortunately, with an ongoing period of transition, that beginner status would end up being phased out, along with the overt fawning within a dozen or so episodes. Tara would eventually be turned into a strong, proficient agent.

A strong case can be made that Tara was a step backwards for the series and for feminism. However, despite those early mistakes and inconsistencies, it could also be argued that from one aspect she could be seen as being equally progressive as her predecessors. (Granted, this is from a hindsight viewpoint). While it is clear that Tara is not as brilliant or accomplished as Emma or Cathy, it begs the question why would she need to be, in order to be a good field agent. Steed's prior partners were never official government employees. Up until now he's never partnered up with someone who was officially a co-worker. Were there not any females already working at the Ministry? And as wonderful as Mrs. Gale and Mrs. Peel were, an underlying negative message can be discerned. An unintentional subtext arose that implies that female agents are the exception and not the norm. And even to be seriously considered for this job, the women have to be academic geniuses or absurdly gifted. How many of Steed's male colleagues are as qualified as Emma or Cathy? How many of them needed to be, in order to be hired? It plays into that adage of having to be twice as good in order to get half as much respect. [5] With Tara and the women who followed her (Lady Diana Forbes-Blakeney; Purdey), the idea advocated is that a woman doesn't have to be near superhuman in order to be good at this or any other profession.

Humour: Brian Clemens has often stated that he created the character of Mother since he deemed Linda Thorson unable to handle the humour the show was renowned for. *Two Fellers* challenges that assertion. The script has at least five scenarios where Steed engages Tara in the same kind of light, easy banter he would often have with Mrs. Peel. Could Linda Thorson tackle the humour with the same skill as Diana Rigg? No. Not at that point in her career. But was she capable of doing a competent job? Yes. It helps to have a strong writer and director on hand. This episode demonstrates that with the right people, Thorson had the ability to handle wit. This is demonstrated particularly with her scenes with William Kendall as Lord Dessington. Their interaction is genteel and awkward yet humorously endearing, with Thorson giving her most assured performance to date. And while she clearly did not have the same degree of chemistry with Patrick Macnee, Thorson could interact with him well enough if the writing was there. She manages to respectably play off of Macnee in their humorous moments, particularly in the final exchange, just before knocking out the mastermind Seagraves. Sadly, those whimsical interactions would soon become almost non-existent, instead being replaced by Steed playing much broader comedy against Mother.

Avengerland: The final significant change for the show lies in the fabric of the world that it resides in. *Two Fellers* presents that artificial mix of surrealism and satire which would today be referred to by fans as subversive. It is the typical world that had become *de rigueur* for the Peel era, but taken to its most extreme degree. It doesn't get any more madcap than this. From this point on, the show would pull back and shift gears. That surrealistic tone would not completely disappear, but by the end of the series that heralded subversion would appear in far fewer episodes or with less prominence. The satire would still remain, but it would end up sharing the spotlight with a darker, more grounded world. Interestingly, the side effect of this is that any humour stands out more and appears more pronounced. A very different world from the one Steed inhabited with his previous partner.

© Frank Hui

1. These opening credits are not, of course, the ones seen in the UK where we saw the 'field of armour' images.
2. Frank is spot-on about the way this episode splits opinion. However, after many viewings, I don't belong in either camp. As a one-off episode I enjoy it, but it lacks some of the key 'subversive champagne' elements I look for in a 'classic' episode.
3. Frank's comments remind me of the villains in *Epic*, an episode which this one has much in common with.
4. While Brian Clemens has suggested that Steed and Tara were never lovers, their on-screen physicality suggests otherwise.
5. I think that these are key observations which challenge many critics' perceptions about *The Avengers*' female leads.

MY WILDEST DREAM

Filmed: April 1968

Exterior Locations:
Peregrine's home: fire escape
Jaeger's office
Winthrop's house: façade, drive
Acme Precision
London streets
Stable Mews

Sets:
Peregrine's home: penthouse living room
Jaeger's consulting room, outer office
Tara King's apartment
Acme Precision: Gibbons' office, Slater's office
Winthrop's house: dark room
Observation unit
Tara King's street
Steed's mews apartment

MY WILDEST DREAM

Main Character List:
Paul Gibbons: vice president of Acme Precision Combine Limited
Aloysius Peregrine: vice president of Acme Precision Combine
Dr. Jaeger: quack psychologist, 'aggresso-therapist'
Janet Owen: villain nurse working for Jaeger
Dyson: henchman
Tara King
Honourable Teddy Chilcott: in love with Tara King
John Steed
Frank Tobias: Acme Precision vice president, mastermind
Slater: optics section of Acme Precision
Henry Winthrop: Acme Precision
Dr. Reece: ministry psychologist

Philip Levene was one of *The Avengers*' most prolific writers, penning a total of 19 scripts. Though he would continue to be listed as 'script consultant' for a few more episodes, *My Wildest Dream* was, sadly, his final *Avengers* script. There seems to be the suggestion that he left the series due to a falling out with Brian Clemens over the direction the show was going and Terry Nation replaced him as script editor. Taking on board that supposition, it does seem that Levene wanted to inject more emotional reality into his episodes and take them away from the more cartoon style of Season 5. There seem to be more consequences for the leads in Levene's contributions. They aren't so detached from the cases. For example, Steed is investigating friends in *The Curious Case of the Countless Clues* and his close colleagues get murdered in *Get-A-Way!*, of whom he says, "I wouldn't be here now if it weren't for them". [1] The more carefree, detached style is evident once Levene left the show.

For *My Wildest Dream*, Levene decided to use a murderous twist on the increasingly popular psychological techniques of cathartic expressions that were very much in vogue in the 1950s, 60s and 70s. There was the widespread belief in the benefits of 'letting it all out' or 'giving vent to your emotions'. The book *Crazy Therapies* by Margaret Singer and Janja Lalich takes a cynical look at the free-for-all approaches employed in this period. The authors noted that many of the venting techniques did little good and in some cases caused more harm. Levene took this into the *Avengers* world and definitely made that the case. Though the idea of living out a fantasy murder of someone the client absolutely hates is an inventive technique created by the 'dabbling' Dr. Jaegar, it unquestionably comes into the category of 'causes more harm'. And when you have a diabolical mastermind around who, with the aid of drugs, brings the fantasy deaths into reality, you have a problem for the Avengers to solve.

Bringing the episode visually to life was new director, Robert Fuest. Fuest had worked on the show previously in the capacity of set designer. Way back in Season 1 he collaborated on many episodes with visionary director Peter Hammond. Hammond was a visual wizard of the early seasons. Despite shows at Teddington Studio usually getting a good size design budget, they couldn't afford to build many large sets. Hammond's creativity came in particularly useful in getting around this problem. As Brian Clemens explained in the 1992 *Without Walls* documentary, "If we were shooting in a bank, we'd just have a grill and some money and shoot through that". Fuest shared on the Optimum DVD commentary for *Game* that Hammond made a big impact on him and was directly responsible for inspiring Fuest to become a director himself. His big directorial break came in 1967 with the film *Just Like a Woman* starring Wendy Craig. As well as writing and directing it, he also designed the sets, giving the film a very unique, Swinging Sixties look. It was this film that brought him to the attention of *Avengers* producer Albert Fennell, ever on the lookout for a director with an *Avengers* touch of style. Fuest would direct eight episodes for Season 6.

The opening scene plays out with the tropes of a thriller adventure as a would-be murderer (Gibbons) makes his way up a fire escape to his intended victim's apartment. The setting is rather drab but it's made to look interesting through the placement of the camera. *The Avengers* is a world of style, a world that always has a twist on the mundane. An ordinary fire escape should be made to look more interesting than it is. We see Gibbons' face appear through the handrail and his hand comes directly to the foreground as he pulls himself to the camera and passes right to left. He goes out of shot but instead of the camera following him, it pans to right and records his ascending shadow on the wall. We see an intense close-up of his eyes through the steps above him. A low shot sees his feet move up to the apartment. Director Robert Fuest favours faster cutting shots, moving away from the more leisurely approach favoured by directors like Don Sharp and James Hill earlier in the season. Cut to studio. A bold blue set decorated with striking pieces of opulent gold paraphernalia. The camera sees the victim through an ornamental spinning gold Ferris wheel. The setting says, simply, wealth. The victim (Aloysius Peregrine) sees Gibbons in the mirror and we see him react in the mirror before turning. As he turns, the viewer becomes the victim. We are staring at up Gibbons as he raises the large piercing knife. The effect is disorientating as it cuts between the victim's reaction and us seeing his point of view. Then the knife comes down to pierce Peregrine but the scene jumps to another location where Gibbons is stabbing a dummy with a photo of Peregrine's face attached. Bass guitar has accompanied the build to the murder. With the cut from this drug-induced fantasy into the reality of Dr. Jaegar's surgery, the music becomes dreamlike.

The Avengers TV show is a dream land; the reality for the series is scored with dream music. We're watching the dream of the writer and the director. Gibbons is led away from the appointment not looking like someone who has benefited from his cathartic release. A handheld camera looks over the roof of his chauffeur-driven car as he exits the surgery. The camera then moves down to look through the open car window as he climbs inside. We're curious about this man and what kind of therapy has taken place so we're looking for clues by peering into the car. He greets the man in the back seat next to him who gives him short shrift. The man is behind a newspaper. He lowers the newspaper and we see Peregrine.

Curious. Then up pops the title, *My Wildest Dream* and things start becoming clearer.

For his final episode, Levene breaks with tradition. Following the episode title, the expectation of the audience is that we will see Steed and Tara as that's how it is nearly always done. As the opening murder was only a fantasy, there's no reason for Steed and Tara to become involved so the scene actually returns to Jaegar's consulting room. Jaegar's counselling is presented like an interrogation in line with the thinking that counselling should be aggressive and direct, as that will aid the client. Fuest opens the scene with a bright light to emphasise this. Gibbons is pulled around, shouted at and injected with drugs. Therapy seems to be a contradiction.

What happens next is actually the villains' big mistake. If they were diabolical masterminds of quality they should have known that involving Steed as the perfect witness was a bad idea. They actually engineered their own downfall.

Jaegar's secretary Nurse Owen phones Steed at Tara's apartment whilst she is pestered for a date by love interest Teddy Chilcott. It's clear that Tara only has eyes for Steed. She gets Steed to fake a ballet date with her which is interesting as she was dressed up anyway. Was this just in the vain hope that Steed would call and take her out? Following Nurse Owen's warning that Peregrine is in danger, they rush off to his aid.

Peregrine's real death is initiated. We see the dummy swinging on a rope with stab marks already present yet we hear Jaegar leading Gibbons through his fantasy murder procedure. He describes the scene just as we saw it previously. Gibbons is so pumped full of drugs that he imagines that what is taking place is fantasy. As he sees the face of his victim, reality and the drug-induced dream mix so he sees the photo face of Peregrine over the real face. Following the murder, Steed and Tara rush into the setting. They remain silent as the confused Gibbons innocently protests that the situation is a dream. He looks at the knife. There is no blood. On one level, he's right of course, it is just a dream. No one has been murdered; Hugh Moxey as Peregrine got up and went home after completing his scenes. Yet as *The Avengers* dream continues, he backs away and falls to his death. In this thicker cardboard version of the dream, Tara reacts to the sight of his fallen body with distress.

As Steed and Tara look over the scene of the crime, Fuest uses the reflection from a glass case to show Peregrine's dead body on the floor (Fuest's inspirational guru Peter Hammond was very fond of mirrors). And, just as with a dream, the conversation continues without pausing even though the setting has rapidly changed to Tara's apartment.

Following a meeting with the shrouded villain Tobias, Steed discusses his findings with Tara whilst she waters her plants with a teapot (wearing a fetching long wig).

Steed: So seriously suspecting...
Tara: ...as we usually do!

They may be dealing with murder and serious issues yet they can still have fun and face their cases with a quirky sense of style and enjoyment at the clichés.

Dr. Jaeger, meanwhile, has moved on to his next client, Slater. His hate figure, Winthrop, is depersonalised just as Peregrine was. A photo of his face is attached to a dummy. The dummy is pushed around and humiliated. Winthrop is a literal 'dummy of a man'. He's no longer an actual human being, he's just a prop. Slater stabs the dummy with a large knife causing sawdust to explode outwards. Fuest shows us Jaeger's satisfaction through a glass tabletop which is promptly covered in the sawdust. The sawdust visually represents the cathartic release. Result!

By so blatantly depersonalising the victim, Levene's making a comment on how the show has used characters as pure fodder for the plot. They don't have an identity other than that of a murder victim. Yet these victims have a life and interests. Peregine appears to be mending a watch in his spare time; he isn't just a board member. The same for Winthrop; he also works at Acme Precision Combine but he spends a lot of time in his darkroom developing photos and is shocked by Peregrine's death. Yet with Jaeger's technique, they are robbed of their lives and are just dummies to be used.

As Slater narrates the fantasy of Winthrop's death, Fuest shows Slater's eye in the reflection of the knife. We see his legs heading towards Winthrop's home but it's his shadow holding the knife. As he imagines that the death is a fantasy, he is not responsible; he's distanced from himself. He enters the darkroom and is framed by a paper cutter and a large photo of Winthrop. He pulls down the cutter, slicing Winthrop's photo in two, a symbolic precursor to the murder. Winthrop turns and is stabbed just as Tara and Steed enter yet again as witnesses. But this time they've interrupted the dream and not the reality. Winthrop is alone and Slater is nowhere in sight. When the murder does finally take place, the dark room's red light illuminates the knife blade in a way that suggests blood, without the reality of it.

Tara goes to Acme Precision Combine to find Slater's office diary in order to check his appointments. On entering the office we are privy to Dyson, Tobias' henchman, getting there first. The camera follows Dyson lurking in the foreground shadows, as Tara moves to Slater's desk. Slater appears in the reflection of a glass panel whilst the camera views Tara. He turns out the light. The next shot is through a glass panel showing the sights of a gun. As Tara appears in the centre, Dyson makes his attack. Tara's fighting approach often involves wrestling and tussling and using whatever comes to hand. She picks up a glass panel containing the gun sights' image and uses it against Dyson. She's not going to be his victim. Great use is made of the elaborate set. Fuest has lots of fun with a variety of stylish camera angles and the set is dramatically lit by Frank Watts with strong shadows. A car chase between the two then follows. The chase scene itself marks a shift in the series' format in that it takes place in central London. [2] Car chases had been previously the province of isolated country lanes.

Robert Fuest's influence is really felt when it comes to the 'Observation' room where Slater is held. The script probably described a standard hospital style bedroom to meet its needs. With a desire to push the visuals in a wilder direction and celebrate the madness of the show, Fuest asked Robert Jones for an expansive white space with the word 'observation' massively dominating the back wall, the letter 'O' becoming a door. Transparent screens surround the bed in the centre. The room is truly dreamlike as it makes no sense in reality. The screens have no function as they are transparent; there's no hiding in this room. It could connect to the wild therapeutic beliefs of the time. Is Dr. Reece hoping for a beneficial reaction by the patient feeling so exposed? Does it have to make sense though, other than offering a wonderfully bold and artistic visual image?

Dr. Reece is knocked out by Dyson, and Slater is manipulated into killing Tobias (as a charade to take suspicion away from him). Reece isn't worried about Slater being missing. Steed's response is interesting. He reacts with anger at this short-sightedness. Dr. Reece is a humorous character constantly delighting in his new experimental drugs and he doesn't seem to comprehend the severity of the situation. Normally such a character on the side of the heroes would be treated with measured calm, regardless of how eccentric they were. Yet here the seriousness of the situation provokes a response of anger from Steed – he's taking it seriously. In line with Brian Clemens' expression, the Season 6 cardboard is thicker.

"And then there was one". Tobias is the only surviving member of the Acme board when he kills Slater, supposedly in self-defence. With the board opposition out of the way, the villains need to deal with their "unimpeachable" witness.

Tara: Are you unimpeachable?
Steed: Well that's beside the point.

Jaegar has so far been presented as the villain; it is, after all, his technique which leads to the murders. Steed's investigation leads to the surgery. He adopts a playful persona to ease his way in. He jokes about his name; it causes him to canter around his club. Nurse Owen says Dr. Jaegar can't help.

Steed: Oh I don't want to be cured. But do you know anyone who'd like to buy seven tons of hay?

All the jollity soon vanishes and he gets to the point of his visit. This is quite a rare scene as Steed calls the self-inflicted doctor out for his technique. It suggests wider implications than just the episode. It could be a comment on amateurs thinking they can develop their own therapeutic techniques as they jump on a bandwagon. It seems to be that at this stage Steed might believe that the murders are just the result of Jaegar's poor counselling and not due to any masterminding. Since Steed does not appear for the rest of the episode until the end, regardless of his use as a witness, one could surmise that he considers it a shut case. Steed's personal storyline is at a dead-end.

The episode's 'Chekhov's Gun' now comes into play: Teddy Chilcott, initially a comic relief character, desperately attempting to woo Tara, only to be thwarted by Steed at every turn. The villains want to use Jaegar's technique on Steed so need someone who hates him. Chilcott really hates Steed for being a barrier to Tara's affections. He blames Steed rather than his own overbearing personality. He is almost a literal gun introduced early in the episode, waiting to be fired by the villains.

Unfortunately the episode becomes weaker from this point and feels like it's going through the motions. Structurally it makes sense but there's no added dynamism. There's no gear change as proceedings race to a climax. The reason why the final act doesn't work is that it prevents Steed and Tara from being Avengers. He disappears from the episode and Tara has a fight with Dyson and a breaking and entering visit to Jaegar's to occupy her. They've been used as pawns throughout the episode but they don't get the advantage as the episode draws to its conclusion. The ball is still in the villains' court until the final moments. It's essentially their story that we're following and Steed and Tara can only react to it. Steed has become a victim in his own show and is treated like all the other faceless dummies/murder victims. It's only his fast spy reactions to Chilcott and then Tobias that see the problem so swiftly dealt with;

the denouement can't be anything more than a disappointing anti-climax.

Of course, the tag scene had to feature a play on a therapy session between Steed and Tara. He shares a story from his childhood, relating to being deprived of champagne. Tara says that this explains his fondness but Steed says, "No, the insatiable craving, the perpetual desire, the uncontrollable urge, to lay my hands on a bottle of champagne, is for a very different reason...I happen to like it."

Was Philip Levene exercising his personal demons after a troubled, unproductive time in therapy? Or did he just think it a load of mumbo jumbo? Who knows? Maybe he just thought it was a good idea for an *Avengers* plot. And with that plot he departed. Mr. Levene, we raise a glass of champagne to you in celebration of all those wild dreams you committed to paper and entertained us with. [3]

© Darren Burch

1. Steed's all-night party is an extremely emotive and atmospheric scene which allows us to feel for the victims in a way which Clemens rarely allows.
2. This is a great example of *The Avengers* 'making it new' in Season 6 as the cityscape of affluent London becomes a semi-regular location.
3. I agree with Darren that Levene's historical importance as an *Avengers* writer should not be underestimated. His reputation as the 'science fiction' writer on the show is a misleading generalisation, as glorious episodes such as *Something Nasty in the Nursery*, *Who's Who???* and *Death's Door* demonstrate.

WHOEVER SHOT POOR GEORGE OBLIQUE STROKE XR40?

Filmed: April 1968

Exterior Locations:
Ministry of Technology: Cybernetic and Computer Division: building, security fence
Urban street
Baines' apartment block
Pelley's mansion: façade, summer house, grounds

Sets:
Ministry of Technology: computer laboratory, research area, waiting area
Baines' apartment: living room, communal staircase
Pelley's mansion: hallway, study, staircase, Blue room, landing, cellar
Steed's mews apartment

WHOEVER SHOT POOR GEORGE OBLIQUE STROKE XR40?

Main Character List:
Tobin: works at MOT, inside man
Baines: works at MOT
Jacobs: gardener/henchman
Tara King
John Steed
Dr. Ardmore: cybernetic surgeon
Electrical Anaesthetist
Jason: butler (imposter)
Sir Wilfred Pelley: George's inventor
Loris: female mastermind
Keller: chauffeur/henchman
Jill: nurse

Tony Williamson's *Whoever Shot Poor George Oblique XR40?* is a master class in what *The Avengers* does best – tell a tale you already know, but tell it from the perspective of the Gun and the Rose: tweak it, quirk it, give it a spin and put it out there. Telling the story of a technology tragedy which leads to a Christie conclusion looks ordinary on paper, unless you happen to have Williamson's talent for dialogue and pace.

As one of only a handful of writers whose output for BBC Television and ITV is almost knock-for-knock, Tony Williamson's body of work is hugely impressive. Standout successes for the BBC include *Counterstrike*, *Adam Adamant Lives!*, *The Revenue Men* (tales of smuggling and customs leaks), *Mask Of Janus*, *The Spies* (his superb script for *If I Can't Win, I Don't Play* is almost a summary of his approach to all spy-detective stories he told: "Espionage is only a game, a game with no rules, no referee and no final whistle. A dangerous game where cheating counts more than honour") and *Codename* ("It's not every day you'll see a Cambridge don oiling his semi-automatic pistol"), while his output for ITV was largely reserved for Lew Grade's catalogue of ITC programmes.

What is particularly significant in reflecting on this episode of *The Avengers*, however, is Williamson's previous submissions for the series itself: the first script for Diana Rigg (*The Murder Market*); the wonderfully Dickensian Emma Peel episode *Too Many Christmas Trees*: followed up by the pure *Avengers* class of *The Thirteenth Hole* (the teaser alone on that episode draws inspiration for the teaser of *Poor George*): and then the electrifying *Positive Negative Man*. His first offering for Tara King, the *Super Secret Cypher Snatch*, is discussed in detail elsewhere in this study, but in drawing these *Avengers* threads together a common theme emerges – take the everyday, throw it away and move away to some distance, tilt the head to the right, view the world from a different angle and try again.

Seasoned, 'veteran' director Cyril Frankel wraps viewers in the customary brooding air of sinister goings-on as the episode opens with the familiar scenario of a security guard prowling the grounds of another super-secret establishment, this time the Ministry of Technology and Cybernetic Computer Division. Amidst that halcyon time when every evening was moonlit with sunlight (day for night at its best still looks a bit too much like day for night no matter how well you disguise it), someone is clambering over the walls and lurking menacingly in the near-shadows, armed and ready to strike. Meanwhile, flustered scientific boffin Baines (Adrian Ropes) urgently calls his colleague Tobin (Frank Windsor, making a departure from the ever-reliable Watt from *Z-Cars/Softy Softly/Softly Softly: Task Force*, etc) to advise that George is throwing some sort of fit after being fed. There is much off-screen panting and agonised gasps as Tobin confirms he is on his way. The intruder, Jacobs (John Porter-Davison), bursts into the Administration wing and fires a twelve-bore shotgun into a vibrating computer bank before knocking the security guard unconscious and fleeing the scene. With the sudden reveal that George has been shot, the two scientists draw a computer printout from the smoking technology mess: "Attention! I have a message of the most vital importance. Help!"

With the familiar scenario of Steed and Tara on the trail of the culprits responsible, mixed with the out of the ordinary identity of the victim as a super computer ("one of the best brains in the country") with a desperate need to talk, the episode itself could be told along fairly linear lines. And some may say that it does indeed do so, rising minimally above the ordinary along the way. However, the episode contains much to enjoy, both visually and audibly – some of Williamson's dialogue bristles here – and there are a few set-pieces which are delicious *Avengers* stuff.

The standout point about Cyril Frankel's approach to directing this story is the skilful employment of low, brooding lighting in the majority of scenes, matched with the fact that Williamson has written an episode of *The Avengers* which scarcely moves away from the three main locations (an additional, albeit briefly-seen, location being Steed's apartment). The majority of the heavy-lifting of the episode falls on the shoulders of Anthony Nicholls as Doctor Ardmore (desperately toiling to save his 'patient' through a series of operations which are at times hampered and at times nearly ruined by the sabotage attempts of Tobin, who is later revealed to be part of a plot to permanently silence George and his rambling computer-feed). A gruff surgeon who lurches from one crisis to another in a bid to put George back on his castors, Ardmore is the lynchpin around which Steed and Tara circulate in a search for clues.

Tara, who enjoys a different costume in virtually every new scene in this episode, from svelte and figure-hugging in a masquerade cat-suit, to donning an easy-on-the-eye ensemble when she later pretends to be a long-forgotten American niece of one of the major players, is given the customary leg-work in this episode: in search of Baines' working notes on the indigestible equation which gave George a dangerous case of irritable bowel circuitry, she enjoys some of the best dialogue in the opening half-hour, exchanges with Baines (whilst wearing her cat suit) of "You don't own a dog, do you?" and, later, as they tortuously navigate the same set of stairs shot from different angles to give the villainous Jacobs enough time to pinch his notes from his high-above-the-sky apartment, there is some nice – corny but the sort of material you'd happily have seen

Emma Peel doing while flipping through the Yellow Pages any day – banter between Tara and Baines, thus:

Baines: To have curves in my place would be sacrilege.
Tara: Well perhaps I better...
Baines: No, no, no. I don't like right angled girls, although I don't mind girls with the right angle.

There is the customary fight in the darkened apartment as Jacobs shoots Baines before fleeing, after knocking Tara senseless with the shotgun, only for a half-conscious Tara to take a tumble or two down the stairs, before losing consciousness and waking later to discover Baines' corpse. There is a growing trend of 'Tara is found/finds something, Tara is knocked unconscious, Tara wakes up and staggers through the next scene' which emerged in this final series. Matched with the hopeless state of the locks on her apartment door – welcome one villain, welcome all! The door is open, feel free! – it became something of a mark on its card for this run.

Further tense operations ensue with Dr. Ardmore doing a variation on *The Gravediggers* in tinkering away with spanners and lances in a bid to steady his patient's condition. (The heart monitor for George resembles a pretty promising nightclub drumbeat for a modern-day audience). Switching over to pure AC, with urgent demands for full power and the occasional mop of a brow, George blows a fuse during the touch-and-go operations, before issuing the cryptic message: "Pelley...Traitor". Ardmore is baffled that George, crying out for his creator Sir Wilfred Pelley (*The Power Game*'s legendary Clifford Evans, all eyebrows and gravelly tones), should suggest he was a traitor. Steed's curiosity is piqued. He later joins Tara at Baines' apartment where they discuss the situation: Pelley's equation fed to George; Baines is now dead; and George is almost finished. What's the connection? This is rather a delicious bit of writing by Williamson, who uses the equation ploy as a metaphor in itself, spelling out the conundrum and awaiting the final solution – just like an equation for Steed and Tara to solve; this is best reflected when Tara makes the aside: "It still doesn't add up".

Suspicious that Pelley will not return from leave to assist in the life-or-spare-parts operation for George, Steed visits the Pelley Estate. There is a terrific nod towards *North By Northwest* in Frankel's direction here as he (and with likely contribution from Director of Photography Alan Hume) captures a shot on Steed's arrival of the right arm of a gardener coming into shot and laying down a brush onto a crowded wheelbarrow (the shot is later reversed when Steed departs to reveal the gardener is in fact Jacobs). Dennis Price is as stiff in upper with lip as his collar is with tip as he plays the part of Jason the Butler, always on hand with a Blackadderesque wry aside and comment during Steed's brief interrogation of the drunken, somewhat confused Sir Wilfred. As Steed leaves, Tobin arrives, demanding that Pelley give him instructions on how to silence George permanently.

Laurie Johnson's music is employed here and there throughout this episode, but unfortunately it can prove to be an unwarranted distraction when viewing the more Howard Blake-themed Tara episodes. An earlier employment of a chord from *The Town Of No Return*, and here, at the end of this scene, using a tune from *The £50,000 Breakfast*, summons recollection of things past rather than easily concentrating on what is unfolding here. The music is still perfect and very much a part of *The Avengers*' body of work, but the recollection of the Peel era makes for an unfortunate distraction. [1]

Although more *Emergency Ward Ten* than high drama, the operating theatre scenes are livened by an excellent chemistry between Linda Thorson (who at times can brightly spring into action and lift a scene; at other times scripts serve her less well) and Anthony Nicholls as Ardmore. Their exchange about how George could calculate the speed of the bullets heading towards him is beautifully counterpointed by Tara's reflection that it was a shame he couldn't duck. Williamson continues adding these perfect light touches when Steed arrives on the scene, peering through the theatre window and making non-verbal gestures to a be-masked woman he believes is Tara. When he suddenly finds she is standing beside him, Steed's terrific, "Well she was saying yes to something" is pure unadulterated class, as is the later exchange between them both:

Tara: The last thing he computed was that 2+2 = 5.
Steed: I always suspected that. [2]

It is a shame that the perfection didn't lend itself to disguising the obvious boom in shot in this scene.

Steed advises Ardmore that Pelley won't be able to lend a hand to the proceedings, requesting the latter's personnel file from a cagey Tobin. When they depart the scene to review the situation (and reflect on Pelley's unblemished service record), Tobin pours acid into George's exposed workings, ruffles up his clothing and, with the aid of a conveniently stowed enormous wrench, prepares to stage a false assault. He is later found by Ardmore and the alarm is raised that George has been poisoned. The grounds are fruitlessly searched. At this point, on the basis that two hard drives are better than one, Ardmore introduces them all to Fred Mark III (George's half-witted, "empty-headed" moronic fool of an ancestor) as a potential solution – putting Frank's brain into George's body and thereby saving George's delicate memory cells in the process. As one operation gets underway, Steed tells Tara he is prepared to put another patient on the table: himself, as bait, to draw Pelley out into the open. His visit is not without incident, and there are some nice quick-cuts in this scene in which Steed takes in the situation swiftly in noting a pair of (rather foolishly) discarded women's leather gloves and a fur coat on the hat stand. Prompting Jason the Butler for the identity of Pelley's paramour, he gets short shrift. After he leaves, the delightful Judy Parfitt makes her entrance as Miss Loris, the fiendish blackmailer and power-player putting the screws on Pelley. She issues instructions to Jacobs, rising to Steed's bait that Baines had other working notes for the equation, to get to the latter's apartment first, find the notes and kill Steed. After a bit of business involving drawn curtains and subdued lighting, Steed and Jacobs have a fight to the death, with Steed using his trusty bowler to deflect a handgun-shot back at Jacobs who dies (deliciously offbeat and quirky, *The Avengers* still manages to serve up an unexpected twist with moments like this – stretch belief, who cares, this is *Avengerland* – and it's fun!).

There is some further nice business between Steed and Tara when he sends her on a mission to impersonate Pelley's long-lost American niece, Prunella, with banter over the fact that he hasn't seen her in years and Tara can pretend to have a touching reunion. Handing her a photograph of said niece (a shot later revealed to be that of a toddler bathing!), he admits to a certain resemblance:

Tara: Where's the resemblance?
Steed: The knees. Good luck!

When Miss Loris learns from Keller that Jacobs is dead, Pelley drunkenly taunts her that their plans are coming unstuck. Later, Tara/Prunella arrives for her reunion with "Uncle Wilfie" where she is introduced to Loris as his general factotum. Parfitt, who could always be relied upon for an icy and brittle portrayal on cue, leaves no one wanting in her short, clipped and dangerous exchanges. Minimalist yet totally compelling. As Tara is ushered off to stay in the Blue Room (shades of a reworked set from *The Forget-Me-Knot* here?), Loris reflects on whether this newcomer needs to be disposed of. Upstairs, we are treated to a delightful musical accompaniment by Howard Blake as Tara retrieves a gun from her luggage and goes on the snoop. If ever a viewer needed to be introduced to the labyrinthine nuances of the world of *Avengerland*, the scene in which Tara ransacks Loris' handbag and discovers a gun and a hypodermic syringe should speak volumes for the calibre of its inhabitants.

Drawing to the business end of the episode, Tara overhears the blackmail plot in which Pelley is being forced to disclose secrets around an anti-missile system or face the consequences. She telephones Steed during a critical moment when George is being powered-up post-operation and learns of the plot. He later renders Tobin unconscious after catching sight of him cutting vital connections to George, with another perfect example of Williamson's bristling dialogue:

Electrical anaesthetist: What did you hit him with?
Steed: With a great deal of venom.

The damage minimal, Ardmore continues to revive George – although he remains unconvinced that Pelley, as Steed espouses, is a traitor. George's sudden uncoded message seems to provide an explanation: "Help me. I am being held a prisoner in my own house. I am being drugged and interrogated daily. Systematically they are milking every secret from me. My staff are being held as hostages, they will kill them if I do not cooperate. Tobin is in with them. Tobin is a traitor. But the ringleader, the man behind it all is...the man who is posing as Jason my butler". SO THE BUTLER DID IT! (Agatha Christie would have approved).

Meanwhile, Tara entrusts another person she shouldn't (said butler, Jason, in this instance) and winds up unconscious in the cellar with the real butler and chauffeur, as Loris and company prepare to flee, having forced Pelley to tell them all. Later, she is laid out in the drawing room before Loris instructs the chauffeur to put her in the summer house and set fire to it, an 'unfortunate accident' in the country. Cue a set previously used from *Mission...Highly Improbable* as Steed arrives on the scene and a fight ensues in the fuel-doused surroundings, leading to an exchange between Steed and the revived Tara:

Tara: Ah my Prince on his fiery Steed!
Steed: An asbestos-clad Steed. An unflammable, unfiery Steed.
Tara: They were going to burn me!
Steed: Yes, just like Joan of Arc.

Williamson is on form once again. The episode rounds off with the villains being rendered unconscious themselves during an athletic bit of seeing-off by Steed and Tara (who does a *Haunted Honeymoon* turn down the banisters). The tag scene, something of a post-Blackman tradition of finishing with a smile and song/a wink and a nod/a smirk and a smack, draws on George's other qualities – namely, now revived from a near fatal gunshot wound and traitor sniffer-outer, he has the recipe for the perfect, most deliciously potent cocktail in the world. Steed adds the final ingredient of a thimble-full of Scotch, and retires gracefully behind the sofa when the noxious brew destroys his living room. Ruminating that the recipe will be consigned to the top secret list, he and Tara resort to that most reliable of *Avengerland* staples: champagne.

By no means a classic, by every means a corker, this is standard *Avengers* territory: take something ordinary and make it extraordinary. It may not convince in terms of realism, but it was never meant to be kitchen-sink drama. As escapist, pure entertainment, done with superior class and a firmly British sense of fun, *Whoever Shot Poor George Oblique XR40?* remains a guilty pleasure and a slice of quirky television.

© Matthew Lee

1. I couldn't agree more and the recycling of incidental music which we instinctively associate with a specific episode is both distracting and jarring.
2. This surreal comment mirrors similar quips made by Steed in the earlier filmed seasons, such as his suggestion in *A Surfeit of H20* that the shape of the puddle left by Sir Arnold Kelly's corpse resembles his auntie's biscuits.

ALL DONE WITH MIRRORS

Filmed: June 1968

Exterior Locations:
Country track
Woodland
Mother's headquarters (swimming pool)
Coastline and cliff top
Carmadoc Research Establishment: security fence, gated entrance
Country roads
Guthrie's cottage: façade, drive and garage
Williams' house and grounds
Lighthouse
Wooded countryside
Rocks
Field of wild flowers

Sets:
Watney's car
Carmadoc Research: security area, laboratory
Lighthouse: base room, staircase, lamp room, secret room
Guthrie's cottage: den
Williams' house: study/workroom

ALL DONE WITH MIRRORS

Main Character List:
Arkin: enemy contact
Roger: agent
Mother
Rhonda: Mother's silent assistant
Tara King
John Steed
Walter Guthrie: local resident
Markin: radio operative at lighthouse, enemy agent
Watney: agent
Major Sparshott: Carmadoc Research security
Professor Carswell: Carmadoc Research
Miss Tiddiman: Carmadoc Research
Dr. Seligman: Carmadoc meteorologist
Emily: elderly housekeeper of Guthrie
Frederick Williams: local radio astronomer
Gozzo: henchman
Kettridge: henchman
Timothy Barlow: Colonel's secretary (imposter/enemy agent)
Colonel Withers: lighthouse owner (imposter/enemy agent)
Pandora Marshall: journalist
Sweeno: henchman
Timothy Barlow: the real one
Colonel Withers: the real one

To those who've seen it, *All Done With Mirrors* might be remembered as 'the one with the lighthouse' or 'the one where Steed cooks a steak on the engine of his Rolls Royce motor car'. It's certainly one of the most stylishly-directed episodes. From the opening scenes, we get unusual camera angles (even for *The Avengers*), and shots of events reflecting in the shiny surfaces of objects close to the camera. This is not directorial indulgence. [1] It is entirely relevant to the episode's plot, which involves reflections and beams of light, but it also harks back nicely to the innovative and trend-setting style of the show's earliest directors like Peter Hammond. Light flares and glares at many times during the story, puzzling the first-time viewer as to the significance of its visual mystery, whilst completely retaining *The Avengers* 'look'.

Style and plot work in parallel, televised film being the ideal medium for this story; the clues to resolving the action are literally light and sound. The first person to die, the anti-British spy Arkin, wears a physician's head mirror in the middle of an apparently deserted wood, whilst conversing with someone who seems to be invisible: a disembodied voice. One mystery is never resolved though, and that is what precise secrets Arkin has been gleaning from the eavesdroppers, the unseen villains who have somehow penetrated the security of the Carmadoc research facility. Carmadoc is working on a research programme into solar power, but the spies have this conversation:

Arkin: What is the density, the velocity of this device?
Man's Voice: That's the real big secret – haven't been able to get hold of that yet. Shall I continue with the equations?

What is the "device"? It's not even a MacGuffin. The plot is solely about discovering the spies and their ingenious method of breaking the research centre's security. Is this episode, as some critics have suggested, beautiful to look at, but shallow? Thematically it has points of interest, especially in terms of gender roles and, through Tara essentially 'going it alone', the perceived capabilities of women versus men. That said, characters' motivations do drive what plot there is, and we don't get a cliché like members of a corporation's board being bumped off in a boring series of revenge killings. Gratifyingly, one of the principal motivated characters who aids Tara's mission is another female investigator.

Steed is under "house arrest" at Mother's outdoor swimming pool. Mother and Rhonda become regulars from this episode onwards. Steed and Tara were clearly filmed at different times and don't appear in the same shots as they converse 'poolside'. Tara's shots look wet and rainy and Steed's are very sunny and dry! There is some nice wit near the start, as Tara regards the arrested Steed, who is surrounded by swimsuit-clad lovelies plying him with champagne (he's already had brandy!):

Steed: I'm innocent. Entirely innocent.
Tara: Yes – but for how long?

Wittiness then takes a leave of absence for some time, barely replaced by Watney's blithering idiocy, until near the tale's climax when wit returns in force alongside the 'violent' action; a pleasing mix.

Mother, perhaps with some fellow-feeling due to his code-name, is very supportive of female agents. He considers that they can offer, "A new intuitive approach to things". Steed seems reactionary and chauvinistic by comparison, which is very out of character for him. [2] Mother takes on Rhonda as his new permanent helper from now on, too.

The music is particularly impressive, combining instruments and building suspense, including adding a layer of percussion for sequences of lurking danger and 'creeping about'. Howard Blake's work is supplemented by some choice Laurie Johnson cues. Inexorable strident flutes and timpani, similar to the Cybernaut-march of previous seasons, are fittingly used for the approach of the giant red-headed hit-man, Gozzo, who kills with his bare hands, or squashes people under tables. Gozzo throws radio astronomer Williams up against a mirror; clearly the terrified Guthrie hasn't told his friend to break all reflective surfaces, even though Williams is supposed to be aware of the 'retro-meter' device and its new owners who have frightened, and then killed, Guthrie. Perhaps Williams' room faces away from the lighthouse, and he cannot be eavesdropped upon or shot by a sniper at a distance, which seems to be the villains' preferred method of termination, despite having the murderous giant Gozzo at their disposal.

Tara's fight with Gozzo is cited as one of the best ever seen. As originally scripted, it ended with the giant being impaled on a scythe. On screen, they energetically skirmish over a huge expanse of lawn until Tara's succession of blows and kicks forces the giant to back-flip into a shed, demolishing it. Gozzo rises but, unseen by both Tara and the viewer, he has the head of a rake embedded in his back. It's a splendid scene, and certainly puts to rest any accusations that Tara's fights generally consist of hitting her opponents with a brick in her handbag. [3] However, there is nothing gratuitously gruesome: the rake allows the viewer to be surprised by the remorseless giant, having risen from the wreckage, reaching for Tara but inexplicably toppling forward to his death. *The Avengers*' fights emphasise aesthetically-appealing action and reaction, not 'crowbar to skull' *Sweeney*-style realism. Even the table 'crushing' of Williams by Gozzo is not explicit but stylish. We see a quivering arm protruding from under the upturned table, not blood and gore. After apparently fatally despatching one of the villains in the lighthouse, Tara smiles grimly at 'death': the card she finds from the pack the man had been playing with. The Ace of Spades, in popular old legend and folklore, is known as the 'death card'. Even Watney inadvertently knocks out the fake Barlow, in one of the several confrontations that ends with a villain being hurled from the lighthouse steps and crashing into the furniture, usually bashing their head against the wall. Perhaps this is an in-joke regarding the restricted nature of studio fights, given the imaginative outdoors action of the lawn/shed fight and the breathtaking stunt of Tara being shunted off a cliff by a murderous motorcyclist. Despite the frequent presence of guns amongst the villains here, they're rarely fired, Ray Austin still being keen on stunts and unarmed combat.

After five seasons of *The Avengers*, we can now well believe an elderly 'granny' with hedge-trimmers could be a danger. Enough to subvert the idea when, far from being menaced, Tara finds the aged housekeeper Emily to be friendly and informative. Emily is maternally devoted to Walter Guthrie (whom she doesn't know is dead). Guthrie fell over the cliff edge "the other day", implying that several days have passed; yet Emily seems unaware, much to Tara's consternation, and despite Guthrie having regular habits, such as taking tea at the same time every day. Does this imply Emily is merely eccentric, or is she becoming senile?

The flexible silvery material Mirrorlon proves its science fiction credentials; lots of 'solar reflector' diamond shapes and strange hanging strips at Carmadoc. Could they be something to do with its famed 'anti-bugging' measures? The Mirrorlon is used to good effect, in a directorial flourish similar to that employed by former *Avengers* director Peter Hammond, when Watney looms up diagonally beside Dr. Seligman; he's actually approaching from behind, but the weird angles disorient the viewer momentarily. The technique of using a light beam to remotely record sound is not pure science fiction, but largely science fact. It probably originated with Léon Theremin in the Soviet Union c.1947, when he developed and used the 'Buran' eavesdropping system which worked by using a low power infra-red beam to detect the sound vibrations in glass windows from a distance. Today, spies use laser microphones that work on broadly the same principle.

The portrayal of the one female scientist at Carmadoc is not clichéd. Although she is not referred to as a doctor or professor, but instead as "Miss" Tiddiman, there is no hint in performances or direction of her being subordinate to the men. Cathy Gale and Emma Peel were also scientists, so the series had a reputation to maintain. For some young viewers, Tara is more identifiable; a government *ingénue* learning new skills, with natural intelligence augmented by some 'spy school' training rather than lengthy post-graduate academia, but thrown in to field work with real secrets and real enemies and traitors. Without being patronising, the script makes it clear that Tara has learnt quickly on the job (well, she is partnered with the UK's best agent). Steed's view of her as a vulnerable neophyte will have to be revised after this mission. As Steed rushes off to 'save' Tara, it is again Mother who has more faith in her:

Mother: She's been trained to take care of herself.
Steed: It's just a game to her. She'll go charging in.
Mother: What I mean to say is, let's both hope that Tara...
Steed: Let's!

There's a slight awkwardness with Steed's continued arrest, in that his name should be cleared immediately when Watney sees the next killing and reports in. Tara correctly deduces that it is an outside job, as soon as she arrives. She is perhaps quick to trust Major Sparshott's assurances of having vetted everyone personally, but as Tara points out the external line of enquiry is a valid one to start with.

The characters are distinctive, even the minor research centre scientists having their own individual appearances, tics and mannerisms. A colonel obsessed by the sea and living in a lighthouse seems an absurd idea; usually in *The Avengers* a retired colonel would be surrounded by obvious militaria. Colonel Withers (we're told) wanted to be a sailor. Edwin Richfield, here playing the fake Barlow, was cast as the 'Brigadier substitute' Captain Hart RN in *Doctor Who*'s *The Sea Devils* a few years later, the commander of a coastal station. Tenniel Evans, playing Carswell at the research centre, is another link with sea; he was a star of the long-running British radio comedy series *The Navy Lark*. A modern viewer can enjoy this series on several levels: connecting or escaping to two other worlds: both the reality of 1960s television production with lots of comfortably familiar faces (Edwin Richfield seems obliged to be in every *Avengers* season), and the fantastic fictional danger of *Avengerland*. This story, especially, is a splendid episode to show to friends who don't know the series well. There are cliff-hangers within the episode and the mystery and danger develop nicely. On broadcast, the commercial breaks act like intermissions in a three-act play. [4]

The big twist comes at the episode's halfway point, as journalist Pandora Marshall arrives as an 'expected' guest whose impending visit seems to have been forgotten by everyone at the lighthouse. This ultimately exposes the imposters who have taken it over. Pandora follows the fake Barlow and Kettridge up the lighthouse stairs and they seem to have disappeared (into the secret communications room halfway up). Pandora reaches the lamp room and sees Tara down on the cliffs. Much of this sequence is dialogue-free, emphasising visual action, with handheld camera work. Tara's 'going it alone' is great fun for her fans. She jettisons the twittish Watney at the first opportunity. The ladies' parallel investigations, and their brief team-up, are enjoyable for fans of action/adventure featuring pro-active women, which must surely include most *Avengers* fans. If Steed's presence is missed, then there are always 160-plus Steed-heavy episodes. Steed, after all, is *one* of the Avengers – but not the *only* Avenger. This change of emphasis is a breath of fresh air. Another such welcome change is the coastal location with its stunning scenery. The lighthouse [5] is one of those bizarre places that *The Avengers* uses so well, juxtaposing rural and nautical Old England with an ultra-modern scientific base. The nautical feel continues indoors, with some attractive set-dressing (ship's figureheads, paintings and ships in bottles). The sets look authentic and largely convincing, except perhaps the summery landscape outside Williams's window. Sometimes it is impossible to tell what is shot on location and what is shot on a set. [6]

There are a couple of things that don't seem to make sense. The real Colonel Withers, the real Barlow, and the captured Pandora are all tied up and kept in the communications room used by Markin. You'd think it would cramp his style a bit as they'd overhear all his secret communications! Why not kill them? Astronomers Williams and Guthrie, who had 'stumbled' onto the truth, were quickly 'silenced' by being killed. One can invent reasons. Maybe Withers is kept alive in case anything goes wrong with the retro-meter device. Maybe the imposters are worried the bodies would be found, exposing the scam. Pandora Marshall had come down solely to interview the real Colonel about his retro-meter, but when she finds it, she reacts with an amazed whistle and remarks "what a handy little device," as if it is new to her. Maybe she did not truly believe the tale of its invention until she used the thing herself. [7]

As the action comes fast and furious near the climax, so does the visual and verbal wit. From the captives forgetting they're chained together, to comic reactions as the telescope-mounted retro-meter spins, causing alarming sounds of violence to randomly erupt right beside all and sundry, including Sparshott, who announces he is "taking the rest of the day off" due to sounds suddenly playing in his shiny head. There is the famous 365-step stair fall (ending with the abuse of yet another unfortunate chair), leading to Tara's leap year gag. See also Tara's exasperated "I've got a friend that can open these at the drop of a bowler hat", all whilst she battles for her life. When Watney arrives, she lets him cover the unconscious Barlow whilst she goes off to deal with "the other five".

It's wonderful to see Tara performing so magnificently, especially in such a sumptuous episode. Is the lighthouse, full of male villains, a phallic symbol? This lighthouse even has unusual Gothic Revival design elements, such as defensive battlements. The numerous arrogant males are briskly emasculated by Pandora and Tara. The uselessness of Watney draws attention to the correctness of Mother's high estimation of female capability and feminine intuition. No wonder Mother decides to keep Rhonda close by, from now on. Attitudes towards gender roles and capabilities changed drastically throughout the 1960s. *The Avengers'* leading ladies Cathy and Emma spearheaded that change. Tara reinforces it here, giving the lie to dismissive and derogatory complaints of brick-in-handbag fighting techniques. [8] We get some of the very best fights in the entire series during this season: particularly in this episode, and the glorious brawl in the optics room in *My Wildest Dream*, amongst many more. This story is a startling *tour de force* for Tara, with her carrying an entire show single-handedly at this point, only eleven episodes into her run (when watched in production order, as the season should be, bar *The Forget-Me-Knot*). [9] There are still over twenty pleasurable episodes to go.

Steed can never again make the mistake of claiming Tara is "vulnerable", because her performance here shows that she has become as capable as any Avenger. Other writers, exploring episodes such as *A Touch of Brimstone*, *Quick-Quick Slow Death* and *The Girl From Auntie*, have examined the series' obsession with eroticism and the psychology of sex and sexuality. *The Avengers* uses sexual attraction and also kinkiness. It has also led the field in terms of gender politics, not least by being decades ahead of its time with strong, capable and independent women. I'm pleased that Tara is one of them. And when she flashes those gorgeous green eyes in any of this episode's big close-ups, I admit that my thoughts aren't entirely analytical...

There is more beautiful scenery at the episode's highest point - the iconic tag scene. In a field of tall meadow buttercups, an immaculately-groomed Steed has prepared a romantic table for two with complete silver service...and provides a sizzling steak for the beautifully-dressed Tara from under the bonnet of his car; "done to a turn" (like this near-perfect episode). It is a unique and memorable scene, encapsulating the joy of summer and the playfulness that *The Avengers* carries off with such *panache*.

Tara: Steed, what can I say. You're unbelievable.
Steed: Very nice of you to say so. I always say that the simplest pleasures of life are the most enjoyable.

This apotheosis is another reason why many reviewers rate *All Done With Mirrors* as the best of Tara's episodes. If *The Avengers* is 'about' sex, and the action rises to an exciting climax, then this scene is the post-coital bliss. Is there any better or more memorable tag scene? [10] It is definitive. Tag scenes, essential to *The Avengers*, are literally a *divertissement* in the sense of the term used by the Académie Royale de Musique, for both *tragédies lyriques* and *comédies lyriques*, with their own required music and light humour, often performed at the close of the performance.

Ultimately, this is another delightful visit to *Avengerland*. The writer of this story, Leigh Vance, later swapped a lighthouse for a windmill, by adapting Clive Egleton's spy novel *Seven Days to a Killing* into the film *The Black Windmill* starring Michael Caine. Although Vance's television work included some episodes of *The Saint* and a *Strange Report*, sadly he wrote no other *Avengers* episodes, which is a shame, since this is one of the best. [11]

© Frank Shailes

1. With the exception of the stylish shot through the pair of glasses on the cliff, which is pure *Avengers* 'aesthetic surface'. (On reading these notes, Frank commented: "The shot through the spectacles is perhaps a bit indulgent, but drawing them to the viewer's attention is important: they're where the sound is being projected from for the 'beckoning' voice which draws Guthrie over the cliff so I think I'll forgive them being 'up front and personal'."
2. Does part of Steed's unease also stem from Tara being coupled with such an idiotic agent?
3. The wonderful location helps create the visual appeal here. Tara/Thorson undermines lots of negative opinions about her in this episode.
4. This is an element of the scriptwriting structure which we tend to ignore, not unlike the serialisation of Dickens' novels.
5. Frank would like to point out that the lighthouse authority, Trinity House, has a web page for Start Point lighthouse (the

location used in this episode) with some fascinating photographs and historical facts.
6. I agree. I'd often wondered whether the lighthouse interior was set or location.
7. This is *The Avengers*, after all, where plot holes are part of the charm and the desire not to be taken too seriously.
8. It is Brian Clemens who has encouraged this notion, as well as inventing it for *The Forget-Me-Knot* episode.
9. I think that Tara's fabulously tomboyish corduroy-denim suit and short haircut help here, liberating her and establishing her as an action hero.
10. I agree. Surely this is one of the best colour tag scenes.
11. Reminiscent of Colin Finbow's delicious one-off, *A Surfeit of H_2O*. Maybe they both did too good a job. (On reading these notes, Frank replied: "Ooh naughty. Yes, sometimes a flower (or a writer) can grow too tall!"

YOU'LL CATCH YOUR DEATH

Filmed: May 1968

Exterior Locations:
City streets
Camrose's surgery
Country roads
Mother's headquarters (high walled terrace)
Padley/Seaton/Herrick's surgery
Anastasia Nursing Academy
Stable Mews
Walsingham House

Sets:
Camrose's surgery: consultation room, entrance hall
Steed's car
Padley/Seaton/Herrick's surgery: hallway, consultation rooms
Steed's mews apartment
Anastasia Nursing Academy: foyer, study
Walsingham House: Colonel's study
Cold Cure Clinic: corridor, deep freeze room, allergy room, laboratory, tunnel & nose
Telephone box

YOU'LL CATCH YOUR DEATH

Main Character List:
Ralph Camrose: private consultant, ear, nose and throat specialist
Farrar: patient
Dexter: chauffueur, henchman
Preece: henchman
Janice: receptionist
Tara King
John Steed
Mother
Rhonda: Mother's silent assistant
Henry Padley: ear, nose and throat specialist
Georgina: receptionist
Maidwell: stationery salesman
Seaton: ear, nose and throat specialist
Melanie: nurse at academy
Matron: nursing academy
Dr. Fawcett: Institute of Allergic Diseases
Butler
Colonel Maurice Timothy
Dr. Frank Glover: head of research at cold cure clinic
Dr. Herrick: ear, nose and throat specialist

Always keep a-hold of Nurse
For fear of finding something worse...

As an actor, Jeremy Burnham held the unique distinction of appearing as a guest star in introductory episodes of all three of *The Avengers'* filmed seasons. The fourth season's two attempts of *The Town of No Return* saw him play the deceptive Reverend Amesbury in Elizabeth Shepherd's abandoned debut, before his return to reprise the role in remounted scenes with Diana Rigg. In the colour Rigg season's premiere installment he played the pallid pottery director White, while in the hastily conceived Season 6 curtain raiser he took on the role of agent Simon Filson. However, Burnham's interests extended beyond the acting profession and by the time he joined the cast of *The Forget-Me-Knot,* he'd begun to forge a career as a TV scriptwriter, having co-written with Dinsdale Landen an episode of the 1967 BBC drama *Mickey Dunne* in which Landen starred as a character not far removed from that played by Michael Caine in the 1965 hit *Alfie*.

While filming scenes with Patrick Macnee during the first week of January 1968, Burnham asked the *Avengers* star if there might be any opportunities to write for the series. Advised by Macnee that the production was looking for writers, Burnham approached Brian Clemens with the germ of an idea for a story set in a cold cure clinic, featuring as a highlight a scene in which Tara King would fall out of a large artificial nose, to which Steed would exclaim, "Gesundheit!" Having also earmarked a cold cure clinic story in his collection of potential storyline thumbnails - albeit without the giant nose - Clemens commissioned a story outline, and having found it to his liking, gave the go ahead for a full script. To assist Burnham in the task, Clemens provided a selection of his own scripts to provide pointers regarding style and presentation - which in his commentary for the Optimum DVD release of *Love All* Burnham recalled came with the proviso 'I don't want criticism, I just want praise'. The scripts proved very instructive, however, and Burnham also found that he and Clemens shared the same sense of humour. Taking about two months to complete, the trial script was presented under the title *Atishoo, Atishoo, All Fall Down* and was accepted for production - although before completion the title would be changed to the catchier *You'll Catch Your Death*. Burnham was now a fully-fledged *Avengers* writer.

Playing relatively safe, the new recruit ticks many of the requisite *Avengers* boxes with his debut story. There is the statutory number of mysterious deaths. Our heroes are aided by an eccentric expert. They follow the clues to a seemingly innocent establishment which proves to serve a far more sinister purpose. A diabolical mastermind with perfidious plans for world domination is revealed to be behind the pernicious plot. One of our heroes is captured, incarcerated and ingeniously escapes. After an inventively choreographed fight, the villain is hoist by his own petard. There is a mordant butler. But what could have been a tired and comatose episode is written with sprightly pep and vigour, breathing fresh life into some of the series' most well-worn clichés.

For an episode inspired by the search for a cure to that most mundane of British medical complaints, the common cold, *You'll Catch Your Death* opens in a location that is anything but common. Forsaking the architecturally anaemic consulting rooms of Harley Street, the production fades in slightly to the north, where the full-blooded fairy tale Nash terraces of Regents Park provide a strikingly elegant backdrop to this week's plot's inciting incidents. Eminent specialists are being struck down by an unknown ailment, and the only clue is an empty envelope. We have already been made aware that no ordinary postman is responsible for the mysteriously-fatal missives. This one is chauffeur-driven to his victims' doorsteps by a Rolls-Royce. As the ear, nose and throat men drop dead like flies, even under the watchful eyes of our avenging agents, Tara finally clocks the 'posh postie' and takes off after his luxurious harbinger of doom. Meanwhile, Steed follows the paper trail via the Anastasia Nursing Academy to the home of crusty ex-colonial Colonel Timothy - a health freak whose wealth has enabled him to establish his own private cold cure clinic, accessible through a secret panel in his drawing room (naturally). Looked down upon by a giant nose, the clinic is seemingly devoted to the colonel's cold cure cause, but by now we know that it masks a sinister purpose, Tara having been delivered into the clinic's clutches after being cornered by her courier quarry. The scenario now builds to a satisfying conclusion as Steed teams up with the colonel to outwit the enemy with the aid of armour-plated headwear - their alliance echoing that of Mrs. Peel and John Laurie's Crewe in *A Funny Thing Happened on the Way to the Station*.

Burnham's script is well served by its director Paul Dickson, an award-winning documentary film maker who, by 1968, had also gained experience with film series production, having directed several episodes of *The Champions* during the course of the previous year. Although he directs *You'll Catch Your Death* with flair and imaginatively stylish touches - including the use of slow motion to capture the deaths of the episode's victims - he would make no further contribution to the series, returning instead to direct further episodes of a variety of ITC productions for Monty Berman, before taking up a career in film education. Dickson's visuals are also complemented nicely by John Hough's location work, which elicits dramatic capital from the grandiose classical architecture of the Regents Park area, a location superbly suited to *The Avengers*' mythical vision of England, and includes a stylish car chase which shows off Tara's striking AC convertible to snarling effect - although his rather cautious handling of Dr. Herrick's car crash is less than convincing. [1]

The episode is also brilliantly served by its guest actors, who have all been perfectly cast in their roles to bring Burnham's script vividly to life. From Roland Culver's tin-helmeted Colonel Timothy and Fulton Mackay's gimlet-eyed Glover, to Dudley Sutton's deadly driver Dexter and Peter Bourne's phoney postman Preece, *You'll Catch Your Death* is populated by a host of off-beat oddballs from all walks of *Avengerland*. In this the episode underscores an increasing departure from the diktat laid out by Brian Clemens during the early days of the filmed seasons' *The Avengers* that the series would admit to only one class - the upper. Of course the lower classes always did have a place in *The Avengers* - servants and henchmen and lackeys of various kinds were essential to the smooth running of any diabolical mastermind's plot - but crucially, they knew their place and were generally stereotypical ciphers with no discernable character or individual motivation. This began to change during the fifth season, which saw the rise of the self-knowing working class antagonist. Clive Colin-Bowler's mod-esque Robin in *The Bird Who Knew Too Much* would be an early example of this kind of psycho-pop class warrior, with *Murdersville*'s Hubert and Mickle being perhaps the most viciously gleeful realisations of the show's master-biting under-dog. Burnham's Dexter and Preece fulfil a similar function - the angelic-faced Sutton making a particularly demonic impression as the casually callous coachman, with Preece looking every inch the disgruntled flunkey. The plebian pleasure they take at the expense of their 'betters' would manifest itself in its ultimate form in *The New Avengers*' episode *Sleeper*, adding another dimension to its depiction of a London at the mercy of uncouth yobs.

But despite its broader than usual social spectrum, *You'll Catch Your Death* is still set firmly in *Avengerland*, and boasts its fair share of dramatically bizarre situations and looking-glass visions of what passes for 'reality'. Burnham also demonstrates that he has a good ear for *Avengers* dialogue, furnishing his characters with some excellent exchanges and wonderful one-liners. Discussing the quality of the deadly envelopes:

Maidwell (a quality manufacturer): It's our big money maker you see, sir. Low cost to make bulk buying a more attractive proposition.
Steed: It's fairly common?
Maidwell: In every sense of the word.

Or Steed justifying philanthropy at the Anastasia Nursing Academy:

Matron: Buying your way to heaven?
Steed: With the meek inheriting the earth, it's the only place left.

And Steed again:

Steed: If one's born with a silver spoon in one's mouth one must see that it feeds as many people as possible.

On encountering Dr. Fawcett:

Fawcett: You ought to be ashamed of yourself.
Steed: I frequently am.

Fawcett: This is chloroform.
Steed: I don't like it.
Fawcett: You're not the only one.

Steed discussing progress with Mother:

Mother: Dirty work?

Steed: Trifle unhygienic I'm afraid.

And on introducing himself to Colonel Timothy:

Steed: I assume you've never had a serious illness in Mozambique.
Timothy: You must be clairvoyant.

The villains also get some good lines:

Preece (after delivering a deadly envelope to Steed): He'll have found the envelope...Sniffed it...
Dexter: ...And snuffed it.

One of the most notable lines is not one of Burnham's, however. As she grips Sylvia Kay's Matron in a suspended leg-lock, Tara utters the lines, "Always keep a-hold of Nurse, for fear of finding something worse". This quote from *Jim - Who Ran Away From his Nurse and was Eaten by a Lion*, by the early twentieth century poet and man of letters Hilaire Belloc offers a telling acknowledgement of one of the most notable literary antecedents of *The Avengers*, particularly in its film series form. Born in 1870 to Anglo-French parents, Belloc possessed a unique talent for poetic social observation and was especially famed for his comic cautionary verses, which cast a black-humoured eye over British life. His vision of the country – and in particular its upper classes – chimes perfectly with the elegantly mannered style of *The Avengers*. In his introduction to a volume of Belloc's work, the critic A. N. Wilson notes that Belloc's poems revealed what he felt about Britain's crazy institutions, from the House of Lords to the Fire Brigade, and that he thought that Britain was a farcical place guided by no true religious or political principles. This vision fits perfectly with the essence of *Avengerland*, and one could easily see any of Belloc's wittily-drawn characters sitting comfortably in an *Avengers* episode.

It is undoubtedly on a similar level - as an elegant darkly comic satire on British obsessions - that *You'll Catch Your Death* works best. It has all the wit and style of a Wildean comedy, if lacking the subtextual depth that other - particularly earlier - episodes possess. Although it may have its weak points - Steed and Mother's exchanges regarding Tara seem rather forced and unconvincing- Burnham's first excursion into the realms of *Avengerland* is certainly nothing to be sneezed at.

© Sam Denham

1. When I think of Season 6's location filming, and Burnham's episodes in particular, I always think of these upper class urban streets which, as Sam suggests, ideally suit *The Avengers,* visually, atmospherically and thematically.

SUPER SECRET CYPHER SNATCH

Filmed: June 1968

Exterior Locations:
Cypher HQ: façade, security fence, main gate, roof
Country roads and open countryside
Mother's headquarters (field)
Block of flats
Ministry building
Classy Glass Cleaning Company: façade, yard
Woodland

Sets:
Cypher HQ: Webster's office, cypher office
Mother's headquarters (purple/ladder set)
Jarret's flat
Ministry building: photo lab
John Steed's mews apartment
Classy Glass Cleaning Company

SUPER SECRET CYPHER SNATCH

Main Character List:
Wilson: agent
John Steed
Tara King
Mother
Rhonda: Mother's silent assistant
Roger Jarret: M.I. 12 agent
Masters: guard
George Webster: director of Cypher HQ
Betty: Cypher HQ
Ferret: M.I. 12
Peters: camp forensics photographer
Myra: cypher office
Charles Maskin: CGC henchman
Charles Lather: CGC boss
Vickers: CGC henchman
Davis: CGC henchman

A number of Tara King episodes centre on high security buildings, including *Split!*, *Have Guns – Will Haggle*, *Whoever Shot Poor George Oblique Stroke XR40?*, *All Done With Mirrors*, *Killer* and *Super Secret Cypher Snatch*. Studio lots, a RAF base, a school and a transmitting station were typical real-life locations used for the exterior shooting. There is a certain sameness about these soulless post-war structures; a sense of *déjà vu* about the all-too-familiar, characterless, 'fenced-and-guarded' settings. The aptly-named Charles Lather, head of Classy Glass Cleaning, clearly agrees: "Double glazed with moulded frame...urgh – ghastly!...All that grey concrete! Quite soul-destroying." *All Done With Mirrors* releases us from the architectural drudgery of the Carmadoc Research Establishment through some wonderful location filming on the Devon coast and the delightful lighthouse set; *Killer* offers us the atmospherically artificial backlot town; *Split!*, *Have Guns – Will Haggle*, and *Whoever Shot Poor George Oblique Stroke XR40?* all whisk us away to attractive country mansions. *Super Secret Cypher Snatch* would need a similar 'location lift'. In addition, with formula fatigue a recurring problem in the colour film era, another challenge for both writer and director would be to raise the story above the mundane and predictable, through quirky or surreal touches in both the script and the direction. As Matthew Lee observes elsewhere in this book, *The Rotters* accomplishes this with panache, largely through the memorable henchmen George and Kenneth. Could accomplished *Avengers* writer Tony Williamson and director John Hough sprinkle similar magic here?

The teaser for *Super Secret Cypher Snatch* adds stylish touches to a fairly routine opening. These range from the strange sight of a spy cycling along a deserted country lane in an old lady's frock and veil, to the panoramic filming of the subsequent fight between biker agent Wilson and the spy. This is seen from both the ground, with an enemy helicopter hovering overhead, *and* from the helicopter's viewpoint, the battling men's clothes billowing in the maelstrom of downdraught. The interesting valley location (Ivinghoe Beacon) makes for an intriguing, almost claustrophobic backdrop. The fact that this was a 'new hook', filmed after Brian Clemens and Albert Fennell decided that the original teaser wasn't interesting enough, demonstrates that applying the right sort of avengerish touches was deemed more important by the production team than saving money. [1] A final flourish is applied as the episode title appears, superimposed on the stolen cypher sheets. The red lettering of SEPET SUCPRE CNCEHC SYPARE transforms itself into SUPER SECRET CYPHER SNATCH. While the font/formatting of the titles was playfully redeployed throughout Season 6, this particular touch adds an intriguing tag to the teaser, tarnished only by the recycling of the *You Have Just Been Murdered* music, a recurring false note in Season 6.

Mother's HQ set is a bizarre mixture of clues and red herrings: large toy lorries manned by plastic workers in white uniforms, a (real) convertible Bentley, a dull concrete floor clashing with a bold pink wall, and a pair of ladders for Steed and Tara to climb down, offering a delightful piece of delayed significance so early on in the story. Equally eye-catching are the first shots of Cypher HQ, first seen from the distance, then in close-up, its weather-worn concrete walls and tall, narrow windows resembling a post-modern castle. (It is a more interesting structure than the other post-war buildings utilised in the series). The clichéd sight of an agent fleeing is nicely counterbalanced by the enemy henchmen: armed window-cleaners in white overalls, with matching white bowler hats and wearing gas masks. (They should remind us of the toy men at Mother's HQ.) Roger Jarrett, the MI12 agent, is gunned down in cold blood. However, none of this is disconcerting for us as viewers. After all, this is *Avengerland*. The strange, stand-out detail is that the HQ security guard watches impassively as the assassination takes place under his very eyes, as does Cypher Supremo George Webster, staring out from his office window. This is the episode's first true hook, and the episode might have been better served with this delightful scene as the teaser. The scene's avengerish ability to turn realism on its head is completed when an arriving employee greets the guard just moments after the killing:

"Hello, Masters. What kind of a day has it been?"
"The usual Monday, Miss, routine and boring."

Mother's second meeting with Steed and Tara provides delightfully staged visual appeal as they pose like fashion models with their respective vehicles: Tara is sitting on her bonnet, Mother is sat inside and Steed is standing – in almost military style – in front. The scene takes place in a field of wild flowers, almost as iconic a location in Season 6 as Tykes Water Lake Bridge was in the Peel era. There is no 'plot point' to this meeting being arranged away from Mother's headquarters but, in one sense, that precisely *is* the point: it is stylishly unnecessary. The scene allows the story to introduce the light teasing of James Bond-style secret services:

Mother: That's MI12 for you...Terrible preoccupation with gimmicks and gadgets. I said no gadget will ever take the place of a man.
Steed: Or woman.

As Margaret J Gordon, Matthew Lee and a number of other critics have observed, there is an on-going battle in *The Avengers* between villains using advanced technology/devices and Steed/partner counteracting with rational thinking, human instinct and simple weaponry: bowler, umbrella, hand-to-hand combat, even a champagne cork. Here, on one level, there are two groups of enemies: the usual diabolical masterminds *and* MI12 who are threatening to take over key assignments, keen to demonstrate and display their elaborate methods of spy warfare. If they are successful in cracking the cypher mystery, the avengers might become obsolete, as Steed has already intimated:

Mother: Can I drop you somewhere?
Steed: The Employment Bureau?

The scenes in Jarrett's apartment work on a number of levels. There is the witty point scoring as MI12's civil servant Ferret and Tara King try to outdo each other in terms of detective/spy skills, culminating in the delightfully-named, pompous Ferret announcing, "I can say quite definitely that Roger Jarrett left here on Saturday", at the precise moment when Tara discovers his corpse in the window seat 'coffin'. There is also a delicious contrast between the dry, dull Ferret and the friendly, camp forensics photographer, Peters, intent on capturing Jarrett's 'better side' for posterity. The gently dark humour continues as Miss King attempts to guess what each personal item found on the corpse doubles up as: comb/high frequency resonator; wallet/survival kit; cigarette case/automatic pistol etc. As the list continues, we should guess, perhaps, that an increasingly bewildered Tara will eventually outwit her rival through a clever retort: "Astonishing that Mr. Jarrett should have all these marvellous gadgets and still disappear." (There is a similar witty quip of hers/Williamson's in *Poor George*.) Linda Thorson delivers the line with aplomb. Indeed, she plays the scene with consummate ease, displaying great comic timing. It is hard to imagine Diana Rigg doing it any better. The conversation demonstrates how far Thorson had developed her ability and her character in a relatively short period of time. It is both fitting and ironic that Ferret's lack of humour allows him to become a comic figure:

Steed: He [Webster] swore on every civil service manual that he'd never laid eyes on Jarrett.
Ferret: Impossible. Webster had a triple star clearance. He can't lie.

As in *Something Nasty in the Nursery*, *Love All* and the *New Avengers* episode *Angels of Death*, the suggestion that some people are 'above suspicion' is playfully satirised. Like an onion, *Super Secret Cypher Snatch* has layers to it: the contrast between Ferret's sobriety and Peters's camp charm; MI12 being watched by the avengers being watched by the Classy Glass henchmen; the continuing mystery surrounding Cypher HQ: is George Webster a double-agent aiding CGC, or simply the victim of a cunning, villainous plot? In an episode which lacks a darker, dramatic underbelly, these layers are vital. They add substance to the froth. The killing of Peters is typical of the episode's style. At the moment when he appears to have solved the puzzle of Jarrett's seemingly mundane photographs, a window-cleaning henchman taps on the glass then silences him – quite literally – before continuing to clean the panes. Once again, there is no need for the writer/director/character to do this; it simply adds a quirky flourish or stylish full stop to the scene. When Steed arrives to investigate the murder scene – cue sinister music – there is another tap on the window…this time it is Tara King on the ladder. As viewers, it is we who are now being played with, in what already feels like a sleek, self-confident episode. [2]

The visually bizarre style continues with the sight of a fleet of CGC vehicles riding along country lanes to Cypher HQ, repeated in the build-up to the story's climax. Steed may rightly claim that they've "known stranger methods of cover" but the spectacle *is* a strange one and prepares us for something even odder a few minutes later when Steed comes under attack from a ladder. These two scenes are separated by a delightfully simple set: the CGC offices. Following the advice that less can be more, a sprinkling of gold-painted stepladders, some panes of glass and inexplicably out-of-place chandeliers make up a self-referentially artificial stage on which the episode briefly moves from froth to farce, with Steed warning Lather that he only has one window left unboarded at the family seat. Lather turns him down as a client, regretting that, "We owe a duty to our employees. The sight of all those boarded windows; men have cracked under less." Just as Linda Thorson demonstrated earlier, here Patrick Macnee reminds us of his comic ability. The contrast between CGC's opulent interior and bland, post-war exterior echoes the mood swing from the humour of Steed's exchanges with Lather to the dramatic car chase which follows. We have already been warned that there will be a gear change by the reflection of a menacing henchman in his van's rearview mirror as Steed entered the building. As Steed leaves, Hough gives us an almost identical shot, like book ends to the interior scene. The chase is on…

Steed's battle with the ladder-wielding Classy Glass henchmen must rank as one of the most daring, dangerous and surreal chases in *Avengers* history. The sequence filmed on the woodland roads of Burnham Beeches, with Steed under attack from these snakes with ladders, offers us a perfect example of 'subversive champagne'; it is both exhilarating and amusingly ridiculous at the same time. With the henchman/stuntman having to duck to avoid low branches, it is no surprise that this involved four separate days of shooting for Hough and his second unit. [3] It was time and artistic endeavour well spent; the chase represents a visual highlight of the season.

When Tara later suggests that CGC could be "a perfectly harmless company", we can back up Steed's judgement that they have "a very lethal line in ladders".

As is usually the case, Steed and Tara's nighttime infiltration of enemy headquarters provides a welcome injection of atmospheric menace, helped by a wonderfully moody musical score. The (literal) uncovering of Ferret's corpse – his face surreally covered by a window cleaner's chamois cloth – adds to the strange spectacle. However, as I suggested earlier, menace plays a very minor role in this episode. What is far more striking in *Super Secret Cypher Snatch* is the stylish pace of the episode, in stark contrast to the leisurely, theatrical approach to *Pandora* and *Take-Over*. It also demonstrates the subtlety of structure Frank Hui referred to in his analysis of *Death's Door* in the previous volume. Each visit to Cypher HQ reveals a little bit more of the mystery, offering a gradual, subtle explanation as to why "tomorrow's yesterday again".

As the episode reaches its climax, what makes *Super Secret Cypher Snatch* a rarity is that all too often the *Avengers* fight finale represents either a disappointing anti-climax or even a post-climax. Here, Steed's battle in the Cypher HQ building *is* the highlight or climax of the entire episode. It is a surreal, visual feast which provides the proverbial icing or cherry on the cake (depending on which side of the Channel you live on). As the gas and the hypnotic recording take effect – "It has just begun to rain. Otherwise, it is a perfectly normal, perfectly ordinary day" – the sight of real life 'mannequins' is bizarrely hypnotic for us as viewers. The way in which the smiling, lead henchman makes a minor, aesthetic adjustment to one of the 'frozen' workers adds a stylish touch and clever fore-echo of Steed's actions once he arrives. The sight of white bowler-hatted guards patrolling the green woodland surrounding Cypher HQ offers us another strange spectacle, as does the leaf-fringed fight which ensues, a balletic battle backed by an upbeat score. (The woodland greenery scenes also literally inject colour, in contrast to the concrete grey of Cypher HQ.) We have reached the final confrontation.

The image of Steed causing mayhem in the Cypher HQ building, bulldozing assailants with the tea urn, while still finding time to ask them if they take it "with or without milk", is a moment of madness which could only work in *Avengerland*. Add in the aural backdrop of the hypnotic tape reminding us that it is "a perfectly normal, perfectly ordinary day" and you have an extraordinary spectacle. Steed even finds time to re-adjust an elderly lady's teacup, mid-battle, cleverly mirroring the henchman's earlier gesture. The tag scene – a tedious weekly add-on once the 'bright horizons' of Season 4 had been left behind – continues the theme of hypnosis, as we are tempted to believe that first Tara, then Steed, is entering a trance-like state. In reality, neither is and nor are we, our attention lost once the 'real' story has been completed. (Tags – like teasers – were necessary devices for the US market but, once again, 'less is more' and the classic charm and simplicity of the monochrome endings was never matched in the colour era.)

Super Secret Cypher Snatch is, like *The Rotters*, one of those Season 6 episodes which often slip under the critical radar. People are more likely to discuss the sublimely innovative *Stay Tuned*, the episodes which playfully engaged with other film and television genres, or even the utterly dismal *Homicide and Old Lace*. However, despite the absence of both a memorable mastermind and a darker, dramatic underbelly, this episode in many ways epitomises Season 6 at its best: witty, playful, surreal, fast-paced action adventure offering viewers a thrilling ride, ladders and all. The inclusion of stylishly unnecessary gestures and touches reflects both a season and heroine at ease. Both Tara King/Linda Thorson and Season 6 had 'found' themselves after the earlier production chaos.

© Rodney Marshall
1. My thanks to Michael Richardson for the teaser re-make information. *Bowler Hats and Kinky Boots*, p. 302.
2. This is despite poor continuity errors with Tara King's hair, as in this scene where she slides back down the ladder and has an entirely new style at the bottom!
3. My thanks, again, to *Bowler Hats and Kinky Boots* for this information.

GAME

Filmed: June 1968

Exterior Locations:
Children's playground
Averman's house: façade and grounds
Rough ground/foxhole/manoeuvres ground
University building
Bristow's country house

Sets:
Bristow's country house: motor racing set, snakes and ladders set, stock market set, hallway, battle stations set, word game set, super secret agent cage, scaffold/safe/six-sided room/hour glass
John Steed's mews apartment
Jig Creations: jigsaw shop
Averman's house: study/office
University building: reading room

GAME

Main Character List:
Monty Bristow/Daniel Edmund: the games king, mastermind
Cooty Gibson: racing car driver, ex-army tribunal
John Steed: ex-army tribunal
Tara King
Manservant: henchman
Dexter: zoologist, ex-army tribunal
Manager of Jigsaw Creations
Henry J Averman: stock broker, ex-army tribunal
Brigadier Wishforth-Browne: ex-army tribunal
Professor Witney: university don, ex-army tribunal

Game was filmed in June 1968 and, like so many Season 5 and 6 episodes, there was an abundance of wonderful exterior locations, be it winding country lanes, a field of buttercups, or Tyke's Water Lake. The seasons of the year were very much in evidence due to these wonderful exterior scenes, and as such there is a lovely summery ambience to *Game*, despite the terror inflicted by this episode's particular diabolical mastermind, Monty Bristow. [1]

Game is a very visual episode, with some extremely inventive sets portraying various games devised by Bristow. Author Richard Harris had cleverly written a script which finds Bristow's victims being forced to play games that all correspond with their chosen career. The first of these is a racing driver enduring a deadly life-size version of 'Speedway'. In long shot, this clearly has the appearance of a toy racetrack, which on the one hand is an indication of the limitations of a television budget, but on the other hand is indicative of *The Avengers'* self-referential approach.

The theme of people being used as pawns in games devised by a superior mind was one used several times during the 1960s. *The Celestial Toymaker*, the *Doctor Who* serial starring William Hartnell, and *Star Trek*'s *The Squire of Gothos* were two such examples, albeit with an intergalactic theme. *Game* was definitely in *Avengers* territory, encompassing the world of espionage and revenge, with one foot in the land of fantasy, the other foot planted firmly in reality.

Game was Linda Thorson's fourteenth episode, almost halfway through her thirty-three episode tenure, and it was filmed around the time of her twenty-first birthday, at a point when she was finding her confidence and strengths as an actress. This was always bubbling under the surface, even in her earlier tentative performances as Tara King, but suddenly it had exploded so gloriously in *All Done With Mirrors*, filmed the month before *Game*. It's a joy to watch her assurance in the role as it blossomed with each successive episode. It's a well documented fact that Linda Thorson was not Brian Clemens' choice. Indeed he has gone on record as saying that he would not have cast anyone as young as her. [2] However, with hindsight it would have been a mistake to have cast a similar performer to Diana Rigg. Thorson's style was refreshingly different, her youth and exuberance going hand in glove with the surreal off-the-wall direction which the series was now taking.

Game exemplifies perfectly the era in which it was made. A celluloid time capsule if you like, encapsulating a fun, surreal, slightly more innocent age. There are some nice examples of surreal humour in *Game*, a style of humour that was very much in vogue during the late 1960s. In one scene Tara visits The Master at Jig Creations, and watches him in a clearly speeded-up segment of film as he assembles a jigsaw at lightning speed. "What do you do on long winter nights?" she then asks him. "Ride a bicycle", he replies. This wacky, pre-Pythonesque sense of humour is evident in *Game* and many other Season 6 episodes, a style of humour that would have been inconceivable only five years earlier during Cathy Gale's tenure. Another scene in *Game* infamously dates the episode to this more innocent age. The scene in question finds Steed pulling Tara from an armchair in order to visit the Brigadier. As he guides her out of his apartment, he playfully pats her on the bottom. I have watched this episode countless times over the years without questioning this scene. It was perfectly acceptable in the more playful *Carry On* days of yore, and as such the episode becomes very much a product of its time. Any displeasure is maybe a reflection of our more cynical times, where the blatantly unacceptable is now deservedly punished, but also, sadly, where overreaction and suspicion can become a way of life. Having said that, I doubt if Cathy Gale would have tolerated such cavalier behaviour from Steed. [3] He could well have found himself flying over the nearest sofa! Tara, however, had quite a different relationship with Steed than her predecessors, and seemed fairly willing to accept such behaviour in the playful spirit in which it was given.

In another scene, Averman is chloroformed by Bristow's butler. Tara herself was chloroformed countless times during this season. Chloroforming was very much a trait in *The Avengers* and similar 1960s series, no longer found in today's more violent nature of entertainment. Not that there was a shortage of violence in *The Avengers*. After Averman's incapacitation, there follows a pretty hefty fight between Steed and the butler, but a proper fisticuffs affair with no weapons or bloodshed. This was a philosophy always adhered to throughout *The Avengers*' entire run.

The Avengers, while being an action series of an escapist nature, also encompassed the right amount of comedy as a counterbalance to the violent aspects, as is evident in an episode like *Game*. For instance, following the aforementioned fight scene between Steed and the butler, Tara brings an icepack over to Steed as he recovers on his sofa. "What's that?" he asks. "You said lots of ice", replies Tara. "I meant for the drink. If I put anything like that on my head, it'll freeze the brain cells."

Avengers plots were clearly more grounded in Cathy Gale's day, and more of an escapist nature during Emma's reign, but there was a broad diversity of styles during Tara's tenure. There were darker episodes such as *Take-Over* and *Requiem* which saw a deliberate attempt to recreate a more realistic *Avengerland*. However, there were also episodes of an increasingly surreal nature such as *Look* and *Game*. *Game* is sheer escapism, complete with off-the-wall plot and atmosphere, and also boasts some of the most memorable and imaginative sets in *Avengers* history. Following the weird and wonderful Snakes and Ladders set, we then find ourselves in the midst of another bizarre one, as Averman is forced to play 'Stock Market' in a bid to literally save his own life. The set designer must have had either the time of his life or a complete nightmare creating such unusual sets within the limitations of his given budget and deadline. As such a visually stunning canvas was created, it was clearly time well spent. [4] The production team devoted a lot of time and resources in their attempts to create this wonderful *Avengerland*, a more perfect and sunny reflection of the imperfect and inclement world viewers all lived in. The Greater London area was often scouted for unusual, eye-catching locations, and we are rewarded with such fabulous scenes as Steed and Tara enjoying a gentle moment in a field of buttercups as they await their rendezvous with the Brigadier. [5] He eventually arrives in true *Avengers* fashion: in a tank, and heading straight for our heroes, before crashing into a tree, the jigsaw pieces in his hand signifying that he has been added to the ever-growing list of victims.

The jigsaw pieces themselves are a clever ploy in author Richard Harris's game of plot development. In so many episodes Steed and Tara are to be found piecing together the unravelling mystery they are attempting to solve. In *Game* they are literally finding the pieces of a jigsaw, which when completed will provide the key to their latest mystery. According to a much quoted saying, there are seven basic plots, possibly too simple a generalisation that even divides literary experts. One of these plot devices, revenge, begins to rear its ugly head in *Game*, as Steed realises that all the victims were on

Sergeant Edmund's tribunal. Steed begins to suspect that not only is it possible that Edmund wasn't killed while trying to escape, but also that he is one of the pawns in this deadly game, as he himself was on Edmund's tribunal.

Tara is used as bait to lure Steed, and yes, she is chloroformed by the butler! Steed shows the assembled jigsaw to The Master, as the plot dovetails neatly into its completed picture. After The Master recognises the building in the jigsaw as Bristow's house, Steed races to Tara's rescue. The house, in reality, is Grim's Dyke Hotel, an impressive 19th Century Grade II listed building in Harrow, North London, which was also used in films such as *The Prime of Miss Jean Brodie*.

The episode reaches its climax, as the most impressive set and the most inventive game of all is revealed. In 'Super Secret Agent', Steed has six minutes in which to rescue Tara, now trapped in a giant hourglass rapidly filling with sand. This game requires all the skills a secret agent possesses: courage, strategy, cunning. As most secret agents hold little store for their own life, a damsel in distress is incorporated into the mix. This is a very iconic and memorable scene, involving one of the most inventive and unusual sets ever created for *The Avengers*. [6]

Steed, being the ultra-skilled agent that he is, successfully completes the first few missions, and is rewarded with a gun containing six bullets, only one of which is live. Bristow, played with a cool sinister charm by Peter Jeffrey, has played all of his deadly games by the rule, or rather by his own set of rules. [7] Steed plays by no rules but his own, and in an act of extreme cunning, he fires all of the bullets at the hourglass, the live one freeing Tara from her fate and enabling her to join him in the climactic fight scene. This is an ingenious and very *Avengers*-like twist that turns the cards successfully in our hero's favour. Steed can clearly play dirtier than the villains he battles, and it's a blessing to the nation that he is on the side of virtue! Even the deadly ace up Bristow's sleeve is no match for Steed's ruthless cunning in *Game*'s exciting finale. Confirmation of Steed's desire to always win can be found in the amusing tag scene, which finds him playing 'Steedopoly' with Tara, a game she clearly has no hope of ever winning!

Game is an immensely enjoyable episode that never slows its rollercoaster pace for a second. It is directed with panache by Robert Fuest, who ensures that every frame of film has something enjoyably diverting to offer. The fun the cast appears to have had with *Game* is infectious. A four-bowler fun-filled fifty minutes, and surely among the top episodes of this hugely enjoyable season.

© Richard Cogzell

1. Perhaps we can go a step further and suggest that the delightful summer landscape is horribly, ironically at odds with the interior horror of the games.
2. He has also gone on record as saying that he didn't rate her as an actress either, which is far less pardonable in my opinion. Ironically, he was to use her a few years later in his atmospheric *Thriller* episode *Lady Killer*.
3. In one monochrome episode, Emma Peel playfully smacks Steed's bottom. Do these moments tell us something about the different relationships which Steed had with his female avengers?
4. There is something darkly fascinating about the stock market indicator being (tantalisingly) composed of his blood pressure/heart pills.

5. As I suggest in my chapter on *Super Secret Cypher Snatch*, the field of wild flowers becomes an iconic image in the Tara King era.
6. We could call it a set of sets, each a visual delight and tease.
7. Bristow is (delightfully) reminded, at one point, by his butler that he must adhere to his own rules.

FALSE WITNESS

Filmed: July 1968

Exterior Locations:
Underground garage
Urban streets
Stable Mews
Suburban street/bus stop
Mother's headquarters (London bus)
Woods
Sir Joseph's house
Field of cows
Fire escape/street
Dreemykreem Dairies Bottling Plant
Country roads

Sets:
Telephone box
Steed's mews apartment
Plummer's flat
Sir Joseph's study
Edgefield's flat
Dairy: Sykes' office, churn area, milk vat room, butter machine
Milk float

FALSE WITNESS

Main Character List:
Penman: agent
Melville: agent
Brayshaw: chauffeur/henchman
John Steed
Tara King
Gould: agent/bus conductor
Mother
Rhonda: Mother's silent assistant
Plummer: witness in Edgefield case
Sir Joseph Tarleton: prosecutor
Grant: lie detector operator
Sykes: dairy manager
Amanda: Sir Joseph's secretary
Nesbitt: witness
Lane: henchman
Sloman: henchman

False Witness offers us a slick teaser in which two agents are on a mission in the heart of the urban jungle. While Penman enters an underground/multi-storey car park – a recurring location in both Season 6 and *The New Avengers* – Melville acts as the look-out. His false information – "No one coming" – is baffling, given the fact that we/Melville see the chauffeur hit-man Brayshaw arrive. Melville must, surely, be a double agent? His lack of warning will be explained and justified later on by the truth/lie drug laced into the milk, but what is never justified is the fact that he simply walks away as the chauffeur shoots Penman, despite the loud gunshots. This is, of course, *The Avengers*, where plot holes are as common as bullet ones, but even so there are unanswered questions or inconsistencies in Burnham's storyline.

The teaser is followed by some delicious location filming: Steed driving away leisurely from his picturesque London mews just as the fatally injured Penman staggers into it; then Steed pulling into a suburban housing estate close to a parade of shops – there are even members of the public seen heading towards the shops or crossing the road – before erecting his very own request stop. It is a wonderfully surreal moment, as is the bus conductor Gould's refusal to allow a member of the public to mount the unpopulated vehicle: "Sorry, full up." "What do you mean 'full up'?" Burnham may have broken an *Avengers* guideline/rule by allowing a member of the public to both appear and speak, but there are limits, even in his version of *Avengerland*. The post-war characterless suburbia offers a visual contrast to the affluent city seen elsewhere in this episode and the bus stop scene is a fascinating one.

Mother and Steed's subsequent discussion of the Edgefield case – "the Department's losing agents and I'm losing sleep" – is reassuringly formulaic yet Burnham's delightful HQ offers us a refreshing change. As stated elsewhere in this book, Mother's quirky, changing HQs are a visual (structural) highlight of the season [1] but here this is taken a step further, allowing a mobility which will ensure that Mother can pop up wherever and whenever the writer/director wants him to. The upper deck has become an office with the public's seats replaced by Rhonda's bar counter, Mother's desk and guests' corner seat, the windows flooding the 'location set' with light and allowing us to watch the suburban landscape drift by as the perplexing case is explained. It is pure *Avengerland*. The Routemaster bus' aesthetic appeal adds greatly to what could otherwise have been a series of tedious 'tell not show' scenes and the HQ contrasts nicely with the Mews scenes which it alternates with.

As the plot begins to unravel, a particularly clever touch is the way in which Steed is investigating key witness Plummer's kitchen for clues while Tara empties the dustbin's rubbish onto the apartment floor, also searching for evidence. The short fight scene with a milkman in Plummer's flat has just offered us a clever moment of delayed significance, although both the episode title and Melville's strange behaviour pre-warn us that witnesses are likely to be unreliable throughout this story. Re-watching the episode with the 'benefit' of hindsight, the fact that both Melville and Plummer take their coffee with milk, while Steed drinks his black, provides another imbedded clue.

Mother's mobile HQ drives out into hilly countryside as the plot thickens, adding a surreal touch as the front destination roller indicates that they are heading towards Piccadilly Circus. The bus reflects the Avengers' mission, struggling to reach a desired destination. In a twist from the more usual situation where Steed expresses his concerns for Tara to Mother, here it is Tara who is worried about Steed:

Mother: The security of the Department's at stake.
Tara: And Steed's life!
Mother: He'll be all right. Forewarned is forearmed.
Tara: Not against a knife in the back.

It is a crisp, emotive exchange in which Tara/Steed's humane reactions in Season 6 are once again contrasted with Mother's more pragmatic approach. Patrick Newell – given a larger than usual role in this episode – sparkles with his dry delivery, offering a self-referential look as he reminds Tara that Steed *"usually* knows what he's up to."

A third of the way through *False Witness* we find ourselves returning to the teaser location of the underground car park for what is both a re-run and an extension of the opening scene, the dialogue and chauffeur chase echoing the teaser, while the agent investigation this time takes place in Edgefield's funky Sixties interior, rather than his car. This cyclical or non-linear approach – the returning teaser – works well in *The Avengers*, as demonstrated by *The Murder Market*, *The Hour That Never Was*, *Stay Tuned* and *Pandora*, allowing the writer/director to either puzzle us or take us further along the plot line. Here, it increases the dramatic tension as we already know what Steed suspects: that Melville will let him down. Rather than bursting the dramatic bubble, it inflates it. Even the music score is suggestive of a relentless repetition, frustrating Department agent and viewer alike. This score reaches a crescendo as a perplexed, furious Steed drives Melville away from the city.

Melville: What did you do that for?
Steed: For services not rendered.

Steed's physical assault in the following woodland scene splits opinion. Some critics, like Sunday Swift, see it as an example – as in

Fog – of a regrettable violence on the part of Steed, at odds with the suave, cool Steed of the Emma Peel era. It is, arguably, further evidence of the emergence of stereotypical gender representation in Season 6: the macho male, the doting, dependent female. On the other hand, Steed's reaction to the false witness within his own department is – on the level of realism – an understandable one, given the fact that his life has been endangered and that only some lousy marksmanship from the chauffeur has saved his life. From this perspective, it could be argued that Steed's return to a darker avenger is an example of the 'thicker cardboard' of the Tara era. I am left undecided so I will fence-sit on this one.

At this halfway point in the episode we are still bewildered by Melville's actions, although by now we can be fairly sure that it is not a simple example of a rotten apple in the Departmental barrel. After all, he isn't the only false witness. As if to mirror the confusion, we get a delightfully odd shot of Mother's bus parked in a field, surrounded by curious cows. Grant's "infallible" lie detector provides us with the recurring leitmotif of unreliable modern technology. After all, as Steed observes, it is "human". The rural idyll of the stream-bordered meadow is contrasted with Tara's urban pursuit of the Dreemykreem milk float through architecturally-impressive Georgian terraces. The sight of Tara's red Lotus Europa tailing the float around Belgrave Square, shot from the dairy van, with milk bottles fore-grounded and elegant London houses as backdrop is – for me – one of the iconic Season 6 images. We also gain our first sight of the dairy's bottling plant as the mystery is finally 'skimmed' off. The dairy HQ and Tara's tailing of milkman Lane are neatly brought together by Sykes' avengerish order: "Special delivery, Lane. Sir Joseph Tarleton. Two pints please."

The Dreemykreem bottling plant is one of the most memorable *Avengerland* sets of the Tara era. The stacked milk crates and chrome churns offer perfect hiding places or ideal weapons for heroine or foe; we have the enormous and aptly-named full-fat henchman Sloman; and we can sense immediately that the large milk vat will become a fighting pool playground. As Tara takes a sample of the milk, the opening verbal exchanges with the villains are a delight: "Worried about lack of vitamins?" "Desperately. I'm just wasting away." "Then we must bring the roses back to your cheeks, mustn't we?" Sloman's dunking of Tara in the milk vat offers a playful echo of Emma Peel's ducking in the Little Storping pond. Now that the plot has been revealed, *False Witness* becomes a frothy, milkshake episode from hereon in, typified by Tara's phone call to Sir Joseph: "This is very unimportant...I don't want to warn you...don't be careful" and Sir Joseph's character summary of the diabolical Edgefield moments later – "the most incorrupt, irreproachable man in the country. An idealist, a philanthropist and a paragon of virtue" – delivered through gritted teeth. Why is it that Sir Joseph seems aware that he has said the opposite of what he wants to, while Melville isn't?

Any sense of dramatic tension has given way to the sort of 'surface *soufflé*' story which Burnham specialises in: visually attractive but rarely hiding dramatic depth. This second half is, arguably, uncomfortably at odds with the earlier style and events. The pre/post-Dreemykreem scenes almost belong to different episodes. The sight of the milkman standing like a cowboy by his milk float charger in Steed's Stable Mews offers us an unsettling image, yet with the tense dramatic cord now less than taut the moment is lost. The following chase scene in which Tara attempts to catch Lane's float is cleverly filmed but is more surface style. As Tara leaves Steed a written 'non-warning' – "the milk is harmless" – Steed advises Melville to take his coffee black in future. In yet another episode where Tara and Steed are rarely together, it is left to Miss King to return to the Batman-esque dairy den and for Sykes to deliver the best line of the episode: "Butter wouldn't melt in your mouth, Miss King. Or would it?" Having said this, his subsequent order to henchman Sloman – "Put her in the butter machine!" – isn't far behind. The final fight scene combines the usual *Avengers* balletic qualities with theatre of the absurd, as first characters engage in a *Wonderland* of nonsensical dialogue and then Tara is ejected, inside a butter pat costume. Steed's "Milk Ho!" rescue of Tara from a physical trap ties *False Witness* to many of the other filmed *Avengers* episodes. The hallucinatory drug theme connects this story to others, as well, including *Something Nasty in the Nursery* and Burnham's *Love All*. *False Witness* isn't as intelligent or innovative as either of these, but it does offer us a quirky, entertaining and visually stunning episode. In addition, Mother's Routemaster provides the cherry on the cake; it is, perhaps, *The Avengers*' equivalent of *Doctor Who*'s Tardis, allowing the sedentary Mother mobility and the viewer a top seat spectacle. [2]

© Rodney Marshall

1. In the nineteen episodes in which he appears.
2. It is unsurprising that the Hollywood film drew upon this.

"Lord Edgefield is the most incorrupt, irreproachable man in the country. An idealist, a philanthropist, a paragon of virtue."

Or in other words...

Lord Edgefield was a frightful cad,
A bounder, who by foul means had
Heaped shame upon his fellow peers
By preying on men's secret fears.

This irked Sir Joseph Tarleton, who
Was good and decent, through and through,
And by any means employable sought
To see Lord Edgefield brought to court.

I could go on with such a rhyme,
But my deadline looms. I'm out of time...

Having successfully delivered his first script for *The Avengers*, Jeremy Burnham was signed up by Brian Clemens to provide further scripts for the series under a two year contract, which would pay him a regular retainer, plus a fee for each script delivered. Either working from thumbnails provided by Clemens, or from his own story suggestions, Burnham would write a further four scripts for the series, before its cancellation in 1969. After an initial meeting with Clemens to discuss how a possible thumbnail would be developed, Burnham would then work from home to produce a first draft storyline which would be discussed at a further meeting during which Clemens would suggest other ideas that might be incorporated. After working out a structure between them, Burnham would then develop the 'one-off' characters needed for the script - an early example being the superior stationery salesman Maidwell from *You'll Catch Your Death* who Burnham thought was perfectly portrayed by Henry McGee as both creepy and funny -

capturing the essential ingredients of the show. No particular rules or limitations were set on the scripts, apart from the display of blood or any realistic representations of authority. If policemen, police cars or ambulances appeared, they had to be fake. On average, a script would take two months to complete, with Clemens usually having further input into the final draft.

For Burnham, the particular appeal of the series was the unique world it was set in, his feeling being that other filmed series of the time such as *The Saint*, *The Baron*, *Man in a Suitcase* and *Jason King* were virtually interchangeable. *The Avengers* he regarded as being completely different, in that even if you saw a clip of it without Steed or his partners, you would immediately know it was *The Avengers*. In his view the series was sexy, funny and had great style; he found Steed and his partner a 'dream' to write for. This obvious enthusiasm for the show is evident in all five of the scripts he turned out during 1968, each of which adeptly captures the essential essence of *The Avengers*. It's also notable that apart from *Fog* - which is a pure murder mystery, albeit in a period style - each of Burnham's storylines is driven by something almost non-existent. In *You'll Catch Your Death*, it's a seemingly empty envelope, in *Love All* a subliminal message in a book, and in the proto-*New Avengers* episode *Who Was That Man I Saw You With?*, most intangibly of all, the driving force is pure suspicion.

In *False Witness*, the plot's prime mover is a harmless-looking colourless liquid. Its effect, however, is far from harmless, and is used to strike right at the heart of the British nation's cherished values of honesty and fair play. In this the episode tackles themes that would become a central concern of Brian Clemens' later productions - the corruption and moral collapse of the British establishment. Up until *The Avengers*' sixth season, the series had largely portrayed Britain's governing bodies as a force for good, and generally to be regarded with respect, even if they might countenance the use of underhand methods. But by the late 1960s the programme began to reflect a growing public distrust with public servants and the ruling classes, in the wake of such high profile scandals as the Profumo Affair. The enemy, it seemed, was no longer at the door, but had taken up residence in the castle, and might even be sitting at the top table.

Moving away from the over-used multiple death/surreally fantastic stories of the colour Rigg and early Thorson period, *False Witness* explores the themes of moral collapse and the disintegration of trust in a far more 'real' world. There are still visually bizarre moments and twisted takes on dramatic situations, but the tale is firmly rooted in a world we can recognise. In what could be seen as another nod to Hilaire Belloc (as noted in the chapter on *You'll Catch Your Death*), and his series of poems about Britain's ignoble peerage, Burnham has conceived as his villain of the piece the smarmily oily Lord Edgefield, a man who has achieved his position and wealth through ruthlessly exploiting the indiscretions of others. This doubly demonstrates that all is not what it should be in the upper echelons of society. The country's so called 'betters' are shown to be weak and open to extortion, in a world where privilege is abused. This insidious moral cancer now proves a further threat when it seems that even those who are genuinely trustworthy can no longer be relied upon. Symbolically representing the virulent nature of corruption, it transpires that these less predictable lapses in otherwise high standards of behaviour are being artificially induced at the behest of Lord Edgefield: through the use of a new drug which instils uncontrollable mendacity in those to whom it is given. As a result, and in another nod to Hilaire Belloc, whose cautionary verses for children included the tale of *Matilda, Who Told Such Dreadful Lies*, Steed's fellow agents, apparently willing case witnesses, and even the head of the investigation into Lord Edgefield's affairs, are effectively turned into congenital liars. The fate of the whole country - if not the world - now lies in the hands of the drug's manufacturers.

In a neat twist on the famous line from Sir Arthur Conan Doyle's classic Sherlock Holmes short story *Silver Blaze*, in which Holmes refers to 'The curious case of the dog in the night-time', it is the curious case of the dog in the day-time which fails to alert Tara to the activities of this week's instrument of chaos. As he had done in *You'll Catch Your Death* with his bolshie postman, and would do so again in *Love All* in the form of an outwardly dowdy cleaning woman, Burnham puts the implementation of his devilish plot into the hands of another servile cog normally responsible for making the nation's wheels go round. This episode's enemy of the people is that every day purveyor of essential goodness, the milkman. In an episode brimming with contradictory imagery and dramatic reversals of behaviour, it is wholly appropriate that the forces of evil are represented by a substance universally associated with well-being and purity. And, once again, in the sixth season it is the lower orders - this time tradesmen - who have taken the upper hand. The drug's inventor, Sykes, is not the archetypal 'posh' *Avengers* villain at all. He is a charmless spiv, complete with pencil moustache, who is happy to sell his goods for no other reason than financial gain, his perversely-named company 'Dreemykreem Dairies' selling what is in fact the stuff of nightmares.

Taking further delight in confounding expectations, the episode turns several other iconic manifestations of the British way of life neatly on their head. Apart from the malevolently menacing lone-handed milkman, seen by the camera in a wonderful crash zoom as he stands in Steed's mews, and watch-dogs that don't bark, telephone boxes and telephones become means of noncommunication, dustbins contain items of great importance, public transport is not available to the public, and even lie detectors can't detect the truth. [1] Perhaps the most visually memorable reversal of the episode concerns Mother's mobile HQ. Unlike the common crook Lord Edgefield, who swans around Mayfair and St. John's Wood in his chauffeur-driven Rolls-Royce, super spook Mother has taken up residence on the top deck of a proletarian double-decker bus, which we first see trundling round a council estate in Borehamwood. This allows us a rare opportunity to see 'The Man in the Street', in a clever gag that has him turned away from the seemingly empty conveyance. Unusually, all the interior scenes are shot while the vehicle is driving around the Elstree area and there is also a charmingly pastoral and surreal shot of the vehicle standing in a field surrounded by the unwitting suppliers of the substance being abused by the diabolical villains. [2]

Verbally, the episode is also replete with contradictions - in the most literal sense of the word - as characters are forced to say the opposite of what they mean in a number of key scenes, particularly Tara, after she falls into a vat of the doctored milk. "I don't want to warn you", she plaintively informs Sir Joseph at one point, and "The milk is harmless" in a note to Steed. Sir Joseph, too, is given a keynote speech in which he is forced to describe the odious Lord Edgefield as a "Paragon of virtue" through gritted teeth. There is also a wonderfully-realised scene in which the lie detector is out-witted by the drug and a climactic fight at the end of the episode which sees the villains unable to assist each other, having had their - for once literally - subversive champagne doctored by Steed.

In only his second script, Burnham has effectively succeeded in moving away from the well-worn *Avengers* plot clichés that provided the basis for *You'll Catch Your Death*, and taken the characters into a slightly more believable *Avengerland*, enhanced by the episode's extensive use of location filming. His treatment of Steed and Tara also presents them as more realistic and down-to-earth characters, with Steed at one point resorting to unexpectedly angry violence and Tara finding life as a spy far from glamorous. In this the episode exemplifies the differences between the handling of Steed's partner in the sixth season and the show's earlier incarnations. It's hard to believe that either Cathy or Emma would have been reduced to scrabbling through the contents of rubbish bins, or would have themselves trapped in a giant butter churner, and this begs the question whether the treatment of Tara as an object of comedy rather than as a character deserving of respect might in some way have contributed to the demise of the series, particularly in view of the penultimate scene in which she is encased up to her neck in a giant slab of butter. [3] Nevertheless, this does set the scene for a wonderful tag gag in which Steed concludes that with all that butter, what better way to toast the success of their mission than with a large helping of...toast. Well, buttered sandwiches, anyway.

© Sam Denham (with grateful thanks to Jeremy Burnham)

1. These all add to the surreal mixture, creating a disconcertingly inverted world.
2. Whether or not the writer/director meant the connection to be made, it is a great one.
3. I think this is an excellent observation/suggestion, offering further evidence of the undermining of Linda Thorson/Tara King.

NOON DOOMSDAY

Filmed: July 1968

Exterior Locations:
Lang's Halt: deserted railway station
Open countryside
Department S: minefield, barbed wire fence, farmhouse, farm courtyard, outbuildings, well
Field and helicopter

Sets:
John Steed's mews apartment
Taxi
Department S: common room, barn, well shaft, corridors, guest bedrooms

NOON DOOMSDAY

Main Character List:
Grant: cowboy henchman
Farrington: cowboy henchman
Mother
Rhonda: Mother's silent assistant
Tara King
Giles Cornwall: head of security at Department S
John Steed: wheelchair-bound
Dr. Hyde: Department S
Dr. Carson: Hyde's assistant, Kafka's inside henchman
Sir Rodney Woodham-Baines: injured diplomat
Roger Lyall: mental breakdown patient
Jules Perrier: injured French agent
Edward Sunley: injured agent
Gerald Kafka: escapee prisoner, mastermind

Noon Doomsday is one of a handful of Season 6 episodes which tackle other fictional genres. More often than not this is done in a playful, satirical fashion, as is the case with *Wish You Were Here* (*The Prisoner*) and *Legacy of Death* (*The Maltese Falcon*). Neither of these episodes makes any pretence at offering a darker, dramatic undercurrent. *Noon Doomsday* shares far more in common with another Terry Nation script, the effectively unpleasant *Take-Over*. Both move at a leisurely pace, with a disturbingly subversive atmosphere – rather than action – creating the dramatic tension. In some ways *Noon Doomsday* represents a greater achievement. While *Take-Over* has an almost theatrical appeal, it is virtually humourless, despite its undeniable style. [1] This episode, on the other hand, creates the perfect mixture of subversion and champagne, with plenty of scenes where wit and drama merge. It offers a fitting homage to the Hollywood classic *High Noon*, but with a satirical wink added for good measure.

One of the delights of *Noon Doomsday* is its cleverly constructed triptych structure: Mother lodging at Steed's apartment, Steed and Tara King at the 'ranch' (the mischievously-named Department S) and the hired henchmen cowboys waiting at the abandoned railway station. The latter has a haunting, deserted *Avengerland* feel to it. The fact that so little happens for so long in the story – the cowboys don't even leave the station until Kafka, the mastermind, arrives just ten minutes from the end of the episode – is, ironically, one of *Noon Doomsday*'s greatest strengths. It is a bizarrely unique hour: almost *The Avengers* meets Western with the absurd banalities of *Waiting for Godot* thrown in. And 'Kafka', of course.

The teaser immediately offers a glimpse of the abandoned train station: weeds infesting the rusting tracks, the timber-framed, rotting station buildings effectively recreating the feel of a frontier town or outpost in a Western. The cowboy music helps to establish this. We then experience a panning vista of rolling countryside, two horsemen galloping across fields and up a hillside. Immediately, however, the Western genre is questioned. While Grant is dressed like a cross between a burglar and Union soldier, Farrington wears a mustard jumper under a tweed jacket, with a bright flower in the lapel. Not exactly your standard cowboy's attire. They tie their horses up by the railway track, warning us that no train will be approaching this station. This lends an almost 'theatre of the absurd' quality to the subsequent scenes which take place here: the cowboy assassins waiting, seemingly, for something which can never arrive. Farrington's announcement that they will be killing John Steed "at twelve noon" has a theatrical air to it, matched by Grant moving the station clock hands to the appropriate time, before the episode title offers us a third and final indication of the simple, diabolical aim. The Western music score has, by now, become playfully over-dramatic. [2]

As the first half hour of *Noon Doomsday* unfolds, we are offered the effective triptych structure I referred to earlier, adding a similarly pleasing '3D' feel to that which we experience in *The Forget-Me-Knot*. Mother's scenes at Steed's apartment are mainly played for laughs, as he makes his way – with both enthusiasm and stamina – through the artificially-colourful liqueurs in Steed's drinks cabinet. These will be playfully redeployed by the director later to indicate the countdown to Tara entering Department S, as the camera pans across glasses ranging from full to empty. The assortment of colour-coded telephones which Rhonda has to deal with adds further light touches to these scenes. However, typical of *Noon Doomsday*, these 'fun' scenes are then given a dramatic edge or twist as Mother becomes aware of the escalating bad news: a prison break-out; the identity of the escapee, the former head of Murder

International, Gerald Kafka; Department S's phone line cut etc. It is symbolically appropriate that Mother's holiday-mode relaxation disappears at the very moment when he has drained the last dregs of the colourful liquids. Both the humour and the apartment have run dry. Lightness is nearly always darkly-edged in *Noon Doomsday*.

The absurd nature of the train station vigil is mirrored by the surreal spectacle of Tara King arriving in a London taxi in the midst of wild flower fields. The sense of an unspoilt, idyllic world of Arcadia is dramatically offset by the unpleasantly ugly atmosphere building up at the station. We effectively flit between the two, with both the music and the images clashing: the colourful array of wild flowers horribly at odds with the sight of glass bottles being senselessly smashed on the tracks; the disturbing music as Farrington menacingly sharpens a piece of wood with his knife cutting through the light, melodic score as Tara King enjoys a carefree ramble. It adds up to a disconcertingly uncomfortable spectacle.

The real identity of Lang's Halt was Stanbridgeford. Both the station and the passenger service had closed in 1962, the line shut in 1964. The location manager who uncovered or chose this spot deserves our appreciation. It is in the perfect state of disrepair – if that isn't an oxymoron: dilapidated enough to offer the sense of a disturbingly deserted *Avengerland*, yet still recognisable as a station where a train might, just *might* stop. [3] (The surrounding, rolling countryside has also been perfectly 'cast', offering us a surreal sense of the rugged Wild West in the heart of leafy Buckinghamshire.) In a clever, further twist in the plot, the opening scenes involving Farrington and Grant make us think that Grant is the violent thug, while Farrington – busy deciding what present to buy for his niece's ninth birthday – is the more sensitive partner. As their moment of departure draws closer, we realise that Grant's impatience is simply nerves, while Farrington is the experienced, chillingly cold serial killer:

Farrington: My goodness, you do get edgy, don't you?
Grant: You don't, I suppose?
Farrington: I *did*. First dozen or so times. But it's just a job of work, sometimes a little messy I'll agree – but not too arduous, and remarkably well paid.

Their weapons of choice match their characters. As Farrington demonstrates with a target can, a knife might seem less dangerous than a gun but it is equally lethal and makes far less noise as it goes about its deadly business.

If the train station location works perfectly in terms of *Avengerland* atmosphere and a sense of theatrical absurdity, it also exudes the feel of a Wild West building. This equally applies to Brian Clemens' farm which was used as Department S, "the most secretive nursing home in the country" according to Steed. Thanks to the musical score and clever direction, we are happy to read 'Wild West ranch' for 'Home Counties farm'. The sense of a Western is reinforced here, partly by the imaginative use of the outbuildings, with the sense that henchmen could be hiding behind the hay bales and the use of a lasso and cart wheel to terminate Giles Cornwall, Department S' security man. The well shaft also provides a memorable set for one of the more dramatic scenes as Tara finds herself caught between a good-but-dead doctor at the bottom and an evil, alive one at the top who is preparing to send her into the same watery grave. It is yet another stylish moment.

The scenes in which she vainly seeks out support for Steed among the convalescing patients combine humour and drama, both elements based on clichés or stereotypes – Jules Perrier, the 'cheese-eating surrender monkey' French agent; Sir Rodney, the upper-class 'pacifist' diplomat, injured yet possessing enough lust-fuelled energy to sexually intimidate or bully Tara. As Steed had suspected from the start, like the Marshal in *High Noon* he will have precious few loyal colleagues to draw upon.

The final showdown contains enough plot twists to keep viewers guessing: Steed intends tying Tara up and fighting the villains alone; Tara knocks Steed out with a champagne bottle; Tara proves equal to the task of eliminating the cowboy henchmen; Steed recovers in time to terminate the diabolical mastermind with the aid of a 'crutch harpoon'. The latter adds a surreal touch to the fight finale spectacle which is atmospherically shot, as figures move in, out and around the cathedral-like barn and other outbuildings. At one point, grain is kicked up from the ground by the chasing villains and it fills the screen, offering us a fleeting, effective image. These moments are stylish but lack the menace of the previous ones, Blake's Western score now upbeat, before becoming clichéd saloon piano playing. Farrington, clearly unaware of the legendary exploits of Cathy Gale, Emma Peel and Tara King, foolishly announces that their opponent is "only a girl"; Grant fatefully orders her to turn around: "I don't like to see the eyes." These are (humorous) stereotype errors for which they will both pay the ultimate price.

There is a stylish slickness about the ways in which we move between the three sets/locations in this episode. An example is the pop of Steed's champagne bottle becoming Grant's gun shooting practice on the rusting train tracks. However, what draws these three places together, thematically, is the fascination with time. The title *Noon Doomsday* resonates throughout as Grant is constantly demanding the time from his fellow cowboy who carries a dandyish pocket watch. The station clock hands never move from their midday position, a constant reminder of the appointed hour. Kafka wants to kill Steed at this symbolic time as a revengeful anniversary 'gift'. Mother and Tara "synchronise" their watches to ensure that the latter can enter Department S unscathed. The sundial in the grounds at the farm is the first thing we see in the initial shot of the farm. Dr. Hyde will later tap it, complaining that it is "two minutes slow". (Ironically, his time is about to run out). Characters are seen looking at – or passing – the sundial throughout the episode, just as Tara and Steed anxiously read the common room clock as the drama unfolds. (No wonder the tag scene involves Steed buying Tara a luminous, surreal sundial!) As in *High Noon*, this is an atmospheric treatment on the subject of the relentless nature of time and the act/art of waiting. Grant wants to speed it up, Steed would like to slow it down or stop it, while Kafka is savouring it. However, it is Tara King who makes the best use of it, starting with the choice to visit Department S in the first place, despite the 'timed dangers' involved:

Mother: One half second the wrong way and you'll be dead, Miss King. Quite dead.

She also uses the preparation time far better than her enemies, ensuring that she is prepared for the midday appointment. *Noon Doomsday* is a thrilling paradox. It playfully yet also faithfully engages with *High Noon*, almost matching the latter's leisurely, suspenseful use of 'real time' as we are left to wait for the brooding atmosphere to develop into action. If John Steed plays the wounded Marshal Will Kane/Gary Cooper, then Tara King comes into her own here in Grace Kelly's role, though lacking the moral dilemma facing the pacifist Marshal's wife. The extended scene in which she vainly seeks out support among the convalescing patients is a perfect example of the clever combination of humour and drama in this script. There is plenty of both in *Noon Doomsday*, an episode which matches the complicated route in to Department S itself. As Tara puts it:

"The approach is the tiniest bit unconventional."

Steed's reply – "charming countryside though" – could equally refer to the enjoyment of watching this fascinatingly different *Avengers* episode. [4]

© Rodney Marshall

1. *Take-Over* does contain elements of humour, of the distinctly dark variety, particularly in the verbal fencing between Fenton and Steed. However, it lacks the avengerish lightness of touch, the frothy wit and charm I associate with the series. One could argue that it is all subversion with no champagne.
2. This episode was scored by Howard Blake, rather than Laurie Johnson, as *Bowler Hats and Kinky Boots* points out.
3. This branch line had been popular among ramblers, out to enjoy the rolling countryside captured in this episode. *The Avengers* filmed between the line closure in 1964 and the track-lifting in 1970. The principal building – not seen on camera – was bought privately and has been restored as a home, now known as Stanbridgeford House. One of the platforms is now part of the garden. The main station building was demolished soon after filming, according to Michael Richardson's informative guide.
4. The only bones of contention I have with this super episode are ones which surface regularly in Season 6. First, the music. Incidental music – funereal or conveying tension, levity etc. – is constantly re-used in *The Avengers*, which is perfectly acceptable. In fact, it is highly effective to have

these familiar standard pieces. However, the Tara era re-use of the big musical scores is disappointingly lazy and, I would suggest, off-putting. In *Noon Doomsday* the recycling of the *Murdersville* score has me mentally travelling back to Little Storping and the ducking stool. As Blake scored this episode I would have hoped for his own (new) creations to dominate throughout. My second problem is Tara King's schizophrenic wardrobe which here offers her something which is far from flattering. It is also ill-suited for the exciting action finale. She looks infinitely better in her tomboyish corduroy jean suit, as worn in *All Done With Mirrors*. The constant fashion style changes did neither the actress nor the character any favours.

LEGACY OF DEATH

Filmed: July-August 1968

Exterior Locations:
Farrer's mansion and grounds
Stable Mews
Country roads
Chinese curio shop
Tara King's street and apartment back entrance
London streets
Solicitors' office

Sets:
Farrer mansion: baronial hall
Steed's mews apartment
Chinese curio shop and back room
Tara King's apartment
Summerhouse
Solicitors' office

LEGACY OF DEATH

Main Character List:
Henley Farrer: mastermind
Zoltan: manservant, 'terrible' wrestler
Humbert Green: searching for the Falcon dagger
Sidney Street: searching for the Falcon dagger
John Steed
Slattery: searching for the Falcon dagger
Tara King
Gorky: Russian searching for the Falcon dagger
Oppenheimer: German searching for the Falcon dagger
Ho Lung: Chinese curio shop
Dr. Winter
Gregor: henchman
Cosher Klaus: 'inferior' assassin
Dickens: elderly solicitor
Baron Von Orlak: searching for the Falcon dagger
Winkler: dwarf henchman

The Avengers' first episode, *Hot Snow*, started out with classic features of a *film noir*. Dr. Keel's life is forever altered by the murder of his fiancé. It so happened that the killers were drug-smuggling mobsters that accidentally got the wrong doctor's office and address. They feared his fiancé would recognise them. Hence she was eliminated and died dramatically in his arms. Existential random occurrences accepted as being the determining factors in life is a key element of *film noir*. There is also the anti-hero, such as Sam Spade in *The Maltese Falcon*: a man with the most ambiguous of morals, a fatalistic outlook, and a sense of alienation from society, not unlike Dr. Keel's new partner in *Hot Snow*, a man named John Steed. His ethics are not based on loyalty to his fellow man, but on his own personal sense of justice. Unlike Keel, he is emotionally indifferent to murder, happy to exploit others, including his new partner, Dr. Keel, in order to achieve the desired outcome. Their common thread is to avenge. In many ways the initial Avengers together represent the quintessential *film noir* detectives: probing the underbelly of society in a world of perpetual night, in search of hidden truths, ironically often concealed in the light of day. On this quest for truth, they discover the essential corruption and disorder of society: drug cartels, prostitution rings...the dirty grittiness of it all, the absence of any purity.

In many ways, *The Avengers* evolved: corruption in the world of high finance, automation, the questioning of the class system in Britain, and even the commercialisation of marriage, to name just a few. However, *The Avengers* was about much more than exposing societal corruption. As *film noir* detectives, they were truth seekers. *Legacy of Death* could easily have been simply a candy-coloured parody, but it has much more beneath its glossy surface, in the form of the tootsie lollipop. Every child knows of its candy-coloured exterior: the layers of hard sugar coating that conceal the rich inner filling. *Legacy of Death* has both. After all, it is not only a parody of *The Maltese Falcon*. It is a parody of all *film noir*. On the surface it is full of gags and absurd humour. It is shiny and bright, full of delicious distractions in the form of sugar coating. Just like the lollipop, *Legacy of Death* conceals its core. On the inside it is a rich chocolate, black and white *film noir*, with messages about the corruption of the society we live in. The colour episodes sugar-coated and disguised the many deeper messages that the monochrome era more clearly exposed.

Henley Farrer is an oriental collector who has a dazzling treasure. However, he is an insecure man. Every thief from far and wide will be descending upon his property to steal his fortune. He is a diabolical mastermind with an ingenious plan: to lure them to their doom by making them compete for the treasure. The few that remain will have a surprise in store when they arrive: death. In preparation, he has his faithful servant administer a drug that simulates death. He peacefully lays to rest in an elegant rose glass-covered casket. After all, if they think he is already dead, they will not kill him. This *film noir* depicts the outcome of greed, and the dilemma of owning vast fortunes in this corrupt black and white world. The possessors are insecure, as at a moment's notice their fortune could be gone. Living a life of insecurity and paranoia is a curse. It is a story that has been around since the dawn of time. Any powerful empire, wealthy individual, or even corporation, can be overthrown. Rome fell, Napoleon succumbed, and Wall Street crashed in 1929, to name just a few. Those who are greedy can never feel safe. They will seek any means to acquire and protect their vast fortune. They are keenly aware that they live in a primitive animal kingdom, where fortune hunters can strike, where morals do not exist, and paranoia thrives: kill or be killed.

The opening scene with Steed and Tara is odd: no mission, no crime to solve, and no action. Steed is idly playing with a toy airplane and Tara enters in top hat and coattails between parties:

Tara: I can't stay. I've just dropped in to have a drink between parties.
Steed: Between parties?
Tara: Yes. Just came from one. Have another four to go.
Steed: I thought you didn't like parties?
Tara: No I really don't. That's why I'm trying to get them in all in one evening. I've met three counts, four princes, eight lords, fourteen baronets, twenty-one viscounts. I danced with them all. I just wish you had been there.
Steed: I am rather busy. I better get this plane flying.

Here the Avengers appear to be a romantic, perhaps even married couple. They represent the idle rich, bored with life and perhaps each other. For Steed, the spying business has become a hobby to the more important job of flying toy airplanes. Tara, seemingly longing for attention, compensates by flirting with nobility, yet is pining away for the man she adores: John Steed. Seeing it is a losing battle to gain his attention, she leaves. First, in one of many visual gags, she pops open the most enormous magnum of champagne:

Steed: Weren't you going to have a drink?
Tara: Oh I can't. I have to dash off and change for another party.

There is an inner rich core to this scene, one of the many *Avengers* spoofs on the British upper class society. This time, the Avengers themselves are the nobility. It is also a sobering message of alienation (a common theme in *film noir*) but seen in the context of a 'marriage'. In addition, the gluttony of the rich is accurately depicted, as Tara leaves a recently opened magnum of champagne behind, without tasting a drop. In *film noir* tradition, it portrays a hero with complex character traits, both good and bad. This is a very different John Steed than in *Hot Snow*. However, he is completely out of character with his usual Season 6 disposition; he is selfish, lazy, and seems more interested in material possessions, as perhaps Tara does. She clearly can't wear the same attire to the next four parties. Here we see that moral decay does not end with the thieves and diabolical mastermind: the Avengers themselves have been corrupted by greed.

Steed soon learns that he has been gifted a dagger from an unknown benefactor. Tara takes the dagger into her own possession, which she eventually brings back to her flat to use as a coat hanger. It has a practical use, after all: changing into the next outfit. In her silk bathrobe, she swirls around, adorning an elegant sequin gown and ready to dance with the next set of royalty. Suddenly a hit-man enters, played by Romo Gorrara. The spy business almost seems to be an unwelcome intrusion, interfering with her next *soirée*. She overpowers her opponent who eventually falls on his sword (dagger) and dies an agonising death. It is an interesting plot device to have the key to the vast treasure as the murder weapon itself: the dagger of a thousand deaths. [1]

What makes this episode unique is the sheer incompetence of its criminals. This is best exemplified by one hit-man who attempts to tackle the Avengers by jumping off a roof top, only to miss completely and splatter himself, ending up face down on the pavement. The Avengers go on to summarise one of the major themes of this episode:

Steed: The inferior type of assassin...The age of the amateur.
Tara: No pride in their craft.

It actually takes a most competent stuntman to play the most incompetent henchman: Alf Joint was both a stunt double for Sean Connery in *Goldfinger* as well as the thug who fights Bond and gets electrocuted, providing the memorable Bond quote, "Shocking… Positively shocking". A stunt man specialising in high falls, he returned in *Star Wars: Return of the Jedi*, and the *Superman* movies.

The incompetent fortune hunters continue to reveal themselves. Steed receives several special visitors. The most memorable guest is the Russian spy, Old Gorky. He makes a judo tumble landing into Steed's flat, the latter showing his opponent his power. Yet Steed, the ultimate gentleman and spy, offers Gorky a glass of champagne. After all, Russians love to drink and alcohol works wonders in the spy world; why not get him drunk? As Steed offers him a celebratory bottle of bubbly, Gorky assumes it is poison; Steed replies: "And ruin the bouquet?" Glass after glass of champagne is imbibed and broken by Gorky, as he gaily tosses them over his shoulder: the ultimate in visual merriment.

The essentials of spying are to remain invisible and not to leave traces behind for the enemy to find. In this wacky world of *Avengerland*, the diabolical mastermind's henchman shows up as if with neon lights signalling his arrival. He is outside Steed's window observing Gorky, in the loudest yellow 'cherry picker' with assault rifle, and in broad daylight. It is as if he is visually screaming out his arrival. Of course, the street is completely empty; after all this is *Avengerland*. There is no one to take notice of this visual spectacle except for Steed. Alas Old Gorky is shot dead. He warns Steed, "Get rid of it or else they'll kill you also." Tutte Lemkow, who brilliantly played Gorky, went on to play an iconic role: as an accomplished violinist, he was the perfect Fiddler on the Roof.

Oppenheimer is the next visitor, posing as a doctor, searching for the dagger. He attempts to pull out a gun to force Steed to give up the dagger as he tells him, "I've got you covered." "With a stethoscope?" Steed exclaims in absolute wonderment. The guests keep on getting dumber. Quite visibly spying outside Steed's door at the same moment is a spy with a neurotic compulsion: tossing peanuts into his mouth. The only problem is that his aim is terrible, as all of them end up on the floor beside him, leaving a trail behind: another visual sight, making tracking of this criminal a matter of following the peanuts. It is no wonder these criminals have a short life. As Steed opens the door, Oppenheimer and Slattery shoot each other dead. The actor who played Oppenheimer, Peter Swanwick, was best known for his role in *The Prisoner*. He was 'the Supervisor' who was perpetually announcing 'orange alerts'. As a real life war hero, he was one of the first troops to land in Normandy as part of the 1944 D-Day invasion. Sadly, he died at the age 56, six days prior to this episode being broadcast in London.

The characters Sidney Street and Humbert Green are a marvellous spoof of *Maltese Falcon* actors Sydney Greenstreet and Peter Lorre. As they enter Steed's flat, the visual merriment continues. The three recent visitors are fresh corpses, lying in front of Steed's couch covered in a plaid blanket. "Excuse the mess. It's been a busy evening," Steed explains. Misinformation and false leads are what drives the *film noir*; this episode is no different. The thugs believe that Steed knows more than he does about the location of the dagger and treasure, which drives this zany plot. As a result, these most colourful eccentrics perceive Steed to be extremely dangerous, misinterpreting the evidence that lies before them.

The visual gags don't end here. Practically speaking, both the San Francisco gumshoe and the band of thugs Dashiell Hammett created have a lot of 'pounding the pavement' and that's hard on the shoes, not to mention cars. Street and Green show us that the business of sleuthing is not all that it's cracked up to be: financial struggles, holes in the soles of their shoes, and cars that fail them, to name a few. As Sidney Street curiously examines the shoes of one of the dead thugs in Steed's flat, he notices the familiar: "Judging from the look of them (a deceased thug's shoes), he's had some hard times". He would know, as we see identical holes on the bottom of his shoes.

Ronald Lacey does a perfect Peter Lorre impersonation, but this time imitating a role as an eerie Dr. Frankenstein-like physician, rather than his character in *The Maltese Falcon*. His physical posture as a hunchback adds to his creepy persona:

Steed: Can I get you a drink?
Green: Nothing, thank you. I may have to operate later.
Steed: Are you a surgeon?
Green: It's just a hobby with me.

The guest appearances in this episode were some of the best the series had to offer. Thirteen years after *Legacy of Death* was filmed, Ronald Lacey, Tutte Lemkow, and Romo Gorrara united once again in Steven Spielberg's *Indiana Jones: Raiders of the Lost Ark*. Ronald Lacey brilliantly plays a psychotic Nazi. [2] However, the brilliant Stratford Johns steals the show here as a gifted snake-oil salesman, Sidney Street. He tells Green that subtlety will be required to manipulate Steed to give him the dagger. Steed listens patiently as Street weaves the most transparent of tales, which only fools his incompetent partner. He wipes beads of sweat off his face after each part of his fantastic tale. His voice quivers with excitement, much like the story telling of an unscrupulous preacher professing to heal an incurable disease. Typical of many *film noir*, the characters have limited abilities, either because of lack of skills, intellect, or willingness to actually work for a living. Their talent lies in the art of manipulation. Recently, the Mayor of Jordan was perturbed that many of the ancient archeological tombs are being robbed: "You combine unemployment and ignorance and this is what happens. In reality, there is no treasure." Even though the time of the black and white *film noir* is past, the story of greed and corruption in society is a timeless one.

There is no one who could satirise the horrors of the Victorian legal system better than Charles Dickens himself. His own father was thrown into a debtors' prison when Charles was just twelve years old. Steed's visit to Dickens, Dickens, Dickens, Dickens, and Dickens perfectly captures a brilliant parody of Victorian law. Steed asks for his benefactor's identity:

Steed: I should like to meet Mr. Dickens.
Dickens: Mr. Dickens passed away some fifty years ago.
Steed: Oh dear, nothing serious I hope.

They pass by a succession of empty old desks, with memorial wreaths; it appears as a veritable family gravesite. As the lawyer tells Steed that the next Dickens is gone Steed chimes in, "but not forgotten". On finally reaching the back of the room, he asks to speak with Mr. Dickens, at which point the lawyer identifies himself, "At your service." He clumsily searches through mounds and mounds of disorganised paperwork, unable to help Steed. Naturally he is shot dead. Here in this Victorian-era law practice, it appears as if the deceased family members are alive and well, ceremoniously in charge. They appear to have more clout than the only surviving member, who honours and obeys his old family tradition....even if they are all dead. The brilliance of the writing here cannot be overstated in this episode that thrives on comedic incompetence and societal corruption. Craftily choosing the Victorian legal system, it was a comedy within a comedy. Victorian law not only involved senseless ceremony in keeping with tradition; it became rather comedic in its utter bureaucratic incompetence and expense. As a keen observer of character and society, this scene from *The Avengers* would likely have amused Charles Dickens. Killing off the last Victorian-era lawyer, symbolically ending this ancient and inhumane practice of law, would no doubt have immensely relieved Dickens; a most honourable nod to this literary genius.

The finale portrays one of the most stunning visual candy-coloured delights, set in the mansion of the diabolical mastermind, Farrer. The Avengers soon learn that the dagger, when used as a key to the treasure, is actually a trap. Suddenly it triggers the rose glass covered casket to move from its horizontal to vertical position. As it opens, the diabolical mastermind, Farrer, comes back to life, with a serene smile, adorning a white raw silk Nehru jacket. To quote Dashiell Hammett, "He looked rather pleasantly like a blond Satan". Whether blond or grey, Farrer was no doubt the devil in disguise. In his hand he holds the treasure: a spectacular and most enormous black pearl. In this comical scene, a cascade of events leads to utter mayhem, and more deaths. A midget pushes a wheelchair-bound villain; unable to see his path (being too short), he finds himself pushing his master through a plate-glass window to his death. Eventually, the chain of events leads to Steed acquiring a gun, killing Farrer instantly. As he dies, the pearl springs from his hand, bouncing across the floor, plopping into a glass of wine and instantly fizzling away to the size of a tie pin. After all, in *Avengerland*, chemistry can be altered; huge gems instantaneously dissolve to become much smaller replicas that flawlessly retain their original colour and shape.

Just like *The Maltese Falcon*, the rich inner core of this *film noir* depicts a black and white world, drained of morality. The audience sees the violence, betrayal, and the evils of gluttony that breed misery to all who seek ill-gotten gains. The treasure may dazzle and delight, momentarily. However, as fate would have it, it will kill you as it is cursed. Strikingly, it is the inanimate object yearned by thieves that is 'cursed' or evil. It is as if those in search are innocent victims, preyed upon by these inanimate treasures. They are devoid of any wrong doing, as it is the treasure that is cursed, after all, not them. In *The Maltese Falcon*, the character played by Sydney Greenstreet unabashedly shows where his loyalties lie: "I couldn't be fonder of you if you were my own son. But, well if you lose a son, it's possible to get another. There's only one Maltese Falcon." In the end, whether it is *Legacy of Death* or *The Maltese Falcon*, it is actually a very moral tale; those who seek ways to steal and deceive simply end up with nothing at all.

Loss is quickly morphed into joy as Street tells Green about their next scheme: "A certain bird – a statuette thing – Maltese I believe..." *Legacy of Death* therefore becomes the *prequel* to the classic film noir, *The Maltese Falcon*. Ironically, the 45 pound metal prop, known as the Maltese Falcon, that appeared in the 1941 film was sold at auction for over four million dollars in 2013: "Heavy. What is it?" Sam Spade aptly answers: "The, uh, stuff that dreams are made of." [4]

© Margaret J Gordon

1. Unlike the Maltese Falcon, a classic MacGuffin which has little relevance to the story, the dagger here works on a number of levels.

2. He also played other memorable *Avengers roles*: the Strange Young Man in *The Joker* and Hong Kong Harry in *The Midas Touch*.
3. *Bleak House*, in particular, exposes the farcical, immoral waste of time and money in Chancery.
4. Even more ironically, there were several versions of the prop made for the film – resin and metal – and subsequently sold to rich and famous people. You can imagine them squabbling over who has the most authentic one of them all.

A cavernous sitting room and hall decorated in Oriental art, finery and lined with metallic Oriental armoury gives way to the arrival of collector Henley Farrer (the wonderful Richard Hurndall) who asks hit butler Zoltan (a delicious nod to Hammer in the name, and a fitting nod to all things *Avengers* with the casting of John Hollis in the role, already well known to enthusiasts of the Emma Peel run from his appearances in *The Cybernauts* and *The Superlative Seven*) if his guests are coming. Informed that they arrived at the airport an hour ago, Farrer reflects that, "Then they are coming...to kill me." Would it be any other way in *Avengerland*? The invitation falling on the doorstep, black-bordered and embossed, "You are cordially invited to an assassination". How else could the best dressed villains of the age respond? With a curious zeal, he prompts Zoltan to bring him an ornately-handled dagger which he does, shortly before being drawn to the window by the arrival of a vehicle outside. Zoltan urgently prompts Farrer to hurry as the man in question kisses the dagger and hands it to his manservant before stepping into a glass-covered coffin, which closes over him and then draws back onto a moving platform. As a knock comes at the door, Farrer exhaustedly boasts that he has cheated them as he closes his eyes and Zoltan rests a folded copy of a Last Will and Testament on his body and seals the coffin.

Entering the hall from a side entrance, the wonderfully caricatured Sidney Street (the powerhouse that was Stratford Johns, taking a welcome turn from his *Softly Softly* persona in a similar vein to his on-screen companion, Frank Windsor, who appeared *in Whoever Shot Poor George Oblique Stroke XR40?*) and Humbert Green (Ronald Lacey, leering and lisping his way across another enormously colourful masterstroke on *The Avengers* tapestry after his appearance in the Emma Peel classic *The Joker*) creep slowly towards the coffin, weapons drawn and preparing to make a kill –

only to be thwarted when they find their quarry lying in state. The dialogue here is beautiful, firmly grounded in that which audiences have come to expect of this world of dastardly deeds and maniacal master-plans:

Humbert: He's dead Sidney. Dead!
Sidney: He can't be. I didn't travel four thousand miles to meet up with a dead man. How dare he die before we've had the chance to kill him! I won't allow it!

At once, it sums up the characters, their motivation and also sets them into the classic identikit of an *Avengers* villain. The adornments of the drawn weapons, the seedy suits (matching pair for Humbert and Sidney here), the limp, the walking cane, the breathless dialogue of the former a direct link to Peter Lorre, the latter asking "Where's the Falcon dagger?" to leave audiences in no doubt that this is, indeed, the line where *The Avengers* meets *The Maltese Falcon*, travelling along the scripting motorway that is Terry Nation as driven by Don Chaffey in the director's chair.

Two creative powerhouses of their generation, Terry Nation and Brian Clemens were to inevitably cross paths through *The Avengers* (and also on *And Soon The Darkness* and *Thriller*) and Nation's contribution of six scripts for the Tara King series (including the wonderfully-crafted *Noon Doomsday*, offering Linda Thorson the opportunity to remind viewers that Emma Peel was gone and Tara King was now the all-action girl – in the best possible way) wrought many of the high points. Clemens' masterly talent for the brilliance of plot, of title and of situation was always going to be challenged (never bettered, but often challenged) by Nation's own brand of deft plotting and ability to craft a fresh concept/conceit. For a man who contributed to six ITC series, to *Doctor Who*, delivering the magnificently re-watchable *Blake's 7* and the satisfyingly grim *Survivors*, his ability to turn a three-card trick with plots and dialogue remains second only to Clemens in terms of his potent factory-line output. [1]

There has often been much comment made on Nation's infamous reworking of the same plot through three different ITC productions, and in part the same criticism could be levelled here with *Legacy of Death* given that he was essentially writing a truncated version of *The Maltese Falcon* into something splashed across *The Avengers* landscape. This criticism, however, flounders hopelessly because Nation is actually *so* good at reworking a plot/situation that one cannot help but applaud his audacious creative powers and enjoy what is brought to the screen. The sense of the everyday (a Hollywood classic with the legendary Peter Lorre) inserted into the far away (*The Avengers* was always proud to be a little left of the norm) makes the series the perfect platform for this endeavour, and Nation succeeds thanks to Don Chaffey's skilful direction.

Chaffey would eventually find himself post-*Avengers* in Hollywood as a much sought-after director on a range of blockbuster series (and rightly so given his talents). Working on five episodes of the Tara King era of the series, he has a very definite style which lends a fresh approach to the series (the use of lighting and of colour are particularly important as a construct to the series, as reflected in the Diana Rigg run particularly, and used in the Tara episodes there is a stronger sense of menace and character infused in certain scenes by Chaffey's skilful drawing on film noir-esque traits).

Back from the teaser, and audiences find Steed piloting a radio-controlled spitfire hanging from the ceiling when he is interrupted by the furtive arrival of Zoltan (spied by the weedy Gorky, played with relish by Tutte Lemkow). Delivering the dagger to Steed and insisting that it has come from an anonymous benefactor, he makes his exit with what must be one of the most gorgeously menacing double-edged lines that grace the series:

Zoltan: I hope, sir, that the dagger will bring you all the things my master wished for you.

Not a surprising remark in *Avengerland*, where the Avon lady will most likely sell you an atomiser filled with hydrochloric acid, and where florists touting that they can say it with flowers are more likely to put them on your coffin post-delivery. Yet it brings another fresh line to the hefty tome of villainous asides, threats and banter that comprise the dialogue unique to this series. Another neat moment transpires directly after this dialogue, where Steed puts the dagger to rest on a nearby table – directly beside an ice bucket festooned with ice and a poised bottle of champagne. Danger and pleasure, menace and beauty, they live side by side in this world.

Fedora atop, pin-striped below, two-toned of feet and tossing peanuts while he witnesses Zoltan's departure, Vic Wise makes a nice appearance as the gumshoe Slattery, approaching Steed's apartment as we witness the breathless Humbert changing a tyre whilst Sidney insists that fate is against them, that their competitors are most likely already closing on Steed and their prize will be lost. A notable point so early on in the episode is the deliberate use of 1920s/1930s American film noir-esque motor vehicles in *Legacy of Death*, a nice nod to the film upon which it so firmly draws and also a departure from the norm in *The Avengers*, where the vehicles were usually the ultimate in luxury, grace and fine living. Indeed, when Tara's car arrives on the scene it is oddly out of place in this world that harks back to a bygone age. Her splendid costume, however, is very in-keeping with what is going on – very much a pseudo *OK Corral* affair meets morning suit and top hat. Witnessed by Gorky and Slattery, she interrupts Steed's attempts to get his spitfire back on course to share a drink with him (from an imposingly large bottle of champagne she has brought with her) as she is between parties (well, four of them on this particular evening). The reveal over the champagne that Steed is endeavouring to repair the spitfire for his nephew's tenth birthday (three years ago) is delightful. Intrigued by the dagger Steed has been bequeathed, Tara takes it with her (back to her place to change for another party) as Slattery sets off in pursuit. There are moments here when one wonders whether Peter Wyngarde could have made a cheeky return as a gun-toting peanut-chomping gangster in this outing ala *Epic*, but perhaps that just harks back to how superb that scenery-chewing performance really was. The bespectacled controller from *The Prisoner* (Peter Swanwick, here as Oppenheimer, always delivers performances of such contained frustration that one only has to see him to believe his characterisations as real) slips out of a doorway from which he has been furtively keeping watch, and he sets off after Slattery.

While Sidney and Humbert are finally making tracks, Steed accosts Gorky spying through his letter slot and plies him with champagne in a bid to draw clues from him as to his actions (there is some rather nice glass-smashing ala *The Correct Way To Kill* here, a customary bit-of-business between the decadent West and the resolute East). Gorky offers him increasing sums of money (half a million, three quarters of a million and then a million pounds) but fails to explain to a confused Steed what he is bargaining for as he is shot by Zoltan with a rifle trained from a cherry-picker raised from the mews outside. Gorky's dying bid to warn Steed to "get rid of it or else they kill you also" leaves him further perplexed. He contacts

Doctor Winter as Oppenheimer eavesdrops from outside. Quite a bit of business taking place across a raft of intercut scenes, this is what Nation delivers in spades in his scripts – short, sharp sequences which cover a great deal of ground in a swift space of time. Chaffey's direction ably supports this workmanlike economy of scale.

Leon Thau's performance as Ho Lung, the Oriental trader that Tara visits to seek advice on the dagger, is a nice slice of the breathy Charlie Chan, in-keeping with the 1920s/1930s style of the piece, and again the set in which this takes place is a delicious confection of colour and shadow; there is a genuine depth to the setting and a realism with *bric-a-brac* and Oriental adornments here and there. Lung recognises the dagger immediately but passes it off as worthless; he panders to her curiosity by consulting his books in the back room to confirm its historical detail. The fiendish *Avengers* twist played out here is when he hastily makes a telephone call to a contact, dropping his Oriental accent and resorting to his regular upper-crust voice and "Old chap" introduction. Identifying the artefact as the "Dagger of a Thousand Deaths", he promises to keep Tara there until his contact arrives.

Michael Bilton's arrival as Doctor Winter ends unceremoniously swiftly when Oppenheimer renders him unconscious and pinches his coat and black bag to gain entry to Steed's apartment under the guise of being his assistant (one almost eagerly anticipates his identification as 'Doctor Summer', though this never happens). Slattery listens keenly outside the apartment as Steed shows Oppenheimer to Gorky, the 'doctor' insisting on "hot water, lots of it". Patrick Macnee's wonderful step towards the kitchen, then momentary hesitation and raising of the eyebrows in an "Oh well, he's the doctor" internalisation is a wonderful little piece, such a small bit of business but so in character. Oppenheimer then proceeds to rifle through Steed's desk. Here, dialogue (such a princely asset to the entire series as a whole, and always a diamond in the crown of a script where writers really know how to deliver menace) shines once again, as Steed returns and spies Oppenheimer's furtive activities:

Steed: Do you want something, Doctor?
Oppenheimer: Just a place to put my hat.
Steed: Don't you want to examine the patient?
Oppenheimer: Ah, the patient. Examine him, yes.
Steed: Well?
Oppenheimer: What symptoms did he exhibit before he collapsed?
Steed: Don't the bullet holes in his suit give you the teeniest clue?
Oppenheimer: Bullet holes...ah, yes! (inspecting the body) This man has been shot, Mr. Steed.
Steed: That's right, Doctor.
Oppenheimer: Never mind, we can work wonders today. Soon have him up and about. (Turning to inspect the contents of his black bag)
Steed: This man is dead, Doctor.
Oppenheimer: He'll not be alone. Don't move, Mr. Steed. I've got you covered.
Steed: With a stethoscope?
Oppenheimer: (Swaps hands) Don't move again.

Not only does the dialogue bristle with every corporeal element that made *The Avengers* television brilliance beyond its competitors, but the bit of business between the hero and the villain, culminating in what could have descended into slapstick silliness with Oppenheimer drawing a stethoscope on Steed before training the pistol on him, is a picture-postcard of why this series stands the test of time. Steed is as cool as custard, never perturbed by Oppenheimer (Macnee's performance is wonderful here: he never takes his eyes off his nemesis for a moment, on edge with suspicions raised and, like Patrick McGoohan's superb John Drake, coiled and ready for action) and their verbal jousting is such a delight.

As Oppenheimer demands to know where "it" is (certain that Steed killed Gorky when he came looking for the very same), Steed asks what he is looking for. Admitting he has no other alternative but to get "it" for him, he spies Slattery hovering outside and throws open the door to the apartment as he leaps behind the door, amidst a lethal showdown of bullets which renders Oppenheimer and the gumshoe dead – nuts strewn across the floor as the pair reel to the ground. As Steed recovers his bearings, so does Doctor Winter who staggers inside and falls into his arms – just as the kettle boils in the kitchen. It could be borderline farce if it wasn't so beautifully played, and Steed's parting line at the closure of this scene is the sort of five-star perfection *The Avengers* often produced: here we have a debonair agent relaxing for the evening when bodies start lining up through no fault of his own and a mysterious bequest of a seemingly worthless weapon. What else could he say but: "I've got a feeling it's going to be one of those days." If life is like this for John Steed, one wonders what James Bond does on his days off.

Not even the promise of Jasmine tea can keep Tara at Ho Lung's beyond the time she has waited for details on the dagger. Despite his protestations, she departs the scene. A black Porsche arrives moments later and Gregor (Romo Gorrara) emerges, only to be ushered away by Ho Lung in hot pursuit. As mentioned previously, the juxtaposition of modern villainy (Tara's car and the sleek Porsche) with old-world fiends (the American gangster-style vehicles and attire) works beautifully here, very colourful and very *Avengers*.

Stratford Johns and Ronald Lacey 'eat the scenery' as they arrive in the mews outside Steed's apartment, and with such gusto and aplomb. They are the perfect villains with a cause, and their own banter about letting one another down, creasing the linen material and how to kill off Steed is as richly entertaining here as the dialogue-rich fiends of *The Rotters*. [2] Their arrival on the scene and their bid to deal with Steed in a subtle way is priceless, particularly coming after Steed has covered the three bodies at the heart of his apartment by draping a blanket over them. When Sidney blanches at the sight of them upon arrival, only in *Avengerland* could the following casual aside be treated as run-of-the-mill: "You'll have to excuse the mess. It's been a busy evening."

The pair recognise Slattery from his shoes and Humbert draws the blanket back to reveal Oppenheimer and Gorky; Sidney ruminates they may have underestimated Steed and that he could be dangerous after all. He probes Steed on his possession of the dagger, a "worthless trinket" which used to belong to a long-deceased aunt, and concocts a story about having bought the article for a shilling to present to her when he was a boy. The poetry of lies goes up in flames when Steed, unconvinced, reveals that he has given the dagger to a friend, the name of which escapes him.

An important feature of *Avengerland* is the stark lack of competent locksmiths. Obviously they were the first to die when diabolical masterminds started their combined bid to control the fortunes of the world, because they certainly seem to have overlooked Tara King's apartment. Gregor enters with ease and engages in a beautifully-shot fight with Tara (one of her more vibrant exchanges with a villain, accompanied by a superb musical score here which bridges the Johnson-Blake divide and harks back to the Gale/Rigg fights of old). As Steed fathoms out that Bodies + Dagger = Tara, he rushes to her aid. Rendering Gregor senseless with a series of deft kicks and punches, there is a moment of pure Tara elegance (and Linda Thorson relishes every moment here, deservedly so) when, as Steed bursts into the apartment, she picks up her evening wear and says, "I was just going to change" as they both inspect the reeling Gregor, who falls to the floor dead – with the dagger in his back. The pair reflect on the connection between the rising body count and the dagger as Sidney and Humbert arrive. They make their swift exit, but are momentarily delayed when a man leaps from the rooftop towards them, only narrowly missing them and collapsing to the ground, unconscious. The dialogue here is again a nice slice of what passes for chit-chat in *Avengerland*, reflecting on the state of play:

Steed: Pretty inferior type of assassin.
Tara: They just don't make them like they used to.
Steed: It's the age of the amateur.
Tara: No pride in their craft.

Resolving to find out his identity, they search his pockets and Steed withdraws a wallet inside which is a note which reads 'Dickens, Dickens, Dickens, Dickens and Dickens re: John Steed'. There is a nice little moment here when, as the man recovers consciousness, Steed hands Tara his bowler and asks, "Would you mind?" to which Tara says, "Not at all" and knocks the man unconscious once again. Steed's reflection that the man seems to know a dickens of a lot of people called Dickens is an obvious (but fun) pun as they leave, with Sydney and Humbert in close pursuit. They recognise the unconscious man as 'Cosher' Klaus (oh what fun it is hearing Humbert mis-pronounce the name as Kosher, a deliberate joke by Nation but one which has its fair place in *The Avengers*. He is corrected by Sidney but the joke is nevertheless worthy).

Accompanied by more splendid music, the scene in which Steed and Tara are followed by a procession of black cars is wonderful. The dialogue between the pair, reflecting on where they are going as the former reclines into his seat, bowler over brow as he dozes off, is amusing stuff. Nation works the law of *Avengerland* as perfectly as Clemens, with the core players largely unconcerned with the death and mayhem going on around them.

Another wonderful musical cue is delivered (albeit briefly here), harking back to *Something Nasty In The Nursery* as Steed returns to his old summerhouse to hide the dagger. The musical connection is a welcome one, a very neat continuity link for viewers in-the-know to the past history of the programme. [3] Steed hides the dagger in the mouth of an ornate wall-hanging affectionately called Harry the Dragon, before Tara sets off back to Ho Lung's store. Steed resolves to pay a visit to Dickens, Dickens, Dickens…and Dickens (somewhat unfortunate that they are a Dickens short in Macnee's dialogue when the cross-cut goes to a door with Dickens, Dickens, Dickens, Dickens and Dickens painted on it, but was there ever a Dickens of a chance of losing a Dickens in a plot like this?).

The incomparable Kynaston Reeves appears as the youngest surviving Dickens of the firm in question when Steed arrives on the scene. Knocking on eighty, he takes Steed on a tour of floral wreaths and tells the sorry tales of the passing of his predecessors. Clutching a corpse of testaments, he lurches back to his desk and checks for anonymous bequests. Meanwhile, Tara returns to Ho Lung's store and, whilst inspecting the storeroom, finds herself pinned to a crate by a masked Lung who throws a hatchet in her direction. Baron Von Orlak (the gloriously evil Ferdy Mayne, who tirelessly appeared in what can only be described as a lifetime achievement-rendering line of roles in film and television across

Europe and America, the singular highlights of which were when he played a villain) emerges along with his diminutive assistant Winkler (Teddy Kiss). He interrogates Tara and insists on the return of the Falcon Dagger. When she refuses, they render her unconscious with chloroform and begin to "prepare her". Meanwhile, Dickens identifies Steed's benefactor but is shot dead by Zoltan, who appears (using the same handy cherry-picker) through the window of his office.

Tara regains consciousness as the Baron's interrogation continues. He reveals the importance of the dagger and why it is so highly-coveted (despite the fact that it has brought death to all who have ever owned it). Subjected to Chinese water torture, her plight is made altogether easier when Sidney and Humbert arrive on the scene (the latter using the water dispenser used to torture her to fill a plastic cup for Sidney to refresh himself). They release her and force her to take them to Steed's summerhouse to locate the dagger, whereupon she poleaxes them and turns the tables on Sidney in particular, using a feather duster to tickle his exposed foot while she demands answers to a few of her own questions. Hysterical with laughter, Sidney reveals that it is the key to a vast fortune of hidden treasure. She demands to know who gave the dagger to Steed, just as the man in question discovers – in sifting through Dickens' scattered papers – that his bequest was from Henley Farrer.

Breaking in to Farrer's home, Tara finds Steed already on the scene. He explains that Farrer was an old enemy, and she reveals that he bequeathed the dagger to Steed – the key to buried treasure. Steed makes a connection between the ornate Oriental pattern on the tiled floor and the pattern cast by the shadow of the dagger on Tara's back by the dim light in the room. Inserting it into a lock in the floor, they remove a tile and start digging, but their progress is interrupted by the arrival of Sidney, Humbert and a large array of other nefarious interested parties, all armed and equally lethal. Sidney reveals that they are digging for the most priceless pearl on Earth, an enormous black pearl that will make them fabulously wealthy. Steed sifts through the sand and recovers a metal box which he finds is empty. They are all aghast when Farrer's coffin re-emerges from its resting place and the man, smiling warmly, welcomes them. Zoltan, emerging with a machine gun, silences those assembled. In fiendish *Avengers* style, Farrer (Hurndall is clearly having a whale of a time performing as the arch villain in this episode) reveals that he faked his own death to draw out his pursuers in a bid for them to either finish one another off, or his trusty manservant Zoltan would kill them as a matter of course.

As the customary fight ensues to round off the episode, amidst the sound and fury Steed shoots Farrer, who drops the enormous black pearl which reels across the floor and tumbles into a goblet of wine in front of Sidney's greedy gaze. It fizzes into oblivion and eventually, when retrieved, they are disconsolate that it has been reduced to normal size. Steed glibly suggests it would make a very nice tie-pin as the pair leave the pearl in the goblet and make their exit. Their departure marks a fitting signature point for Nation, pushing the envelope firmly into "This is what the pair did on their next fiendish adventure" and positioning a sharp nod at *The Maltese Falcon* in the process:

Humbert: Surely there's something else we can steal, hmmm?
Sidney: There comes to mind a certain bird, a statuette thing. Maltese, I believe. Belonging to, ah, some brothers.

They make their way from the scene as Steed and Tara toast their work over the world's most expensive drink. After such a lively, tongue-in-cheek episode, it seems hardly surprising that Nation delivers a somewhat lacklustre tag scene. Tara arrives at Steed's apartment to find him deeply engrossed in an instruction manual, muttering the mysterious "Roget pins left to me" as he discusses another bequest left to him. He reveals that the problem with the model spitfire was that the Roget pins were the wrong way around, and that he is sure that this time he has got it right. Her maiden flight soon becomes a catastrophic journey of "the last of the few" when it crashes through the window of the apartment and out into the mews. "Never mind," Tara coos, handing Steed a glass of champagne, "To the first of the many".

Imitation is always the best form of flattery. *Legacy of Death* imitates *The Maltese Falcon* to great effect, reworking it into *Avengerland* and beautifully crafting another tale of the otherworldly firmly wedged into the cityscape and countryside of old England. Rather curiously, for a series upon which so much imitation would follow in its wake – largely unsuccessful, for *The Avengers* was always a unique blend of creative genius behind and in front of the camera, the likes of which British Television has never seen again – this episode is a rare attempt to imitate a product of the ordinary world beyond the extraordinary which was *Avengerland*. As with *The Winged Avenger* before it, this truly was the real world knocking on the door for a guest appearance in a world populated by dashing heroes, beautiful heroines and the most diabolically upper-crust villains.

Broadcast on a night where its long-standing competitors were transmitting professional tennis and a heavy-duty sitting of Dennis Potter's *A Beast With Two Backs* for *The Wednesday Play*, in a week when *The Champions* turned their hand to a little *Upstairs, Downstairs* as servants in *The Iron Mask* and when Patrick Troughton's *Doctor Who* would continue to fend off the villainy of Tobias Vaughn and the Cybermen, *Legacy of Death* was another colourful diversion into the unique take on British life which was *The Avengers*: larger-than-life villains, a high body count and a clever pair looking for clues and rounding off a case with aplomb.

© Matthew Lee

1. As stated elsewhere in this book, I am less convinced that Terry Nation ever understood *The Avengers*. We know that *Take-Over* was "recycled" from a Clemens *The Baron* script. According to Michael Richardson, Clemens had been "less than impressed to find that he needed to rewrite large sections" of *Noon Doomsday* and gave his script editor "a verbal kick in the pants" (*Bowler Hats and Kinky Boots*, p. 307). Richardson claims that, for *Legacy of Death*, "Brian Clemens had developed the initial concept for this together with Nation" but that this time he had "no rewriting to do". (*Bowler Hats and Kinky Boots*, p. 310) Like Matthew, I love *Blake's 7* and some of Nation's other dystopian works, but *The Avengers* was a very different show. The awful *Invasion of the Earthmen* demonstrates Nation's *The Avengers* when Clemens wasn't there to put him right. *Thingumajig* is not much better. To be fair to Nation, *Legacy of Death* is far more impressive.
2. Stratford Johns' character warns Lacey's that "subtlety" is what is needed when dealing with Steed, but this is surely something which – generally speaking – is missing from this humorously over-the-top episode.
3. It is on occasions like this that the recycling of music genuinely works, adding a clever intertextual layer as Matthew observes.

THEY KEEP KILLING STEED

Filmed: August 1968

Exterior Locations:
Earthworks
Open water
Hotel façade and village green
Street
Country road/bridge
Country roads
Baron's palace

Sets:
Arcos' headquarters
Hotel: Tara's bedroom, corridor, foyer, Steed's bedroom, Nadine's bedroom
Dusty/dingy/seedy guest rooms
Mother's headquarters (bathyscaphe or bathysphere)
Palace: entrance foyer, reception rooms, side room
Tara King's apartment (fake beach)

THEY KEEP KILLING STEED

Main Character List:
Zerson: Arcos' assistant
Arcos: surgeon, mastermind
Mother
Rhonda: Mother's silent assistant
John Steed
Tara King
Baron Von Curt
Helga: in love with Curt
Miranda: in love with Curt
Bruno: henchman
Perova: enemy agent
Captain Smythe: security
Nadine: enemy agent
Mintoff: enemy agent
Bowler: enemy agent
Georgio: enemy agent
Conference chairman

Doppelganger stories are nothing new, but no writer could be faulted for utilising a premise that allows him to play so liberally with his characters' identities, and to conceal enemy minds behind familiar faces. This makes them an ideal fit for the spy genre, rife as it is with tales of double agents and counter-espionage. On a long-running TV series like *The Avengers*, doppelganger stories also provide the leads with the opportunity to 'stretch their legs' and take on a new role, or, in the case of *They Keep Killing Steed*, several roles, as Patrick Macnee (physically) plays a number of Steed duplicates (though his voice is overdubbed by the actors portraying the enemy agents posing as Steed). The episode's featured method of creating the doubles is "instant plastic surgery", whereby individuals inject themselves with a formula to change the molecular structure of their skin, and then don masks bearing a cast of the face of the man they are meant to impersonate in order to remould their features. This technique is a particularly vivid example of the series' occasional forays into 'body horror'. There is something visceral, even stomach-churning, about the idea of human flesh being quite literally 'remoulded' like soft putty. The horrific nature of the technique is brought home through the fate of the 'failed' fake Steed, who dies from the treatment, face half-formed.

At the opposite end of the spectrum, the "instant plastic surgery" premise 'injects' the episode with some over-the-top comedy. There is black humour galore to be found in watching multiple Steeds react in surprise at the sight of their counterparts, and then proceed to bump one another off. (It is also rather amusing that the greeter manning the door of the peace conference never appears to twig to the fact that he has admitted the same man to the conference several times over!) "Look, the woods are full of them!" Baron Von Curt (Ian Ogilvy) exclaims, in one of the episode's best lines, but just about every room inside the peace conference venue also contains a Steed, living or dead. [1] Further comedy arrives spliced with character moments and a modicum of tension, as Steed attempts to convince Tara that he is the genuine article, recounting an adventure that took them to the Himalayas, only to realise that he shared it with someone else entirely! Steed's story is told in a disingenuous tone, as though he is trying too hard to play the role of himself, giving both Tara and the audience reason to doubt his identity, and Tara's repeatedly-brandished gun emphasises that the stakes are high. He eventually proves himself with the innocuous phrase "strawberry shortcake", the significance of which, in true *Avengers* teasing fashion, is never elaborated upon (just as the audience is never told who, exactly, accompanied Steed in the Himalayas).

Further absurd humour, unrelated to the doppelganger plot but worthy of note, is provided by Mother's headquarters of the week, an underwater base which he and the faithful Rhonda reach by rowing out into the middle of a lake and unceremoniously pulling a plug in the bottom of their boat. Tara's entrance is just as off-kilter, involving a dive off a bridge, followed by a short, albeit difficult, swim, Mother's belated directions proving less-than-illuminating: "Straight downstream, turn left at the salmon nets..." Fore-echoing the central plot device of *The New Avengers* episode *Forward Base*, it provides an ideal setting for Mother, a man on a never-ending quest for a location with the requisite peace and quiet to soothe his fractious personality.

This episode is also of particular interest as it features a third, guest lead in the form of Baron Von Curt. Steed and Tara were often split up in their stories for the sake of the tight production schedule, which made the efficiency of shooting two scenes (one per lead) simultaneously advantageous. By necessity, this meant that there were fewer scenes per episode showcasing the Steed/Tara dynamic, compared to the number of shared Steed/Emma scenes in the previous season. Depending on one's opinion regarding the Steed/Tara relationship, this could be seen as a good or a bad thing, but the Tara King character was certainly afforded more freedom to 'breathe' away from Steed. Many of her showcase moments come in episodes where she is mostly, or almost entirely, on her own and able to demonstrate her capability as an agent, and an individual, to her full potential. In contrast, her scenes with Steed are often, by necessity, shaped by their respective roles of mentor and pupil, and this fundamental inequality makes it difficult for the characters to engage in the back-and-forths that Steed enjoyed with Emma Peel and Cathy Gale. For this reason, it works to both characters' advantage for them to spend large amounts of time apart, reuniting at crucial moments in the plot to share information and unravel the mystery.

However, even if running on parallel tracks suits the dynamic of this particular Avenging duo, the lack of shared scenes requires the leads to trade *bon mots* with incidental characters rather than one another, and this can sometimes prove less-than-engaging. Hence the introduction of Von Curt, who assumes the mantle of Tara's 'partner' for the bulk of the story, just as Lady Diana Forbes-Blakeney would fill in as Steed's partner in *Killer*. Von Curt immediately establishes a different dynamic with Tara than the one she shares with Steed. He is younger, which enables them to act as peers and equals, rather than as mentor and pupil. Their exchanges are punctuated by coy, knowing smiles, and as Von Curt flirts, Tara flirts back as a mutual participant in the game, with none of the awe or hero-worship that often accompanies her exchanges with Steed. In fact, the dynamic is revelatory for Tara's character. Often other male characters' interest in her is not reciprocated, and the audience is afforded few opportunities to see her truly flirt with anyone other than Steed. Here, Tara is shown to be fully capable of engaging in a back and forth with someone she is attracted to, and of doing so in a way in which she is confident and self-assured in her ability to set the tone of, and control, the situation. Her comfort level with Von Curt, a man she has known a matter of hours by the end of the episode, speaks to both her ability to gauge his trustworthiness, and her own personal interest in him. This is amply demonstrated by the fact that she agrees to pose as his wife mere seconds after meeting him, continues the charade later on, and allows him to play a role in the assignment, to the point of letting him accompany her to the site of Mother's underwater headquarters. [2]

Aside from what he brings out in Tara, Von Curt is also interesting in his own right. A wealthy, titled playboy with cars and real estate to match, he is a swashbuckling adventure hero cast in the classic ITC mould, with more than a hint of Roger Moore's Lord Brett Sinclair, from the then-forthcoming series *The Persuaders!*, about him (rather fitting, given that Ogilvy would assume the mantle of Simon Templar in *Return of the Saint*, carrying on from Moore in the role he was still occupying at the time of *The Avengers*' final season). However, it is also highly likely that Von Curt was a dry run for what would eventually be the character of Mike Gambit in *The New Avengers*. Following the departure of Diana Rigg, Patrick Macnee's enthusiasm for the series had begun to wane. Had the series not been cancelled in the United States, and continued for another season, it is entirely conceivable that Macnee, whose loyalty to the series was perhaps strong enough to ensure that he would never voluntarily leave it behind, would have asked for a reduced role in order to pursue other projects, and a third, younger male character would have been introduced to pick up the slack. The episode is penned by Brian Clemens, the eventual creative force behind *The New Avengers* and the character of Gambit, and there is something of the Purdey/Gambit dynamic in the relationship between Tara and Von Curt. Their exchanges are light and teasing, with Tara rebuffing Von Curt's advances while not outright dissuading him. Von Curt also shares Gambit's characteristic of making his interests known without becoming physically imposing or demanding, nor taking any particular offence at being rebuffed. Indeed, Von Curt is decidedly non-tactile, and any physical contact is initiated respectfully. He is also not dismissive of Tara's obvious affection for Steed, and attempts to reassure her of his safety rather than use his absence as an opportunity to compete with him. As a major player in the plot, he is quick to offer his assistance to Tara, despite the obvious risks involved. He is bemused by Tara's impromptu jump off the bridge, but rather than react with alarm, he instead awaits her return. He subsequently rolls with, and accepts, the episode's increasingly bizarre series of events, taking in his stride a multitude of manufactured Steeds, living and dead, before emulating the original by arming himself with a rapier for some swashbuckling fight scenes. His aristocratic, refined background speaks to Steed having a measure of influence on his character, which is unsurprising given that Steed was the only male *Avengers* lead to grace the series after the departure of Jon Rollason's Dr. Martin King in 1962. This would make Steed the obvious template for any new male lead character, though Brian Clemens would move in a new direction when developing Gambit, whose working class roots put him in a very different social circle than the Baron and Steed. Nonetheless, they all bear a collection of what could be called the hallmarks of an *Avengers* 'boy': an adventurous streak, a predilection for (or at least ability to handle) the bizarre, a sense of humour, a nobleness of character, and a healthy respect and appreciation for the opposite sex.

With Tara spending the lion's share of her screen-time with Von Curt, Steed faces the majority of the episode partnerless, though this does not prevent him from engaging in some noteworthy exchanges. Held captive by diabolical mastermind Arcos (Ray McAnally), developer of the "instant plastic surgery" technique used to manufacture the countless Steed doppelgangers, the Ministry's top agent cannot help but interact with his kidnapper. Arcos is one in a long line of adversaries who not only respects Steed as a professional, but admires him on a personal level, and would enjoy having him as a friend had their loyalties happened to fall on the same side. Despite using Steed for his own ends and vowing to kill him once he is no longer needed, Arcos does not mistreat him, even when he attempts to escape. "He hit me," complains one of Arcos' henchmen, defending himself against his boss' ire when Steed attempts to escape. "He shows wisdom," Arcos snaps back, before returning his attention to Steed. Their exchanges are civil, almost congenial, though also infused with alternate meanings, and often initiated as a means for Steed to distract his captor from his attempts to escape. [3] At one point, they engage in a game of chess that involves 'reading' the meaning behind each other's moves. Arcos notes Steed's preference for his knight, which Steed puts down to its versatility (naturally, every good Steed needs a knight); Steed counters by observing, quite cleverly, that Arcos relies heavily on his pawns and hates to lose, classic traits of a diabolical mastermind.

Most interestingly, Arcos laments at one point that it is a pity that he did not meet Steed earlier, as he could have helped him reach his full "potential": "One must concede that you have a certain wit, a certain talent. But your potential has never really been developed." Steed, surreptitiously working at freeing his hands, frowns slightly at the comment, and prompts Arcos to continue. Alas, Arcos does not elaborate on what he means by 'potential'. It could simply be a matter of, in Arcos' eyes, following the 'wrong' ideology, but Arcos, with his interests in sculpture and science, seems rather too enlightened to be a candidate for indoctrination. If that is the case, it is interesting to speculate regarding in which area he believes Steed to be lacking. Is it a professional failing he speaks of, or something more personal?

Steed's response is also interesting. Given that Steed has a penchant for witty ripostes, it is surprising that he simply asks Arcos to continue. Even if he means to keep Arcos talking so that he can loosen his bonds and affect his escape, there is also perhaps a slight interest on his part in what Arcos has to say. His expression seems to indicate a measure of reflectiveness above and beyond his current situation. Is Steed, now well into his career and his life, already beginning to feel the first touches of melancholy that would mark his character in *The New Avengers*? Is he now regretting some of his choices in life? There is no way of knowing, of course, and his reaction could be interpreted in any number of ways, but it is interesting to speculate. When Arcos, mistakenly killed by his own side after he adopts Steed's face for himself, reverts back to his original features in death, Steed stares at him, disturbed and entranced, while Tara looks away. It might be the sight of his own dead visage or the morphing of his features into Arcos' that holds his gaze, but perhaps Arcos's words are also echoing in his mind. In Arcos' eyes, Steed's face with Arcos' mind behind it would likely be the fulfilment of that unelaborated upon 'potential' in ways that Steed himself cannot fathom, and for a brief moment, Arcos melds the two, subsuming Steed's identity in the process.

Steed's captivity also showcases his innovative, and inherently professional, nature. Free from his bonds and having rendered his guard unconscious, Steed finds himself at liberty in Arcos' hideout, but unable to leave. Realising that it is only a matter of time before he is recaptured, he forgoes making hopeless attempts to save his own skin; instead, he chooses to make up a number of kits for delivery to Arcos' agents, ensuring the creation of a multitude of duplicate Steeds, which he hopes will attract attention at the peace conference. He then calmly awaits recapture. It is a small, but notable, character moment in an episode that, in some ways, is a preview of things to come in *The New Avengers*, but still features plenty of original *Avengers* touches, and showcases a diabolical mastermind who gets under Steed's skin in more ways than one. [4]

© JZ Ferguson

1. This is, surely, one of the very best Tara King era lines.
2. The fact that Steed is also happy to go along with this white lie suggests that he shares her confidence in the young aristocrat.
3. It is fitting that Arcos asks Steed to taste the wine which his henchman mistakenly thinks has been poured for him.
4. These *Avengers* touches might well have been lost had the original intention to film parts of the episode in Spain gone ahead, with Arcos' atmospheric quarry base becoming an animal pen beneath a bullring and Mother's quirky submarine destined to be a gypsy caravan! This 'European plan' also pre-echoes *The New Avengers*. (My thanks to Michael Richardson's *Bowler Hats and Kinky Boots* for this information).

WISH YOU WERE HERE

Filmed: September 1968

Exterior Locations:
Elizabethan hotel: façade, grounds, shrubbery
Office block and car park
Country roads

Sets:
Elizabethan Hotel: lounge area, reception, terrace, Tara's room, corridor, Brevitt's room, lift, games room, service corridor, laundry chute/basement room, Charles' room, manager's office, kitchen
Uncle Charles' office: outer office
Mother's headquarters (balance chair/cardboard cut-out photos)
John Steed's mews apartment

WISH YOU WERE HERE

Main Character List:
Brevitt: hotel guest
Charles Merrydale: hotel guest, Tara King's uncle
Mellor: waiter
Parker: hotel manager
John Steed
Tara King
Maple: Charles' chief clerk
Kendrick: company secretary
Maxwell: guest, mastermind
Miss Craven: hotel employee
Mother
Rhonda: Mother's silent assistant
Basil Crighton-Latimer: Mother's nephew
Vickers: henchman

Two prisoners discuss an escape attempt, the shadow of the barred window cast upon the wall behind them. One of them, Brevitt, makes a run for it, across the hotel lobby! Parker, the manager behind the desk, asks him where he's going; when Brevitt says he's leaving, Parker indicates that his luggage is waiting for him. There's a crash and a cry from outside and Brevitt is carried back in, Parker apologising obsequiously for the over-polished top step. His friend stares through the bars of the lounge bar. This is a nice opening scene with misdirection of the audience; the closing reinforcement of the prison bar motif for the freeze frame under the titles is clever and understated.

Tara and Steed visit Tara's uncle's chief clerk, who is worried that Kendrick is taking over the company while her uncle is out of contact during his holiday. Kendrick returns and claims he spoke to (Uncle) Charles that morning, and has a postcard: "Having a wonderful time, place is absolutely captivating, wish you were here." [1] Outside, Tara is still worried and decides to visit her uncle while Steed goes to see Mother.

Tara arrives at the hotel and checks in. She surprises Parker by asking for her Uncle Charles, who is in the lounge. Dudley Foster, playing Parker, is so superbly thin-lipped in his malice that his mouth is in danger of disappearing altogether. Charles, the man from the opening scene who *didn't* try to escape, is overjoyed to see her but chastises her for coming, under his breath: "And what stupid idiotic impulse brought you here?" He tells her he's being held prisoner; the hotel is not what it seems and the guards could be everyone, anyone; he's not sure.

Tony Williamson delights in borrowing lines of dialogue from Patrick McGoohan's masterpiece, *The Prisoner*, with that show having the same basic premise – people of interest being held against their will in a seemingly idyllic village (or hotel), never being sure who were fellow prisoners and who were their captors. [2] Indeed, the working title of this episode was *The Prisoner* and we will see more references to it later. The director, Don Chaffey, also worked on McGoohan's show as well as its predecessor, *Danger Man*.

Brevitt makes another attempt to escape - a screech of tyres and the porters carry him back in on a stretcher. Tara still thinks it's coincidence and decides to prove it; she tells Parker she won't be staying and goes to her car, but it won't start. Parker rings for the village taxi, and then says it must be out. Tara declares she'll walk to the bus stop but a bucket of water is dumped on her by the window cleaner above the front door; she's whisked off to her room to dry herself. This is a weak device as Tara is a strong character but here she is completely submissive and easily cowed by a bucket of water. [3] Tara then learns that her cases were 'accidentally' taken away with her car and when her suit is returned the middle has been burnt out with an iron. Accepting the truth at last, she agrees to see Brevitt. Charles recommends she put some clothes on first and she finds a wardrobe full of striped uniforms – another reference to *The Prisoner*, where the villagers wore bold Edwardian hooped shirts.

The set design for the hotel is superb; Robert Jones and Simon Wakefield really evoke the *cliché* of the sort of dowdy hotel that would call itself *The Elizabethan Hotel*, all black and white with the exposed beams and carved woodwork. The choice of the Edgwarebury Hotel for the location also fits the script to a tee. This episode is such a dramatic contrast to the dreadfully rushed *melange* that we see in the reworked Bryce episodes. The lighting is astutely done – a hint of menace in every interior of the hotel with looming shadows in the corners, the play of light across exterior walls, with leaves and branches etched in blurred outline across them.

Meanwhile, Steed is with Mother, trying to unmask a double agent. Mother is swinging around the room on a large pair of scales, clearly meant to suggest the controller's pendulum in Number Two's office in *The Prisoner*. This makes for hard work for the camera operators, who struggle to keep him in focus and Patrick Newell is unfortunately completely out of focus when he delivers his, "I will not be thwarted in my quest to unmask him" hyperbole.

The set design here is not so good; the extreme artificiality and the smallness of the set make it less impressive than the others. In fact, these scenes with Mother are the low point of the episode, due not only to the set but also to the delivery of the lines, the rapid cuts and the overplaying of the 'stupid boy' aspect of Basil. Mother wants Tara's analytical mind on the case and is infuriated to learn she's taken a holiday. He's more infuriated a moment later when his nephew, Basil, sinks a golf ball into his whisky.

"Sorry, Uncle!" Basil exclaims.
"I'm not your Uncle, I'm your Mother!" Mother growls.

Steed is dispatched to look into a hit-and-run case, whom he discovers to be Maple. This is poor scripting, simply for plot expediency: Steed would never be sent to a hit-and-run. Was a line changed, where Maple had asked for Steed or Tara? Mother only mentions that Steed hasn't much time.

Tara, meanwhile, discovers Brevitt's body in his room (accompanied by perhaps the only bad piece of music in the whole episode) and she and her uncle take Maxwell to Brevitt's room to prove to him that they really are prisoners. However, henchman Vickers is now lying on the bed and he fights off Tara when she tries to roll him over. Parker enters and tells them Brevitt checked out a few minutes ago and left the hotel. They ask Maxwell to try to leave the hotel and get help but he staggers to their table a few moments later, saying someone had left a roller-skate on the steps, and that his car has been stolen.

Throughout the episode, Howard Blake's incidental music, interwoven with some of Laurie Johnson's famous stings from *Escape in Time* and *The Hidden Tiger* and judicious use of subtle sound effects such as the birds twittering in the trees make this episode resonate with England in the summer; this is what *The Avengers* is about and we can see (or hear) a real return to form for the series. [4]

Steed hangs up the telephone and tells Mother he's now been given five excuses for why Tara can't come to the phone, one being that she was in the swimming pool; yet the Elizabethan Hotel has no swimming pool. The exchange that follows with Mother and Steed sharing the words: "Funny", "Silly", "Stupid", "Odd", and "Crass" is unfortunately too long and labours the point.

Steed explains that the hit-and-run was connected to Tara's uncle so Mother decides to send Basil to the hotel, observing, "Well, if she is in trouble she'll be grateful". Steed grimaces in reply, "And if she isn't she'll never forgive us". [5] (Ironically, Patrick Macnee is on holiday for much of the filming and his scenes would have been filmed in a separate block; he's only on camera for a short time.) The undercurrent of family runs through this episode, with Tara and Basil as polar opposites; she is efficient, resourceful and intelligent while he is the bumbling idiot nephew.

Another escape attempt is made via the laundry chute while Maxwell guards the door but Uncle Charles is knocked out by an unseen assailant. In the morning, Charles is annoyed to discover that Tara didn't take the opportunity to escape, electing to stay and help him instead. He questions where Maxwell was but Tara is oblivious to the suspicion.

Basil arrives in a little vintage car, jam-packed with different sporting equipment in a conscious echo of Steed's appearance in *The Girl from Auntie*. [6] Basil 'introduces' himself to Tara but, like her before him, doesn't believe she's being held captive. She decides to prove it to him and leads him to the front desk, where she loudly says she hadn't realised he'd come to see Charles and then challenges him to leave. He discovers that all his tyres are flat, and then has a bucket of paint dropped on him. This is a major flaw in the plot as – for a second time – Tara throws away a clear chance of escape by putting Basil under suspicion; she would have been better served to order him to report the facts to Steed. After Basil is daubed in paint, we have a flaw in the camerawork to match, with a rather wobbly zoom out.

Kendrick arrives, having decided he no longer needs Uncle Charles kept alive, a plan Parker is queasy about but Vickers is happy to put into action. Basil makes a break for it and is chased by two porters. He's about to escape when an attractive girl wearing a swimsuit (did someone say *Benny Hill*?) claims to have caught her foot in a trap; Mellor coshes Basil when he goes to help her. [7]

Tara and Charles are disappointed when Basil staggers back in, holding his head. Basil apologises for doubting Tara and says it's like no prison he knows: no locked doors, bars or warders. Tara realises that this may be the villains' downfall and drags Basil off to the front line: the kitchen. She explains that a hotel needs food and water as they barricade themselves in. Finding the main power switch, she plunges the hotel into darkness, prompting the innocent guests to all leave. Tara declares that now they know who the enemy really are: anyone not in the kitchen.

"Correction!" announces Maxwell, who has produced a pistol and reveals himself as the mastermind. However, his hubris is his downfall. Tara knocks him down with a serving trolley then knocks him out. Unfortunately, I'm sure that the entire audience could see Maxwell's betrayal coming a mile away as it's hardly subtle.

Tara plucks the hotel safe key from Maxwell's pockets and they realise that they now have the upper hand. She and Basil ransack the safe so that when the others arrive they think Maxwell has made off with the loot. They are easily hoisted by their own petard at the front door, Basil polishing the step and Tara smacking them with a frying pan.

Tara is often rather unjustly lampooned for using a brick in her handbag in *The Forget-Me-Knot* but her use of improvisational weapons here is perfectly in context, if a bit slapstick. The fault in *The Forget-Me-Knot* is that her action is accompanied by a dreadful sound effect, as though we had accidentally tuned in to *Benny Hill*. There is worse slapstick in another episode. Maxwell coshes Charles *again* and tries to escape. He leaps over the polished top step but finds the tyres of his car are all flat. He rushes for a bicycle down the side of the hotel and is ambushed with a bucket of paint and a banana peel. [8]

Steed finally arrives in his Rolls and requests a room for "a weary but successful viper hunter". He tells Tara her holiday has done her a world of good, but she declares she wants to come back to work, in order to have a long, long rest.

In the tag scene, Tara discovers that Steed is being held prisoner in his flat. When she refuses to leave, he interprets it as an offer to hold the fort alone and says he's off to the pub; she can mind the neighbour's baby until he gets back!

So: high production values, an enjoyable plot that has enough post-modernism to keep you entertained, although it doesn't quite realise the potential of the concept. [9] Tara, once again, demonstrates the mettle that she previously showed in *All Done with Mirrors* and proves that Linda Thorson can carry an episode while Patrick Macnee is on holiday. Sadly, several lapses in the script and the camerawork and one truly glaring piece of music mar an otherwise good episode. It's worth watching again, though.

© Piers Johnson

1. Is the use of 'captivating' a hidden clue from the character – if he did write the postcard – or from the (mischievous) writer?
2. Or who are there as bona fide guests, free to leave when they want to.
3. It is also one of many examples where the episode becomes silly, rather than surreal.
4. Howard Blake's role in the music of Season 6 is often neglected by fans and critics. Much of the original music – in a season saturated by recycled scores – is composed by him.
5. This is a totally unrealistic response from Steed given his paternal concern for Tara throughout Season 6.
6. This in turn is mirrored by the scene in *The New Avengers'* *The Eagle's Nest* where Steed arrives on the island of St. Dorca weighed down with a ridiculous amount of holiday gear.
7. As Piers observes, this seems more *Benny Hill* than *The Avengers*; I would add *Carry On* to the mix.
8. By this point, I'm afraid, any sense of avengerish atmosphere and subtlety has long since been lost, in my opinion.
9. I wholeheartedly agree with Piers here: the concept had great potential which the finished product fails to realise. This episode could have offered a genuinely disturbing undercurrent but buckets of water, paint and banana skins

are neither subtle nor avengerish. Why construct such an atmospheric set, only to employ *Benny Hill*-type antics? If the aim was to satirise *The Prisoner*, the result was – in my opinion – simply to undermine *The Avengers*' subversive, darker qualities.

KILLER

Filmed: September 1968

Exterior Locations:
REMAK Factory façade, drive, grounds and gated entrance
Stable Mews
Graveyard
Wilkington's cottage
Abandoned village film set
The Pirate pub, Lower Storpington
Woods
Country roads

Sets:
REMAK Factory: reception area, factory rooms, tunnel area, processing room, control room
John Steed's mews apartment
Mother's headquarters (exotic drinks set)
Wilkington's study
Fancy Frills Limited
The Pirate pub bar
Coach (with dummies)

KILLER

Main Character List:
Arthur Wilkington: electronics/computer expert
Merridon: mastermind
Brinstead: henchman
Trouncer: undercover agent
John Steed
Tara King: going off on holiday
Mother
Rhonda: Mother's silent assistant
Lady Diana Forbes-Blakeney, temporary partner for Steed
Clarke: forensics expert
Freddy: camp Fancy Frills Limited packager
Gillers: agent
Paxton: false contact/henchman
Calvin: agent
Ralph Bleech: business partner of Wilkington
Lawson: agent
Chattel: agent

Killer is, on the surface, a well-made but essentially formulaic Season 6 episode. A series of agents are bumped off; an all too familiar, soulless post-war building houses the mastermind and his technological know-how; and there is yet another unfriendly pub where our Avengers meet the enemy. If the plot sounds instantly recognisable then so too is the real location of the REMAK 'factory'; the approach to Haberdasher's Askes School had been used in numerous *Avengers* episodes. Even the music – as was the case, unfortunately, throughout most of this final season – is recycled from previous seasons. [1] Bearing all of this in mind, what possibly could make *Killer* stand out from the crowd?

There are a number of stylishly surreal scenes, locations and touches but the most significant is the use of Jennifer Croxton to play Lady Diana Forbes-Blakeney. While Ian Ogilvy's role in *They Keep Killing Steed* offers us a tantalising image of what a young, dashing male partner for Tara King might offer, Steed still played a prominent role – or roles! – in the episode. In *Killer*, 'Forbes' *replaces* Tara. The official history is that the main role was written for Linda Thorson but, in order to allow her to complete her filming of another episode – delayed by a recent illness – Croxton was brought in. This is certainly the suggestion put forward in Michael Richardson's engaging *Bowler Hats and Kinky Boots*. [2] However, I am going to be slightly mischievous and provocative here. We know how unreliable *The Avengers*' official history can be. Brian Clemens was never a fan of actress Linda Thorson or the character she portrayed. Years later, while making the second season of *The New Avengers*, he even commented: "I think Linda wasn't very good in the part" (*TV Times*, October 22nd, 1977). By casting an Emma Peel-type in terms of physique and style, was he taunting the audience and previous producer Bryce by showing them what he felt they were missing out on? The tag scene seems to add to this theory, as a puppy-like Tara is seen to have been writing a postcard an hour to Steed while she was away, like an obsessed, lovesick teenager. It is a very odd moment in an unusual episode and one I will return to later. Croxton offers sex appeal and a cool charm, even if she lacks Diana Rigg's sophisticated and stylishly sardonic acting ability. However, there are plenty of critics who have noted the physical similarities, including David K Smith:

"Jennifer Croxton...put[s] in a plucky performance with plenty of Emma-isms...so slender and athletic, she even sports similar hair and fighting styles. Clearly the producers had resurrected the ghost of Emma." (*The Avengers Forever!*).

Smith is not alone in sensing that the similarities between Rigg/Peel and Croxton/Forbes are entirely and provocatively deliberate. The Steed/Forbes partnership allows for a different dynamic between the leads in this one-off episode. Mother – this time dwelling in a less than memorable headquarters kitted out like a minimalist upmarket bar – quickly undermines Steed's patronising advice that "active duty is a little different from training school." Forbes has arrived from 'Special Service' and is already an experienced agent. Steed won't need to play the paternal role in this hastily-assembled partnership.

The following scene in a graveyard introduces us to the first packaged corpse: wrapped in polythene and tied up with a decorative pink ribbon. If the presentation is oddly surreal, so too is the forensic scientist:

Steed: How did he die?
Clarke: In alphabetical order: he was clubbed, poisoned, shot, spiked, stabbed, strangled and suffocated. And his ear drums are damaged.
Steed: His neck's broken as well.

As so often, Steed notices details missed by the so-called experts and closes the conversation with this darkly impressive final flourish. The formulaic structure of a series of agents/corpses being discovered is freshened up by the strangeness of the gift-like spectacle of agents who are "washed, sterilised, dry cleaned" or, as Steed sums it up succinctly, "packaged". If REMAK represents the ultimate killing machine, it also demonstrates its owner's desire to display its capabilities, showing off his unique powers. The following scenes see action and surreal display taking it in turns as they vie for our attention.

Even if she did inherit Tara's lines, Forbes is anything but a Tara substitute. She arrives at the dead man's house in a stylish, white MGB. Her outfit is designed to display her slim figure: a pink mini-skirt, purple blouse, turquoise neck tie, red buckle belt and red boots reaching up to just below her knees. Her fight with Brinstead offers us a cross between the art form of Emma Peel and the physicality of Tara King.

Meanwhile, over at Fancy Frills, the overtly camp and stylishly attired Freddy announces himself as a "packager extraordinary", a tag which could naturally refer to REMAK itself. (The villains are, presumably, buying their ribbon from him).

Killer revolves around five locations/sets which we constantly flit between: Mother's HQ, the wonderfully-atmospheric disused film set where the informer meets agents, the Pirate pub run by a grimfaced landlord wearing a patch, the 'factory' in which the automated killer is housed and the graveyard where the bodies are delivered and displayed. Everything is fake, from the pirate landlord, the village where Paxton meets agents, the factory and its (mannequin) workers, to Mother's bar. The graveyard mourners – Steed and Forbes – are there simply to seek information, not to pay their final respects. Even the killer our Avengers are seeking out isn't real, in the sense of being a human who can be brought to justice.

The ITC Pinewood set is a delight, taking *The Avengers'* fascination with sets-within-sets to its ultimate extreme. On one level, the set is a 'real' working one which was used by a number of television drama series. [3] It allows Paxton/the double artist the opportunity to offer us a series of spectacular stunts, including tumbling down an exterior staircase and crashing through a plate-glass window. These displays not only have to impress the viewer; they have to convince a series of agents as well, adding a delicious extra layer of artificiality. [4] Even Steed is taken in by Paxton's performance. When yet another agent arrives at the real/fake village set he too joins in with the spectacular stunts, bouncing down to the ground from a tall building with the use of a rope. Why? It makes no logical sense. However, this is *The Avengers* and it adds to both the surreal, visual spectacle and the odd humour. These scenes are simultaneously highly amusing and yet also dramatic: the perfect recipe for avengerishly 'subversive champagne'.

When Forbes and Steed uncover dead Fred at his shop he too is on display, with a pink ribbon tied round his neck, the 'packager extraordinary' extraordinarily packaged. The surrealism is mounting and it increases, rather than detracts from, the dramatic undercurrent.

As we reach the final scenes, the elegant Croxton is now sporting a black silk roll-neck top, wine-red cardigan, salmon-pink trousers and a fashionable black hat. She looks ready for the catwalk rather than a fight finale. However, Forbes' pursuit of the factory coach leads to one of the most atmospheric scenes in this or any other *Avengers* episode. As she approaches the parked vehicle, the camera focuses on her apprehensive eyes, then the driver's empty seat, then back to her eyes which transform from wary to incredulous: the coach seats are full of stern-faced male mannequins sporting jackets, ties and an assortment of hats. The music here is fittingly borrowed from the scene in *The £50,000 Breakfast* when the henchmen attack the female owner of the ventriloquist shop. Just as the Litoff Organisation's urbane hit-men hide behind disturbing masks – in a chillingly atmospheric scene – here Paxton is camouflaged among the factory dummy workers, poised to pounce. For a change, the recycling of music from a previous era carries a clever, intertextual resonance. The struggle between Paxton and Forbes lasts under ten seconds but the visual appeal of this short piece lives far longer in our minds than the half minute which the entire scene takes up. Like *Killer* itself, it is more about stylish visual display rather than subtle storyline. [5]

Steed's showdown battle with REMAK – which in a sense the entire episode has been building towards – offers us a stark contrast between his approach and that of the helpless men who went before him. Whereas the less experienced agents charged in 'blind' and treated it as a physical battle, Steed treats it as an intellectual/psychological one requiring a mix of strategy, common sense, timing and perseverance. It is like a point/counter point, deadly game of chess with Steed anticipating or working out each of the machine's seven attacks.

The suspense is combined with delicious moments of subtly surreal humour, such as when Steed bends over REMAK's typewriter to note that he has even been given a reference number, part of the machine's highly organised process, before nodding to affirm that he is impressed that his collar size has been correctly recorded! These are the sort of stylish touches which take *The Avengers* well beyond the realm of more mundane or traditional spy-fi and sci-fi television dramas. Steed once again proves that the free-thinking human can overcome the pre-set computer, in this case taking advantage – as he did with the cybernauts – of a killing machine's lack of loyalty: "They'll take orders from anybody". Forbes and Steed are even left with a Mr. Benn-style souvenir in the form of REMAK's gold plaque. [6]

As I mentioned earlier, having enjoyed the novelty of the 'Emma Peel Mark 2', Forbes, we are then provided with a tag scene which reinforces one of Tara King's less endearing characteristics: her puppy-eyed emotional dependence on Steed. The mountain of postcards left on Steed's door rug – "miss you", "wish you were here" – offer a stark contrast to Forbes-Blakeney's seductively cool charm. The contrast between the two women couldn't be greater and the producers are clearly asking us to draw comparisons and possibly even make a choice of preferred female lead. The postcard detail is a strangely bizarre one given that Jennifer Croxton's appearance was never going to amount to anything more than a one-off role, in a visually impressive yet formulaic episode. We would be left with Thorson/King for the remainder of the season, making it an odd ploy to display her as desperately lacking independence and being so emotionally reliant on her male partner. [7]

Killer, ultimately, stands out in Season 6 because of two memorable sets – the 'disused' film village and the avengerish mannequin factory bus – and a series of stylishly surreal images. Jennifer Croxton/Lady Diana Forbes-Blakeney – at the risk of sounding sexist – is part of the unique, visual display or packaging, thematically linking her to the episode's plot. Her sex appeal is a major component of *Killer*'s attraction. Whether – like Smith – you are left wanting more of her is a matter of individual taste. Personally, I enjoy it as a one-off diversion.

© Rodney Marshall

1. As Piers Johnson's wonderfully informative website *Mrs. Peel...We're Needed!* notes, the music here was borrowed from a large number of previous *Avengers* episodes, including *The Hidden Tiger, A Funny Thing Happened on the Way to the Station, The Winged Avenger, From Venus With Love*, and *Never, Never Say Die*. (*The £50,000 Breakfast* can be added to this list.)
2. Jennifer Croxton suggests on the Optimum/Studio Canal commentary that Thorson was on holiday.
3. Piers' website points out that this real set/fake village was part of the ITC Pinewood set used in *Danger Man, The Saint* and *The Avengers*. *The Morning After* episode re-used some of the village streets.
4. The initial display has to fool us, which it does. After that, they simply have to entertain us which they certainly do. The plate glass is clearly already broken, allowing us to enjoy the artificiality/artistry of the spectacle.
5. Mannequins are effectively employed in so many *Avengers* episodes. They add to the unsettling, surreal atmosphere in *The Murder Market, Man-Eater of Surrey Green, Pandora, Target!*, and *K is for Kill* among others.
6. In the case of the BBC children's TV series, Mr. Benn was allowed to take away a souvenir from each of his adventures, thanks to the generosity of the mysterious shop keeper.
7. In terms of *The Avengers'* countercultural sexual politics there are times, such as this, when Tara King's character undoes the radical work which went before to establish the female lead as physically, emotionally and intellectually stronger than the male. Here she comes across as emotionally dependent and almost desperate.

THE ROTTERS

Filmed: September-October 1968

Exterior Locations:
Department of Forestry Research: grounds
Block of flats
Country church
Country lanes
Wainwright Timber Industries Head Office
Road junction/woods
Forsythe's country Cottage
Sawbow workshop/London mews
Clearing in the woods

Sets:
Department of Forestry Research: corridor, Pendred's office
Mother's Headquarters (plastic)
Pendred's apartment
Institute of Timber Technology: wall, mound
Church belfry
Steed's mews apartment
Sawbow's workshop
Wainwright Timber Industries: open plan head office, laboratory
Forsythe's cottage: patio, living room

THE ROTTERS

Main Character List:
Sir James Pendred: Forestry Research, senior scientific advisor
Kenneth: a rotter, Wormdoom Ltd
George: a rotter, Wormdoom Ltd
Mother
John Steed
Tara King
Rhonda: Mother's silent assistant
Carter: Pendred's secretary
Beale: Pendred's manservant
Professor Palmer: Institute of Timber Technology
Reggie Pym: expert on timber decay
Mervyn Sawbow: dodgy antique dealer/restorer
Sonia: Wainwright Timber Industries
Parbury: British Burial Caskets
Wainwright
Sandford: henchman
Mrs. Forsythe: Forsythe's mother
Sandford: henchman
Jackson: henchman
Victor Forsythe: timber research expert

Position Vacant: Self-starter with drive, cunning and initiative wanted for a rewarding opportunity in Avengerland. Heading up a corporate start-up, the successful candidate will be responsible for the day-to-day running of a thriving blackmail/extortion/assassination/revenge bureau with extensive foreign travel. A strong awareness of class and its importance as the driver of all things is a critical competency, as is the ability to recruit a team of reliable support staff to carry out broader company policy (murder, assault and stress-tested driving at high speed to name but three). Previous experience as a diabolical mastermind will be highly regarded.

Every fictional hero has a Moriarty, a seething molasses of envy and thwarted ambition contained in an immaculate suit or sharply-lined dress. James Bond tangoed with Blofeld. The Doctor locked horns with The Master. Based in some far-off corner of reality, these fiends fight their way across the screens and usually wind up serving their dues in some correction facility or other for all their hard work.

When unreality is the foundation, when otherworldly takes centre stage and over-the-top teeters that bit closer to the hues of black and white that are menace and laughter, how does an immovable object sidestep an unstoppable force? In *Avengerland*, they do it with the only way possible for the cultivated, urbane, well-lived and seasoned English villain: with upper class and lower contempt. Brilliant as a bounder, classic as a cad, these men and women from the School of Gentle Knocks and Light Fingers knew their place in the world as per the school motto (*Above the rest whom we detest*) and never doubted that they would one day conquer their corner of the world – and very possibly the pillar box sitting on it as well.

Villains in *The Avengers* rank as some of the most memorable, most colourful, most diabolical and most perfect of all time and in any form, whether that be film, television or theatre. Whilst a good deal of this can be attributed by the casual passer-by to the actors who inhabit the skin from the script and flesh it out on screen, this is a disservice to the enormous tapestry woven by the creative genius of a mafia of writers, producers and directors who shot holes in the genre with lightning wit, a superior style and a sense of the English manner of murder which would resonate outside the series and influence all which followed in its wake.

For an *Avengers* villain to be wholly successful, they need a plan: not just an ordinary Point-Gun-And-Demand-Cash routine; this would be beneath them. They require guile and ingenuity, mastering the weather, shop dummies, department store bombs, ferocious felines, computers, robots, treasure hunts and aliens to bend to their will. These upper-crust socialites/businessmen/aristocrats/scientists/geniuses would wile away their spare time with the occasional world-domination plot. Their casual approach to popping off the odd rival, their attitude that life is only worth living if everyone who gets in the way keels over, their resolute belief in the continuing life of an Empire and their place in it are their cornerstone. Some of the best villains to emerge across the face of 1960s British television found their home in *Avengerland*. Nathaniel Needle, lurking in a haystack, is a reminder that you don't need to hide on an international space station to be a cad with a cause. Cuddle up to a Teddy Bear in *Avengerland* and you might find yourself assassinated. Play a Joker in bridge and you won't want to look behind you. When comforting nannies turn into something nasty in the nursery, you know you're in familiar territory. The familiar is the key to the success of the English villain throughout a decade of the series: a nanny, an elderly knitting circle, a doctor, a dentist, a soldier, a politician. On the surface, this scarcely contains the hot-bed of greed, avarice, revenge and fiendish plots which simmer to the boil beneath the surface. These men and women are deadly, the smiles a veneer. Very often, the casual and comforting phrase is laced with an undertone of menace which gets the message across without the need for physical violence. Murder comes with an apology, and a bill for the cleaning with a polite request for immediate payment.

Dave Freeman's *The Rotters* introduces audiences to the latest in a long line of fiendish foes, but on this occasion they are so deliciously bad, so potently worthy of their place in the pantheon, that they lift an out-of-the-ordinary episode into the stratosphere with their casual, class-based banter and general amusement that they can make a living by disposing of other people, in a world where the occasional death over breakfast is brushed away with the egg cups and the folded newspapers. The murderous henchmen, George and Kenneth, wear the attire of the classic English country gentleman on a summer stroll to the Lamb and Flag for an afternoon pint. They seem innocuous, unlikely to receive a batted eyelid from the passer-by, yet murder is on their mind and they spend much time discussing the trials and tribulations of being a gentleman and a murderer rolled into one: they are quintessential *Avengers* fiends – all class and serious substance. Their dialogue – which is discussed later in this piece – is one of the greatest high-points of the sixth and final run of *The Avengers*, a rich stream of darkly comic invective which is a tribute to Freeman's creative talents and a showcase of what the man could achieve in basically his sole dramatic work. [1]

The Rotters represents a high-point in the season as a whole and a landmark achievement for *The Avengers*: a comedy of manners with a deadly punch-line. The core of the success of the episode lies in the script, with dialogue that sparkles with such aplomb that one could be forgiven for thinking that Freeman has been a consistently reliable hand for *The Avengers*. The tone and shape of the episode, the dialogue bouncing between the principal players, and even the sets in parts (namely Mother's surreal office locale in this episode) are not a million miles away from what Steven Moffat has been trying to engineer for some time with his efforts for the re-booted *Doctor Who* series for BBC Television.

Banter is King, but performance is Queen. Were it not for the wholly convincing performances of all concerned, ranging from Macnee's lightly mocking bewilderment at the absurdity of the villainous plot around him, to the steely stiff-upper-lipped conviction of Gerald Sim and Jerome Willis, the script would teeter into uncontrollable farce. The key here is director Robert Fuest's assembly of the totally familiar: *Avengerland* landscapes of thatched cottages, cosy lanes and roads, lush woodland and government organisations festooned with boffins with a potently eccentric streak. This extends to the casting of a host of familiar faces previously seen in the series: Sim (*Mission to Montreal, The Wringer* and the *tour de force* that is *Dial A Deadly Number*), Willis (*Intercrime* and *How To Succeed...At Murder*), Harold Innocent (*The Medicine Men*) and John Nettleton (*The See Through Man*). Securing familiar foundations facilitates an opportunity to branch out into the extreme fringes of the characters which populate *Avengerland*, pushing the patriotic and maniacal envelope until it reaches the postage stamp.

The sense of familiar is apparent from the outset: the teaser opens with Sir James Pendred (Garry Marsh), Director of Studies for the Department of Forestry Research, running for what seems his life. He emerges from woodland and staggers into the grounds of a nearby dwelling, a mysterious electronic crackling noise pursuing him. He arrives at the Department of Forestry Research, lurches into an anteroom, the door to which he firmly bolts behind, and he hurries into his office as the electronic crackling noise gets closer. Heaving a sigh of exhaustion, he switches on the light and then proceeds to turn the lock in the door to his office when the electronic crackling booms loud. He is left holding the door handle, lock and key, but the door has completely vanished. Standing before him are the identically dressed and becapped George (Jerome Willis) and Kenneth (Gerald Sim), the former carrying a gun, the latter a steel cylinder with a directional funnel. George fires directly at Sir James who slumps dead at their feet. They casually admire the empty door hinges and lock which remain in place, the door having vanished, and they briefly chuckle at their handiwork. [2]

In a cross between an inflatable palace and a Persian harem, Mother's latest headquarters plays host to Steed and Tara as they reflect on Sir James Pendred's recent demise, Rhonda pumping up Mother's inflatable chair. [3] They discuss Pendred's death as "Murder most foul". As a senior scientific advisor, he telephoned the Prime Minister ten minutes before his death, insisting on an urgent meeting on a matter of national importance. With Steed taking Pendred's office and Tara sent to his apartment, the pair go their separate ways in search of an explanation.

Steed arrives at Pendred's office and marvels at the empty hinges against the door frame. He meets Carter (Noel Davis), Sir James' secretary, who holds the lock to the non-existent door in his hands. Steed asks if any secret documents may have been stolen but Carter assures him that their department does not trade in such material. Again, Freeman's strong sense of what passes for banter in *Avengerland* is spot-on:

Carter: We don't deal in secrets in this department. We plant trees. When they grow up, we cut them down.
Steed: What a full, rich life you must lead.

A cursory inspection of files – on annual leave and damage rendered to wood by field mice – doesn't point Steed in a conclusive direction, particularly given that Pendred tried to reach the Prime Minister.

A green utility van bearing the fiendishly worthy hallmark of WORMDOOM LTD pays a visit to Sir James Pendred's residence, emerging from which are George and Kenneth, who have furtive business in hand. They push past the late Sir James' butler with lofty indifference and enter the apartment, announcing that they are in attendance at Sir James' request. When the butler advises them of his passing, Kenneth counters, "I was quite aware of that, old fruitgum. We were there". Confused, the butler soon insists they leave. George, pouring himself a brandy, admires the apartment as a "charming place", Kenneth smiling and admitting it "has character". [4]

George demands that the butler (whom he addresses as "old bean") produce a photograph which was taken before the war of a group (students at the Institute of Timber Technology), a picture they must acquire. When the butler informs them the picture is in an album in a nearby desk, Kenneth insists that he shouldn't trouble himself (referring to him through clenched teeth as "old trout") and he and George seek out the album themselves. Behind them, the butler tries to flee but is swiftly gunned down by George. Creeping over to the sofa against which his body has collapsed, they indulge in glasses of brandy and a little light banter. [5]

Kenneth: You know I do *despise* the working classes. They're so... so...
George: Working class?
Kenneth: Quite.

En route to the Institute of Timber Technology, Tara spies Professor Palmer (John Nettleton, late of *The See Through Man*) sitting atop a hill, camping out and smoking a pipe as he keenly monitors the progress of precious seedlings and planted mighty Redwood – which Tara nearly mistakenly crushes underfoot in greeting him. Here the sense of tradition in *Avengerland* rises to the surface once again: the higher the bureaucracy or intelligence, the stronger the eccentricity. The bigger they are, the more bonkers they get. [6]

Outside a village church, George and Kenneth are surveying the area before making their move on Reggie Pym, the leading authority on timber decay. They admire their surroundings as they engage in menacing banter. Again, Freeman's free-flowing dialogue between two of the best villains the programme ever produced is nothing short of Brian Clemens-like in its perfection:

Kenneth: Lovely old place, isn't it?
George: Mmm, charming. I adore the countryside. You ever strangled anybody, old chap?
Kenneth: Strangled? No, no I can't say I have. The trees are awfully nice at this time of year aren't they, don't you think?
George: Mmm, awfully nice. Just a hint of autumn in the leaves. I wonder what it's like?
Kenneth: What?
George: Strangling.
Kenneth: Oh, rather unpleasant I should imagine. Not a method a gentleman would use.
George: Oh, quite, quite. Awfully vulgar. Mmm, country air. Jolly invigorating.

Kenneth: Makes one glad to be alive.
George: Mmm. Shall we do it now?
Kenneth: I don't think so, no. Just get a good look at the geography and come back tonight. It's always better in the dark.
George: Much better. More sort of...dramatic.

Wainwright Timber Industries is an impressive business in a stately old home which Tara visits in pursuit of clues. On this occasion, she has arrived far too late. She meets a taciturn gentleman in funereal black (Harold Innocent) who escorts her to Mr. Wainwright – who happens to have curled up his toes and is resting in a casket behind a discrete curtain (where staff can pay their last respects). Where on Earth other than *Avengerland* would one attend an appointment and find oneself meeting a corpse rather than a client? Equally avengerish is the exchange between Tara and a sinister staff member (later to be revealed as Wainwright), who seductively strokes the top of the casket and slaps the side of it in flirtatious delight. Linda Thorson is nothing short of being a delightfully expressive actress, and she makes much of this scene to great understated comedic effect. Tara departs, but not before she is seen leaving by George and Kenneth, who raise the alarm. The receptionist, Sonia (Toni Gilpin), contacts Sandford and assigns him to deal with her. In a particularly well-constructed chase scene – the music working superbly well with a chase through the woods here, captured to great effect by director Robert Fuest – Sandford blocks the path of Tara's car with his van and then advances on her with an axe, chasing her into nearby woodland as she runs for her life.

Fuest fore-echoes the claustrophobic tension of his work on Brian Clemens' superlative *And Soon The Darkness* with a chase through a tangled maze of trees, with lots of tight shots of the aggressive Sandford and the tense, panicked Tara. [7] When he strikes at her with an axe and it imbeds itself in the tree, we see genuine flashes of the Gale/Rigg action of old as Tara strikes him to the ground and, as she endeavours to pull out the axe, Sandford dashes back out of the woods and steals her car. The shade of *Avengerland* brilliance which tips the scene into *par excellence* remains the car speeding up to a closed gate, Sandford leaning an arm out and pointing the same silver cylindrical weapon Kenneth has been using at the gate. It vanishes without trace, allowing him to drive off and leave her stranded. In this world, even the laws of physics don't stop a villain! [8] Nursing her tired feet after an eight-mile pursuit of her stolen car, Steed nonchalantly reflects that Tara got the car back; his attitude is that she is fussing over nothing. If this had been Mrs. Peel, would he have been as ungallant?

Visiting a thatched cottage in the country, Steed is greeted by Victor Forsyth's mother (Amy Dalby) in the garden pruning roses. There is another delicious *Avengerland* touch when Steed admires the scent of a rose and Mrs. Forsyth wrenches it from his hand, throws it away and presents him with an immaculate fake, remarking, "I always prefer plastic flowers. They last so much longer." Where else would a seemingly gentle, elderly spinster be so flinty and disposable? She shows Steed into the sitting room to wait for Victor's arrival, whereupon he is introduced to two more of her son's "friends" who are waiting to see him: George and Kenneth.

The exchange between the three men here is a brilliant confection of style and substance which further highlights the class of the series: they exchange shallow pleasantries about the weather, Victor as a "splendid" chap and his dexterity on the piano, violin and clarinet, but each is carefully monitoring the reactions of the other and there is precious little interest in the discussion; they are watching one another to gauge why they are there, their motives and their level of potential threat – a super-secret agent meeting two super civil assassins. [9]

Mrs. Forsyth returns and is confused; she never knew Victor could play an instrument. The word-play and bluff have fallen apart. Kenneth demands to know what game Steed is playing. He draws a gun on Steed and the tense proceedings are interrupted by Mrs. Forsyth's return (he hides the weapon beneath his cap). As she wheels in a tea trolley, Steed instructs Kenneth to lend her a hand and he manages to keep the weapon trained on him through the cap as he does so. Having forgotten the sugar, Mrs. Forsyth leaves the room as Steed, pouring out tea, throws the entire contents at Kenneth and does battle with George. Fuest delivers a directorial touch which has all the clever hallmarks of *The Doombolt Chase* (upon which he worked) when Steed grapples with Kenneth for the gun. The three-shot static hit against the piano is a hugely effective and minimalist approach after the earlier destruction of the tea service and general rough-house scenario as the three men fight one another. The culmination of the fight – with Steed being trapped under the piano while it disintegrates and crashes down on him off-camera – is a beautiful effect, matched by dialogue *The Avengers* always produced with unashamed panache:

George: Interesting sound.
Kenneth: Yes. They don't write tunes like that anymore, you know.

Mrs. Forsyth admonishes a very naughty Steed when she returns, instructing him to put the piano back together, as meanwhile Tara engages in a pursuit of shady 'antique' dealer Mervyn Sawbow. Fuest makes extensive use of wood, water and mud in the location work mounted here. Sandford terrorises Sawbow. As Tara creeps too closely to the scene, Sawbow's execution is temporarily delayed whilst Sandford's companion seeks out Tara. She unsuccessfully tries to render him unconscious by striking him with a branch, which results in the customary fight on both counts: Tara and the man, Sawbow and Sandford; the latter ends when Sawbow is gunned down in the back as he flees the scene. Having hurt her ankle, Tara flees to a nearby woodshed. Thinking she is safe, she peers through a crack in the door and suddenly, amidst the electronic sound which is emitted from the silver cylindrical weapon, the entire shed vanishes and Tara is knocked unconscious and exposed, captured by her oppressors.

Meanwhile, Mother receives a call that Forsyth has arrived in London and is waiting in Steed's apartment to meet with him. He sets off at great haste. There is much to appreciate in the lighting and foreground in this scene, with Mother taking centre stage amongst his inflatables. Fuest again draws the action into the living room of the viewer with the bright red 'hot line' virtually leaping from the screen as Steed effectively cools his heels in the background.

Sonia advises George and Kenneth that Tara is working with a man called Steed, who is being worked on in his apartment as they speak. There is a delicious sense of character here as the pair seem put out that someone else is handling their job of menace and mayhem. Tara pours acid onto her chains but they do not readily yield as Sandford enters the room to retrieve her dinner tray. Their banter here is pure *Avengers* material, casual and menacing all in one:

Sandford: You weren't thinking of clobbering me with that wine bottle, were you?
Tara: Oh, it had crossed my mind. I get so few pleasures down here.

The discussion seems to have dealt with the menace, but Tara still manages to throw the bottle at the back of Sandford's head when he departs and she strikes a direct hit, rendering him unconscious as she returns to her acid-melting work. Lesson Number 164: Never turn your back on The Avengers. Stealing his gun, she stealthily tries to make an exit from the building but when she overhears approaching voices she hides in the anteroom in which Wainwright's casket lies. She is appalled when Wainwright rises from his grave – "Not dead, Miss King. Merely resting" – and draws a gun on her as George and Kenneth close in.

Also being held at gunpoint, Steed learns that Forsyth paid a visit to the apartment to meet with a chap named Steed, who promptly tried to kill him, but wasn't quick enough. The real Steed swiftly disarms him and then engages him in conversation about the members of the Institute of Timber Technology and the secrets they held to themselves. Forsyth confirms that they discovered a mutation of dry rot that spreads like wild-fire and that Wainwright is actually alive and well. He also produces a spray gun, a similar silver metallic cylinder to the one Kenneth has been using. Steed probes him with dialogue which bristles with *Avengers* edges:

Steed: What have you been doing in the week since you left the plane in Paris?
Forsyth: Ah, well, now that's a rather funny story.
Steed: I'm dying to hear it.
Forsyth: There was this awfully pretty girl...
Steed: I've heard it.

Meanwhile, George and Kenneth are weighing up the task of ending Tara's life, and they're having a crisis of culture and conscience:

George: No offence, Miss King, but killing girls is, well...ah...

Kenneth: Well, it's not cricket, you see? It just isn't done.
Tara: I'm glad to hear it.
George: You see, there are certain ethics…Standards of behaviour …Certain actions which a gentleman would never consider.
Tara: I wouldn't want to put you in an embarrassing situation.
Kenneth: That's dash decent of you, Miss King.

Tara suggests that they should untie her and let her go, but it would be impossible for them to do that. They are caught in a criminal quandary. The pair avoid a "sticky moment" by delegating the task of assassinating Tara to their 'lesser rank', Sandford. With a "Toodle-Pip" and "Chin-Up" the pair depart, leaving Wainwright to advise Tara that, regrettably, her usefulness has come to an end. A hostage is not required, Steed has been disposed of and Tara will be joining him very shortly. Wainwright recounts his evil scheme: to fill the world with his rot vapour from targeted pillar boxes, activated by a single device and destroying the wooden foundations of the entire world. He will hold the world to ransom for £100,000,000, a modest sum he feels sure Tara would agree. Cue Tara: You don't believe all this rot, do you? [10]

Steed arrives at Wainwright's premises (with Laurie Johnson's stalking chords from *The Superlative Seven* to carry him over the threshold) before he meets, fights and eventually defeats George and Kenneth in the foyer. He even overcomes a sword-swishing Sonia with the aid of the rot-gun, which blasts wood away from a suit of armour on the wall which falls onto her head, rendering her unconscious. Bursting in on Tara's holding cell (aka the kitchen), he is thrown off balance by Wainwright hurtling a pillar box at him in order to make his escape. Steed releases Tara with the aid of the rot-gun and then they both follow in hot pursuit. As Wainwright mounts the stairs, shooting at them as he does so, Steed blasts the underside of the staircase with the rot-gun and the floor gives way beneath Wainwright, who collapses into his casket: "The quickest undertakers in the business" quips Steed as they beat a hasty retreat, the building in ruins. [11]

The episode rounds off with possibly the only misfire in the production: a tag which doesn't seem to have a strong enough connection to the content around wood and disintegration and is, perhaps, the writer taking the rise out of the magic mushroom trend of the late 1960s. Tara is putting the finishing touches to the assembly of ingredients for Steed's Crusted Omelette of Mushroom, as the man in question relaxes on the sofa, reading a good book. She retrieves an enormous mushroom from the sitting room and carries it into the kitchen as Steed, incredulously, watches on.

The Rotters is the sort of class everyone aspires to. It is the Rolls Royce of Season 6, the diamond-encrusted bracelet of the overall programme and a positive jewel in the crown of British Television from the 1960s. It contains a stylish pair of cut-glass cads of the Terry Thomas mould who would be sorely displaced outside *Avengerland* but, within its tooled-up streets and champagne-swilling drawing rooms, they are the masters of all they survey. Comedy and surrealism are fused into a priceless work of art, sketched out by the sheer poetry of Dave Freeman's script and ably supported by Robert Fuest's technical know-how: the lighter shades of the villains going about their gentlemanly brand of rotten bounderism is counterplayed against the darker hues of an axe-wielding maniac pursuing our heroine through a tangled, complex maze of brooding woodland. Like *The Correct Way To Kill* before it, this episode showed that the sun never went down on the Empire while there was life in *Avengerland*.

© Matthew Lee

1. I agree with Matthew about George and Kenneth, the snobbish assassin henchmen. Like Needle, their obvious enjoyment and darkly amusing dialogue add both sparkling champagne and dramatic subversion to the episode, lifting it above formula fatigue, just as *You Have Just Been Murdered* represents a similar high point in the previous season.
2. I love this bizarre moment at the end of the teaser, but – as is the case in *Something Nasty in the Nursery* – how are we meant to react? To laugh with them? Empathise with their victim? Or, somehow, do both?
3. I presume that the plastic palace works as a piece of delayed significance, warning us that in this disturbing world where wood is 'doomed', plastic is the safer (if less aesthetically pleasing) solution.
4. The featureless modern apartment block seems a strange one here, lacking the character which the villains compliment it for possessing.
5. Here the darkly comic humour is more dark than comic.
6. The oddly camp eccentrics dressed as boy scouts – *Silent Dust*, *The House That Jack Built* etc. – always die, an unwritten law of *Avengerland*.
7. *And Soon the Darkness* (1970) is a wonderfully bizarre thriller, filmed in France, which brings together Clemens, Terry Nation, Robert Fuest, Albert Fennell and Laurie Johnson. Available on DVD through Optimum/Studio Canal, it remains a fascinating, atmospheric spectacle.
8. The special effects work well in this episode, as they had in the Peel colour season.
9. This fits in with Harold Pinter's vision of subtext for seemingly banal conversation: that "underneath what is being said, something else is being said".
10. Is Tara, on one level, asking us as viewers the same question about this bizarrely surreal episode?
11. Steed defeats Wainwright's entire team in under a minute.

THE INTERROGATORS

Filmed: October 1968

Exterior Locations:
Urban street
Open countryside
Earthworks
Minnow's apartment building
Caspar's apartment block
Fields
Country house

Sets:
Country House: corridor, interrogation room, bar, reception
Mother's Headquarters (through telephone box)
Caspar's apartment
Minnow's apartment
Tara King's apartment
Helicopter

THE INTERROGATORS

Main Character List:
Sergeant Blackie: fake TOHE unit
Lieutenant Roy Caspar: military intelligence
Colonel Mannering: fake TOHE leader
Tara King
John Steed
Mother
Rhonda: Mother's silent assistant
Corporal Rasker: fake TOHE unit
Wilson: informer
Izzy Pound: one-man-band, informer
Norton: forensics
Charles Minnow: military intelligence
Fillington: informer
Puffin: balloon seller, informer
Captain Soo: Mannering's second-in-command
Paul Mullard: trained with Tara King
Toy: henchman
Ling Ho: henchman

Rounding off the landmark fifteenth series of *Dixon of Dock Green* for BBC1 in December 1968, NJ Crisp's *Beserk* embodies a mission statement of the television which would follow in its wake:

"Any job. Any time. This is what we ask of our police. Most of us have some idea of the crises we may be called upon to face within any twenty-four hours. But what warning do they have?"

Edges were hardening on the drama landscape, a grittier view of the emerging world seen through the jaded eyes of a new generation. Detectives pushed to the brink, no longer comfortable behind a desk and facing criminals with fiendish nous and the violent wherewithal to mix it with the best of them. Private investigators with their own means, fighting back as best they could against crime and sinister goings-on.

The Interrogators represents the strongest foretaste of *The New Avengers* the original series proper would offer. Richard Harris and Brian Clemens' contribution to the sixth and final series of *The Avengers* is every bit as hard as the *Hot Snow* which melted almost eight years previously to give way to an iconic future. Often cited by Linda Thorson as one of her favourite episodes, this is probably down to the fact that she has some important work to do in a production which reduces Steed to second fiddle, remaining as he does for the most part confined to one set. [1]

The combination of the writing talents of Clemens and Harris seems an unusual one. Harris was a seasoned television and film veteran with a host of successful productions under his belt; he had also been responsible for the shape, tone and form that became *Man In A Suitcase*. It is perhaps his success in this ITC venture which brought him back into the *Avengers'* writing sphere after his contributions to the initial season with *Square Root Of Evil* and *Hunt The Man Down*. Later, he penned both the Diana Rigg episode *The Winged Avenger* and Tara King's *Game*. *The Interrogators* does not reflect the balance adopted in his other productions, where shades of light and dark are played out in concert. Was Clemens' role to level out the dark with a shade of the (at times absurdist) light and wrench a workmanlike script into *Avengerland*? [2] Boasting guest appearances from Hammer legend Christopher Lee (Dr. Frank N Stone in *Never, Never Say Die*) and Cardew Robinson (sinking his teeth into a second *Avengers* outing after digesting a slice of the scenery in *The £50,000 Breakfast*), the pieces of the puzzle fit together neatly under the directorial gaze of Charles Crichton (a past master of *The Avengers*).

Teasers are traditionally an appetiser before the main course. They hint at things to come; they tantalise an audience's televisual taste buds and lure them in with a hook. The 'dentist teaser' which unfolds here bucks the convention, and is essentially just the start of the episode itself. There is nothing particularly extraordinary or in sympathy with the *Avengers*. The interrogation could easily have sat in the episode proper as it does not contain a hook or *Avengers* quirk to make it a standout reason to continue viewing. [3]

Brian Clemens' influence is very much in evidence as the episode opens. Clemens has an economy with words and a brilliant mind when it comes to fashioning otherworldly within the ordinary world, the quirk within the plain and the menace behind the smile. Here, his contribution is clearly the nice touch of Steed driving into an average London street in which a bright red telephone booth is the landmark. Stepping inside and dialling zero, the entire rear panel of the booth opens as a door and within can be seen a cavernous room with a staircase. Tara hurries past him as he enters and their brief exchange of "Hello. Goodbye" "Urgent business?" "Very, Mother will tell you" is the sort of banter one expects from the leading players. One could almost conjure an image of Steed asking "Is there honey left for tea?" and Tara replying "Yes, in the pot that dead man slumped over the dresser is carrying" as gentle, over coffee chat. Part *Get Smart*, and undoubtedly *Avengers* movie, this is the stuff of *Avengerland*: the wheelchair-bound Mother (Patrick Newell) like a bloated bee buzzing around tall-stemmed plastic daffodils which his secretary, Rhonda, waters for no reason.

Crichton achieves an effective close-up shot during Caspar's continuing interrogation scene as Blackie throws a bucket of water over him while he sits in the dentist's chair. The water splashes against the camera lens and as a tight close-up of Philip Bond (as Caspar) fills the screen, water drips down the right-hand side of the shot in an impressive connection with the intensive framing of *The Ipcress File*. With Christopher Lee menacing in the background as Caspar wearily repeats his name rank and number, this is an effective and claustrophobic torture sequence. Continuing the *Ipcress* theme, Lee makes nice work of "Look at me, look at me" dialogue, smirking as he notes Caspar's pleas to rest. There is a powerful sense of light and dark, both thematically and in terms of lighting across this scene, especially in Lee's close-up shots when he recounts that he knows Caspar is responsible for running a string of informants gathering information, that their names are known only to a select few and that he wants those names. The tension of the scene could have been played out further but Harris and Clemens turn the tables on the audience when Rasker (the brilliantly gravelly Neil McCarthy) interrupts proceedings with tea and refreshments to revive them after "thirsty work". The entire mood changes, as Caspar is suddenly revived, engaging in banter over milk and sugar. Even Mannering changes his persona, playfully reminding Caspar not to forget where they left off, with the captor prompting the captive to admit that he was asking him about a chap who was a keen archer...

...who happens, at this time, to be practising his talents by firing an arrow into a large bullseye in the middle of a field. Striking the successful target, he lays down his bow and arrow near a tree and wanders off to collect the one imbedded into the target. Unseen by him, an arm reaches around the tree and steals his bow and arrows. As he retrieves the arrow from the target, he turns and is shocked to see his own bow and arrow trained on him from behind the tree. He cries out but is impaled on the target. Clemens' nice touch of the over-the-top verging just inside the credible and lending itself to telling the business end of murder, this scene is terrific in its visual execution as Crichton mounts a shot in which the arrow is seen to impale the man against the target, the arrow head jutting through the target as the camera pans down to the handful of arrows he releases as he slumps forward. The episode starts to fall into the repeated pattern of Mother/Steed are appalled/aghast/confused about what is going on, an informant is executed, Tara does something interesting somewhere, there is another interrogation /torture scene, and then the whole cycle starts all over again. Some scenes bristle with better dialogue than others between Mother and Steed during this process – the excellent retort from the former of "Confound it, Steed, one of his undercover informants was uncovered and killed!" is terrific stuff, and though it may lack subtlety, the identity of Caspar's next informant, Izzy Pound and his Incredible Marching Sound, is a card-carrying *Avengerland* resident in his own right.

His solitary scene in *The Interrogators* is a standout exercise in the utter madness of a man doing what he is doing where he is doing it and what happens to him as a result, matched with its perfect placement in the pattern of *The Avengers* as an overall tapestry. A discarded poster hailing Izzy and his talents, warning "No Visitors. Keep Clear" is always going to be an attraction for an assassin with too much time on his hands between engagements. A man blowing a trumpet, pounding a drum and marching around a disused quarry wearing a Rule Britannia hat and playing an accordion is having the (last) time of his life. He marches proudly back and forth whilst, high above, Blackie arrives with a rifle and gun-sight and prepares to take up a position to gun down Izzy (Johnny Laycock). Steed arrives on the scene and tries to summon Izzy's attention as a first shot rings out (but is muted by the trumpet) and then a second shot strikes home and kills Izzy. In one of those deliciously black *Avengers* touches, as the body tumbles down a small hill each thump against the earth renders a 'parp' from the accordion.

As the forensic team looks for clues in Caspar's apartment, Clemens and Harris make a brilliant nod towards Sir Arthur Conan Doyle's Sherlock Holmes with Norton (Neil Wilson) regarding the cigarette end found in Caspar's apartment:

"Hand-rolled. Custom-made. Mixture of Virginian and Turkish with a preponderance of Oriental herbs. Smoked by a right-handed male of medium build. Of course that's only in the nature of a wild guess at this stage. I'll need to get back to the laboratory to confirm my findings."

As the episode unfolds, viewers are introduced to the bar at which a series of unnamed officers relax over drinks between bouts of interrogation. A bewildered and beaten Caspar finds solace there over a not-too-dry martini with lots of ice and an olive. His surprise return to his apartment after the forensic team has left, encountering Tara (despite a continuity error in which Caspar does not bear any bruising or marks but later has a sticking plaster on his face and bruises), is a neat twist. He is later interrogated again by Steed and Mother in a bid to ascertain where he has been and why he has no recollection of events beyond a touring holiday by car to the south coast. Steed recommends summoning Charles Minnow, with whom Caspar trained, in a bid to stir memories. Mother sends Tara to pick him up. Arriving at his flat, Tara is fobbed off by Minnow (David Sumner) with an excuse that he will answer the door shortly, but in reality he has just met with Mannering and the pair make their escape via the service entrance, leaving her waiting. One can't imagine the delightful Emma Peel ever being kept waiting on any man's doorstep!

Act Two of the episode presents a near 'more of the same' routine. However, some of the dialogue does lift above the recurring theme, with a delicious address by Mannering through an opaque screen to Minnow somewhat summarising the strategic point of the story:

Mannering: Which do you think is worse, Minnow? The sound, or not knowing when it will begin again? You become your own torturer really. 'When?' your brain keeps asking. When will it start again? You steel yourself against the moment. You tense every nerve. But the sound doesn't come. Then suddenly...!

Minnow crumples to the floor, enduring another supersonic assault on his senses. There are strongly familiar *Avengers* traits here, with hallmarks of the Cathy Gale episode *The Wringer* here (where Steed underwent a similar form of psychedelic cat and mouse interrogation). Once again, Tara joins the forensic team at Minnow's apartment, and once again a cigarette end is discovered. The unfortunate repetition is, however, lifted above the ordinary in two delightful comic touches when Tara lunges for a recently fingerprint-dusted telephone to call Mother with news of the discovery, and his distasteful reaction to same:

"Any man who smokes such a revolting mixture must be evil incarnate!"

While Tara and Mother agree that a link has been found and that Minnow will talk and betray his contacts, viewers witness the further interrogation of the man in question under stark lighting and, literally, underfoot of Mannering. Steed reports back on the literal dead end he has found with Caspar's body and Mother reveals that Tara is pursuing the next lead, Phillington, who is Minnow's Number One contact. Steed hopes he is still alive and kicking ...

...and to a certain extent his hopes are well-founded. Resplendent in a bright blue tracksuit, Phillington exercises his football skills in the middle of a field, as he bounces the ball from foot to knee to head in practice. Totally absorbed, he fails to notice Blackie taking a hidden position behind some scrub bushes, before waiting until Phillington performs an aerial overhead kick and then gunning him down. Tara catches the ball as the assassin's bullet ends another life. She, like Steed, is (nearly always) too late. A nicely macabre and correct way to kill in the genuine style of *The Avengers*, the largest logistical problem with the episode is that the murders pile up too easily, with little or no traction made by Steed and Tara which weighs down the plot from moving beyond the Standard Scene 1 + Standard Scene 2 + Standard Scene 3 = Standard Scene 3 + Standard Scene 2 + Standard Scene 1 eternal loop.

The same cycle returns in Act Three as Tara reports on Phillington's death to Mother and requests the name of Minnow's second contact. This is followed by another interrogation scene (Mannering aggressively questioning Minnow), but at least there is a slight change of tempo when Minnow tries to make a break for it and the restrained tension of interrogation changes sharply to swift violence as Mannering strikes Minnow down and nurses a sore hand, for which he winces with distaste at actual physical violence. Here, Harris and Clemens bring something new to the table: the proposition that an interrogation without violence, an assault on the body and the mind without recourse to physical violence, is acceptable in the modern world. It is violence of a physical nature as a last resort which Mannering finds repugnant: a fascinating spin on the genre. Later, when he and Minnow have the tables turned again and they are reflecting on escape attempts being acceptable as par for the course and how Mannering used to box for his battalion, viewers witness Mannering's change of approach to more violent means as, after a conversation about Nosher Wright being a splendid chap, 'salt of the Earth', he strikes down Minnow once again and resumes the interrogation.

The life of an informant not being the lucrative living on easy street they may have hoped for, Mr. P Puffin ekes out a living with 'Balloons For Every Occasion' on a stall which mysteriously has no customers. Perhaps the fact that every man, woman and child in *Avengerland* can gainfully employ themselves with weapons readily to hand may have something to do with his recession-based trade. Tara pays the man in question a visit, warning him of imminent danger and that Mother has sent her to protect him. They are soon under siege when a shot rings out and Blackie, brazenly in the open, approaches them for a better, second shot. Tara uses a pair of scissors to burst a huge balloon in front of him and a fight ensues. A rather neat twist on the usual theme, the fight ends when Puffin retrieves Blackie's discarded weapon and fires a parting shot into his back.

Tara receives unexpected guests at her apartment: Mannering and Soo. Presenting bogus identification papers to gain admittance, they request Tara present her own credentials. This leads to a rather neat little exchange, pure Clemens class laced with Harris malice and menace in the undertone:

Mannering: You watch others, Miss King, we watch you.
Tara: Big brother?
Mannering: We had hoped that our interest might be slightly more paternal.

Here the hallmarks of Clemens' influence on a script emerge, with the nice *Avengers* touches of Mannering's instruction to escort Tara to Centre 53 to attend TOHE Course A7, which is covered by Secret Security Section 47 Subsection QR4932. Tara queries that the course is to begin immediately and she admits she is tired after her recent assignment. Mannering insists tiredness is the key to the training course, testing her limits. He insists higher authorities have drawn her away from her recent assignment to attend the course. He invites her to consult Mother if she needs verification. Tara counters, inviting him to telephone Mother instead. Mannering counter-counters by advising she has committed a cardinal error in even acknowledging Mother (as he dials a number). It is delicious stuff and worthy of the series.

Citing that she will now have ten demerit points against her name, he pretends to converse with Mother about a potential Bridge game in the near future. When she takes the telephone, it is revealed that Mannering has been speaking with Rasker, who activates a tape recording of Mother's voice, insisting he selected

Tara for the course and would be obliged if she attended and followed Mannering's instructions. Completing the call, Tara asks what a TOHE course is, and Mannering smiles, explaining it is "a Test of Human Endurance". [4]

All the plot cards are on the table and, with the chips down, the final gamble on a race to the finish gets underway. Minnow becomes the mouthpiece through which there is plot exposition, with Mother and Steed learning that he was hoodwinked into the interrogation by a sound recording of Mother's voice and taken to a house in the country at an undisclosed location in a closed van (this story is told in concert with the real-time events of Tara being taken to said same location). Mannering escorts her to her room, espousing the virtues of the course and the 'fine bunch' of men participating. As they advance down a corridor, Tara witnesses the brutal assault of an RAF officer. The dialogue is pure *Avengers* here as Mannering says "We do try to make their stay as pleasant as possible" and then the carrying of a semi-conscious soldier to a room by two oriental guards as Mannering admits "I'm a great believer in physical well-being".

Mother: Only forensics would make a special trip to say they hadn't found anything.

This is a beautiful aside between Mother and Steed when Norton arrives on the scene as Minnow realises he must have let secrets slip when his guard was down at the bar. Norton announces that he visited Tara's apartment to report his lack of findings, only to find she had disappeared – and so had her toothbrush. All that remained was a familiar discarded cigarette end. For a man intent on breaking the secrets of the opposition, Mannering needs to be awarded The Order of the Ashtray when he returns to the East!

Tara's interrogation begins with Mannering asking for everything she knows about John Steed, restraining Soo's more brutal methods for "later". Steed urgently presses Minnow for details of where the country house is so that they can reach her in time. When Minnow reveals that he was left with instructions to anticipate further tests beyond TOHE and that, if all went wrong, he was to release a pigeon and Mannering would contact him within the hour, this piques Steed's interest. The country house must be scarcely an hour away — "as the crow flies". Cue the flight of the fine feathered friend as Steed, with a "Follow That Pigeon!", boards a helicopter and sets off in pursuit of Minnow's pigeon (to the accompaniment of Laurie Johnson's 'Follow That Car' music of the Peel era). As Tara painfully endures a supersonic interrogation, the pigeon comes home to roost for Rasker as the helicopter descends on the grounds outside. Tara's interrogation is interrupted as Rasker raises the alarm that Minnow's pigeon has returned and he has spied Steed in the grounds. As all the officers and agents under interrogation assemble before Mannering, he issues firearms and explains that this is in the nature of a fresh test: they have arranged for an intruder to penetrate the area, and it is their job to deploy and fight him. Mannering lies, advising that the weapons are loaded with blanks, and instructs them to shoot to kill if they find the intruder, with ten merit points for the lucky winner.

There are strong shades of *Game* in this sequence and one can see where Harris' line of reasoning lay in the plot, a neat conceit but perhaps a little overused by this stage in the history of the series. As the episode draws to the business end of a punch and a kick, Tara overhears Mannering identifying the intruder as Steed. She later spies Soo lighting a cigarette that bears the hallmarks of the discarded cigarette ends she has witnessed being found. She renders him unconscious and endeavours to break out.

Armed with bayonet rifles, two oriental soldiers anticipate Steed's arrival through the French windows in the bar. He creates a diversion by pushing a discarded tree trunk through the windows and emerges through a different entrance where one of the officers lunges unsuccessfully at him with the bayonet and is parried by Steed's trusty bowler. The sheer delight of this series is that even the most menacing and lethal attacks are defeated by aid of bowler, champagne bottle and the like. The ordinary often defeats the extraordinary in *Avengerland*, and quite rightly so.

Steed finds himself cornered by a sea of armed agents. Sportsmanlike as ever, Mallard discusses that there are ten of them and if they all shoot Steed as once, they can claim a point each. Tara leaps in front of Steed to protect him and tells the men that the guns are loaded. It is a nice touch that Steed nonchalantly checks Tara's watch to see the time. Mannering arrives, insisting Tara is lying to claim the points for herself, and in a battle of wills Steed watches from behind her; Mannering increases the stakes by instructing the men to shoot both Steed and Tara; Steed intercedes and makes a suggestion around who is really bluffing: he recommends Mallard point the gun at Mannering and pull the trigger. If the weapon is loaded with blanks, Mannering will be safe. As Mallard fires, Mannering attempts to flee but Steed trips him up and he lands against the nearby wall, unconscious. Confiscating the weapons, Steed recommends rounding off proceedings with a drink – 'on the house'.

The tag scene – often superfluous in the Tara era as they do little more than make a fairly lacklustre comedic take on the overall episode seem somewhat painful in execution, unlike the brilliance of those performances in the Diana Rigg episodes – here is of secrets and interrogation, fitting for an episode which spends most of its time trying to argue its way out of four sets. Resplendent in evening wear, Tara is being interrogated by Steed at her apartment. He must have an answer – and by six o'clock! He insists she tell him the secret – of the recipe for a delicious soup they have just consumed. Tara reveals that the secret is yoghurt, which Steed, toasting her success with a glass of champagne, finds incredible. [5]

The Interrogators has a black heart of stone at its core and this works particularly well in sharpening the edges of the everyday and presenting a tale not too far from *The Professionals* and *The New Avengers*. As the world emerged from the 1960s into the grittier and harsher brown light of the 1970s, this sort of content would become the order of the day. As a sea-change from the quirkier aspects of the final run of *The Avengers* as an original series, Harris and Clemens deliver a script with a nice line in the bizarre (informants) and the bewildering (interrogators) with our heroes (Steed and Tara) always in hot pursuit, the prize flowers of Mother's plentifully-watered garden.

© Matthew Lee

1. Thorson considered herself "privileged to have worked with both Charles Crichton and Christopher Lee" (*Bowler Hats and Kinky Boots*, p. 322).
2. Michael Richardson suggests that Harris wrote the original draft script but that Brian Clemens "rewrote it not just for content but also for structure, to allow the leads freedom to work on other episodes concurrently." (*Bowler Hats and Kinky Boots*, p. 321).
3. I agree that the teaser is neither quirky nor self-contained, although the fact that a seemingly routine visit to the dentist becomes an intensive torture interrogation arguably adds a darkly avengerish twist.

4. There are shades of *Requiem* here, with a dark menace as a confused Tara is being interrogated, pre-interrogation.
5. The tag scenes in the monochrome Season 4 are beautifully simple, with our heroes heading off towards that 'bright horizon'. I would argue that the Peel colour tags are often closer to the Tara ones.

THE MORNING AFTER

Filmed: October-November 1968

Exterior Locations:
Ministry of TSI
Town streets
Rostarn Trading Company
Macey's Garage
Car park
The Eastern Hemisphere Trade Commission Building

Sets:
Rostarn Trading Company: office, corridor
Telephone box
Steed's car
Castle's Bank
Garage
Jeep
The Eastern Hemisphere Trade Commission Building: cellar
Van
Steed's mews apartment

THE MORNING AFTER

Main Character List:
Tara King
John Steed
Jimmy Merlin: 'quadruple agent'
Sergeant Hearn: soldier
Harold Thomas Cartney: nuclear bomb expert
Gregor Parninski: 'Major Parsons'
Brigadier Hansing: nuclear bomb expert
Jenny Firston: journalist
Yates: journalist

One of the noteworthy aspects that has arisen during the evolution of *The Avengers* is the breezy dynamic Steed maintains with his compatriots during each adventure. No matter how vile the villain, how dangerous the mission, how brutal the circumstances, the Ministry's top man can be always counted on to keep his cool, make time for a lighthearted quip and occasionally produce a flute of champagne to share with his partner. This whimsical, nonchalant relationship is at the core of the surreal world that the programme had come to reside in. Steed anachronistically engaging in witty banter with Cathy, Emma or Tara amidst a bizarre crisis greatly enhanced the sense of fantasy that is distinctive to the show.

Such arch interactions were not confined to just the people regularly partnered with Steed. In a show known to be littered with eccentric and entertaining characters, there have been a number of guest characters who have played off him just as well as any of the show's leading ladies. Notable examples included Kim Lawrence in *The Charmers*, Georgie Price-Jones from *The Girl From Auntie* and Hickey in *The Hour That Never Was*. Perhaps one of the best and most laudable of these 'substitutes' is James Merlin, a quadruple agent who is the master of the double, double, double, *double* cross. He made his appearance in *The Morning After*.

Merlin is a top ranked agent-for-hire who will provide any service for any client as long as the price is high enough. He's an opportunist who is always looking for the chance to make a bountiful sale, regardless of how he acquires his merchandise. Such a disposition of course doesn't make for a great foundation for loyalty or a stable relationship. Merlin is cunning, creatively resourceful and gifted, with a mischievous sense of humour. He exudes a cavalier manner and his own special brand of charm that often leads others to greatly underestimate him. In other words, he is a worthy counterpart to Steed. Even Steed, being totally on his guard, can still be outmanoeuvred by him. Rarely do we observe such a real match.

Consistent with his name, Merlin is a proficient trickster, producing such items as playing cards, keys and even a useful plot device. He performs sleight of hand so skilfully and so frequently that they become reflex actions serving as commentary on the circumstances of the plot.

While Merlin sadly makes only a single appearance, it happens in a story that is structured to make maximum use of his character. *The Morning After* is a smartly plotted episode that is in the same vein as *The Hour That Never Was*. Steed and Merlin fall victim to an experimental knockout gas that Merlin was attempting to exclusively sell. When they awake they find the town, where they are at, completely deserted and the mystery begins to unfold. Brian Clemens' script shares a number of similarities to the earlier story. We have the mysteriously empty location and atmosphere of bewilderment as the two men try to assess the situation. There are stark, barren buildings and the echoing silence of abandonment. There is even a moment with an empty milk float, soon followed by an unknown man inexplicably gunned down by soldiers enacting martial law. The first half of the episode is focused from the perspective of Steed and Merlin trying to discern the truth. It is later uncovered that the town has been evacuated owing to the discovery of a live nuclear bomb, with government soldiers tasked to dismantle the offending object.

Halfway through, the story shifts gears, integrating the classic hoax motif so often used on the show. The militia present are discovered to include a number of mercenaries who our hero initially suspects may be there to sabotage the dismantling efforts. In a further twist, it is revealed that these brutes are in fact under the orders of the commander in charge, Brigadier Hansing. He is an embittered mastermind who has plotted the bomb scare and evacuation as all part of an elaborate ruse to, in fact, *assemble* an atom bomb that will be used to extort the country out of untold millions.

It is interesting that Merlin's part in the script plays more like a substitute Mrs. Peel than a Miss King. A person who is more mature, sophisticated and witty. The script does have more of a feel of a monochrome Emma Peel adventure with the duo working together in true partnership to resolve the situation. Granted this partner did not have much choice in helping Steed out. Merlin comes off in many ways as very different. Being male and technically an adversary, Steed's dialogue with him is at times antagonistic and more sarcastic. There is also a bit of disapproving contempt and distrust that is not confined to a pair of handcuffs. We have Steed who, for all his off-the-cuff and decadent demeanour, is still very much a patriot and a loyal servant to her Majesty's government. This sensibility easily clashes with a man whose own allegiance is only towards money, however charismatic he may be. There is a constant push and pull between the two that is energetic but subtle, with each getting a chance to push the other's buttons. In a way the two are very much alike, but having taken different paths. Steed's agitation with Merlin may partly stem from looking into a dark mirror he would prefer not to gaze at. Such a conflict allows the viewers to see a different side of Steed and allows Patrick Macnee a rare chance on the programme to stretch his acting muscles in a more nuanced fashion. [1]

Despite the verbal jabs and Merlin's sense of self-preservation, the two of them make a highly effective pairing. They are both such seasoned operatives, they know how to communicate with each other through body language and work together. This is exemplified by their first encounter with the alleged Sergeant Hearn (played by a typically boisterous Brian Blessed) and his men where they skilfully outmanoeuvre these soldiers and avoid getting shot, all while still being bound together. In between their bickering, the two men point and counterpoint each other to effectively ascertain the truth. Merlin is even the one to realise that there are hired killers infiltrating the troops. For the purposes of this story, having an association with the unsavoury proves beneficial. [2]

Even after all the surprises of the story have revealed themselves and other characters have been introduced, the focus remains on the Steed/Merlin relationship. The Brigadier and his mercenaries are only given as much attention as needed to unveil each plot twist and layer of the extortion plan. Not much is given to their characters. The weight of the Brigadier's villainy and how dangerous an opponent he may be is never firmly established. By the final scene, it is clear he is not presented as much of a threat at all.

More time is given to the gradual, but not unexpected, softening of Merlin, where he becomes genuinely fond of Steed and in this instance turns into a true ally. At first he manages to escape, leaving Steed at the mercies of one of the villains. But Merlin has a moment of conscience (which he firmly denies) and returns to save him. He even provides the means to defeat the villains. Ever the greedy opportunist, Merlin had stolen several samples of the sleep gas with the intention to sell exclusively to several governments.

Despite any consternation, Steed and Merlin come together in the end to round up the villains. They are no match for our heroes and the conflict is resolved rather quickly. This might be Steed's most formidable team-up over the course of the series. After all, he is basically fighting alongside another version of himself. As two Englishmen who are urbane, smart and dangerous, an assault from

Steed squared is more than any group of opponents can handle. It is a fitting end that Steed softens enough in his attitude to let Merlin go. However, Merlin can't help but pull one last piece of trickery to remind Steed that regardless of what may have occurred, they remain 'best enemies', at best.

© Frank Hui

1. The idea of Merlin providing a 'dark mirror' for Steed is an intriguing one, reminding us of the videotape and monochrome Steed who was, arguably, a more consistently complex character.
2. Ironically, it proves to be vital and Merlin's presence blurs the boundaries between hero/villain. Possibly Steed does as well, as Frank suggests.

LOVE ALL

Filmed: November 1968

Exterior Locations:
Ministry building
Suburban street
City streets
Roberts' house: façade
Bellchamber Brothers perfumiers
Tara King's street

Sets:
Ministry building: corridor, co-ordination and control room/Sir Rodney's office, Tait's office, Roxby's office, phone booth
Mother's HQ (manhole entrance)
Casanova Ink: corridor, office, printing room
John Steed's mews apartment
Bellchamber Brothers perfumiers
Tara King's apartment

LOVE ALL

Main Character List:
Martha Roberts: cleaner
Sir Rodney Kellogg: missile re-deployment
Tait: missile re-deployment
Basil Roxby: missile re-deployment
George Fryer: missile re-deployment
John Steed
Tara King
Mother
Rhonda: Mother's silent assistant
Metcalfe: security
Frances: ministry employee
Nigel Bromfield: inventor of Rosemary Z Glade, mastermind
Freeman: henchman/printer at Casanova
Bellchamber: perfumier
Grimshaw: policewoman
Thelma: Casanova Ink
Athene: Casanova Ink

Steed: I know love is meant to be blind, but this is ridiculous.

Philip Levene was the second most prolific scriptwriter in the film era of *The Avengers*. He had, most famously, created the Cybernauts, but was also responsible for a number of other classic plots. He contributed exactly half the stories for the Peel colour era and wrote three early episodes for the Tara King season, including the delightful *Get-A-Way!* He had been installed as the season's script editor, providing the filmed *Avengers* experience which incoming producer John Bryce lacked. However, following the production chaos highlighted elsewhere in this book, he sadly departed, amidst disagreements with Brian Clemens who wanted to take back editing control/responsibilities – despite ostensibly replacing Levene with Terry Nation as a 'figurehead' script-editor. With both Roger Marshall and Levene now consigned to the '*Avengers* past', Clemens sought fresh creative input for this troubled season. A number of writers penned a single episode; however, the vast majority of the stories were written by just four men: Clemens, who was obviously an old hand by now and who could 'turn around' a script in a couple of days if need be; Tony Williamson, who had contributed two of the best Peel monochrome episodes, *The Murder Market* and *Too Many Christmas Trees*; Nation, whose efforts veer wildly from the magnificently moody and surreal *Noon Doomsday* to the sci-fi flops *Invasion of the Earthmen* and *Thingumajig* [1]; and a surprise fourth writer, Jeremy Burnham.

Burnham had been involved in the very first filmed episode, *The Town of No Return*, delighting viewers in the role of Jonathan Amesbury, a seemingly charming, bumbling vicar who turns out to prefer funeral requiems to the Wedding March. He went on to appear in both colour seasons, in *The Fear Merchants* and *The Forget-Me-Knot*. Burnham was keen to transform himself from actor to writer and Clemens' decision to hire him to write five scripts turned out to be a master stroke. Burnham's vision of *Avengerland* fits the psychedelic Tara King era perfectly. His Routemaster bus in *False Witness* is Mother's best HQ, a highlight of the season. It is, arguably, *his* episodes – such as *You'll Catch Your Death* and *Love All* – which best capture the new spirit of the show, with affluent London street footage and witty drug-related plots in which the real and surreal playfully merge.

Love All's teaser sets up a perfectly realistic scenario: we enter the 'fag end' of a dry, top secret ministerial meeting. Sir Rodney Kellogg seems to epitomise the stereotypical trustworthy, upper class civil servant. However, as the second part of the pre-title sequence demonstrates, there is another side to this minister of the crown. Sir Rodney may operate within an office called 'Co-ordination and Control', but he appears to have no self-control when it comes to the cigarette-clenching cleaner, Martha, who professes to be interested in everything about 'Rodders', especially his "secrets". Not for the first time in the series, *The Avengers* is poking satirical fun at the precariously thin veneer of respectability and feeble security in exclusive *Avengerland* settings. Here, it is Steed who describes as "impossible" security leaks coming from a department – missile re-deployment – where everyone has a "top Q.R. Security Rating". Mrs. Peel said much the same thing in *Something Nasty in the Nursery*. In both episodes these top government ministers have been duped by mind-altering drugs, but there is also an inference that no one – regardless of social background or professional seniority – should be automatically deemed 'above suspicion'. In *The New Avengers* episode *Angels of Death* this will be taken a step further, with both Gambit and Purdey concluding that the inside worm *must* be someone labelled as 'above suspicion'.

The playful nature of the drama is demonstrated early on when Steed arrives at the Ministry. Having heard three shots fired, he discovers Sir Rodney holding the used gun: "Three shots – very civil. You even shoot people in triplicate." The light-heartedness extends to the faintly ridiculous sight of the zombified, middle-aged Rodders 'in love' and then Mother batting in a cricket net while complaining that they are on "a sticky wicket". Even the security guards are part of the farcical spectacle as they are dressed in formal attire like London commuters, with matching bowlers. Much of the humour derives from the fact that Tara – without even leaving HQ – has second guessed the root of the problem – "infatuation" – simply from Steed's description of Sir Rodney: "looking into infinity with an idiotic smile on his face." Mother rejects the suggestion out of hand. Like Steed, all he can see is that 'unimpeachable' polish of social veneer: "Whoever heard of a respectable gentleman like Sir Rodney losing his head over a woman. I've near heard anything so ridiculous in my life." While Sir Rodney's behaviour *is* ridiculous – and for the time being inexplicable – it is not as silly as Steed and Mother's dismissal of Tara's continuing suggestions of love conquering all, particularly as they have no better suggestion for why a 'respectable' civil servant would jump through a window twenty feet from the ground.

A more subtle humour comes when the 'real' Martha answers the front door of her 'aunt' to Sir Rodney and manages to suppress any hint of surprise that the infatuated knight has tracked her to her home. Veronica Strong – writer Jeremy Burnham's wife – plays the two roles with aplomb, almost convincing us that they are two different characters. Martha's murder of Sir Rodney, moments later, lacks a disturbing dramatic undercurrent, the darkness simply belonging to the gallows humour which prepares us – though not love-sick Rodders – in advance:

Rodney: You'll never regret this, I promise.
Martha: But you might.

When Martha is picked up by the mastermind, both the writer and director ensure that we don't get to see his face, which is similarly kept off-camera in their earlier telephone conversation. The episode may be one of the lighter Tara-era soufflés, but mystery plays an important role and the clever plot, like an onion, will only be revealed one layer at a time. The first clue has been left by Martha, spraying herself with 'Reckless Abandon' in more than one sense. It seems odd that it is left to the inexperienced Tara to warn old timer Steed that "in cases like these you've got to consider every -" ...line of inquiry, or *scent* in this case.

Bellchamber Brothers' 'Perfumiers Extraordinary' boutique offers the episode's first memorable set. Drawing on the show's videotape past, it demonstrates how simply a well-made set can be created. A pair of gothic pillars, matched by a pair of glass arched French windows, a central chandelier and a table of elaborately-shaped, coloured perfume bottles fore-grounded suffices. The Bellchamber brother who is present provides us with an *Avengers* stock character: the quirky, eccentric shop owner. In this case, a man who states that no one ever asks for him:

Bellchamber: You see, I've got no personality.
Tara: What! None at all?
Bellchamber: Not an iota.

The list of 'Reckless Abandon' clients allows *Love All* to return to the running gag of Mother's snobbery and naivety about the possibility of respectability and villainy being bed-fellows. The Honourable Malvena Treadworth Smith cannot possibly be a suspect, for example, as she is a Platoon Leader in the Girl Guides. If the story pokes fun at the socially exclusive world in which the Avengers often step, it also satirises the male chauvinism of the ministers themselves. These are men who – as Tait informs Steed/us – are "confirmed" bachelors, for whom women are an "anathema", "extraordinary creatures" who simply don't "tick" in the same way as these dry civil servants. And yet, at the same time, they are falling in love, like a house of cards, with an unattractive, working class 'scrubber'. As in Shakespeare's *A Midsummer Night's Dream*, where a little fairy dust can make a nobleman fall in love with an ass, there is a suggestion here that men mistake lust or infatuation for 'love', and that whatever 'magic' is being used, it seems to work all too easily on these top-secret ministers. The episode's title hints at the sixties' sexually permissive culture. The ministers may be educated gentlemen from 'good families' but is their "dedicated" misogyny simply covering up a fear of women? Does it represent an unnatural suppression of a natural desire? Later on, the micro-dots will excuse them for their reckless abandon, but it cannot explain away their usual attitudes and behaviour. They even carelessly leave the top-secret dossier out on desks in unlocked offices!

The fight scene at Tara's flat once again reminds us that this is a delightfully light soufflé, Freeman's battle with Miss King taking place while an ill-tempered Mother is kept waiting impatiently on the other end of the telephone line. Tara's flat is a perfect 'playground' set for action-adventure, Freeman crashing through the banisters before a final tussle on the lower floor. Linda Thorson is at her comic best as an out-of-breath Tara, apologising to Mother for keeping him waiting. Never mind, the dead henchman's ring has revealed a second clue: Casanova Ink.

The Casanova Ink outer corridor is a gloriously surreal, delightful set, with giant-size book spines revealing ludicrous titles: from the unlikely – such as *Love in an Igloo*, *Love in the Bernese Oberland*, *Love Among the Pigmies* – to the clichéd *Love Makes the World Go*

Round and the banal (or softly pornographic) *Love in an Upstairs Room*. Even the entrance is through one of these spines, opening to reveal a woman in mid-flow, discussing sexual bondage:

"I know you're there. I sense the aura of evil that surrounds you. I beg you, untie my hands. I can hear you. Your breathing."

Thelma's theatrical performance – played with comedic skill by Patsy Rowlands – is amusingly over-the-top, but it is simply the *entrée* for the wonderfully avengerish reveal that pulp romantic fiction writer Rosemary Z Glade is actually a piano-shaped computer: "every romantic situation in the world is built into her memory circuits. The keys activate the situations." The piano, as Thelma puts it, creates "instant romance". On one level, this amusing scene takes the plot forward, yet on another it offers us a critique of the capitalist 'romance industry', not unlike the marriage bureau in *The Murder Market*. The books consist of randomly assembled pieces of clichéd dialogue and hackneyed description, rather than heartfelt emotional literature. What does this tell us about Casanova's readers? [2] Romance/love becomes an automated piece of pulp fiction, consumed – presumably – by sad, lonely people who naively believe in 'instant romance'. (Or *Love on the Moon*, come to that.) It is as artificial and hollow as the 'love' generated by the micro dots stored in the back offices. As Steed leaves Casanova Ink, the mastermind of the diabolical love plot is finally revealed, two thirds of the way into the episode. Once again, rather than darker drama, his appearance gives rise to more wit and humour:

Thelma: Mr. Steed, this is Mr. Bromfield.
Steed: *The* Mr. Bromfield? The mastermind who created Rosemary?
Thelma: Mr. Bromfield's a genius...
Steed: I agree.
Thelma: And ever so passionate!

Steed: I'll take your word for it.

The love drug is used for comic effect throughout *Love All*, both before and after the secret 'formula' is revealed. When Tara first encounters Bromfield, for example, we get the wonderful exchange: "I love you"; "Who doesn't?" The formulaic reveal by the mastermind is a fascinatingly plausible one: micro-dots projecting subliminal messages through the pages of a book. I also like the reason given by Bromfield for choosing the emotion of love:

"Love is the most potent emotion in the Universe. Unlike jealousy, hate, fear, love is the emotion of co-operation. The man or woman in the thrall of love is as easily manipulated as soft putty."

Love All is, as I have suggested, a light comic recipe, in stark contrast to the action adventure of *All Done With Mirrors*, or the psychologically dark and powerful films such as *Stay Tuned*, *Requiem* and *Take-Over*. However, herein lies the one fly in the ointment, which arrives in the build up to the fight finale. It is as if the writer and director suddenly worry that they have cooked up a fluffy story without enough substance. As Bromfield and his Casanova team prepare to flee – mission accomplished – the mastermind tells Tara to throw herself from the fifth floor window:

"You don't like heights? But if I asked you to, you'd step out onto that ledge, wouldn't you?...If you knew there could never be anything between us; if I told you your love was hopeless...There'd be no point in your continuing to live would there?"

The scene is played unpleasantly straight, the increasingly sinister score confirming this. Even murderous Martha is shocked. It is so unavengerish and out of keeping with the rest of the episode that it represents a 'wrong' ingredient which threatens to spoil Burnham's otherwise perfect recipe. When Steed saves Tara from dropping to her death, the darker moment continues. [3] A furiously bewildered

Steed demands: "What's the matter? What are you trying to do?" "Trying to end it all – you should have let me fall." The scene does not 'spoil' the entire episode, of course, but its three and a half minutes certainly tarnish it, representing a false note in an otherwise faultless episode.

At the halfway point of *Love All*, Mother complains that "this wretched affair's taking on a pattern and I don't like the picture." His comment works on a self-referential level, reminding us that there is a formulaic approach to Burnham's script. Nevertheless, the liberal sprinkling of verbal wit and humour; some memorable sets and location shooting in cosmopolitan London; a cluster of eccentric guest characters; an almost absurd fusion of surrealism and realism; and a subtle unravelling of both the plot and the mastermind's identity ensure that – despite Mother's reservations – we enjoy an almost perfect 'picture'.

© Rodney Marshall

1. Nation's scripts were often heavily re-written by Brian Clemens, or taken from an original Clemens idea. Nation never 'got' *The Avengers*, unlike Burnham who instinctively understood where the show had evolved to at this stage.
2. I might have added, what does this tell us about the industry itself which financially benefits from its flogging of pulp fiction to these people? Like the Togetherness marriage bureau, they pretend to offer a sensitive 'romantic service', but are only interested in making money.
3. Patrick Macnee injured himself in the filming of this dramatic sequence, later discovering that he had cracked some ribs. (*Bowler Hats and Kinky Boots*, p. 326). I can't help but read this on a symbolic level. The scene represents a harmful break in the episode's otherwise perfect structure.

TAKE ME TO YOUR LEADER

Filmed: November 1968

Exterior Locations:
Airfield
Cremorne Hotel: façade
Urban streets
London mews
Rehearsal building
Tara King's street
Train station luggage entrance
Church

Sets:
Shepherd's apartment
Mother's HQ (warehouse): screen room, makeshift hospital bedroom, warehouse store room
Giant crates
Hotel: corridor, bedroom
Rehearsal building: doorway, rehearsal room
Telephone box
Tara King's apartment
Colton House: outer room, karate room
Timber store
Crypt

TAKE ME TO YOUR LEADER

Main Character List:
Holland: agent
Shepherd: enemy agent
Mother
Rhonda: Mother's silent assistant
Tara King
Captain Andrews: agent
Howard Trent: enemy agent
Phillipson: 'scarecrow' agent
Major Glasgow: gadgets expert
Dr. Stanmore: doctor in hospital
John Steed
Condon: enemy agent
Audrey Long: teacher
Sally Graham: precocious child
Colonel Stonehouse: department leader
Cavell: enemy agent
Captain Tim: karate expert
Williams: enemy agent
Jackson: enemy agent

One of the characteristics of *The Avengers* that has become a staple of the show is the array of eccentric or offbeat characters that populates their world. *Take Me To Your Leader*, like most of Terry Nation's scripts for the series, exemplifies this aspect very well. *Take Me To Your Leader* is a lighthearted rift on *Mission: Impossible*, one of the most popular spy shows ever created in the US. The signature motif of the programme was that each episode's assignment was delegated through a tape recorder. After the instructions were given out, the recorder would self-destruct in ten seconds.

The script applies a similar gimmick to this tale where Steed and Tara are tracking down an arch-villain through a chain of contacts. This chain extends between an enemy organisation and a traitor at the Ministry who has been passing on important secrets. Each set of instructions is passed along using a voice-imprinted briefcase that progresses with each successive key that is applied to it. It is also rigged with explosives to prevent tampering. Such a plot setup allowed Nation to litter the script with a broad mix of characters, the majority being typically of the colourful or offbeat variety. Under close examination an intriguing pattern emerges with this assortment of baddies that our heroes cross swords with. It's a pattern that may or may not have been part of a deliberate plan conceived by the writer. Throughout the story, Steed and Tara encounter characters who are presented with personality traits or in circumstances that align to each of the Seven Deadly Sins of Christian teachings. It is a rare instance where one can infer such a complete representation of the Cardinal Sins.

IRA or wrath (Part I). Wrath is something the audience witnesses both in the prologue and the first major scene. It comes in the form of lethal violence, courtesy of the musician-agent, Shepherd. A Ministry agent invades his home to acquire the briefcase in question. Shepherd does not take kindly to an intruder entering his domain and doles out a quick, deadly response. Further emphasising this air of angry consequences is Fang the wonder dog. Fang appears in the initial act and is the first link in the chain, delivering the case to his contact, Howard Trent. However, the hound quickly detects one of the Ministry agents who is camouflaged and spying on them. Fang pounces and reacts with full ferocity. No surprise since, after all, most folks don't care for voyeurs.

ACEDIA or sloth. Sloth is traditionally categorised as physical or even spiritual laziness. Sloth has also been defined as a failure to do things that one should do or has been tasked. In this circumstance, we can apply that to the above mentioned Trent. He is the second link in the chain and crashes his bike while trying to escape from Ministry forces. Net result is he becomes hospitalised and bedridden, unable to complete his assignment.

AVARITIA or avarice: What are little girls made of? In traditional rhyme:

> *Sugar and spice and all things nice*

In *Avengerland*:

> *Securities and gold and every coin she can hold*

Ah, avarice: the unending yen for material possession. Shakespeare wrote that a love of money is the root of all evil. And no greater consort to coinage was ever presented on the show than Miss Sally Graham, the fourth link in the chain. Money is her god and, as she tells Steed, her susceptibility to bribes is one of her few failings. Her exchange with our hero is one of the highlights of the episode. [1] Steed offers her 10 shillings for information on the case. She counters with a demand of £25. We're talking about an amount that would be ten-fold that today. She stingingly warns Steed that he wouldn't want to take advantage of her just because she is a little girl. Small wonder that he suspects she's one of the gnomes of Zurich. There is little doubt that Sally was destined to grow up to be a yuppie corporate raider. It would also come as no surprise if she became one of the financial architects whose maneuverings led to the economic collapse of 2008.

LUXURIA or lust. The next link in the chain is a man name Cavell. Although characterised as a highly skilled combatant, he is little more than a vain, lecherous weasel with a bad toupee. He is even deficient in the fortitude to face someone he is about to kill. He is quite open about his desire for Tara, explicitly 'hitting on her' in a patronising manner. He is still aroused by Tara when ordered to eliminate her. That passion proves to be his undoing as Steed and Tara use it to outwit him and find out the location of the sixth link in the chain. He is left handcuffed and humiliated but still admiring his beautiful assailant. [2]

SUPERBIA or pride. Our next link is Captain Tim, a highly adept karate expert. Captain Tim has quite the masculine ego. He's suspicious when Tara shows up to drop off the case. He cannot possibly believe this mere girl is his contact Cavell. He's been told that Cavell is the only person who could beat him in a fight. In his perception, there's no way Tara could be the one. She is forced to do battle in a fiercely choreographed fight that is made all the more tense with its lack of an accompanying score. Captain Tim is a dangerous and brutal opponent, as seen by Tara receiving a painfully realistic punch to the face that would automatically evoke a wince and grimace from any viewer.

With some discreet assistance from Steed's bowler, Tara wins the fight and ends up breaking the Captain's knee. He is sufficiently humbled and begs Tara to take his place to deliver the case, owing to his injury. It is a moment that can be symbolically viewed as paying deference and yielding to a superior opponent. They say prides comes before a fall. It is no different with the Captain and fall he does. The final blow to his sin of pride comes with the man pleading with Tara not to reveal to anyone that he lost a fight to her.

IRA or wrath (Part II). The seventh link is the violent Shepherd who appeared in the prologue. Steed engages the man but tries to reason with him, saying how opposed he is to violence and asks him politely where the next key for the case is. Of course he says all this after delivering a powerful blow across Shepherd's jaw. Rather than try to be patient and outwit Steed, he goes with his first instincts and resorts to killing. The audience knows how foolish that will be and our murderous musician ends up dying flat and off-key.

INVIDIA or envy. Envy, like some of the other sins, represents an insatiable desire. It is a form of jealousy where one covets another's place or standing. While that could easily apply to many a secret villain, in this case the eighth link in the chain actually fills that role with a bit of dramatic license. Link eight presents itself in the form of two different men appearing with the same case. They diverge, with Steed and Tara separately trailing each one. So we have the true case and a fake: a decoy agent carrying a doppelganger, a mere pretender hoping to fool others that it's real.

Sadly, Tara follows the envious imposter and barely manages to escape fatal consequences. After doing so, she commandeers a car from a local clergyman. In keeping with all these abounding sins, Tara pays this man of the cloth for his vehicle with a bottle of champagne. This can almost be seen as an exchange of sacramental wine, cleansing our heroine as she flees from the clutches of envy.

GULA or gluttony. Gluttony is the over-indulgence and over-consumption of anything to the point of waste, to the expense of those in need. While traditionally associated with sustenance, it can also be interpreted as selfishness; essentially placing concern with one's own interests above the well-being or interests of others. What better way to describe a traitor in Steed's organisation than someone whose own greed and desires are fulfilled at the expense and safety of various agents? Colonel Stonehouse is that traitor. He fits the scenario of the ageing civil servant who longs for more than his severance can afford. He wants the luxuries and indulgences that can be provided by the vast payments for his dastardly deeds. That desire, like with many of the others in this episode, proves to be his downfall. The man might have actually escaped with his crimes, but his greed got the better of him and his judgment. Too anxious to see the payment for his evil acts and too rushed to handle the means of his future paradise, he fails to realise he has mistakenly opened one of those doppelganger cases of envy, and dies from its trap.

© Frank Hui

1. Am I alone in thinking that children are out of place in *Avengerland*?
2. Does the need to eliminate her actually *increase* his desire, in a sadistic form of sexual power game?

STAY TUNED

Filmed: December 1968

Exterior Locations:
Urban streets
Country roads
Father/Mother's driveway

Sets:
Steed's mews apartment
Psychiatrist's office
Tara King's car
Father/Mother's office
Taxi
Tara King's apartment
Kreer's house: hall, conditioning room, villains' study
Forensics garage

STAY TUNED

Main Character List:
John Steed
Proctor: henchman
Tara King
Doctor Meitner: psychiatrist
Father
Collins: agent
Taxi driver
Travers: forensics expert
Sally: driver of Italian car
Kreer: hypnotist villain in Fitzherbert Street
Lisa: villain
Wilks: henchman
Mother
Rhonda: Mother's silent assistant

As the old saying goes, variety is the spice of life. So true, and certainly true of Season 6 of *The Avengers*, the most varied season of all. This was mainly due to the wealth of talented writers who contributed to it, as opposed to only two writers who had written the bulk of the previous season. There was a rich diversity of styles in Season 6, from the slapstick of *Look Stop Me* to the dark horrors of *Take-Over*. One particular genre that *The Avengers* regularly returned to was the psychological thriller. *Too Many Christmas Trees* was a Season 4 highlight with Steed battling against a mysterious intrusion of his mind. *Death's Door* was a standout Season 5 episode and quite unlike the rest of the season, dealing with several inexplicable mental breakdowns. An earlier Season 6 episode, *My Wildest Dream*, explored the frailty of the human mind in quite a disturbing fashion. *Stay Tuned* returned to this concept in a darker fashion as it explored the susceptibility of one mind in particular. Our hero, John Steed.

Stay Tuned could very easily have been called *Déjà vu*. Evoking memories of *The Hour That Never Was*, the teaser where Steed informs the operator that he is going away is repeated in virtually the same way, except that the carnations are now dead, and on opening his front door he is not confronted with his unseen assailant, but by Tara informing him that he's already been on holiday.

Steed's visit to the psychiatrist offers theories as to Steed's amnesia, such as emotional stress, and even the token blow on the head, but the psychoanalysis is wisely kept to a minimum in *Stay Tuned*. Writer Tony Williamson cleverly offers us clues in this scene, without revealing too much of the mystery too soon. In his Austrian accent (echoes of Freud!), Dr. Meitner informs Steed that as he has no history of amnesia, his condition is temporary. "You will see visual triggers that will ignite sparks and then a conflagration, and your memory returns with the blanks filled in." By alerting us as to how Steed will regain his memory, Williamson has cleverly planted a seed in the viewer's mind.

The theory of psychological triggers now firmly planted in our subconscious, we are then taken completely by surprise in the following scene, which finds Steed grabbing the steering wheel from Tara in order to crash the car. The word 'Bacchus' triggered this sudden and destructive reaction, adding a new far more sinister layer to this deepening mystery.

Steed and Tara's visit to Father could be viewed as a presentiment to Steed's condition of being unable to 'see' what is happening around him. Father is holding the fort while Mother is away, and in true *Avengers* fashion Father is a woman. It is never made clear what department Steed is actually working for, but presumably it is a neighbouring department of MI5 or MI6. Even though Father is only the temporary head of Steed's department in *Stay Tuned*, this creates a situation 27 years prior to Judi Dench's role as M in *Goldeneye*, which of course in itself echoes the real life appointment of Stella Rimington as Director General of MI5 in 1992. Bless *The Avengers* for always pushing the boundaries of acceptance, and this liberal attitude which was years ahead of its time in the 1960s also creates a situation of not only a woman running Steed's department, but a blind woman. After Steed leaves Father's office, she summons Collins, whom she assigns as Steed's shadow, providing a witness to Steed's 'blindness'.

No psychological thriller worth its salt is complete without a word association scene. Tara's attempt at this popular practice is seemingly fruitless, resulting in a frustrated Steed uttering "It's no good. I can't remember. I just want to be in Tibet." A strange statement to make admittedly, but it provides Steed with the trigger his memory needed. Steed slips out of his apartment while Tara is making coffee, and there follows a beautifully filmed scene, possibly the most darkly atmospheric sequence to ever grace an *Avengers* episode. Hearing chimes from outside his black cab, Steed asks to be dropped off. He then walks along a deserted street, which in itself places this scene firmly in *Avengers* territory, the solitude of a deserted location adding to the tension, and successfully creating a world of mirrored reality. The whistling and the footsteps that follow Steed along the street add menace to an already suspenseful scene. The fact that Steed is unable to see his pursuer indicates to the most discerning viewers that some form of hypnosis has likely taken place, but this only adds another interesting layer to an already intriguing mystery. [1]

The opening scene is repeated a second time, which creates an air of increasing *déjà vu*, yet as with the first repeat, the scene then cleverly veers off in a new direction. On this occasion, Steed notices the dead flowers and places the phone down, suggesting the first crack in the wall of manipulation that has been built around him.

Hitchcockian elements abound in *The Avengers*, and never more so than in *Stay Tuned*. Parallels of the psychiatrist's unraveling of the patient's tormented mind in *Spellbound* can be found in *Stay Tuned*, but there are also traces of *Vertigo* to be found here, as it becomes increasingly clear that Steed's mind is being manipulated and guided by another's will, albeit in *Stay Tuned* with the aid of hypnosis.

What Steed needs at this point is a stroke of luck, and this he receives from the lady who tracks him down after grazing his Bentley. Life's dilemmas can often sort themselves out by unexpected happenstance, and this sudden turn of events offers Steed his first real breakthrough. It also offers a lighter moment in the midst of this dark unsettling episode, reminding us of the fine balance of comedy and suspense *The Avengers* always created so successfully. After Steed kisses her and promises to take her out for the best celebration she's ever had, she utters, "Gosh. Then honesty is the best policy."

The combined efforts of two agents is surely preferable to one working alone, yet in *Stay Tuned* Steed and Tara decide to infiltrate the house with the Chinese doorknocker separately. [2] This could be viewed as a dramatic ploy that offers a more perilous situation. After all, there would be no suspense awarded to a scene whereby all the villains are neatly banged to rights.

After Tara has entered the house in Fitzpatrick Street, it isn't long before she's confronted by Kreer, played with a suitably satanic charm by Roger Delgado, a role that appears to signal his future role as The Master in *Doctor Who*. If ever an actor had been required to portray The Devil himself, then a director need have looked no further than Delgado. A sinister and deadly charm literally oozes from his every pore, and it's just a pity the role of Kreer wasn't expanded more in order to cast a sinister shadow over the whole affair. Brief though his role was, Delgado still provides a memorable villain in *The Avengers*' rogue gallery.

After defeating Delgado, Tara is confronted by another memorable villain in the shape of Lisa, played with exquisite wickedness by Kate O'Mara. O'Mara had a most interesting face, and had the allure of an untamed exotic beauty with almost feline qualities. She looked far too wild and bad to ever be an Avenger, but she had all the makings of a perfect *Avengers* villain, and as with Delgado it is a pity her role isn't bigger. She did, of course, play the main villain in the stage version of *The Avengers* in 1971.

The mystery of Steed's unseen assailant is explained to Tara by the very man himself, Proctor, played by Gary Bond with appropriate smugness. Post hypnotic suggestion is behind Steed's condition, explaining why he is unable to see Proctor. Steed was conditioned to believe Proctor doesn't exist. It seems feasible for a man to be conditioned not to see another, but to condition a man to kill enters the world of psychological fiction (as opposed to science fiction). Most, if not all, psychologists maintain that a normal law abiding citizen cannot be compelled to commit an act that contradicts their core belief system. It is improbable that Steed could ever be compelled to commit murder, but if one suspends disbelief for the story's sake, it makes for a most intriguing and suspenseful piece of psychological fiction. Some experts have argued that while you cannot hypnotise someone to do something that goes against their core belief system, it may be possible to change their beliefs and influence the subject's actions accordingly. Hence, hypnotism itself isn't dangerous, but some hypnotists can be. Although Steed turning into a murderer is an actual improbability (I've avoided the word impossibility), Stay *Tuned* nevertheless illustrates just how damaging a dangerous hypnotist can be.

The teaser is repeated for a third and final time, again with differences to the versions before it. This is an unusual and intriguing method of plot development that imbues *Stay Tuned* with a unique flavour. As already mentioned, *The Hour That Never Was* had a famous repeated scene, but no other *Avengers* episode had the same scene played out four times. This technique does have a slightly hypnotic effect on the viewer, reinforcing the post hypnotic suggestion Steed is undergoing. The fourth re-enactment finds Proctor guiding Steed to fulfil the act he has been conditioned for, even reminding him to take his gun.

With her new found freedom, following an impressive fight scene with O'Mara, Tara plays a tape which reveals, "When you hear Bacchus, you will kill Mother." Of course it had to be Bacchus, the God of wine, and also Steed's chosen alias in *The Danger Makers*.

This neatly leads us to the grand finale, where Steed finally meets Mother. The scenes featuring the two Patrick's were among the most amusing of Season 6, showcasing both actors' flair for comedy, timing and deadpan delivery. Their scene in *Stay Tuned* doesn't disappoint. When Bacchus is finally mentioned (which you just knew it would be!), Steed fires his raised gun at Mother and walks out. The shot of Patrick Newell's sweat-drenched face outlined by bullet holes in the wall behind him before uttering, "Steed always was a superb marksman", provides a welcome moment of humour after such a dark and haunting episode.

Stay Tuned is undoubtedly one of this season's highlights. [3] A most hypnotic, eerie, yet beautifully filmed episode, that both disturbs and delights. As far removed from the surreal and wacky *Look Stop Me* as it is possible to get, it illustrates perfectly the wonderful diversity on offer in this superb run, surely the most varied season of television ever made.

© Richard Cogzell

1. I agree that this is a classic *Avengers* scene crackling with atmosphere.
2. I love the twinned build-up to this as Steed and Tara record their near-identical thoughts and concerns as they prepare for their night mission in their respective apartments.
3. I would go as far as to suggest that there isn't a better structured or more entertaining episode in the Tara King run.

FOG

Filmed: December 1968

Sets:
Streets and alley complex
John Steed's mews apartment
Telephone box
Mask & Face theatrical costumiers
Osgood's house
Gaslight Ghoul Club: entrance hall, corridor, members' lounge, Black Museum
Armstrong's house: study, hall
Hotel: façade
Hansom-cab garage
Tara's apartment

FOG

Main Character List:
Blind man
Knife grinder
Mark Travers: secretary of Gaslight Ghoul Club, arms dealer
John Steed
Haller: World Disarmament Committee
Sretlslov: World Disarmament Committee
Gruner: World Disarmament Committee
Valarti: World Disarmament Committee
Carstairs
Flower seller
Tara King
Mother
Rhonda: Mother's silent assistant
Rag and bones seller
Fowler: Mask & Face theatrical costumiers
Mrs. Golightly: Osgood's housekeeper
Charles H Osgood: Gaslight Ghoul Club
Sir Geoffrey Armstrong: President of Gaslight Ghoul Club, surgeon
Wellbeloved: curator of the Black Museum
Rowley: Gaslight Ghoul Club
Batholomew Sanders: hansom-cab hire service

"I think I'll just soak up the atmosphere." – John Steed

Fog is a relatively poorly received episode of *The Avengers*. As the plot focuses on a retelling – or, rather, a re-invention of the Ripper myth – the episode is aesthetically far darker than most *Avengers* episodes. The bright sunshine yellows, lavender, plum purples and cherry reds, all so integral to the surreal image of the programme, are replaced with grey-green, steel blue and gaslight yellow. On *The Avengers Forever!* website, David K. Smith calls the episode 'a one-note samba that fails to stir much interest', arguing that 'the overly-enthusiastic use of dark, shadowy, foggy scenes leave the entire episode – much like the script – impenetrably murky'. Guest critic Joseph A.P. Lloyd on *The Avengers Forever!* website argues that, 'London is just not like that any time of the year. It is just wrong to have *The Avengers* 80 years out of date from everything else...A cold, lonely failure, which seems to have no intention of greatness'. [1]

What Lloyd fails to recognise, however, is that whilst it is true that at no time of the year does London look like a Victorian penny dreadful, there is no time of year that London looks the way any other typical *Avengers* episode might portray it, either. Arguably, the cornerstone to the success of *The Avengers* is maintained because of the bizarre, post-modern brightly coloured, absurdly surreal world which Rodney Marshall refers to as 'fashionable froth'; the bright, colourful Britain that is, as Linda Thorson suggests in the documentary *The Avengers Revisited*, 'the England everyone wants to know instead of the England that was'. *Avengers* promotional material promised a 'picture-postcard Britain illustrated in tourist brochures', relying on sharp style and atmospheric aesthetics to maintain pure surface. There was never any attempt to maintain a realistic version of Britain; it is not London, England that is portrayed, but London, *Avengerland*, an under-populated world where everyone is upper class, beautiful, and charming – including the villains. [2]

Much of the appeal of *The Avengers* lies not only in this bizarre Never-Never Land, as Brian Clemens refers to it in *Avengers Revisited*, but in the dry wit and tongue-in-cheek banter between Steed and his partners. Gale and Peel could easily match (even surpass) Steed's ability to deliver a clever, snappy quip, and there was a wonderful gender inversion between Steed, Gale and Peel, that, although not necessarily visually recognisable, was nevertheless an inherent staple within the show itself. As Patrick Macnee argues in *Avengers Revisited*, '[Steed] was the woman, and she the man'. Whereas Gale and Peel were Steed's equals, apprentice Tara always seems to lag behind. With the lack of snappy wit in the King era, the bizarre, surreal 'style over substance' nature of the programme becomes more prominent, I would argue, as distraction for the lack of chemistry between Steed and Tara. The gender inversion that was a cornerstone of the programme for the Gale and Peel eras, however, is erased entirely within the Tara season: with Tara playing it 'all girl'. This is even more complicated as US executives, concerned Steed was too effete, forced Steed to abandon his androgynous, reactive Dandyism for that of a more foppish, action-orientated masculinity that does not suit him. [3]

Fog highlights some of these issues, as Steed attempts to play a more action character. When wishing to interrogate what he believes to be the Ripper murderer – rechristened here as the 'Gaslight Ghoul' – Steed opts to knock the gentleman over, aggressively barking questions at him with his knee pressing on the man's chest. Rather than the anticipated swordstick the real killer carries within the carpetbag, there is only an assortment of sandwiches, proving that he is not the villain they seek. Uncharacteristically, Steed is out-gentlemaned by the poor fellow he's pinned down, who tells him, "Is it incumbent of you to be so rough?...If you're some species of cut-purse, you're welcome to my wallet. I detest violence". Steed, as it turns out, has violently bowled over Mr. Osgood, a player in an exclusive Gaslight Ghoul fan club. In previous seasons, Steed would have enjoyed questioning him with casual conversation over a drink rather than resort to violence. Steed even cheats in the final fight with the villain by punching him out cold during a sword fight – something Steed would have been reluctant to do within the Gale and Peel eras. [4]

Not only is the witty banter absent; in forcing Steed into the role of an action hero, some problems arise. Steed has never been one to rush about - for the majority of *The Avengers*, his character was based on maintaining a stationary reaction to events, and, as Patrick Macnee himself intended, to be involved in as little of the action as possible. *Fog* is a perfect example of this: the pace of this episode relies on Steed strolling through foggy streets and reporting back to Mother. Tara and Mother ultimately prove to be rather a useless distraction, and Steed, as always, relies on costume to solve the crime. Steed's charm and wit is suffocated within the fog; the plot is trapped within the prefab cobbled streets, barely illuminated by the prominent gaslights.

And yet, it must be remembered that *The Avengers* has always had absurdist plots, and the fame of the show is dependent on the stylish methods utilised to carry out those plots. Using the Ripper myth as inspiration, *Fog* attempts to reconcile the dark, gloomy atmosphere of the Ripper myths with the surreal, bizarre emphasis on surface and artificiality *The Avengers* was famous for. Using specific aesthetic signifiers, *Fog* attempts to explore the Ripper murders at a safe distance, relying on the audience to infer the connections to the Ripper myth without ever specifically addressing it, just as Marie Belloc-Lowndes did in her fictional novel, *The*

Lodger (1913). Curiously, Bellock-Lowndes rechristened her murderer 'The Avenger', though, in *Fog*, the Avenger is not the villain but Steed, the hero who unmasks him. An 1888 wanted poster for the Ripper-like Gaslight Ghoul reads:

100 GUINEAS
REWARD
FOR INFORMATION LEADING TO
THE ARREST OF THE PERSON
KNOWN AS THE
GASLIGHT GHOUL
PERPETRATOR OF MANY VILE & GRISLY
MURDERS NEAR GUNTHORPE STREET
LONDON DURING THE MONTHS OF
OCTOBER & NOVEMBER 1888.
HE IS TALL, BEARDED AND HAS
BEEN SEEN CARRYING A LONG
CARPET BAG.

Here are overt references to Ripper: Martha Tabram was murdered in early August of 1888 in George Yard in Whitechapel – a street later renamed Gunthorpe. The main period of activity for the murders attributed to the Ripper is actually only seven weeks – end of September to mid-November 1888 – and *Fog* places the Ghoul's murders within the same time frame. Several newspaper articles referred to Ripper as a 'Ghoul' during the crimes, and offered the general vague description of a tall bearded man that has become a staple for the cinematic representation of Ripper. The primary suspect throughout most of the episode is a surgeon, as suspected with the Ripper myths. *Fog* also contains more subtle references to the Ripper myth: the villain is ultimately recognised by Steed as he quotes Edgar Allan Poe, who it is occasionally claimed was the inspiration for Ripper to commit the murders. One of the few pieces of forensic evidence attributed to the Ripper case was a disguise burnt in a fireplace, and, as *The Avengers* has a great affection for costume, *Fog* exploits and exaggerates the importance of disguise. There are also more broad references not just to the factual Ripper murders, but fictional representations. [5] *Fog* references Conan Doyle's Sherlock Holmes (the 1966 film *A Study in Terror* was originally titled, coincidentally, *Fog)*, with Sherlock Holmes attempting to solve the identity of the Ripper murders. *The Avengers* often utilises techniques such as specific camera angles from Alfred Hitchcock, but this episode draws on one of the earliest Hitchcock productions, a 1927 adaptation of Belloc Lowndes' *The Lodger*. Hitchcock added the subtitle and atmospheric device, 'The London Fog' to his film adaptation: whilst heavy 'pea-soup' fog was a staple for the Victorian penny-dreadful, and, indeed, has become something of a tradition for many Ripper-inspired films like Hitchcock's, fog played no part in any of the actual Ripper murders. [6] Indeed, the artificiality of the fog is even acknowledged by a Gaslight Ghoul Club member who tells Steed, "Don't forget to turn the gas off. And the fog." [7]

The fog, coupled with the emphasis on costume, emphasises a 'hidden' London. For the actual Ripper murders, this meant the criminalised, destitute area of Whitechapel; for *Avengers*, this means a hidden part of the brightly colour-saturated, artificial 1960s Postcard London that transforms into the darkly colour-saturated, artificial Victorian penny-dreadful. This results in a setting that would delight any Gaslight Fantasy novelist but, as it is so aesthetically different to the typical *Avengerland*, it is no surprise that *Fog* is considered a failure by some, who expect the fog to lift and offer substance to the story.

The Avengers, as pure surface, offers nothing: lifting the veil of fog and costume reveals only more artificiality and surface. Steed, always a mark of the past, serves strangely as a mark of the future within this episode; in this corner of *Avengerland*, Steed's Edwardian garb takes on futuristic associations surrounded by the 'Victorian' atmosphere. Steed is only able to solve the murders by using a fabricated diary entry describing an 'undiscovered' 1880s Gaslight Ghoul murder. He is eventually forced to abandon his iconic Edwardian suit, bowler and umbrella in favour of the Victorian Inverness caped coat, black topper and a swordstick. By indulging in the counterfeit fantasy, Steed can infiltrate a society of counterfeit Gaslight Ghouls to find the counterfeit Ripper murderer – "a wolf in wolf's clothing", as Steed says.

Although *Fog* uses enough signifiers to make the parallels with the Ripper myth obvious, there are also deliberate choices made within the episode to distance and subvert the myth and conform to the expectations of *Avengerland*. *The Avengers* tends to be focused on the upper classes, usually avoiding direct references to any working class element, as well as female victims. With the Ripper victims being impoverished female prostitutes, this presented a problem. The victims in *Fog* are transformed from destitute women in a sexual industry, into men – powerful, foreign political delegates in town for a disarmament summit. Not only is the class representation changed from the destitute to the upper echelons of Britain, but the murders are also de-sexualised and re-politicised from class and gender to the foreign militarised masculine. [8]

Underneath the costume, the Gaslight Ghoul copy-cat murderer is really an affluent, white-collar businessman who fears losing his comfortable lifestyle and 'going extinct as the dodo bird'. Whilst this is a repeated theme throughout *The Avengers*, usually shown within the realm of mechanics overtaking man, here there is a specific irony to the villain's methods: by dressing as the Gaslight Ghoul of the Victorian era and insisting on living in the past, the villain ultimately proves himself to be part of an extinct era that cannot be maintained within the 'futuristic' peaceful 1960s. But it is a past that has never been – he clings not only to a bygone era of the 1880s, but also to the fantasy of one that exists only within *Avengerland*. He murders people in order to save himself from the future, but the 'past' world he is attempting to both reflect and protect is as counterfeit as the beard Steed wears to infiltrate the club.

The poly-form brick walls, the fog machine, the cartoonish extras like the woman selling lucky heather, the pianola in the street – even the Hansom cab rushing away on the prefab lacquered plaster cobblestones – these are all designed to maintain a superficiality. Focusing on the idea of extinction and repetition, the killer attempts to repeat the Gaslight Ghoul murders of the past. The Gaslight Ghoul murders are both representing the Ripper murders effectively, but also subverting them: repeating Ripper murders they might be, yet they are also murders that have never happened.

The 'never-never land' house style of artificial, stylised, bright 1960s London appears to be subverted in favour of the trappings of a gloomy 'gothic' 1880s London. The employment of the Penny-dreadful gaslight fantasy, however, regardless of critical reception, simultaneously subverts the normal *Avengers* artificial aesthetic, but also conforms to it. [9] In employing the Ripper myth (influenced by Poe, Hitchcock and Doyle's Sherlock Holmes), instead of transforming *The Avengers* to 1880s London, *The Avengers*, in turn, transforms these influences into pure artificial surface. Rather than lend the programme any form of depth or substance, these influences are employed to maintain absolute superficiality.

© Sunday Swift

1. It should be noted that both Smith and Lloyd are pro-Peel

'Tara bashers'. For example, their reviews of *Killer* demonstrate their pleasure of the use of an Emma Peel-like co-star for Steed. Smith asks, "Where was Jennifer Croxton when we needed her back around October '67?" while Lloyd comments that "we finally dispose of Tara...Croxton should have been introduced into the series immediately, and made to re-shoot all the King episodes so far produced". Their views on the Tara era in general are, arguably, tainted with frustration that Emma Peel was no longer there.
2. *Avengerland* is always a fantasy land, whether it is the Stable Mews of the 1960s or a *fin-de-siècle* Victorian London.
3. The sexual/textual revolutionary qualities of *The Avengers* are largely lost in Season 6 which is a great shame, taking away some of the series' countercultural appeal.
4. This is a different Steed from the one we find in the Peel colour season. It is, in some respects, a return to the 'darker' side of the Gale era. (He has always cheated, though!)
5. The working title for Jeremy Burnham's *Fog* script was *Ripper!* Clemens decided that this was too close to reality for *The Avengers*. (Source: *Bowler Hats and Kinky Boots*.)
6. The fog becomes, arguably, an example of the literary device of pathetic fallacy, with fog representing both a metaphor as well as a means of adding a certain (artificial) atmosphere.
7. *The Avengers* on film loves adding this type of self-conscious fictionality.
8. This is, arguably, the key change which *Fog* makes in avengerising the Ripper myth/history.
9. In this sense, *Fog* is not as 'different' as some critics have suggested. It reinforces – more than it undermines – traditional *Avengers* leitmotifs and themes.

WHO WAS THAT MAN I SAW YOU WITH?

Filmed: January 1969

Exterior Locations:
War Council building
Tara King's road
Suburban street
Country roads
Castle (Mother's headquarters)
Urban road and underground garage
Stable Mews

Sets:
Fairfax's car
Alleyway
Boxing club
War Council: sentry box, reception, lift, lift/ventilator shaft, war room
Tara King's apartment
Telephone box
Castle: dungeon (Mother's headquarters)
John Steed's mews apartment

WHO WAS THAT MAN I SAW YOU WITH?

Main Character List:
Jimmy Fairfax: agent
Perowne: agent
Gregor Zaroff: henchman
Dangerfield: mastermind
Kate: Dangerfield's companion
Tara King
Powell: agent
Hamilton: agent
Gilpin: war room
General Hesketh: war room
Mother
John Steed
Rhonda: Mother's silent assistant
Aubrey Phillipson: agent
Gladys Culpepper: lip-reader

John Steed is a traitor.

This would seem to be a highly improbable state of affairs. The idea that John Steed, a man with an impeccable service record, both in the war and throughout his long career in espionage, would turn his back on Queen and Country borders on the ridiculous. And yet, throughout the course of the series, his loyalty was questioned countless times by his own people, though their suspicions always proved unfounded. Painting Steed as a traitor makes for a dramatic plot device precisely because Steed himself would seem to be beyond repute, but the series' writers could be accused of utilising it perhaps a touch too liberally throughout the show's run. This is especially true given the fact that the show always had at least *two* leads. Each of Steed's partners was just as unimpeachable as the man himself, but they all also possessed back stories rife with the potential for ulterior, traitorous motives.

What of Cathy Gale, with her connections to the Castro regime in Cuba, and her presence in Kenya during the Mau Mau uprising which cost her husband his life? Emma Peel, head of the board at Knight Industries, surely would have been an ideal target for accusations of corporate espionage. Purdey was a good candidate for double agent status given that her father was shot as a spy and her ex-fiancé was a man with terrorist leanings. Mike Gambit's sketchily-defined past certainly would have left him open to any number of accusations of treachery. And yet, none of these characters was ever framed in the course of an episode. This is what makes *Who Was That Man I Saw You With?* a unique episode in the series' history. For once, Jeremy Burnham went against the grain and chose to shake up this basic premise by calling Tara King's loyalty into question, providing a new perspective on each of the series' leads in the process.

All Done With Mirrors is often cited as Tara King's finest hour, and indeed it is an extremely significant story for her character. Tara is provided with the opportunity to single-handedly solve a case and engages in multiple physically-demanding fights. She also demonstrates a scrappy resilience, surviving a perilous fall from a cliff and swimming back to shore against the tide. But *Who Was That Man I Saw You With?* is arguably just as significant a milestone for her character as *All Done With Mirrors*. In a sense, it brings her full-circle. Tara's first appearance in the episode finds her in military gear, her face blacked out commando-style. This echoes her introduction in the episode *The Forget-Me-Not*, in which the trainee Ministry Agent 69, decked out in similar garb and with a blackened face, mistakes Steed for a target on the training range. As Tara proceeds to infiltrate the security of the War Room, her route takes her through a ventilation shaft, and she crawls through dusty, cobwebbed vents reminiscent of the spider-laden tube she clambered through in *Invasion of the Earthmen*, one of her earliest adventures. However, in both of these early appearances, Tara was portrayed as a green, inexperienced agent, attacking the wrong target in her training course and becoming visibly-panicked within the confines of the tube as the spiders rain down from above. The Tara assaulting the War Room, in contrast, has developed and matured over her tenure into an innovative, strong, capable agent.

Unlike her fellow *Avengers* women, Tara did not subscribe to any particular fighting style. While Cathy Gale relied mostly on Judo, Emma on Kung Fu and Karate, and Purdey developed her own take on the French martial art of Panache, Tara utilised several methods, along with a not-inconsiderable amount of improvisation. The episode provides numerous opportunities for Tara to showcase this resourcefulness. In her opening assault on the War Room, she disorients a guard by spinning him in his office chair before knocking him out, and then ensures that he will remain immobile when he regains consciousness by handcuffing his wrist to his ankle (in the absence of a handy piece of furniture). She escapes the agent holding her under house arrest by throwing her drink into his face, and then sends him sprawling backwards into a chair. Even when her arms are tied to the ropes of a boxing ring during the final fight, she manages to assist Steed by restraining Dangerfield (Alan Wheatley) with her legs. [1] When Zaroff (Alan Browning) captures her at Steed's flat, her first instinct is to reach for a bottle of champagne to use as a weapon. This creative use of props not only adds a quirky visual element to Tara's fight scenes, but also provides an insight into the way her mind works, suggesting that she operates best under pressure. The picture that emerges is one of an observant individual who is keenly aware of, and constantly taking in, her surroundings, perhaps to a greater degree than either the audience or her opponents realise.

However, Tara's resourcefulness is most apparent when she successfully 'frames' Steed in her bid to make a case for her own innocence. On the run with the Ministry's best agents on her tail, she not only manages to evade capture, but also concocts, sets up, and executes an elaborate plan of her own. She arranges for Steed to receive a phone call that leads him to acquire a mysterious envelope, sends cases of champagne to his flat with an incriminating card, and photographs him talking to an anonymous man, before finally arranging for Steed to arrive on the scene just as she stages her fake suicide. When she presents the evidence to Steed, demonstrating how she could easily set him up in the way Zaroff did her, she argues her case forcefully. Despite her continued love of, and admiration for, Steed, she proves eminently capable of speaking her mind by means of a forthright, relentlessly logical argument. She is not disrespectful toward Steed, but she certainly does not defer to him as her 'better', either. Instead, she speaks to him as an equal, with conviction and authority, and without suffering from any apparent intimidation, a sign of an evolution in their partnership from their days as mentor and pupil. When Steed asks her who the man in the photos is, she enigmatically replies "a friend". Whereas throughout the majority of Season 6, Steed was portrayed as possessing the resources and the connections to move the case along, Tara has now developed connections and resources of her own to draw upon when she is in a tight spot, a sign of her development as an agent.

The episode also displays another aspect of Tara's character, namely her open, straight-forward, good-natured personality. Potentially a liability for an agent, Tara has managed to turn her natural warmth into an asset. She cloaks her deceptions and double-plays in open, friendly conversations in which she often asks outright for the information she seeks, but the straightforwardness and seeming lack of guile in her inquiries often buy her more success than elaborate subterfuge. This episode takes her strategy to extremes, as she wanders around the War Room asking questions of Gilpin (Alan MacNaughtan), a man who is completely aware that she is attempting to penetrate his security. However, even with this advantage, he still falls victim to Tara's 'open subterfuge', as she makes inquires regarding the value of certain files, and then proceeds to photograph them once she has been assured of their importance. She is 'caught' with a miniature camera, but her open and obvious 'failure' conceals the fact that she has, in reality, entered the War Room with two cameras, and her sigh at the fate of the first camera's exposed film eliminates Gilpin's suspicions and causes him to drop his guard, allowing Tara to walk away with the film in her second camera untouched. Her friendly straightforwardness therefore enables her to successfully penetrate the impenetrable, Steed-designed War Room. She later employs her open personality again, to a different end, when asking Dangerfield to explain the nuances of his plan. "I can accept you killing me. It's an occupational risk," she says, with complete frankness and no apparent fear. "What I can't accept is not knowing why." Dangerfield obliges with an explanation, allowing her to unravel the plot while also giving Steed a chance to move in. In many ways, this echoes Steed's chosen method of information-gathering, in which he feigns a cheerful, non-threatening, over-the-top persona that allows him to 'blunder' through doors without seeming to recognise the gravity of his actions. It is possible that Tara has picked up on the success of this strategy and spliced it with her own natural, friendly disposition. The fact that Tara herself is an inherently decent human being, one who shows a genuine affection and concern for her fellow agents and the people she encounters in the course of her investigations, means that her friendly inquiries are not always entirely feigned, which contributes to their success.

Also worthy of examination in this story is Steed. The fact that, for once, he is not the one under suspicion provides him with the opportunity to take on the role normally reserved for his partner, and allows him to grapple with the question of Tara's potential guilt. Perhaps because he has been subjected to similar schemes so many times over the length of his own career, Steed unwaveringly approaches the situation from the position of a sceptical disbeliever. He certainly does not wish, from a personal standpoint, to believe that Tara has gone over to the other side—indeed, he is extremely, almost paternally, protective of her, and harbours no small amount of affection for her. But at a basic, instinctual level, the idea simply does not seem plausible to him. Steed's reliance on his instincts would play an increasingly significant, visible role in *The New Avengers*, but here his faith in them is just as prevalent.

Despite the fact that he witnessed the delivery of Tara's flowers and pearls from Zaroff himself, and arrives on the scene to find her near Fairfax's dead body, he is reluctant to accept the seemingly-obvious conclusion that Tara has 'turned'. This does not mean that Steed is completely biased and incapable of dispassionately evaluating the evidence. He bears witness to Tara's interrogation by Phillipson (Bryan Marshall) and maintains a grim professionalism, resisting the urge to interfere or jump to her defence. He also does not attempt to deny the veracity of the evidence mounted against her. But what distinguishes Steed as an agent from his contemporaries is his ability to push on with an assignment long after all of the 'obvious' conclusions have been drawn. Rather than questioning the existing evidence, he asks for more, driven by the instinctual sense that if something feels wrong, it probably is. He refuses to be deterred in his search for that evidence until he finds it, which he usually does. In this case, in the form of Miss Gladys Culpepper (Aimee Delamain), lip-reader extraordinaire. Perhaps he senses the inherent goodness of Tara's nature, but regardless of his reasons, he makes clear to Mother that he will trust to his intuition and investigate her apparent betrayal "officially or otherwise." The only moment he can truly be said to doubt his instincts is when he finds Tara seemingly dead by suicide. He utters but one word, "Tara", before she reveals the subterfuge, but the intonation conveys his shocked disbelief, both at her death and at the idea that she has, in fact, been working as a double agent, ultimately driven to suicide when her treachery was uncovered. He does not have time to let the grief sink in, but he is clearly disconcerted by the idea that he could have so horribly misread Tara, and her motivations.

Mother, in contrast, does not have the luxury of following his instincts. He must remain a professional, capable leader and take a hard line, reducing Tara's security rating despite his own personal misgivings. A generally unsentimental character, even when it comes to members of his own family, it is telling that Mother is visibly upset when confronted by Fairfax's (William Marlowe) evidence of her treachery. In his years in the service, Mother has no doubt borne witness to any number of betrayals in the form of lost friends who were either turned or killed by the other side, and has developed a thick hide and cynical attitude toward the espionage business. It is also highly likely that his own disability, almost certainly accompanied by chronic pain, was earned in the field, perhaps due to a betrayal by a fellow agent. This has done nothing for his fractious temperament. However, in spite of his prickly exterior, there is a sense that Tara has become a 'favourite daughter', one he has watched grow and develop as an agent, and who has managed to penetrate his defences and worm her way into his affections in the process. Her good-natured character has prevented her from being put-off by Mother's attitude, and, as was made apparent in the episode *Requiem*, she is genuinely saddened at the thought of his death. Mother's anger at Tara's apparent betrayal suggests that the feeling is mutual, and that Tara working for the other side pains him at a personal level, as well as a professional one, even though he has 'seen it all' and should no longer be surprised by these sorts of developments.

In contrast, Mother appreciates Steed because his long career in the service has given him a level of experience equal to Mother's own, allowing Mother to have meaningful exchanges with someone on his wavelength, even if they do not share the same rank, something that cannot be said for many of the other agents under Mother's remit. Tara cannot claim to be Mother and Steed's equal in terms of experience, but she does bring a fresh, unjaded perspective to their dynamic, complementing Mother's cynicism, and Steed's experienced professionalism. Without her, Steed and

Mother have lost not only someone they care about, but the mutually complementary triangle of perspectives on which they have come to rely. That loss even appears to affect the silent Rhonda, who hovers unobtrusively in the background, looking grim rather than impassive. [2]

Turning the tables and targeting Tara as the traitor allows for a new perspective on all three of the season's leads, and their combined dynamic, one that would not have been possible had Steed's loyalty been in question as per usual. The episode is notable for other reasons: the upside-down, prototypically Avengerish idea of Tara openly trying to break into the War Room, to the point of admitting her desire to steal top secret papers; the comically vain diabolical mastermind Dangerfield and his extensive array of beauty treatments; the extremely well-choreographed fight between Steed, Zaroff, and Dangerfield at the episode's climax; and the lovely visual of the champagne fountain in the episode's tag scene. But ultimately, it is the exploration of Tara's character and her impact on those around her that is at the story's heart, giving her a chance to shine even as her season drew to a close. [3]

© JZ Ferguson

1. On a realistic level, the boxing ring serves no purpose, yet it offers us an intriguing set-within-a-set and we instinctively know that it will become a fighting arena in the final battle.
2. Rhonda may be mute but she frequently offers the viewer an interesting sounding board through her facial responses.
3. This episode and JZ Ferguson's essay both highlight the character development which allowed Tara to escape – most of the time – from the arguably irritating, overly dependent character who is awestruck by Steed earlier in the season.

PANDORA

Filmed: January 1969

Exterior Locations:
Tara King's car bonfire site

Sets:
Lasindall house: dining room, Pandora's bedroom, upper landing, hallway, Uncle Gregory's quarters
John Steed's mews apartment
Tara King's apartment
Antique shop
File room
Juniper's clock shop

PANDORA

Main Character List:
Rupert Lasindall: mastermind
Henry Lasindall: filing 'controller'
Miss Faversham: hired housekeeper
John Steed
Tara King
Xavier Smith: antique shop owner
Mother
Rhonda: Mother's silent assistant
Carter: filing clerk
Simon Henry Juniper: WW1 operative 'Fierce Rabbit'
Gregory Lasindall: WW1 operative 'Fierce Rabbit'
Hubert Pettigrew: WW1 operative 'Fierce Rabbit'

Artistic innovation and commercial popularity are, arguably, sometimes at odds with each other in *The Avengers*. The series' well established formula is often seen – by critics of the colour era – as tired and predictable by Seasons 5 and 6. Yet, as David K Smith observes, it is precisely this familiar formula which helped to establish the show's unprecedented global appeal. When episodes attempt to break away from the tried and tested formula the critical response is, interestingly, mixed. *The Hour That Never Was*, *Epic* and *Stay Tuned* are, generally, seen as groundbreaking masterpieces, while late-Season 6 scripts such as *Pandora* and *Take-Over* are sometimes viewed as disappointingly 'unavengerish'. The latter two have the feel of leisurely-paced stage plays, where fights are kept to the strict minimum and where a claustrophobic, studio-bound atmosphere of stricture and confinement dominate. Neither contains much in the way of light-hearted wit and humour – the 'champagne' of the show [1] – and instead concentrate on the subversive and the surreal, providing an unsettling, unpleasant, theatrical atmosphere. There is a potential paradox at play, then. When the later Tara-era *Avengers* episodes stick to formula they are accused of flogging the tired – rather than dead – horse; when they break free and offer something startlingly different they are seen as failing to provide the viewer with the traditional or 'pure' *Avengers* product that s/he has tuned in for. Damned if you do, yet also damned if you don't.

While *Take-Over* is praised and enjoyed by *some* fans – despite or even because of its unavengerishness – the critical response to *Pandora* is, generally speaking, 'lukewarm' at best in both the UK and the US. David K Smith awards it a single 'bowler', describing Linda Thorson's performance as the episode's "greatest liability" and lamenting "a lack of production creativity". In France, where the Tara era tends to be far more popular, there is more support for this episode. The critiques of the webmasters on the French *Le Monde des Avengers* website sum up the split opinion. Denis Chauvet describes it as follows: "A soporific episode offering an indescribable boredom...What is avengerish in this episode?" Like Smith, he awards it one bowler, while the other two webmasters wax lyrical and give it the maximum of four. "A completely atypical episode; a complete success" states the Miami-based French webmaster. Bernard Ginez argues that while a series such as *The Avengers* needs to develop a specific identity through its fictional world – *Avengerland* – its themes and its characters, it is equally important from time to time to head off in an alternate direction in order to break from the potential predictability or "monotony". This difference of opinion is fascinating and highlights the subjective nature of critical analysis, even among fans sharing a common love for a television series. Is *Pandora* a welcome diversion from typical *Avengers* fare or does it represent an hour devoid of avengerish style? Is it even as revolutionary or 'different' as some critics have made out?

The cleverness of the teaser does not become (fully) apparent until thirty-seven minutes into the story, offering us a cunning example of delayed significance. At the time we are simply thrown into a confusing time tunnel. As the Lasindall brothers discuss the merits of 'Rag Time' music over breakfast, Rupert warns Henry that "we must move with the times". This refers just as much to us as viewers as we find ourselves plunged – seemingly – into a Great War period piece. Robert Fuest films the brothers' discussion with 'Pandora', the third figure at the dining table, fore-grounded. She neither moves nor enters the debate and the mystery is (partly) explained as the teaser ends, with Rupert bending down to speak to her: she is a seated mannequin with a bandaged, almost mummified face. The opening scene may be unavengerish, but this final, surreal detail/twist offers a classic *Avengers* touch. As the titles appear on her face, we hear the first of several hauntingly mysterious pieces of music, warning us that this episode will take a different approach. [2]

Tara King's kidnapping takes place on an avengerish set, a deserted antique shop with an eclectic collection of objects: a Napoleonic figure – half statue, half scarecrow – a stuffed zebra head, Oriental figurine, tribal mask etc., all silent witnesses to the drugging and abduction. Tara's imprisonment in the Lasindall's period house places *Pandora* within a successful *Avengers* tradition including *The House That Jack Built*, *The Joker* and *Epic*. Even if Bernard Ginez is justified in describing the episode as "atypical", there are plenty of familiar leitmotifs and themes at play.

Brian Clemens' script is keen to emphasise the breaks with tradition in *Pandora*. Mother – whose headquarters is a balloon which we *don't* visit – is forced to visit Tara's flat for a *rendez-vous* with Steed:

Mother: This is utterly unprecedented, Steed. Sending for me, dragging me down from my Headquarters, well it's like – it's like –
Steed: Like a cuckoo leaving the nest.

The appearance of Mother in one of the Avengers' apartments isn't, of course, "unprecedented" and neither is *Pandora* as revolutionary as some critics make out. It does offer us an alternative episode but one which also draws on familiar material, a fact alluded to as Carter, the clerk, looks back through files with 'Mrs. Emma Peel' and 'Mrs. Cathy Gale' written on the covers. From now on the episode will crisscross between Tara's Edwardian prison and Steed's investigation of her mysterious disappearance. This dyadic structure allows *Pandora* to offer an intertwined narrative which combines what we might call 'interior incarceration' and 'exterior exploration', even if the latter is still studio-bound.

The scenes in which a confused, drugged Tara King tries to make sense of her new life and character in the Lasindall household draw on the conventional country mansion trap at the heart of other Clemens scripts, yet the period puzzle adds interesting further layers, allowing *Pandora* to offer us a more profound mystery. Rather than the malevolent revenge themes of *The House That Jack Built* and *The Joker*, here the *Avengers* girl's involvement is purely coincidental: the freak similarity between Pandora's portrait and Tara King's physical features. Somehow this makes her capture and psychological torture/brainwashing seem even crueller. The constant conflict between the Lasindall brothers also adds a further element of drama, with Henry disturbed and revolted by his younger brother's "mad" determination to take the experiment/plan to its unnatural conclusion, whatever that may be. The wonderful Edwardian set with its sealed, shuttered windows, claustrophobically heavy, patterned wallpaper and art deco flourishes; the disturbingly mournful music; the scraping sounds and wild, desperate mutterings of the deranged Uncle Gregory – a madman in the attic as it were – combine with the wonderful acting performance of Julian Glover as a disturbed, dangerous mastermind to make these scenes powerfully unsettling. We are made to feel as trapped as Tara is; more so perhaps as, unlike her, we haven't been sedated!

Glover's sparkling performance as a man who can't abide "raised voices", yet is happy to shout at everyone else, is almost matched by that of ex-agent Simon Juniper (John Laurie) who manages to combine a humorous sense of the eccentric with more than a hint that he – like Rupert Lasindall – is angry, unhinged and seeking 'justice'. Contemptuous of the "modern resources" which agents like Steed have at their disposal, his decision to investigate Tara King's disappearance himself performs a number of functions: it adds a further investigative layer to the plot; it ties together the public world of 1960s spy-fi with the private one of the Lasindall's WW1 house [3]; and it also demonstrates that old-fashioned detective work is what Steed will require in order to unravel the mystery. [4]

Pandora reaches two powerful dramatic climaxes long before the final twist. First, with the mental breakdown of Tara King as her 'real' and her drug-induced personalities begin to merge in her brain. This is psychologically disturbing [5] in a far more naturalistic way than the mental torture of Emma Peel in *The House That Jack Built* and *The Joker*. Once again, *The Avengers* demonstrates its ability to defy genre and provide a viewing experience which cannot be simplistically labelled as 'light entertainment'. The second climax commences with the skeleton in the rocking chair wearing Tara's clothes. It offers us a dark echo of the mannequin in the teaser, before becoming blurred – Tara is fainting [6] – and seamlessly transforming into the grinning 'ghost' driver of Tara's doomed sports car. This is set on fire and leads to Mother's conclusion that she is now dead. It is the only location scene in the entire episode, confirming the importance of studio stricture in this disturbing drama. This time it is Steed who is disturbed by the drama, rather than us. Patrick Macnee's performance when Mother tells him that Tara is almost certainly dead demonstrates his ability to throw off the fun, frivolous Steed for one who is in genuine, heartfelt shock. (Look carefully at Macnee's eyes as Pettigrew apologises for his drunken behaviour and one can see that it is acting of the highest order; the scene resonates with emotion.)

It is between these two climaxes that the teaser is replayed, with Tara King replacing the mannequin. It is a masterstroke on the part of Brian Clemens. The timing could not be better as the final pieces of the puzzle slip into place. In a break with *Avengers* tradition, the dramatic finale takes place without Steed, and with Tara King a mere dazed spectator. As Rupert unwittingly destroys the "priceless Rembrandt", the meaningful action has been played out *before* Steed arrives; the subsequent half-hearted fighting is short and meaningless. *The Avengers* formula still makes an appearance but the masterminds have already self-destructed without Steed needing to intervene. The twist in the tale/tail is unavengerish, more *Tales of the Unexpected* than *The Avengers*.

Pandora is a one-off, memorable episode in which Linda Thorson produces an impressive acting performance, matched by those of John Laurie, Julian Glover and Patrick Macnee. Combined with a subtle script – not always Brian Clemens' strength – an innovative music score and Robert Fuest's clever direction, the result sees *The Avengers* exploring a different type of story in terms of genre, style and theme. However, avengerish touches are not totally absent: mannequins, a sinister country house trap, the kidnapping of the female co-lead and eccentric guest characters are all reassuringly familiar touches and, while the leisurely pace would not work on a regular basis, it makes for a fascinating theatrical spectacle. It is little wonder that *Pandora* is Thorson and Fuest's favourite *Avengers* 'hour'.

© Rodney Marshall

1. The retired 'Fierce Rabbit' agents Simon Juniper and Hubert Pettigrew do provide welcome moments of humour with the former's eccentric anger at being forced to retire and the latter's alcoholic mis/behaviour in Steed's apartment.
2. For once the score is an original one which is an enormous plus in a season where too much of the music was simply recycled from the Emma Peel era.

3. As, of course, does Henry Lasindall's public function as the Ministry 'Controller' of the filing department which we become aware of near the halfway point of the episode.
4. Is this another example of *The Avengers* questioning modern day technology?
5. It is as powerful as the brainwashing of Tara King in *Requiem* and John Steed in *Stay Tuned* and represents a genuine strength in terms of both Linda Thorson's acting abilities and the psychologically-powerful quality of (some of) the Season 6 scripts.
6. Both David K Smith and Denis Chauvet suggest that *Pandora* over-plays the chloroform/drug cliché which is, of course, used on numerous occasions in this season. However, given the theme, it seems appropriate here, rather than being tacked on as a lazy plot device.

THINGUMAJIG

Filmed: January 1969

Exterior Locations:
Country church
Country roads
Woods, meadow pond and bridge
Earthworks/quarry
Brett's house

Sets:
Church: interior, tunnels, ladder/entrance to tunnels
John Steed's mews apartment
Tara King's apartment
Brett's house: bedroom
Kruger's Caravan
Truman's laboratory

THINGUMAJIG

Main Character List:
Inge Tilson: archaeologist
Greer: archaeologist
John Steed
Tara King
Teddy Shelley: vicar
Major Star: local ex-military type
Bill Reston: archaeologist
Professor Harvey Truman: electrical science expert
Dr. Grant: medical doctor and archaeologist
Phillips: archaeologist
Williams: archaeologist
Brett: archaeologist
Norman Pike: angler
Kruger: mad villain scientist
Stenson: foreign buyer of the electric boxes

Thingumajig could most politely be described as 'not a favourite' amongst *Avengers* fans. In fact it has sometimes been called the worst episode of the entire series! So what exactly is wrong with it? And is anything *right* with it? Is it worth putting in your DVD player more than once? On paper, *Thingumajig* seems to have all the elements of a successful, albeit more than usually way-out episode. *The Avengers* has often been assigned a 'science fiction' label, but that is merely one of the genres in its arsenal, a genre which really dominated only a handful of episodes – *Thingumajig* being one of them. [1]

Linda Thorson was medically signed-off with a cold, which prevented her appearing in most of this episode. Contrary to some reports, the cold was not written in to Tara's portrayal, but it meant that Steed and Tara were separated (similar to the double-banked episodes where either Steed or Tara had to feature very little, due to filming commitments on other stories in simultaneous production). This made the episode less fun than it could have been, with Steed acquiring a couple of ersatz assistants and Tara seeming fairly impotent aside from one spectacular 'crisis' scene.

Apart from Tara's electrically-sparking fight against a black 'brick' (not a brick in her handbag), this episode doesn't have the fireworks of other stories in the season. Pacing is a concern. The title *Thingumajig* implies a mysterious unnamed object; perhaps the build-up of the mystery goes on too long, and perhaps the object's revelation does not match the level of suspense that has been generated. [2] Suspense there undeniably is, though. Even its detractors admit that the episode starts atmospherically. Unfortunately, the pace never really picks up later on.

Horror tropes abound. Director Leslie Norman favours lots of scared-face close-ups and overt signs of supernatural goings-on: a spooky church in a desolate, wintry landscape; the church organ playing discordant sounds by itself; catacombs with slurring, dragging sounds like the footsteps of an eldritch undead stalker; and inexplicable whirring, whining noises around the scene of each death. There is little music, but much unsettling sound design. Technologically, this church has everything from an electrically-powered organ to a telephone and a cement mixer; it gains the entire detritus of a dredged pond during the episode! Powerful electric lights illuminate its nave, alongside old candelabras, now dimmed. A gaping hole in one wall leads down to the prehistoric catacombs, the source of this week's deadly mystery: one incongruous element among many. The catacombs themselves are riddled now with amateur archaeologists, bright lights, and a generator.

In terms of supernatural threat, this story doesn't go as far as *Warlock* in the Cathy Gale era, which implied that black magic is real. The weird self-playing church organ is not due to poltergeist activity: it is explained as the Thingumajig box somehow remotely feeding on the organ's circuits. No mice here, unlike in *The Town of No Return*! Gothic imagery is plundered: mental possession (or a trance induced by shocking deadly events), the lonely church with strange tiles and murals hiding hideous savage relics beneath, its ominous organ portending death. In terms of science fiction, this story is the most bizarre of the series, besides *Man-Eater of Surrey Green*; though that story's plant-possession is echoed here by the apparent possession of Brett. Viewers with little tolerance of sci-fi may therefore not take kindly to a story which relies heavily on that genre. *Thingumajig* isn't too derivative of any previous story in *The Avengers* or in science fiction – aside from the BBC's series *Doctor Who* which had featured electrical 'rats' called Cybermats. The Cybermats were remotely-controlled by their masters. These

Thingumajig boxes are clearly out of control, and very dangerous. Terry Nation, who wrote *Thingumajig* and script-edited some of this season of *The Avengers* had written for *Doctor Who* since its beginning, and may have noted the potential of such creatures. [3]

The boxes, we're told, are electrical animals, that hunt for and feed upon electrical power, and have murderous minds of their own, albeit not very clever ones. One of the escaped boxes enters a lake for no apparent reason, and drains itself of power whilst electrocuting lots of fish. They have been compared to the famous Daleks (also created by Terry Nation), but actually here the story structure is closer to Nation's 1970s TV series *Blake's 7*, particularly its opening episodes which feature people cut off in tunnels, evil conspirators, and a device which repeatedly kills people off-screen but is kept mysterious to heighten suspense (the defence mechanism of a deserted spaceship). Electrical power being sought by a relatively dormant but growing threat features in several of Terry Nation's *Doctor Who* and *Blake's 7* stories – the latter's *Time Squad* (mislaid cryogenic assassins gradually thawing out) and in *Doctor Who* with the Daleks (static electricity provides the evil pepperpots with life, and the ability to zap everyone else to death). The boxes' aggression here seems to be programmed-in, solely because of their creator's malign intent. [4]

A word or two on the excellent direction by Leslie Norman: the catacombs, despite being brightly lit, are disturbing – there's a very effective 'dust storm' towards camera, aimed at no character but us, the audience. Brett later emerges coated in dust, walking dazedly and automatically like a zombie. Despite bed rest, he never fully recovers, and later returns to the site of his trauma to die, apparently reacting to the discordant and self-playing organ; a disturbing and inexplicable scene. Visually, colour is an important ingredient in *The Avengers* of the late 1960s; here it is offset by the desolate coldness, and the midwinter references; Steed even mentions Christmas. There are flashes of colour but lots of near-monochrome, not least in the locations. Vernon Dobtcheff hunched over his tiny heater encapsulates how we are made to feel, with brief moments of warmth (Steed's little joke about his bedknob, the brief Tara scenes) set against the bleak extents of dead and denuded countryside, and harshly-lit catacombs as parched as ancient bone. The crackle of electricity is not a warming energy, but the threat of death.

Two of the fights are very good: Steed's final fight has a lot of exertion and some lethal weapons (not least Steed's flame-cutter gun); Tara's fight features power cable plugs and streams of champagne onto an electrical emitter. Don't try this at home, and also don't try putting a live electrical device in a bath of water as Professor Truman (Willoughby Goddard) suggests. Truman is a rather broad eccentric (in more ways than one), wearing a screwdriver in his buttonhole and taking snuff, whilst having chronic rhinitis, one particularly dreadful sneeze destroying the long-suffering Tara's newly-iced cake. However, the eccentricity in this episode is rather laboured; another element that may grate with viewers used to more ingenious characterisation. We get an apparently Eastern Bloc sponsor who is suffering from the cold weather, and who describes the English weather in terms of a refrigerator, but Steed finds nothing odd about a holiday caravan tootling around in the depths of winter, near the scene of the crime. [5] There are touches of quirkiness in Steed and Tara, notably Tara using her cake-icer to decorate Steed's telephone number onto her ornamental bottle. Thanks to Linda's cold, Steed gains the forgettable fur-wearing temporary assistant Inge Tilson (played by Dora Reisser): most notable for scared faces, smiling perfunctorily at Steed's tedious 'Auntie' anecdote, and being patronised about what side of the car/road to use. Steed never really connects with Inge, although he takes her to the pool of dead fish, and a quarry. He certainly knows how to show a girl a good time!

On the writing front, Terry Nation was originally known as a comedians' gag writer, working with the likes of celebrated comics (and writers) Spike Milligan, Ted Ray, and John Junkin. After broadening his appeal with a comedy play, he adapted three stories for the TV anthology show *Out of This World*. This led to his famous Daleks story for *Doctor Who*, and to later work on series such as *Out of the Unknown*, *Survivors*, and *Blake's 7*. Keen to be seen as a dramatist rather than solely as a comedian, he wrote for action-adventure series *The Baron* and *The Saint*, then becoming script-editor on *The Avengers* and *The Persuaders!* At last, America beckoned, with shows like *MacGyver*. Sadly, Steed's crate of anti-electrical goodies are sent to him, not improvised *MacGyver*-style; only Tara gets to improvise during her fight with the box, using everything from a vacuum cleaner (how many *Avengers* ladies do we see vacuuming?) to copious amounts of champagne. The shot of the Thingumajig box coming down Tara's stairs is actually rather impressive. Nation stated:

"I believe I have the lucky thing of the common touch: the thing that I want to watch is what the public want to watch. I'm a very simple viewer: I don't have high demands. I am like the audience, and so I write for me and know that they will join me."

In the engaging and varied sixth season of *The Avengers*, as well as in numerous other exciting TV shows, Terry Nation proved that populism is a beneficial trait for any aspiring writer or script editor. On the subject of writing *Doctor Who*, Nation said: "I always try to establish a mysterious and moody atmosphere and then inject swift action. I always try to split the Doctor and his companions up, then have them each becoming involved in separate (but related) adventures." In script editing most of Tara's season, and indeed in his own scripts, there was often no choice but to split up Steed and Tara. Here, at least we get to see Tara in some scenes, and she is ultimately put in danger (Linda Thorson was around long enough for a decent scene) and gets herself out of it. However, Steed never seems to be in much trouble at all. Nation also stated that he never did research for science fiction scripts. As the writer he wished to define his own worlds, without interference. If he wanted his world to have trees that talk, or rocks that roll, then that is what they did. In *Avengerland*, metal boxes can roll along for no reason, if he wants them to. Can we accept a box that moves and kills? Ultimately, whether you enjoy the episode depends on whether you can take seriously the idea of electrocution by means of deadly 'electrical animals' in the shape of small black boxes. The writing formula is slightly less visible than in *The Avengers*' fifth season; although some of the cannon-fodder victims barely get a word of dialogue, we otherwise get a collection of actors who react realistically to a confusing and confounding mystery; so it becomes quite gripping. The plot becomes almost irrelevant, and moments like Steed seizing upon a bedknob, or making impenetrable remarks about some of the other dredged-up detritus, becomes a part of the enjoyable oddness of it all.

Patrick Macnee and Jeremy Lloyd (playing Steed's friend, the vicar Teddy Shelley) work hard to give Steed and Teddy a sympathetic relationship, but the script allows little interaction. Nevertheless, Steed has some nice lines to Teddy: "You baptize and bury them and I'll try and see that the interval between the two is as long as possible." Why couldn't it have been the enjoyable Teddy, instead of Inge, that accompanies Steed throughout? The series requires female glamour, but Tara is gorgeous anyway and still appears. Inge is left out of the finale, when Steed could have used her help in the final fight. Steed once again eschews a gun (nearly fatally) but wields a kind of arc-welder/heat-gun. The rest of the cast is certainly strong. Wouldn't any actor love to portray a character called Major Star? Hugh Manning is delightful as the gung-ho ex-soldier who wants to put his village on the map. Perennial television doctor John Horsley is the humane Doctor Grant and seems to be popping in from another, more sensible episode. Willoughby Goddard is as comically pompous as he will be in *The Mind of Mr J. G. Reeder*, and less vicious than we knew him in the surviving *Avengers* first season episode *The Frighteners*. Iain Cuthbertson has won considerable praise for his performance as Kruger, 'lifting' the episode somewhat – he's huge, in physical size and screen presence, and very unnerving in his first scene with Jeremy Lloyd's Teddy. Kruger never introduces himself, instantly raising the hackles of *Avengers* viewers: very ungentlemanly behaviour. Big, ursine, and always grinning, he wears heavy gloves, and is always armoured in layers of protective clothing: an imposing and dynamic villain, who turns out to be scientifically brilliant but utterly mad – the classic Diabolical Mastermind.

So to the themes of this episode. There is death – lots of it – and since Tara is not around, we frequently get an unwelcome dose of Brian Clemens's *Thriller* – the camera lingering upon a woman looking very scared indeed. Sadism? Not in the league of episodes like *Take-Over*, but part-way there, due to its oppressive feeling of the cheapness of human life. Or, at least, the fragility of human life. We don't see any mourning, and Major Star ensures things are moved on briskly – and brusquely – after each death. The main theme seems to be loss of control to unseen powers, and the loss of one's mind (in Brett's case). Also, of course, loss of life: the human victims, the pool of dead fish, the dead winter landscape generally, the constant coldness. The pool of dead fish indicates a destruction of the environment that was once conducive to human and animal life; Nation returned to these themes in his incredible post-pandemic saga *Survivors*, and mixed it with supernatural and humorous elements in his children's book *Rebecca's World* - a modern classic that is well worth seeking out since it features a lot of *Avengers*-style whimsy (and eccentrics).

Science fiction has often invoked the horror of modern man confronting 'ancient' powers that possess more advanced knowledge and technology: Nigel Kneale's *Quatermass and the Pit* with its Martian genetic engineers mutating our prehistoric ancestors, evidenced by an excavation team digging up strange prehistoric skulls. Skulls are featured here, too. The organ playing by itself is reminiscent of the telekinetic movements around the Quatermass archaeological dig when ancient forces are disturbed – indeed, a fugitive from Quatermass's 'poltergeist' activity vainly seeks refuge in a church. The boxes are vampires, feeding on modern power, generators and technology, and like the best Gothic monstrosities they kill indiscriminately. They were created for money, and are the ultimate expression of greed – for money, power (literally energy) and egotism. Kruger is an egotist. He was laughed at for his theories of projected power and delights in being proved right – planning to release "hundreds and thousands" of boxes with the power to move and to kill. Like Terry Nation's later character Davros (creator of the Daleks, and thus an evil alter-ego of the writer), Kruger is turned upon by one of his creations. As with *Frankenstein*, the creator finally falls victim to his own scientific hubris. In making his creatures eager to kill and feed, Kruger is proved right in his narrow views, but wrong in his morality. Magnificent fight, though!

Electrical animals remain a very interesting concept, and huge competition exists nowadays in creating robotic 'life' forms with more and more autonomy. In this episode, Inge mentions a vacuum cleaner that can plug itself in after cleaning a room – these are now common. What if the Thingumajigs (who seem to have simple minds of their own, if very aggressive ones) were capable of true animal life – development, even reproduction? How long before some lunatic makes a computer 'virus' that can move – and kill? If it can happen, technologically, experience tells us that one day it will. The Cybernauts were electrical men, but had no minds of their own. Thingumajigs are potentially scarier. We glimpse more than twenty Thingumajig-like boxes in Kruger's caravan, seemingly without insulation, unlike the 'active' ones from the wrecked van. They're not hunting – yet. Are they deactivated? Are they prototypes? Maybe they will be awoken in the future; after all, Stenson and the caravan seem to survive the episode. Broadcast power is still a holy grail of science; no longer the province of cranks. There is definitely enough food for thought to provide a sequel.

Unlike many other episodes, *Thingumajig* is difficult to interpret in psychosexual terms (save the possible interpretations of entering an underworld as a parallel for confronting the fears in the human subconscious). There is little human contact or flirtatiousness, even between Steed and Inge. The main problem with the story is that Steed is supremely fearless and confident throughout, undermining any sense of threat. He's a superman of the kind which Terry Nation usually tried to avoid when developing his own characters, who were more heroic because of having to overcome their human frailties. There is also a perceived lack of wit; yet Terry Nation, as a comedy writer in his earlier career, had churned out scripts with a joke in every other line. Clearly the script could have been filled with quips galore, but *Thingumajig*'s bizarre premise required a hard-nosed realism in the attitudes of the characters who were immediately threatened, to offset any hint of whimsy in the concept. Steed and Tara's separation only allows some light humour by telephone – Steed's 'clairvoyance' regarding Tara's cake icing, for instance. Truman's sneezing fits and off-colour remarks about "pinching" have to substitute for badinage.

The attempt to reinstate more 'down to earth' stories for this season, under replacement producer John Bryce, quickly failed. However, the series did eventually re-establish some danger and drama, and managed to lose some of the candy-coloured frivolity, whilst retaining an element of surrealism and skewed logic. Perhaps the wintry 1969 episodes were paving the way for a grittier direction into the 1970s. The episodes made after *Fog* have an undeniably grimmer, and perhaps less palatable, style than earlier episodes; see *Take-Over* for the furthest extreme of this trend. *The Avengers* had frequently changed its direction before, but whether or not the new style is successful is a matter for the individual viewer to decide.

© Frank Shailes

1. Frank's comments raise an important question. While science fiction seems a more than adequate label for a one-dimensional episode such as *Invasion of the Earthmen*, does it really fit an hour such as *The Cybernauts* which includes sci-fi elements but is more about both the dangers of nuclear weapons and the debate about the 'white heat' technological revolution?
2. From this perspective, the episode belongs to a mini-sub-genre including *Man-Eater of Surrey Green* and *Gnaws* where atmospheric build-up leads to the anti-climactic/absurd visual revelation. The episode title was Clemens' creation, replacing Nation's working titles *It* and *Little Boxes*.

3. Terry Nation replaced Philip Levene as script-editor on Brian Clemens' return. However, knowing how Clemens always wanted full control of the series, I doubt if Nation was anything more than a figure head. As a script writer – as I suggest elsewhere in this book – I simply don't think he ever understood the subtlety and style of the show, unlike Season 6 regulars Jeremy Burnham and Tony Williamson. He is far more at ease with 'pure' science fiction and *Blake's 7* remains – for me – the most philosophically intelligent sci-fi or space opera show of all time.
4. Nation is infamous for recycling creative material, both his own and other writers', such as his re-use of a Clemens *The Baron* script for *Take-Over*.
5. I agree that *The Avengers* works far better when it employs quirky subtlety rather than slapstick.

HOMICIDE AND OLD LACE

Filmed: completed January 1969

Exterior Locations:
Urban street
Scaffolding (old footage)
Trees and lake, fire post (old footage)
Village pub (old footage)
Country roads
Fields and unmarked grave
Urban street
Earthworks/quarry (old footage)
Intercrime building: front entrance
Top security warehouse: fire escape, yard
Busy city street
London images (stock footage)

Sets:
Old ladies' house: living room
John Steed's mews apartment
Intercrime headquarters: Dunbar's office, control room, cell
Jeweller's safe room
Country cottage (old footage)
Tara King's apartment
Top security warehouse: vaults, Corf's office
Mother's headquarters: art-filled penthouse

HOMICIDE AND OLD LACE

Main Character List:
Georgina: old lady, Mother's aunt
Harriet: old lady, Mother's aunt
Mother
Rhonda: Mother silent assistant
Freddie Cartwright: contact
John Steed
Tara King
Dunbar: Intercrime president
Jackson: Intercrime
Osaka: Intercrime
Fuller: Intercrime henchman
Rossi: Intercrime henchman, fake window cleaner
Kruger: Intercrime henchman, fake window cleaner
Dubois: French safe cracker for Intercrime
Colonel Corf: in command of security warehouse
Sergeant Smith: security warehouse
Lumba: Intercrime henchman

Once upon a time there was an unloved episode of *The Avengers* that committed the dispiriting crime of being unwatchable. 'Unwatchable' is surely the most damning crime for any *Avengers* episode to commit. However, the nature of the production of this episode surely makes it a fascinating episode in itself. It is two visions of the show bolted together in a very rushed 'that'll do' fashion; an episode made to fill a broadcast slot so that (to quote Terrance Dicks, one half of the authorship of *The Great Great Britain Crime*) they didn't have to show the test card.

Season 6 of the show was in the final third of production when the chop came; the Americans no longer wanted any more episodes. No sale to America meant no to a continued making of the show in the manner to which it had become accustomed; going back to black and white film or even a studio-based videotaped series was never an option. [1] Jeremy Burnham's excellent, bold, and confident *Who Was That Man I Saw You With?* showed the series safely nestled in its new identity but, on completion, they knew they would be drawing the show to an end. Their hearts must have gone from the show to an extent - there was no future to look forward to. It's very telling that the last few episodes of Season 6 bear strong similarities to the writers' past work on shows like *Adam Adamant Lives!* and a number of ITC action series. Not that there weren't some strong episodes amongst them, but there is a sense of the remainder being a contractual obligation. With so much recycling of plot lines going on it seems inevitable that Clemens would choose to resurrect the dusty film of *The Great Great Britain Crime* from the vaults to give the team more time in the increasingly fraught production schedule.

The Great Great Britain Crime had the distinction of being the episode that, of all the John Bryce produced episodes, Clemens and Fennell originally considered too awful to adapt for use. *Invasion of* the Earthmen and *Have Guns Will Haggle* had something that they could salvage, given a bit of tweaking but not, it seems, this episode. Only desperation seems to have caused them to use this poor, unloved Bryce child.

Producer John Bryce was brought back to inject some reality into the plots so, on the surface, *The Great Great Britain Crime* seems like a solid idea. Malcolm Hulke and Terrance Dicks had already written for the show back in Seasons 2 & 3 and had shown themselves dependable scribes (the Intercrime criminal organisation featured here had previously appeared in Season 2's eponymously titled episode). What was their crime that made this such a black sheep? The plot: a large international crime organisation...Ah. International. That's a word that the show wasn't really embracing by this stage. The fictional world of *The Avengers* was celebrating quiet country lanes, manor houses and secret government projects; the show didn't talk about foreigners unless they were part of a British Empire colony or heavily Anglophiled. The African characters featured in *Have Guns – Will Haggle* got through by the skin of their teeth in a similar 'transmission rush' but *Crime* was positively overrunning with foreigners: Japanese, Africans and (gasp!) Americans. Would the episode have found greater favour were Intercime an organisation purely British-based? Anglocrime?

The idea of a crime organisation manipulating emergency protocols to ensure that all the UK treasures are removed to one safe location in order that they can easily rob them is a rather fantastic one. With little tweaking, the script could have quite happily sat in the John Bryce-produced Season 3, alongside heist episodes like *The Gilded Cage*. Under Bryce, it's easy to see the show heading out into a wider arena than the rather claustrophobic, heavily stylised and clichéd one of Season 5. The second unit director was sent to capture footage of Buckingham Palace, Tower Bridge and Trafalgar Square, amongst other locations. The show was possibly starting the transition to a more tourist-pleasing aesthetic by including these recognisable locations. John Bryce's brief reign seems to have been moving the fictional world of *The Avengers* back to areas it had once existed in during its videotape days. Even when Clemens and Fennell were reinstated you can still see elements of what Bryce started leaking back through, such as the greater use of London locations.

Despite this new embracing of a more urban landscape, by the time he came to use the footage, the episode still presented an *Avengers* world that didn't tally with Clemens' own vision. His solution to the problem was quite a novel one. With episodes like *Invasion of the Earthmen*, *The Curious Case of The Countless Clues*, *Have Guns – Will Haggle*, although stylistically they don't bare much similarity to Clemens' vision, they were self-contained enough to not need much adjustment. *Crime* had a broader canvas, with more of a sense of a busy cosmopolitan world (e.g., an extra is seen on a busy London street near Marble Arch). Clemens decided to make it an exaggerated fiction within the fiction of the show. This wasn't merely a clip show (although it certainly starts that way); this was Mother creating his own fan fiction, with a fantasy blonde Tara King no less!

Experienced director John Hough was given the job of shooting Clemens' linking material (he'd worked on the original episode in his usual capacity as second unit director). He's showing us Clemens' *Avengers*. This is a world of empty, atmospheric streets, threats from seemingly innocent looking old ladies, low shots, depth of field shots; stylistically, it's wonderful to watch. Hough is quoted in Marcus Hearn's *The Avengers – A Celebration* as saying how interested the producers were in the way something was shot. The teaser fools us into imagining what kind of episode this could be. One of the old ladies had previously appeared in Season 4's *The Girl from Auntie* where she was ruthless with a knitting needle. Was this another episode about killer grannies? Of course not, but it makes for a fun introduction. There is a lovely touch for the individualised title caption with *Homicide and Old Lace* framed by doilies. Clemens very swiftly breaks our first impression by these old ladies being both harmless and actually Mother's aunties. It's interesting to note that Clemens avoids the issue of them ever referring to him by name; he's simply "nephew". [2]

Patrick Newell makes for a superb narrator. He'd already made this clear from Mother's melodramatic imaginings of a fictitious diary account of a Gaslight Ghoul killing in *Fog*. Is his recounting of the *Great Great Britain Crime* any less fictitious? Would the head of a spy organisation casually recount a top secret case; he'd surely have a top hush or button lip classification (ref. *The Positive-Negative Man*). With such a stylistic difference – even, as noted, making Tara King blonde – it can only be the imaginings of a creative mind. As his aunts are fascinated by detective fiction, it probably runs in the family.

"Now look here, Aunts, this is MY story and if I wish to make Tara King sky blue pink, I will!"

For a surprise birthday party, it seems rather cruel that the recipient has to do all the work. Surely it should be his aunts entertaining *him*. As listeners they are rather ungracious, picking holes in every detail and pulling the plot apart. Could it be that the aunts are a mouthpiece for Clemens' own opinions of the original plotting, or are they a way to cover what Clemens removed from the story? The original footage apparently ran to 63 minutes, whereas the average episode length was 50 minutes. The heavy plotting would have needed some severe cutting to make it ready for broadcast. Maybe what Hulke and Dicks plotted was too intricate for Clemens' more linear *Avengers* style of the time. (Would it have worked better as a *New Avengers* plot?).

Mother starts his story in familiar Clemens' *Avengers* territory with clips from *The Fear Merchants*, *The Bird Who Knew Too Much* and *Murdersville*. It would have been a bit strange if Clemens had gone for black and white clips from Season 4, so was limited to the previous colour season. These clips are all without dialogue so Mother can narrate over the top. By choosing moments from disparate episodes to weave into his tale, even including the hardly anonymous Christopher Lee from *Never, Never Say Die*, this adds further fuel to the idea that Mother is inventing the whole scenario. [3]

Vernon Sewell was the original director of *The Great Great Britain Crime* and his style couldn't be more different from Hough's. There are countless wide shots that fail to communicate any sense of style, or pace or drama. His visuals are very flat and undynamic. To add insult to injury, at one point he even shoots off the set. When Tara is escorted to the chief villain Dunbar's office, to be tested in her skill at safe cracking, the guard opens the door to reveal the studio fourth wall. It's no surprise that Sewell wasn't invited back. For all that the script might have lacked of Clemens' *Avengerland*, the direction is chiefly to blame, spoiling many potentially exciting moments. Whilst he fails on the dialogue scenes, the car chase when Dunbar's men ambush Tara in a multi-storey car park is very dynamic and exciting. It doubtless helped that John Hough's second unit camera crew were involved at points. For all the faults of the brief Bryce period, car action is not one of them; *Invitation to a Killing* (aka *Have Guns – Will Haggle*) features a similarly stylish car chase.

As much as the framing device allowed Clemens to have fun at the expense of the original episode (and actually use some of it), it does no favours to the viewer's engagement with the story. In order to cut through what was presumably a complicated plot, we see very little of the story, as Mother races through with his exposition. It breaks the much repeated maxim of 'show, not tell'. We don't get the chance to connect with any of the characters or with what is going on. Even when the action becomes clearer, with the actual heist, too much time is still spent on the narration. As stated earlier, one can surmise that Clemens felt the original plotting was too complicated for *Avengers* viewers used to its (by that stage) normally linear approach; he compressed it into narration to simplify it. *Crime* seems to have had a bit of cat-and-mouse shenanigans as Steed inveigles himself and Tara's way into the Intercrime gang (similar to how Cathy Gale became a member of the gang in the Season 2 episode). The framework ultimately fails as, when the viewer tries to engage with the story, it cuts back to Mother's narration and/or his aunts picking at the storytelling which only serves to irritate. The flippant style of the framework doesn't gel with the generally serious style of the Bryce material, despite attempts to use the silent movie style piano accompaniment to add playful musical colour. The narration framing might have worked within Season 5 which had a more jovial approach. The contrast simply makes the differences even more awkward and apparent. It also does a disservice to *Crime* which on its own terms might have been a serviceable episode. There are some very glib and cheap attempts at humour which the show normally didn't sink to. For example, when Tara overpowers a guard in her prison, the shot is a freeze frame of the door over which comedy sound effects are played, the final sound a cork popping. Further to this, when Tara overturns the secretary's desk, a cry of "Aarrggh, you've laddered my stocking!" is dubbed on. These types of thoughtless additions sadly remind us that the end is in sight and the production team thought, "That'll do". Whether they consciously did or not, it's insulting to a series that was known for its sophistication. It's trying to stamp a joke on to something that wasn't meant to be funny.

For all the straight forward playing of the Bryce footage, it's clear that this still had its own moments of light avengerish humour, such as Cartright constantly saying, "Old man" which Steed mimics. [4] Also Colonel Corf's response to being told to surrender by the baddies; he declares that they can't say that as he had said it first. There are even playful moments such as villain Dunbar going to light his cigarette with a lighter he had just explained doubles as a grenade, which causes the other international members of Intercrime to duck. And Steed claiming he couldn't get the French safe cracker Dubois into a security establishment as the man's a criminal and looks like a criminal.

With so much of the running time of the old footage given over to plot, there isn't much chance for Steed and Tara to shine. From his memoirs, we know that Macnee was struggling with his new role in the show but Steed seems strangely bland much of the time. Tara gets some action sequences but contributes very little dialogue. This Tara, of course, is the original non-spy version. Linda Thorson's performance is still in her rather stilted phase, before she'd relaxed and looked like she was finally enjoying herself. She wasn't helped by the atrocious wardrobe choices. After showing such confident, mature performances, it's a shame they had to dredge up her uncertain one. [5] Even hearing the new voiceover she contributed to the discussion of the potential Buckingham Palace robbery demonstrates her performance progression.

The other main cast members are fine, dependable actors. For all that the linking material irritates, Joyce Carey (who starred in the 1945 film *Brief Encounter*) and Mary Merrall are utterly charming and likeable in isolation, delivering some amusing gags. Patrick Newell gets to show his softer side, after recent episodes where he was simply furious the whole time. Rhonda Parker is allowed to show some personality...albeit still silent. In the original material, Keith Baxter as Dunbar makes a strong impression, even when surrounded by the weaker cast members. The BBC's Adam Adamant, Gerald Harper, gives an amusing turn as Colonel Corf. And Donald Pickering makes a second appearance in the show, as Freddie Cartright, with his convenient bullet-proof vest. It's a shame that we don't get to appreciate these performances in an untainted way.

The whole episode is topped off, or should that be bottomed off, with a tag scene that appears like a blooper or deleted scene. Macnee and Newell seem to have improvised it and break character as it draws to a conclusion. And in a display of appalling editing, a snatch of Izzy Pound playing the National Anthem from *The Interrogators* segues into a crowd cheer and a piano version of *The Avengers* theme for the closing titles. It's as if quality control was no longer important.

In conclusion, it's very easy to see why it is considered unwatchable. As charming as the added framework can be at times, it never lets us into the proper story. The real Great Great Britain Crime is that we'll probably never be able to see the original footage and make up our own minds about the episode. But from what remains it seems that the direction and the overall aesthetic was criminally bad for a series that prided itself on quality productions. And the ultimate responsibility for that belonged to the original producer, John Bryce.

© Darren Burch
1. Given that *The Avengers* was now being exclusively bankrolled by the US network ABC and that monochrome filming was not much cheaper, I presume that the production company had no option other than to stop.
2. This is an excellent observation which I have never noted on my (admittedly) rare viewings of this episode.
3. Just as I dislike the recycling of music in Season 6, I imagine that I am not alone in feeling much the same about watching previous footage. It is, possibly, acceptable in *Return of the Cybernauts* and *Who's Who???*, but here it is uninteresting and taken to an extreme.
4. I presume that this is an intertextual nod to *James Bond*, to the foreign agent on board the train in *From Russia With Love*.
5. I agree wholeheartedly. Unearthing this early 'effort' at such a late stage in the 33 episode run almost resembles a slap in the face for King/Thorson and the viewer.

Homicide and Old Lace represents an irresistibly caustic rewriting/reworking of the previous John Bryce style and a dazzling demonstration of the corrosive power of humour. Brian Clemens also offers us an enthusiastic portrait of Mother, an irreplaceable asset of the season.

Its prototype structure of future 'clip shows' which would pepper many television schedules could lead to us undervaluing the quality of *Homicide and Old Lace*. However, once again – as elsewhere – the series was offering us proof of its *avant-garde* spirit! Above all, the episode represents an accomplished and exhilarating rewrite. In effect, Brian Clemens brilliantly converted *The Great Great Britain Crime*, an episode of the Bryce era, which he deemed unusable for transmission in its original form. In the first place he develops a style which fits the happily transgressive spirit of *The Avengers*. To achieve his ends, Clemens is firing on all cylinders, using a frenetic montage, giving the whole a cartoonish aspect, ironically emphasising the stiff side of the story. He also makes all the music and sound effects parodic. Secondly, Clemens undermines the stilted or constrained performances, tedious discourses, the constant lack of rhythm and inert deadness of the direction and stagecraft characteristised by the previous production team, perfectly illustrated by *Invasion of the Earthmen*.

One laughs openly, especially at Mother's bombastic storytelling, as he fully participates in this caustic irony. This is particularly the case when he points out – in an over-the-top manner – the absurdity of certain situations in his off-camera voice: for example, the use of a Japanese villain as the least likely man to attract attention in a busy European street. Happy to be cruel – and certainly one can question the lack of fair play in the process – Clemens exploits Mother's 'charming' aunts. Their theoretical role as enthusiastic, passive listeners is soon pierced: they are formidable critics, pointing unerringly to the narrative weaknesses of *The Great Great Britain Crime*: they represent a masterpiece of mischief and trickery on the part of Clemens within the narrative. Poor Mother is, moreover, obliged to remind the aunts several times that it is he who is telling the story, a villainous way of highlighting the original script's many misinterpretations and shortcomings.

However, Brian Clemens does not limit his role to that of a vitriolic rewrite. *The Great Great Britain Crime* is a great tribute to the endearing figure and undeniable trump card of this sixth season: Mother. It is with youthful enthusiasm that our friend seeks to satisfy his aunts by embroidering for them (from scratch) the most sensational story possible to satisfy their craving for thrills. For this, he draws on his memory, justifying the use of fragments of past missions, before expanding his remarks to the main section of the story. This dynamic 'work in progress' perfectly illustrates his sympathetic character, and his truly youthful passion for a job – of espionage and spying – which he always strives to paint in a shimmering, epic light, rather than in its sad and banal reality. *Homicide and Old Lace* demonstrates its ability to avoid the faults of later 'clip shows', offering us a plot which is both clever and logical; after all, it had already been established in *The Forget-Me-Knot* that Mother has known Steed for a long time and is aware of his adventures of the previous season.

Enthusiastic, passionate and colourful, here we find Mother revealed in his most intimate reality, the 'high ideal' or boss of the Avengers in their imaginary realm. It is a tribute that is climaxed by the hilarious tag scene which expands upon both his friendship with Steed but also with the indispensable Rhonda. Mother deserved the 'marshal's baton' that constitutes an episode dedicated to a secondary character. *Homicide and Old Lace* brings him the just reward *in extremis*, as we approach the final instalments of a series that would conclude with style. Patrick Newell demonstrates from start to finish an irresistible humour and vitality, in perfect harmony with his colourful and sparkling partners.

© Bernard Ginez (© translation by Rodney Marshall)

HOMICIDE ET VIEILLES DENTELLES

Homicide and Old Lace constitue une irrésistible récriture caustique du style John Bryce et une éblouissante démonstration du pouvoir corrosif de l'humour. Brian Clemens nous propose également un enthousiaste portrait de Mother, irremplaçable atout de la saison.

Sa structure de prototype des futurs clips shows émaillant de nombreuses séries pourrait déprécier la qualité d'*Homicide and Old Lace*. Encore que là comme ailleurs la série s'avère avant-gardiste ! Surtout, l'opus va s'avérer constituer un travail de récriture aussi abouti qu'enthousiasmant. En effet Brian Clemens va brillamment détourner *The Great Great Britain Crime*, un épisode de l'époque John Bryce qu'il estime irrécupérable pour une diffusion classique. En effet, sous sa version littérale il développe un premier degré massif, totalement exogène à l'esprit joyeusement transgressif des Avengers. Pour arriver à ses fins, Clemens fait feu de tout bois, ayant recours à un montage frénétique conférant à l'ensemble un aspect de Cartoon, accentuant de manière ironique le caractère figé du récit. Mais il agrémente aussi l'ensemble de musiques et effets sonores tout à fait parodiques. Dans un irrésistible second degré astucieux et incisif, Clemens fustige ainsi les interprétations figées, les péroraisons fastidieuses, le constant manque de rythme et les mises en scènes inertes caractéristiques de l'équipe précédente, dont *Invasion Of The Earthmen* propose un éloquent témoignage.

On rit franchement, d'autant que la narration volontairement emphatique de Mother participe pleinement à cette caustique ironie. C'est notamment le cas quand il souligne de manière enflammée l'absurdité de certaines situations, en voix off (*Ayant fait astucieusement appel à un Japonais comme l'homme le moins susceptible d'attirer l'attention dans une rue européenne très fréquentée...*). L'ironie du contraste s'avère dévastatrice. Volontiers cruel (et, certes on peut questionner le manque de fair-play du procédé), Clemens va jusqu'à instrumentaliser les charmantes tantes de Mother. Derrière l'enthousiasme de leur écoute percent rapidement de redoutables critiques, pointant infailliblement les faiblesses narratives de *The Great Great Britain Crime*, un chef d'œuvre de malice et de rouerie de la part d'un auteur se trouvant de tranchantes porte-paroles au sein du récit. Le pauvre Mother se voit d'ailleurs contraint d'asséner à plusieurs reprises que « c'est lui qui raconte histoire », une manière assassine de souligner en contrepoint les nombreux contresens et lacunes du scénario original. *Homicide and Old Lace* s'impose autant comme l'ancêtre des clips shows que comme celui des décapants détournements chers à Canal Plus.

Mais Brian Clemens ne limite pas son entreprise à cette seule réjouissante réécriture au vitriol. *The Great Great Britain Crime* représente en effet un superbe hommage à cette attachante figure et incontestable atout de cette sixième saison qu'aura toujours été Mother. C'est avec juvénile enthousiasme que notre ami s'attache à satisfaire ses tantes en leur brodant de toutes pièces l'histoire la plus sensationnaliste possible visant à satisfaire leur envie de sensations fortes. Il puise pour cela dans sa mémoire, justifiant le recours à fragments de missions passées, avant d'élargir son propos au segment principal. Ce tonique *work in progress* illustre à merveille la sympathie du personnage, ainsi que sa passion véritablement juvénile pour un métier qu'il s'attache toujours à rendre plus chatoyant et épique que la triste et banale réalité. *Homicide and Old Lace* se montre exempt des défauts caractérisant nombre des clip-shows ultérieurs, avec une mise en situation astucieuse et logique, puisqu'il est établi dès *The Forget-Me-Knot* que Mother connaît Steed de longue date et donc est au courant de ses aventures de la saison précédente.

Enthousiaste, passionné et haut en couleurs, voici Mother révélé dans sa vérité intime, l'idéal supérieur des Avengers en leur royaume de l'imaginaire. Un bel hommage que l'hilarant tag de fin élargit à son amitié complice envers Steed mais aussi envers l'indispensable Rhonda. Mother méritait bien ce bâton de maréchal que constitue pour un personnage secondaire mérite de voir dédier un épisode. *Homicide and Old Lace* lui apporte cette juste récompense in extremis, alors que l'on aborde les ultime opus d'une série qu'il saura conclure avec saveur. Patrick Newell se montre de bout en bout irrésistible d'humour et de vitalité, en parfaite complicité avec ses pittoresques et pétillantes partenaires.

© Bernard Ginez

REQUIEM

Filmed: February 1969

Exterior Locations:
Underground car park and slope
Street and car park
Steed's mews
Country roads
House and warehouse, grounds, drive
Graveyard
Suburban street and Cleaver's house
Village streets
Gated entrance to Fort Steed

Sets:
John Steed's mews apartment
House and warehouse: locked room, Steed's wrecked apartment, hospital room and corridor
Fort Steed: play room
Hearse
Mother's fake Fort Steed: living room

REQUIEM

Main Character List:
Rista: henchman
Murray: henchman
Miranda Loxton: key witness against Murder International
John Steed
Tara King
Mother
Rhonda: Mother's silent assistant
Bobby Cleaver: agent
Firth: fake Major
Wells: fake doctor
Jill: fake nurse
Barrett

Murray and Rista lie in wait for Miranda Loxton, witness in the case against Murder International, but they wind up killing her bodyguard instead – she is disguised as a clown with a moustache, he is in a ball gown and masque. The freeze frame under the opening credits is a shot of the dead bodyguard in drag, a suggestion of the misdirection of the audience to come. This is a Brian Clemens script, directed by the inimitable Don Chaffey, so we know we can expect something special. Clemens once said, "Nothing is straight in *The Avengers*" and this script, like *Epic* before it, takes that to artistic extremes.

Tara is surprised to find Mother at Steed's flat and Steed "checking a gun". Mother pompously declares that it's an important case but it's Steed who fills her in; he has been assigned the task of protecting Miranda at what he calls Fort Steed, which causes a pang of jealousy in Tara. (Tara's crush on Steed is a minor subplot of Season 6.) He heads off to *rendez-vous* with Miranda while Mother scoots over to examine the liquor cabinet.

I love Patrick Newell's performance as Mother in this episode; he suits the twinkle in the eye and cheeky theft of liquor more than the brusque authoritarianism of *Wish You Were Here*. Mother's demeanour is a charade; he is often brusque in the company of his male agents but relaxes when he's alone with Rhonda or Tara. Does he prefer the company of women? Or are male agents a painful reminder of his former self, before whatever put him in a wheelchair happened? [1]

Steed is ambushed when he meets Miranda but he has anticipated this and another agent, Cleaver, decoys the attackers. Tara, meanwhile, is captured and forced to drive to the Elstree props storage area. This is an almighty clue for the coming action, a foreshadowing of the plot, but is subtly done – no attention is drawn to the props, they are just there in the *mis-en-scène*. She fights her captor, noticing the flower tattoo on his right hand, but is knocked down. The tattoo is an annoying failure of this episode. Sadly, it appears to be drawn in biro and it changes from scene to scene, presumably as it was redrawn for each day of filming; it should have been done properly by make-up.

Tara overhears the crooks discussing a booby trap in Steed's flat; on the third ring of Steed's all-clear signal, the bomb will explode. This is another minor plot flaw – how did they know Steed was going to let the phone ring three times then hang up for his signal? Come to that, how do they know what his flat looks like? The only possible inference is that his flat had been infiltrated and bugged. She escapes through a window but comes over faint as she reaches the car, oddly coming to in the corridor outside Steed's flat. The phone rings and she rushes in, too late to stop the bomb from exploding, knocking her out again. She comes to in a burnt and shattered flat, Mother apparently lying under a piece of the fireplace; she shouts for him then faints again. When she revives a third time, the flat is full of emergency workers clearing the damage and carrying out a body. She is sedated and taken to a hospital.

This episode is all about misdirection and the sets here are excellent. I think we can safely assume that all the scenes in Steed's unaltered flat for *Requiem* were completed before the set was redressed and partly rebuilt for the bomb damage in this episode. Otherwise, they would have had to re-construct the set and redress it again, which seems unlikely given the tight production schedules that they had. (The final two episodes do not feature Steed's Stable Mews apartment). [2]

With Tara being sedated, we see the escalation of the drug subtext of the episode – whenever Tara moves, she is sedated. This trope was a little over-used in the Tara era but is perhaps a product of its time. Don Chaffey enjoys losing focus and snapping back in to suggest the sedation.

When she wakes in hospital, the doctor tells her that both her legs are broken but that she has no spinal damage – she must rest. Major Firth introduces himself and says they need to find Steed. Tara suggests he ask Mother, to which Firth replies, "I can't ask Mother…Mother is dead." This dramatic confirmation that the body in the flat was indeed Mother is excellently played – Firth is downbeat and turns away after telling her, unable to hold her gaze. Tara can only stare in astonishment. [3]

Meanwhile, Steed and Miranda arrive at Fort Steed, the use of music from *Something Nasty in the Nursery* reinforcing the childhood association of the location. Angela Douglas, pleased to be out of her clown disguise, establishes great rapport with Patrick Macnee in these scenes even though the boom microphone dips into shot a couple of times. [4] Steed has a great line in the car as they escape: "Why don't you make yourself comfortable? Take off your nose!"

There are minor continuity errors throughout the episode which are mostly due to post-production editing and the tight filming schedule: Steed changing stance in a cut-away, presumably because a line was cut; a long shot of the van following Steed's car showing a puff of smoke from Rista's gun without a gunshot effect; and so on. Nothing major, but not something which (observant) modern audiences would expect.

Miranda hints at her knowledge of military history and Steed challenges her to recreate Déclair's retreat, then the Battle of Trafalgar and finally a game of chess, all of which she overwhelmingly defeats him in. She confesses to having capable relatives in all these fields, reminiscent of Steed's many and varied aunts. These scenes are the comic relief for the episode, interwoven with the much more serious hunt for Steed. [5]

Firth's lieutenant (another subtle clue here, he's wearing insignia of a cavalry regiment, while Firth is grenadier guards) comes in with the plans for another bomb they found in the flat, this one in a gold pencil – identical to one Tara gave Steed for Christmas. The hunt for Steed is now a race against time.

Tara begs Firth to let her attend Mother's funeral and she is once again sedated for transport there and back but this scene exposes a major script flaw – Tara never seems to wonder why she is the only agent there, and everyone else at the poorly-attended ceremony is from the hospital. This is, of course, another clue for the viewer that all is not what it seems, a central theme of Clemens' scripts throughout the years. Tara suddenly remembers that Bobby was on the assignment with Steed, and Firth radios this in to HQ (rather unsubtly, it must be said, as he's clearly hinting at something when he relays the message – he might as well have said, "Nudge, nudge, wink, wink.")

Murray and Rista get there first and Cleaver dies before he can reveal anything to Firth. Once again, we have a plot flaw, moments after the last. Why do they kill Cleaver at all? Had he revealed he had no knowledge of Fort Steed? Given the lengths they're going to with Tara, you would expect a more concerted effort to extract information from him.

Tara remembers some more snippets: Steed talking about watching the Henley Regatta from near his childhood home and urns on a high wall. She guesses it would be a big house, revealing further gentrification of Steed. There has been an increasing revisionism of Steed's history during Season 6 and the latter part of the previous season. He is given a new persona and background to match his more dapper appearance, which is fine for the casual viewer who might associate his image with a man about town, rather than the harder, more cynical operative of the early years. Certainly, his wardrobe and the set of his flat have gone more upmarket in the last couple of years. I wonder if Clemens was tapping into natural British snobbery or pandering to an American expectation of a class system.

Tara suggests that Steed's flat might jog more memories and is once more drugged for the journey; Howard Blake's suspense theme from *Invasion of the Earthmen* plays when they enter the destroyed flat, setting the mood nicely. Tara spots some flowers and remembers Steed reminiscing about roses around the door and swinging on the iron gates with comedy/tragedy faces.

Back at the hospital, Tara notices Murray's tattoo when he tends to her and summons Firth, who knocks him down – onto Tara's supposedly numb legs, and she feels the pain, but is distracted by remembering a cannon-shaped weathervane on the house which can be seen for miles. Delighted, Firth rushes off to search for the house, leaving Tara alone. She realises her legs ache and examines them, finding the plaster is crumbling off. She peels away the plaster and gets out of bed, bracing herself for a shock of pain which never comes. A nearby staircase leads to the burnt-out replica of Steed's flat she recently 'visited', the door beyond opens to the room she was first locked up in. Realising her folly, she turns to escape. [6]

The artifice comes crashing down and the plot is finally revealed. All those clues that had been scattered throughout the episode now reveal their meaning. I can't recall exactly what I felt the first time I saw this episode, it was too long ago, but I wonder if I experienced a sense of relief as all the supposed shortcomings of the episode were at this point revealed to be intentional.

Requiem is reminiscent of *Epic* in its deconstruction of the usual suspension of disbelief that television normally strives for and here, as there, we are taken backstage to see the sets as sets. This episode is a perfect example of the set-within-the-set theme that we often see in *The Avengers*, and which justly makes it famous for the self-referential and post-modern.

Tara defeats those still at the hospital and returns to Steed's real flat. To his astonishment, she gives Mother a big kiss on the cheek. Appraised of the plot, Mother calls Special Services and gets them to dress a prominent house in the attributes Tara had described – but accentuated so it can't be overlooked. Is this another subtle self-referential dig at *The Avengers*, where caricature and parody is the 'thicker cardboard' of every episode?

Steed, meanwhile, has finally beaten Miranda…at Ludo, thanks to the skills passed on by his cousin, Demon Desmond; not a Ludo Champion as Miranda guesses but a Dice Loader! Delighted, Miranda gushes, "Groovy, baby!" It's played for laughs, but this is more in line with Steed's history – devious chicanery rather than the upper-class toff.

Firth and his men enter the house they think holds Steed – it sounds like dice are being rolled in the next room, but they burst in to find Mother and Rhonda, who easily take care of them. This is a pointless last attempt at suspense; the audience already knows Firth has been tricked and that there won't be time for another plot twist. Tara meanwhile finds the correct house – smaller masks on the gate, smaller urns, and a *canon* shaped weather vane, which anyone would take to be a Bishop.

Sadly, the tag scene doesn't live up to the rest and seems forced. Tara finds Steed researching his family tree and he claims to be descended from "King Noffin of the Fens". Is this a send-up of the middle-class obsession with finding illustrious ancestors, an attempt to further ingrain the revisionist history of Steed, or subvert it by revealing it to be totally false?

Requiem is a terrific episode and has many elements of a classic Brian Clemens story. Clemens loves a good plot twist and here he uses it to deconstruct the show completely, going beyond the intentional artificiality of the sparsely populated *Avengerland* to reveal that the entire show is a façade.

Don Chaffey has a great outing with this episode, calling on all his directorial prowess. He is clearly relishing a more serious plot and producing a finer result than we saw in *Wish You Were Here*. His use of the loss of focus trope to suggest sedation is well measured, despite its frequent repetition. The intercutting and depth of field changes in the bedside chats between Firth and Tara brings the scenes to life and engages the viewer. Chaffey also makes good use of a handheld camera in the hallway outside Steed's flat as Tara staggers towards the door, an unusual sight in Sixties television. Chaffey's panning shots (almost never tracking, perhaps due to the sets), judicious zooms, and tightening on the subject makes the vision sing, coupled with well-shot location work throughout.

We have a lovely tight focus on the tin soldiers and then zoom out to find Miranda. The shot is repeated with Steed, from Miranda's point of view, which mars the drama somewhat; but I suspect that this was an error in the editing suite; Chaffey would naturally film both shots but expect only one to be used in the final cut.

What was wrong with the episode? Murray's tattoo; a couple of silly continuity and plot errors that could have been avoided; Katja Wyeth, who merely stands around smiling; the final pointless attempt at suspense; Murder International seemingly consists of only six people, plus a few passers-by at the hospital and the clean-up crew, hardly an outfit warranting a major court case; the forced tag scene. Not enough, thankfully, to mar the excellence of the rest of the episode which remains a highlight of the last season of *The Avengers*, as befits the work of both writer and director.

© Piers Johnson

1. Is Mother an embittered, disabled ex-agent? Is he an asexual man most comfortable with female company?
2. This is backed up by *Bowler Hats and Kinky Boots*, in which Michael Richardson comments: "As the apartment would not feature in the final couple of episodes, the set dressers were allowed to run riot and totally ruin the set for scenes showing the aftermath of a bomb explosion." On another level, of course, as Piers observes, *Requiem* is revelling in its own self-referentiality, Clemens revealing Steed's flat as a set, just as he had done with Mrs. Peel's in *Epic*.
3. *Requiem* is, indeed, one of those episodes where the dark, disturbing, subversive drama comes bubbling to the surface.
4. Piers notes that 'while we can see the boom microphone on modern televisions, it was outside the viewable area of the day and almost any director or editor of the time would not consider it worth reshooting.'
5. The champagne to go alongside the subversion, reflecting *Requiem*'s deserved status as a 'classic' Season 6 episode.
6. The stripping back of the fourth wall is a delightfully artificial moment which somehow *increases* the dramatic tension.

TAKE-OVER

Filmed: February 1969

Exterior Locations:
Country roads
Fields
Bassett's country house: façade, driveway
Countryside, woodland, swampy ground

Sets:
Grenville's Rolls Royce
Tara King's apartment
Country House: hallway, living/dining room, staircase, landing, Steed's bedroom, Bassett's bedroom, turret room
Land Rover

TAKE-OVER

Main Character List:
Ernest Lomax: chauffeur henchman
Fenton Grenville: diabolical mastermind
John Steed
Tara King
Sergeant Ronald Groom: Bassett manservant
Gilbert Sexton: chef henchman
Laura Bassett: friend of Steed
Circe Bishop: Grenville's medical assistant
Bill Bassett: wartime friend of Steed
Norman Clifford: Special Branch
Corby Trainer: Special Branch

"Do you think I'm pretty?" the blonde surgeon asks. A radio-detonated phosphorus bomb has been skillfully, surgically implanted in the necks of her three victims. The disfiguring scars are covered so as not to raise suspicion. It is an interesting question to ask about oneself...particularly after performing such an ugly act. Circe, an attractive blonde woman, has had multiple plastic surgeries herself, in search of physical perfection. Yet, it is not an exaggeration to say that such a quest for beauty corresponds to a vital need to escape from a profound sense of ugliness. That ugliness is beautifully and graphically captured in *Take-Over*. Just as she tells Steed that she finds him attractive, she begins a most telling dialogue:

Circe: Do you think I'm pretty? I think I am. I think I could be very pretty.
Steed: Who am I to argue with a lady?
Circe: I'm not a lady. That's why I was expelled from medical school. It's my name. It affected my whole character.
Steed: Ah, the Greek goddess Circe, who could turn men into wild beasts.
Circe: Except I can't. I need to have my nose altered you know. Then I'll be really pretty.
Steed: It's a very nice nose.
Circe: It's alright. The second one I had was the best though. I spend all my money on new noses.
Steed: Well everyone should have a hobby.
Circe: I spend practically every penny I get on new noses. Every penny.

After Circe bids him good night with a kiss, she asks Grenville, "Are you going to let me operate on him?"

It is striking, the repetitive compulsion she has to maim people. After she has expressed her physical interest in Steed, she seeks to mutilate him. (It is a nice touch by the writer/s for Steed to note after dinner that she is named after the Greek Goddess Circe, who in Homer's *Odyssey* turned Odysseus' men into swine through witchcraft, after inviting them to a feast.) Circe is a wonderful construct of the 'pretty villain', much like the mastermind in *Who Was That Man I Saw You With?* We first see him sporting a green clay beauty mask. In contrast, Tara's face is black. It is a symbolic gesture of good versus evil. As Tara was all too convincingly being framed by the villain, she was perceived as a most ugly traitor to Mother. As she tells Steed, "It was the best bit of framing since the Mona Lisa." Meanwhile, with his toes and nails all perfectly manicured, and a fine tailored suit that even Steed envied, Dangerfield became the 'pretty villain'. (Were there homosexual overtones in his search for beauty?). Just like Circe in *Take-Over*, Tara's arch enemy, Dangerfield, was a sight for sore eyes. I found myself admiring his impeccably fitted tan suit and matching shoes, planning my next shopping expedition. In many ways, both are reminiscent of Oscar Wilde's Dorian Gray: a man whose painting gets uglier after each amoral act he commits. One can similarly picture both of these pretty villains' portraits of their inner souls becoming uglier with each amoral act *they* commit.

It is speculated that Oscar Wilde wrote *The Picture of Dorian Gray* (1890) very much identifying with the central character himself. As art imitates life, Wilde's real life experience may have shaped his own future as well as his literary works. It dealt with an ugliness he faced as a young boy. Indeed his father, a famous surgeon and ophthalmologist had been accused by one of his patients of having abused her while she was under anaesthesia. At that time this caused a scandal that the mother of Wilde (he was still very young) was able to stifle, by bringing the person in question to trial for defamation of character. She won the case. It is speculated in psychoanalytic papers that this internal feeling of ugliness that really belonged to his father, was symbolised in the portrait of Dorian Gray: an evolving grotesque ugliness that deepened after each amoral act committed. As life imitates art, it is strikingly reminiscent of Circe in *Take-Over* who, like Oscar Wilde's surgeon father, violates her unwilling surgical victims under anesthesia. She continually portrays insecurity about her beauty, while committing violating acts as an unlicensed surgeon on a most unwilling set of patients.

Throughout the episode, there is a sense of brutality and ugliness in the amoral acts of the group that has taken over the home and bodies of the Bassett family. What is striking about *Take-Over* is the villains' elaborate method of controlling their victims: their home, their friend Steed, their bodies. What is all this madness about? For what possible purpose would they employ such efforts to take-over this quiet, unassuming English country mansion?

The answer lies in a Hitchcockian level of suspense that is maintained by only divulging the reason for the take-over in the third and final act: to launch explosive missiles at a nearby peace conference and therefore assassinate the foreign ministers of several countries. This part of the story is a common enough dramatic theme on television during the Cold War period.

The coincidence of the site chosen also proves Hitchcockian. It so happens that Steed's friends' home is the only house in the district with an unimpeded line of fire to the peace conference for the villains to implement their deadly plan. Most *Avengers* plots are quite deviously planned and purposeful. In contrast, this episode is unusual, but well suited for *Avengerland*, in the bizarre, random way Steed is put in harm's way.

For many fans, *Take-Over* and *Murdersville* are the most violent and morally corrupt *Avengers* episodes. What is it about these episodes that creates this ugliness and depravity, which makes them the most disturbing episodes of the series? I would argue that what perturbs viewers the most in this episode is how their hero, Steed, is violently and cruelly attacked; more than in any other *Avengers* episode. Steed is not only targeted himself, but he soon learns that his friends are being held hostage. We empathise with his concerns when he sees his dearest friend's wife hiding a disfiguring scar on her neck. [1]

Initially, Grenville, the head villain, portrays to Steed an air of friendly competition over dinner. He is introduced to Steed as a business associate of his WWII buddy, Bill Bassett, who Steed is visiting. Initially, Grenville asks Steed to join them in a hunting expedition; he offers a wager of 100 guineas for the first 'kill' of the day. The visual imagery in this scene is quite stunning, recreating the thrill of a hunt. However, a gnawing sense of foreboding chills the air. Steed is the hunted beast and Grenville is his number one predator. [2]

This episode has similarities to *Murdersville*, where Mrs. Peel is viciously hunted down with primitive savagery by a depraved 'community' of villagers. Likewise, she is seen for the first time showing affection to a childhood friend she meets, who is brutally murdered by the very same town's people. In both these episodes, our heroes' vulnerabilities are viciously exploited by the villains. Their attachment toward close friends is likewise brutally used to exploit them.

Most importantly, there certainly were overtones of a Nazi-like regime. After all, they not only 'takeover' the Bassett's home: it is transformed into a concentration camp of sorts, with torture of its victims through depraved human experimentation and complete loss of autonomy and control. In fact, the depravity Grenville and Circe display is very much characteristic of Adolf Eichmann and Joseph Mengele respectively. I would argue that this is what makes these episodes rate high on the 'disturbing' scale for *Avengers* fans. Its profound sense of ugliness, just like Oscar Wilde's *Dorian Gray*, lies in its perversion. In fact, I would go as far as to suggest that it is precisely this which makes this episode so compelling: its perversity.

The Avengers is known for its bizarre and depraved criminals and their ingenious weapons. In *Dial A Deadly Number*, we learn that the murder weapon is a bleeper which injects poison into the hearts of its victims. In *Take-Over* we have an equally disturbing perversion. The Bassett's home is transformed into an operating theatre. The head surgeon, Circe, who has been expelled from medical school, heads the team, fully prepared with gas mask and scalpel at hand.

The viewer is exposed to a most violating assault. As a gas mask is forced over the intended victim's mouth, we see the scalpel blade ready to make the first cut. This female Jack the Ripper – we discover later – has devised a unique surgery only available in *Avengerland*. In fact, on one level the surgery *is* the weapon: a radio-detonated phosphorus bomb implanted into the victim's neck that explodes at the flick of a cigarette lighter. Once again, one of the many phallic symbols used in *The Avengers* is employed as a tool for a perversion of sorts: a 'rape' of the neck. This episode breaks the proverbial glass ceiling because the 'rapist' is a woman: the pretty villain Circe. *The Avengers* has no gender barriers.

What makes this episode even more chilling and unsettling for the viewer is the fact that Circe is indeed psychotic. She speaks in a bizarre, weird manner and is preoccupied with some very strange thoughts. Her character is full of so many disparities. She is physically beautiful; she is obviously both intelligent and capable, getting into medical school and creating a new type of surgical implant. Yet she presents as insecure and childlike. She is obsessed about maiming Steed (by surgically implanting a bomb in his neck), appearing almost sexually excited by the very act itself. She even tells Steed how insecure she is, as if somehow incapable of attracting a man.

I would argue that Circe's surgical prowess is her form of mating. It is her surgical yet almost sexual act of implanting exploding bombs in her mate that gives her a sense of sexual domination. Through this act, she is no longer a 'dumb blonde', but has mastered – through perversion – a way to be sexually dominant, exuding immense and complete control over her mates. From this perspective, Circe has taken on a traditionally male role.

However, in reality, Circe appears male-dominated. She is controlled by Grenville. She has to ask him for permission to 'mate' (perform surgery on Steed). She appears as if she lacks the ability and will to control her own destiny, needing a man to tell her what to do. The disparity in her character is vast. From this vantage point she appears weak, as if much of her insecurity is from a Freudian castration anxiety of sorts. Here she represents a phallic female surgeon hitman whose phallus is her surgical scalpel. Without her scalpel in hand, she feels castrated.

Grenville, on the other hand, seems more sexually thrilled by the notion that he can control life and death at the flick of a switch. He appears to establish ownership of his victim with the use of Circe's radio-detonated bomb implants in their neck. It is as if these implants are the phallic extension of Grenville, ready to explode at the flick of his switch. It is a destructive fantasy of Grenville's, as if in his mind he and his sexually powerful exploding bomb implants are one. Just as the phallic building in *Death At Bargain Prices* is aroused to ejaculate its atom bomb, likewise is the radio-detonated phosphorus bomb neck implant in *Take-Over*. Steed not only has Grenville as his vicious Oedipal predator, he also has Circe as his sexual predator. Her odd flirtations and preoccupation with Steed make her the proverbial female praying mantis, ready to 'mate', before devouring the male.

While Mrs. Peel in *Murdersville* is endangered by Mickle and Hubert's veiled threats of rape, here Steed is equally in danger of a 'sexualised' assault by Circe. The phrase 'going for the jugular' succinctly describes Circe's veiled 'sexual' threat of neck surgery on Steed. [3] Either way, Steed is an endangered species in *Take-Over*. He is both a hunted beast in a most vicious oedipal attack by Grenville, *and* a potential male praying mantis ready to be devoured by a female mate, Circe.

Steed's ingenuity saves his life. While being savagely hunted by Grenville, he has a plan. He puts his glove on a sinking branch in a marsh to indicate to Grenville that he has become that first kill of the day. In an episode displaying sophisticated technology, it is ironic how Steed once again overcomes his enemies with the use of rather clever yet low tech devices. In *Death At Bargain Prices*, a toy-pellet gun undermines the high-tech machinery; in *Dial A Deadly Number*, the use of a champagne cork wins the day. [4]

What is similar in both *Take-Over* and *Who Was That Man I Saw You With?* is that Tara brings beauty back to the story. In both episodes, her courage and strength help to regain a sense of morality that has been sorely missing. It is Tara that senses Steed's vulnerability when she sees his bowler hat left behind. It is Tara that outfoxes Circe to regain control. Her presence has been missed through the majority of the episode.

What is entirely missing from this episode, however, is light humour. While television viewers in 1969 were watching the savage takeover of Steed's friends' home, a very different kind of hostile battle had been unfolding. Around the time of the episode's creation, there was a struggle taking place over the future of the show itself. Just as Steed had Grenville trying to kill him off on a hunting expedition, someone actually succeeded with *The Avengers* itself. The show was killed off when the American ABC network decided against future orders. At £50,000 an episode, a lack of US investment spelt an end to production. Within weeks, there was a takeover (from Warner Brothers by EMI films) for the ownership of ABPC, including Elstree Studios and the rights to *The Avengers*. In 2014, with the announcement that the Teddington Studios where *The Avengers* began is due for demolition, it recaptures something of that sense of loss back in 1969: the end of the original series; a bleak future, with no further episodes to look forward to.

Who exactly is the creative genius behind *Take-Over*? In part, is it a recycled *Baron* plot of Brian Clemens' (aka Tony O'Grady) called *The Maze*? Michael Richardson suggests: "It appears that Nation, who at that time had been script supervisor on *The Baron*, simply recycled the idea for his screenplay." (*Bowler Hats and Kinky Boots*, p. 345) [5] Rodney Marshall comments: "When you look at the episode, and compare it to earlier Nation offerings, it's pretty clear to me that this was a Clemens idea and I am fairly sure that most of this was his writing, rather than Nation's." I too have a hunch that Clemens was very much involved in the scriptwriting of *Take-Over*. 'His' show had just been killed off. Over the years, like Steed, he had beaten off competitors, on a series he ended up also script-editing and producing. I can imagine that, seen through Clemens' lens, the fierce competition on American television must have made him feel like Steed did facing diabolical masterminds such as Grenville. Placed against rival shows *Rowan and Martin's Laugh-In* and *I Dream of Jeannie*, *The Avengers* had been outgunned and was hunted down as the first kill of the day. Steed always wins his battles but Clemens had lost this final challenge. Was this on his mind as he edited the script of *Take-Over*? Certainly, violent and brutal images were being conceived with the working knowledge that the show had just been 'killed off'. No wonder this episode is disturbingly depraved. The proverbial atom bomb had been dropped on the show. The series had become a casualty of the American Ratings wars. As with any war, there were human casualties – the lead actors and 'permanent' crew – and a more general sense of loss. The next episode would be the last; there would be no more froth, no more champagne.

© Margaret J Gordon

1. The theatrically disturbing atmosphere; a lack of light music; the absence of wit and charm are also key ingredients. Also, the fact that the Bassetts are well-rounded characters and close friends of Steed, not simply cardboard cut-out agents or 'associates' of Steed. This is a strength of Season 6 when compared to the Peel monochrome/colour eras.
2. For me, once Steed visits the Bassetts in their bedroom, he is as ill at ease as we are.

3. How would this be applied to her earlier operating on Mrs. Bassett and her attempted surgery on Tara King?
4. As Matthew Lee comments: "Even the most menacing and lethal attacks are defeated by aid of bowler, champagne bottle and the like. The ordinary often defeats the extraordinary in *Avengerland*, and quite rightly so."
5. Clemens recycled the idea once again in his 1970s *Thriller* episode *The Eyes Have It*.

BIZARRE

Filmed: March 1969

Exterior Locations:
Snow-covered open countryside, railway line
Happy Meadows: gated entrance, Paradise Plot
Hospital façade
Urban street
Rocket taking off/in flight (stock footage)

Sets:
Humpington Hospital bedroom
Mother's headquarters (billiard room)
Happy Meadows: Happychap's office
Train: guard's van
Paradise: living quarters, mystic's area
Mrs. Jupp's house: kitchen
Mystic Tours: office
Grave
Rocket

BIZARRE

Main Character List:
Helen Pritchard: witness of man alive in coffin
John Steed
Tara King
Captain William Cordell: investigating Pritchard mystery
Bagpipes Happychap: funeral director
Jonathan Jupp: 'dead' financier
Bradney Morton: 'dead' financier
Charley: henchman
Shaw: Mystic Tours, villain
Tom: gravedigger
Bob: gravedigger
Mrs. Jupp: financier's 'widow'
The Master: 'charlatan' mastermind

If a work of art is good, it is remembered. If a work of art is excellent, it is revered, admired and critiqued. If a work of art is perfect, it becomes interwoven in the cultural fabric of the period; scarcely can one be mentioned without the other. If the 1960s was to leave a televisual legacy from British shores, it would be through two productions which were the most creative and enduring products of their time, borne of a cultural identity which would never entirely fade away. *Doctor Who* and *The Avengers* are both firmly established as icons of British television. This is no casual overstatement: they embody an essential British essence which those from distant shores wish to imagine will forever be 'Little England': the picture postcard villages with thatched cottages and public houses, where the sun always shines and the women are always lovely, where the men are dashing and the class is upper.

Brian Clemens' overarching vision for the series always kept a watchful eye on this emerging landscape, and often his contributions to the latter stages of the programme – exemplified most notably with the cult classic *Murdersville* – would twist and turn the conventions of what 'Johnny Foreigner' would expect of 'perfect Britain' into something either darker and more menacing, or else simply more bizarre.

This leads to a broader reflection on the positioning of the final episode of the series proper. Gambling on an audience reaction of "Oh, how bizarre" upon viewing the finished product, Clemens scores dividends in every quarter throughout a fiendishly entertaining example of the quirkiness he so readily infused into the twilight of *The Avengers*. *Bizarre* lives up to its name, but the episode title itself is more a statement of expectation than a statement of intent: Clemens anticipates the audience reaction to what plays out in the episode itself with the use of the title, but the content itself is very familiar territory. Toying with the idea of death is like shooting fish in a barrel to this series; guns to pick one's teeth with and assassination over the kippers at breakfast would hardly raise an eyebrow in *Avengerland*.

On the basis of the tapestry to work with and the landscape to play out on, could a show like *The Avengers* ever really not finish on a bizarre note? The series had opened at the start of the decade as a hard-edged noir thriller production centring on an innocent doctor who became swept up in criminal events and found an outlet to avenge his fiancé's murder by stepping in to stop crime where he saw it and bring culprits to justice. Shadowed by a ubiquitous Man from the Ministry type in John Steed, the programme balanced rough and right against a backdrop of shadows and sassy musical scores. By its end, an impressive eight years and one-hundred-and-sixty-one episodes later, it was a bold, brash and colourful statement on the changing ways in which lives were lived at the end of a cultural and social revolution.

Seen through the lens of an otherworld, not too far from our own, but far enough removed to keep cads in their cosy comfort and portray spies as thwarting world domination between social engagements, *The Avengers* could always be relied upon to be escapist entertainment which touched on social issues of the day, subverted a good deal of the norms, and was larger than life on the small screen.

Its endless ability to reinvent itself – best reflected in the second season which spent time on a revolving circuit of three companions for John Steed until the popular groove was struck with the potently independent Cathy Gale as portrayed by the seductively gravelly Honor Blackman – would firmly influence its closest rival in the longevity stakes, *Doctor Who* – a programme which would score endless opportunities to inject new capital into a standard framework with the concept of regeneration for its principal character.

For *The Avengers*, the constant barometer and mainstay was John Steed, quintessential English gentleman and part of the cool culture sweeping both the nation and the globe. His succession of male, then female, companions reinvigorated the template of the series and, with a host of writers with a similar take on the curious state of the world, the programme went from strength to strength. When far removed, some of the eccentricities and foibles of the British were shunted into sharp relief.

So how, with its dying breath, did the final episode of the series manage to polarise views around whether it was merely surreal served up as surreal for surreal's sake, or whether it was indeed a fine summary of all the best quirky elements of the programme, doffing its cap and mocking its own steps towards the grave? Coming as it did halfway through the final dramatic televised adventure for Patrick Troughton as the genuinely 1960s *Doctor Who*, the galactic hobo, had Steed's time and place finally run out as well? As an embodiment of the cool and the suave, had his character found itself an Edwardian obscurity out of step with the next round of pre-1970s cultural changes?

Perhaps it was simply a case that, like Patrick McGoohan's envelope-pushing masterpiece, *The Prisoner*, sometimes a potently memorable concept and programme can never have a conclusion which would be anything other than either off-the-wall or ordinary and ignored. *Bizarre* is a delicious mixture of black comedy and sixties kitsch rolled into a tale which sends itself up marvellously on more than one occasion and boasts brilliant examples of the sort of dialogue exchanges which always set this series apart from the common herd.

The production is a wild mixture of styles: the teaser being an endeavour to touch on the harder edges of the original season, the tag a celebration of how far the series pushed reality at times, and the material in between a concertina of menace and mirth, wrapped around the premise of whether there is a promise of something better after the end. [1] There are comic-book touches along the way, but these are far from exclusive to the Tara King era and would find their place, now and again, as far back as the Cathy Gale era.

Clemens positions the shades of light and dark beautifully throughout the episode, with death portrayed as full of life: vibrant of colour and of expression, the Happy Meadows' Paradise Plot and its potently playful proprietor with his nice line in dialogue and marketing; and life portrayed as claustrophobically lifeless: the dreary washing-up kitchen-sink-drama-style life of a dreary housewife, the endless repetition of billiards. Even the framing of shots by director Leslie Norman matches this juxtaposition, with open and airy scenes casting off the cobwebs of morbidity and yet the scenes where there is life and where there is vigour are near fish-eye-lensed, squatting uncomfortably for room to breathe.

The episode opens with a teaser carved out of the face of writer Clemens' forthcoming seminal production, *Thriller*, and also harks back to the foundations of *The Avengers* and the title of its opening episode, *Hot Snow*. As snow thaws on a vacant field beneath a crisp blue winter sky, a blonde bare-footed young woman in a nightdress, Helen Pritchard (the delicious Sally Nesbitt, who will always be remembered as the wild-eyed wonder who dangerously toyed with Emma Peel in *The Joker*), walks dazedly onwards. She suddenly collapses, lying on her back and with a dead-eyed stare into the sky above. A solitary tear rolls down the side of her face...

Steed and Tara mount a bedside vigil at Helen Pritchard's side as a tape recorder is activated, trying to ascertain how she came to be in the comatose state she is in. The whole situation just doesn't make sense by Steed's reckoning. [2] Mother announces that Captain William Cordell (James Kerry) is investigating at the scene. Spying a speeding locomotive in the distance, he later reports back to Mother that the young woman may have fallen from a train, which would explain the nightdress. They reflect on the age-old question, "Did she fall, or was she pushed?" over a game of billiards.

Cordell later joins Steed and Tara as Helen regains consciousness. Clearly distressed, she rambles about a train, a coffin and a dead man: "A dead man in a coffin...A dead man who wasn't dead!" Cordell comments to Steed that it is quite a coincidence, as his investigation into passengers on the train around the time Helen collapsed in the field revealed that a coffin was indeed aboard the train, transporting a dead man to the Happy Meadows for burial.

What more appropriate businesses than undertakers and funeral parlours to thrive and prosper in *Avengerland*? The darkly comic and deliciously quirky perspective of writer Brian Clemens shines beautifully here as viewers are treated to the sign proclaiming The Happy Meadows with the tag-line THE 'IN' PLACE TO BE BURIED 'IN' (with a small note to the effect that there are "SPECIAL TERMS FOR PARTIES OF MORE THAN TWENTY" and that one can purchase Souvenirs and Guide Books *en route* to the afterlife).

Steed arrives at Happy Meadows just as the proprietor, Bagpipes Happychap (Roy Kinnear), consults the order of business for the day. In another fiendish touch of reality and unreality melding into *Avengerland*, resplendent in gold leaf on the walls of an archway behind him are the words "HURRY HURRY HURRY, GET IN WHILE THE GOING'S GOOD", with coffins nestling beneath the proclamation in gold of "THIS MONTH'S BEST BUY". This tottering into the surreal and sublime continues as Steed enters Happychap's gaudily-coloured office and the archway leading inside bears the promise that "WE GIVE TRADING STAMPS" and the recommendation to "SAVE FOR THAT FUNERAL NOW". [3]

Their banter on how he came to obtain his name and the solemnity of their surroundings is tremendously underplayed by Happychap busying himself measuring Steed's potential pine-box dimensions. He enthuses that his timing is perfect as he can just squeeze Steed in between two peers of the realm or Jolly Jack Tar's Last Jesting Ground. Kinnear launches his solid, diminutive frame into the superbly dark line: "We like to make death fun!" Happychap also provides the tantalising opportunity for Steed to be squeezed between an admiral on his port, a midshipman on his starboard and a submarine commander astern. Steed is having none of this, guiding the discussion to the recent arrival of the coffin from the train. Happychap consults his records and gushes that it was buried in their most exclusive area: Paradise Plot.

Frolicking through the funereal family he dotes over, Happychap virtually hops and skips as he escorts Steed to the grave of Jonathan Jupp, beautifully commemorated with a white marble headstone and gold nameplate. The name seems vaguely familiar to Steed but he cannot place it. Later, he returns to Helen's bedside and, after Tara and Cordell's fruitless attempts to prompt her memories,

Steed presents her with a series of random black and white photographs. She fails to recognise the first two, but then is suddenly horrified at the third picture; Steed consults the back and notes it is Jonathan Jupp (John Sharp, making a second villainous turn in *The Avengers* after portraying the wonderfully unpleasant landlord, Prewitt, in *Murdersville*).

Near-hysterical, Helen's memory wrenches her back to the events which transpired on the train. We see her travelling to the guard's van to feed her dog. She is horrified to witness the man in the photograph clamber out of a coffin. Distressed, she tries to escape but the man takes hold of her and throws her from the cabin. Later, over a game of billiards, Steed and Mother reflect on whether she is telling the truth. Steed points out that she positively identified Jonathan Jupp, a notorious financier who was on the verge of prosecution for major fraud. His somewhat convenient death circumvented the need for a trial, but Steed wonders whether he may actually be dead at all: he has seen the grave, but not inside it. Mother agrees to arrange an exhumation order.

Brimming with smugness, Happychap asks Steed if he is satisfied when the coffin lid is taken off and the pristine body of Jonathan Jupp lies in state within. Steed retorts that he just wanted to make sure that he was there, much to Happychap's evident chagrin. Meanwhile, Tara intrudes on Helen being assaulted by a sinister gloved assailant, Bradney Morton, who draws a gun on the agent and in the ensuing fight a report rings out and the man slumps painfully to the floor, dead, as Helen lets out a violent scream in distress.

Steed interrupts a billiards game between Mother and Cordell (the former is decidedly pleased he is winning) to reveal that Jupp's body was definitely in the coffin, so 'that is that'. Cordell explains that Helen has been attacked in her hospital room, Mother adding that the assailant was a financier on the brink of being prosecuted for fraud. Officially, Morton died six months ago of a heart attack; his body is buried at Happy Meadows!

Whilst the content of the episode proper brims with all the traditional hallmarks of the surreal spot-welded onto the chassis of the ordinary that makes *The Avengers* what it is, the unfortunate use of so many in-studio mock-exterior scenes around Happy Meadows detracts from the *Thriller*-esque sweeping winter landscapes for which many of the other exterior scenes are mounted. Indeed, director Leslie Norman could be accused of an unusually pedestrian approach to the appearance of these scenes. Gaudy colours and bright lighting lacks any sort of mood and tempo in the Happy Meadow scenes, which fail to mirror the solemnity versus farce which is so brimming in Kinnear's performance. It is certainly a niggle in a final outing which deserved the panache (and budget relaxation) of a parting shot.

Happychap is appalled at Steed's proposition of another exhumation, poo-pooing his morbid curiosity with the dead and heartily recommending that he takes up gardening to exorcise his obsession with digging. He reluctantly agrees to Steed's demands, and Bradney Morton's coffin is exhumed. When the lid is lifted and the coffin is found to be empty, Happychap can barely contain himself: "He's been stolen, taken away, there's a thief in our midst," he blusters, as Steed makes a cursory inspection of the surrounding headstones and then sets off to use Happychap's telephone.

Steed reports to Mother that Bradney Morton's body is missing, and Mother is aghast that body-snatching is alive/undead in this day and age. Steed reveals he has been making a record of the headstones: John Ash; George and Tony Barter; Patrick Vernon. Between them, they make the connection that these gentlemen were all notorious financiers involved in shady deals – and all of them are buried in Paradise Plot. Agreeing that there is no other way but to exhume them all, Steed lays a comforting arm around 'Baggers' and escorts him to the gravesides as he breaks the bad news: Happychap is hysterical. With a thunderously amusing apology sign of "HAPPY MEADOWS REGRET THE INCONVENIENCE TO THEIR PATRONS" around the exhumation barriers, the sound of toiling shovels and the sight of discarded marble headstones play out across the scene. Surrounded by a soiled sea of empty coffins, Happychap is beside himself:

Happychap: This is awful, simply awful. There's no *body* left!
Steed: The great *grave* robbery.
Happychap: What do we do now?

He is appalled when Steed explains that they will need to exhume Jonathan Jupp – again! Clemens' family tree of super spies and their superiors continues as viewers witness Mother speaking to Grandma with assurances that Steed is digging something up. What with Father already having appeared, this delightful linguistic nuance turns the M, Q and R terms of the James Bond era on their head. As Jupp's coffin is opened and is this time found to be empty, Happychap is at a loss to explain what is happening. Steed jumps into one of the open graves and hammers against the soil with his umbrella but to no avail. Could the situation be any more bizarre?

Indeed it could, for the afterlife offers a delicious blend of hip tunes, pampering and grapes as Jonathan Jupp relaxes in the splendour of a form of paradise, surrounded by a beautiful bevvy of women catering to his every whim. Henchman Shaw intrudes on his indulgent relaxation to check that he has everything he wants, and Jupp cannot help amusing himself at the thought of what his wife's reaction would be to seeing where he is right now. "I bet there would be egg all over it!"

Cordell interviews Mrs. Jupp (Sheila Burrell) in his search for clues in her kitchen as she cooks a meal (there is a wonderful non-verbal nod to throwing salt over one's shoulder for luck, as performed by James Kerry, which is a terrific touch). Mrs. Jupp recounts how she found her husband's body after his heart attack and how distressed she was that it should happen when he had planned to take her away. This piques Cordell's interest. She explains that she overheard her husband speaking to Mystic Tours, arranging to go away somewhere special as she heard him remark that, "Where I'm going it will be paradise. Absolute paradise."

At the offices of Mystic Tours – where the promise of a "GATEWAY TO NEW AND EXCITING PLACES – ESCAPE WITH MYSTIC!" is emblazoned on the walls – Shaw emerges from behind his desk and discusses a European junket with Cordell, who is pretending to be a customer interested in a package deal. He lets slips that he is having a spot of business trouble and wants to get away to somewhere cool for a while, as he anticipates a 'hot spell' if he remains in this country. Shaw verbally fences with him on his hopeful destination, and Cordell says he is seeking 'absolute paradise'.

Over another game of billiards, Steed and Mother try to fathom out what has been happening to date:

Mother: How are they doing it? And why?
Steed: Who are they and where are they?

Mother: A whole graveyard looted...coffins dug up! How on earth?
Steed: My guess is it happens at night.
Mother: There's no night guard at Happy Meadows?
Steed: No. Well why should there be? There's no reason to believe that the inhabitants are going anywhere.

It is a superb reflection on Clemens' powerful use of dialogue in order to play, tease and toy with the audience through light banter. The reactions between Patrick Newell's Mother and Macnee's Steed are priceless here; all about what you see in the eyes rather than what is emoted through the voice. Their discussion is interrupted by a call from Cordell which Mother puts on the nearby speaker-phone. In hushed and hurried tones, he breathily reveals that he is on his way to paradise before the line goes dead.

Happychap is on the brink of being Sadman when Steed comes to call again, though he is greatly relieved when he learns that this time all he wants is information. When Steed prepares for a call from Cordell, Happychap delightedly reveals that he is already there – and when he lifts the lid off a nearby coffin, Steed is shocked to see the fellow agent within. Happychap explains that he was knocked down by a car, but that his dying wish was to be buried in the Paradise Plot.

Steed reports to Mother that Cordell is definitely dead – ice cold to the touch. He suggests mounting a night vigil to catch the grave-robbers in the act. Mother is impressed, espousing the virtues of Steed's dedication to the mission even at the sacrifice of his own sleep, only to find Steed dozing off and revealing that he gave the task to Tara – who currently sits not far from William Cordell's marble headstone in the Paradise Plot waiting for action. Rugged up and shivering, her unlikely companion is Happychap, who complains about the cold as Tara reflects that Cordell is a lot colder...

...but in actuality, the man himself is smoking a cigar, surrounded by beautiful women, as rock music floods through the air and he savours his own special brand of Paradise. He is soon joined by an exhausted and heavily-perspiring Jupp, who has given up chasing a young nymphette in favour of banter with another person who found it too hot in the other world. While Shaw checks that they both have everything they need (and Jupp complains he will need a jolly good holiday after this), Charley enters the room and recognises Cordell from his earlier recce of the Humpington Hospital building. Shaw draws a gun on the agent, tut-tutting, "Naughty, Mr Cordell".

As dawn approaches, Happychap is adamant that nothing is going to happen. He and Tara inspect Cordell's graveside and marble headstone, the former insisting it has been a complete waste of time. Much to his appalled chagrin ("If you put money into a bank, a reputable bank, you don't keep withdrawing it to see that it's still there!"), Tara arranges for the coffin to be exhumed once again. When the lid is opened, Happychap is delighted to see Cordell's body still inside – and still dead! Only this time – Tara observes as she notes a charred hole in his coat – he has been shot. This is a gloriously Clemens touch, worthy of his later series *Thriller* which often spun on the nuances around these sort of interesting set-pieces. One could be forgiven for thinking that this was a teaser to one of the episodes of that wonderful series rather than a plot twist in *The Avengers*, such is the mutual synergy between them.

Mother: Shot?
Steed: Shot??
Tara: Shot!
Mother: I wonder if it's too late to hand this whole case over to another department...after all, it's an open and shut case. Open the

grave, shut the grave...I could dress the report up, make it seem simple and straight-forward.

This is another delightful example of Clemens' envelope-pushing of the world of *The Avengers* into the world of its contemporaries. [4] One could gleefully imagine a scene in which Mother approaches Sir Curtis Seretse (Dennis Alaba Peters) of ITC's *Department S* with a job so unusual, so very bizarre, that it is definitely the line of country of Stewart Sullivan, Jason King and Annabelle Hurst (Joel Fabiani, Peter Wyngarde and Rosemary Nichols). The exchange takes place as Steed and Tara reflect on Cordell's demise; Mother confirms that the dead agent spoke to Mrs. Judd, and Steed sets off to see her. In so doing, he uncovers the same lead and connection between Paradise and Mystic Tours.

Paying the tour operators a visit, Steed endeavours to secure a pathway to Paradise, aided by a winning smile and a bag full of money: "They say you can't buy your way into Heaven, but I aim to try!" The gesture certainly impresses Shaw, who conveys him to the "inner sanctum" of Mystic Tours, wherein a complex array of jagged sculpture work adorns a room in which a mystic is in spiritual meditation, lying on his back in contemplation of a far-off place. This is the Master (Fulton Mackay), who has been in a deep state of trance since last Friday. Shaw recommends waking him with the rustle of crisp pound notes, which instantly revives him. Coming as it did in the same year that Johnny Speight's short-run sitcom *Curry And Chips* would feature a blacked-up Spike Milligan in the role of a mystic wise man from the East, it is no surprise to see Mackay playing a similar role here. [5]

Espousing hollow words of wisdom, his keen eye is, however, drawn towards the bag full of money. There is a delightful gear-change in his heavily-tanned character when Shaw reveals that what Steed actually wants is a fast route to Paradise and not words of mystic wisdom. The Master immediately drops the act and the fake Indian accent, and leaps from the bench.

The Master: You won't live to regret it, I promise you.
Steed: I sincerely hope I do!
The Master: Mmm?
Steed: *Live*.

The deal brokered, Steed is barred from leaving by the pensive, tea-swilling Shaw as the Master explains that his death ("violent, but quite painless") has already been arranged. He cannot leave, nor contact anyone. Steed's protests at not even being able to telephone 'Mother' fall on deaf ears. Outside, Shaw escorts Steed into a lane where he saves him from unnecessary injury when a car swiftly turns a corner, and then proceeds to throw him in front of the next approaching vehicle. Inside, the Master smiles and reflects "Next stop – Paradise!"

Tara delightedly informs Mother that Steed has been located at Happy Meadows and she sets off to join him. Her delight turns to incredulity when Happychap reveals he is in Paradise Plot – surely he cannot be digging up another coffin...then the realisation dawns.

Steed: The mind boggles...What would it be like, I wonder, if I had led a completely blameless life? This is really living.
Jupp: Don't you mean dying?

Steed awakes in Paradise amidst a gaggle of girls running here and there, his forehead being stroked by a beautiful young woman, a young girl playing a harp and a couple dancing to the music in the background. He immediately recognises Jupp, who is concerned until Steed passes himself off as a fellow financial fink on the run from his troubles. Clemens once again plays with the conventions of the medium, with a delicious Adam and Eve moment when Steed is offered an apple by a beauty at his side and he remarks, "No, I don't want to spoil things" and he returns it to her with a knowing smile. He learns that the Master was responsible for him reaching Paradise. A de-blacked Master, now wearing a jewelled turban, explains his mastery of the talent of suspended animation which, to all intents and purposes, convinced the world above them that Steed was dead – and buried. The Master points out the coffin-shaped entrance above his head to illustrate his means of venturing from one world (of troubles) to another (the catacombs below Happy Meadows, and on to Paradise). In what must be one of the catchiest swinging late 1960s pieces of incidental music to grace the Tara King season, we witness the party to end one's life with.

As Tara and Happychap are greeted by the sight of Steed's empty coffin, the former leaps into the hole in the ground and tries to dig down for a clue, just as Steed endeavours to open the entrance but is discovered by Shaw and ushered away to a more relaxing past-time. However, he does not fail to hear Tara scratching at the entrance with a rock and when he returns to his work on the entrance, the pair manage to make a connection by wrenching a large knife through the slot.

Steed's activities are noticed and he is cornered by the Master, Shaw and others, a weapon trained on him and the Master reflecting that they can't take any chances; he will now need to make a very real death take place. Literally a fight to the death ensues as Steed sees off all those around him apart from Charley, who trains a weapon on him at just the moment Tara breaks through into the catacombs and renders him unconscious. Shaw then attacks her and as Steed fights his way through, past and around a bevy of screaming beauties to apprehend the villains, the fight comes to an end with Steed marching out a chain-gang of handcuffed men and women, all of whom slowly make their way from the open grave, to Happychap's bewilderment. Steed remains underground with one of the beautiful 'angels' of the Master; Tara escorts the criminals away, assuring Happychap that "Steed is alive and well, but he's staying on in Paradise".

Saving the most unusual tag scene for the final curtain-call, viewers were treated to an off-beat end-note. Splendidly dapper in finest dinner jacket and preparing for an evening on the town, Steed impresses Tara by showing her around the small spacecraft that he has constructed in his back yard. Mother arrives on the scene, camera in hand and enthusiastically taking photographs as Steed reflects that he has always wanted one of these. When Mother ventures outside to take a picture for his album, Tara inadvertently presses the ignition button and the craft is launched into orbit.

Always able to make the best of a situation, and despite Mother's protestations through the communicator, Steed reflects that he can get them down eventually, there is no hurry, and he pours them both a welcome glass of champagne. Mother, addressing the audience, assures viewers that, "They'll be back, you can depend on it" before frowning, staring heavenwards and realising "They're unchaperoned up there!" as the craft disappears out of view.

Broadcast a month before the first moon landing, it comes as little or no surprise that this final tag scene of the final series of the original run of *The Avengers* should be true to its enduring character right to the death: a dedicated setter (for whom many others followed) of fashion, always with an eye on the trends and changing moods of a generation across the most potently creative decade the world has (to date) ever known, what better way to reflect the events of the most remarkable and truly bizarre new world into which man was about to step than have Steed and Tara launched into space?

Apollo 11 may have been one small step for man, but *The Avengers* was one giant leap for British Television: often bizarre, occasionally kinky, sometimes surreal but always undeniably British, this was the programme which set the tone, made the name, cast the shadow and fitted the fashion for a generation.

© Matthew Lee

1. I would suggest that there is far more mirth than menace in this light-hearted farewell.
2. We have to question why Steed and the Ministry have been called in to investigate this case, given that no murder has taken place and that the woman is someone 'of no importance' in *Avengerland*.
3. As in Roger Marshall's *Dial A Deadly Number* and *The £50,000 Breakfast*, there is a gentle critique of the social exclusivity and snobbery of funeral enterprises.
4. Is this a positive thing, though? *The Avengers*, in earlier seasons, had been innovative and ground-breaking, rather than sharing the creative territory of 'rival' shows.
5. I think that any suggestions of racism would be wide of the mark. After all, The Master is, by his own admission, a complete fake.

WORDS OF ONE SYLLABLE: THE FAILURES OF THE TARA KING ERA

When Diana Rigg left *The Avengers* at the conclusion of Season 5, the popular show faced a production upheaval behind the camera, and the need to get a new team in front of the camera. Bringing Rigg back for a single 'transitional' episode to remove Emma Peel from the scene, the series attempted to reinvigorate its arguably flagging formula with a change in format, a shift in style, and a new, younger partner for our ageing spy. While maintaining some of the pastiche elements of Season 5, Season 6 found Steed and his partner in the midst of a wider organisation called The Ministry, with new superiors, new villains, and new serious (and not-so-serious) plots to baffle them. The change of formula from Season 5 to Season 6 might have reflected similar transitions between Cathy Gale's final Season 3 and Emma Peel's first Season 4, or the move from the monochrome of Season 4 to the pastiche-driven and slightly psychedelic elements of Season 5. Unfortunately, some of the more glaring problems already nascent nearing the end of Emma Peel's tenure come to full fruition with Tara King, as a combination of the serious, the mundane, and the insane never come together to form a cohesive whole.

The Avengers was no stranger to a combination of the real and surreal, as episodes as disparate as *The Joker* and *Man-Eater of Surrey Green* prove. But Season 6's attempts at pastiche lack development. Ultra-serious episodes such as the home-invasion-themed *Take-Over* are placed side by side with episodes like *Look, Stop Me If You've Heard This One*, featuring a final fight sequence impossible in the real world. Episodes like *False Witness* begin in a serious, realistic vein, and veer into a madcap territory shorn of narrative consistency. The tones and styles of these episodes jar with one another; far from providing the viewer with a sense of off-kilter fun or variety, they never return us either to a surreal *Avengerland* or to a recognisable reality. They are in-between, bouncing between realism and a surreal style without apparent direction or meaning. Surrealist aesthetic itself requires an implicit criticism of the prevailing culture, and here we find none. Instead, Season 6 is the most quintessentially conservative of any *Avengers* era, reinforcing gender, cultural, and sexual categories with few of the subversive aspects inherent in earlier incarnations.

The most polarising alteration in *The Avengers* formula is the introduction of a very different type of partner for John Steed. Tara King is conceived as a 'fledgling' Ministry agent, assigned to Steed for field training. She's set apart from the Avenging past by already occupying Steed's world of espionage, rather than being drawn into it as his civilian partner. Her knowledge and capabilities are grounded in her training as an agent, with no apparent external education or life experience. She's also significantly younger than either Cathy Gale or Emma Peel, and much younger than Steed. This element of youth will be emphasised throughout the season by unironically costuming Tara in schoolgirl outfits and, in one notable episode, something that looks like a baby-doll dress. She is neither an independent agent nor an experienced woman.

In departing from the formula of the "talented amateur" to a semi-professional (if un-vetted) partner for Steed, *The Avengers* might have reinterpreted the partner relationship, revealing Tara's growing experience and abilities in conjunction with her 'education' by Steed. However, one of the primary elements of previous seasons was the notion of equality. From the season's start, Tara is Steed's professional subordinate who must be educated by her male superior. In many of the early production episodes, Steed teaches his young partner everything from how to throw a man through a plate-glass window to lock picking to judo throws. He occupies the position of teacher or mentor; the partnership is secondary, characterised by Tara's lack of professional experience. This forms a decided contrast to the professional women of earlier seasons.

Tara's grounding as an agent means that she does not bring prior knowledge to the partnership. She possesses neither the educational nor professional background to make a significant intellectual contribution. Tara's predecessors were 'amateur' spies, but retained degrees and experience in other venues. Cathy Gale was an anthropologist, once employed by the British Museum, while Emma Peel was a former CEO, scientist, and mathematician. Cathy Gale and Emma Peel's esoteric scientific, historical, or experiential knowledge will often come to bear upon the mission; in the case of Mrs. Gale, her specialised knowledge is frequently the reason for her involvement in the first place. Tara is not stupid, but she never pursues intellectual interests beyond her professional capacity, and sometimes insists on topics being simplified for her benefit. In *Split!*, she abjures a character who veers into technical jargon to speak in "words of one syllable." [1] She rarely contributes knowledge that Steed, the more experienced member of the partnership, does not already possess. A number of episodes even feature exposition scenes in which Steed tells Tara the plot thus far - usually without much, if any, input from his partner. This places Tara in a position of intellectual as well as professional subordination. She not only does not know more than Steed, she often knows a good bit less.

The structuring of Tara's character as a professional and intellectual subordinate contributes to the confused personal relationship that develops between her and Steed. A broad character and relationship arc can be traced throughout the Gale and Peel seasons, as the partners learn from each other and grow in affection, respect, and understanding. But Tara, given one season to impress us, suffers from an undefined character at the start that gradually becomes more defined as the season progresses. This definition, however, fails to translate to her relationship with Steed. At times she and Steed are teacher and student, and he treats her with a mixture of sympathy and condescension. At other times, they appear to be lovers. But this attitude varies from episode to episode (even if watched in production order), from moments of Steed expressing annoyance with Tara's inability to grasp some concepts, to moments of obvious respect between the pair. Tara's unabashed adoration for Steed is the only clear factor in an otherwise confused relationship. She blatantly begs him for attention, telling him that she'll "write every hour, on the hour" when she goes off on holiday (*Killer*), and embracing him at the end of many cases. The respect and tension present in Steed's earlier relationships are eliminated in favour of cloying affection; a crush, perhaps even a sexual relationship, but certainly not an equal or even very adult one. In effect, the season places Tara in a quintessential position of the damsel, with emotional and physical dependence upon her male counterpart. [2]

The damseling of Tara King develops via plot complications and her treatment by the camera eye. *The Avengers* always skirted the edges of the voyeuristic, the more objectifying episodes veering dangerously close to kinky titillation. Tara is certainly not the only *Avengers* woman to be bound, gagged, or handcuffed. In this context, it may seem odd to state that Tara King has less command over her sexuality than Emma Peel did, standing around in a corset and dog-collar. In the case of Tara, however, the plot does not place a dominant figure into a submissive position for a scene or group of scenes; it rather 'damsels' an already submissive character for the purposes of voyeuristic titillation. She's on her knees with a gun jutting into her face in *Have Guns- Will Haggle*, subject to implicit sexual threats and sadistic domination in *The Curious Case of the Countless Clues*, subdued by butter in *False Witness*, and tortured in *Legacy of Death*. Banter, a major element of previous *Avengers* seasons, falls by the wayside in scenes with 'diabolical masterminds' where Tara is rendered incapable of speech. She's often unconscious, gagged, or placed in a position where her voice cannot be heard and acknowledged, either by her partner or by the villains (*Look, Stop Me If You've Heard This One, Game, The Morning After, Stay Tuned*). This silencing of the lead female is expanded upon in *False Witness,* where a drug makes her unable to tell the truth; she is literally robbed of her ability to express her own mind. The literal and metaphorical silencing of Tara draws out one of the more disturbing aspects of *The Avengers*, hitherto only hinted at: that the woman is a plot device driving the male hero to action. The resolution of the plot requires not her active participation, but her silence. [3]

For all the subordination of her character, Tara has undoubted moments of strength, and these are often the best episodes in the season. Episodes like *All Done with Mirrors* give her a sovereignty otherwise unknown, showcasing her developing fighting skills. Her physical prowess is laudable, and much credit should be given to Linda Thorson for engaging so effectively in the fight sequences. Yet the instances where Tara expresses a sovereignty of purpose and a competent capability in physical and mental combat are all too few and far between. They are the exceptions, and not the rules, and often serve only to highlight the moments when she is suddenly and inexplicably bested. Even in the instances where she's right about certain elements of the plot, Tara's male superiors often ignore her *(Love All)*. She ultimately looks up *to*, and not *at*, her male partner. She does not discuss things with him; she obeys him. She is to be used and enacted upon, rarely an enactor in herself. She exists to be defined against others.

It is not Tara alone who bears the brunt of Season 6's multitudinous problems – she is merely a symptom of a greater illness. Part and parcel of the changed format for Season 6 was the introduction of Mother, Steed's immediate superior. A Ministry superior is nothing new in *The Avengers:* the early seasons are awash in them. In Mother, however, a new development occurs: he becomes a major recurring character with a marked influence on numerous plots. Steed's earlier superiors most often appear once or twice in an episode and rarely interfere with the interplay between Steed and his partner. Mother is a force unto himself, anchoring *The Avengers* in the 'real world' of the Ministry. Mother's helper Rhonda represents a further development of the 'silent woman' motif: she has no speaking part, present to provide amusement and to cater to Mother's whims.

While he does not appear in every episode, Mother almost becomes a member of the triumvirate, interfering with the partner dynamic that characterised earlier seasons. Mother provides the comedy lacking in Steed's interactions with Tara, which further relegates Tara to secondary character status in a number of key scenes throughout the season. In *Fog*, the banter between him and Steed is comic relief that in earlier seasons would have been given to the two lead partners. While Steed will keep a good bit of screen time, Mother's appearance often reduces Tara's screen presence, and certainly reduces her opportunities to interact with her partner. This in itself reinforces the growing gender divide, as the male spies interact to the detriment of the female. [4]

Mother's presence further places Steed himself in a deeper position of subordination to an overarching organisational machine, removing much of his professional independence. This might be argued to be a return to the origins of Seasons 1-3, where Steed was sometimes seen answering to a shadowy superior, or interacting with fellow agents. The difference in Season 6 lies in the execution. Steed in Seasons 1-3 is often just outside the purview of his superiors. He's known for going off on his own, choosing his own partners (his superiors often make a show of disapproving of 'amateurs'), and largely operating with little (if any) official oversight. When the Ministry does get involved, it often turns out poorly: Steed is tortured by his own people in *The Wringer* and *The Nutshell*, defies orders in *The Outside-In Man*, and is reprimanded for insubordination in *Man in the Mirror*. Despite being one agent among many, Steed is far from a 'company man'.

In Season 6, the reappearance of the Ministry as a major entity fully absorbs Steed into his organisation; he no longer possesses apparent or implied professional independence. Episodes focus on the inner workings of the Ministry, including the involvement of traitors in their midst (*The Interrogators*) and even suspicion of Mother and Steed (*Take Me To Your Leader, Stay Tuned*). When Mother tells Steed not to go after Tara in *You'll Catch Your Death*, he obeys until the last minute — a far cry from the insubordinate operator that Cathy Gale once knew, or the agent who would risk all to save his partner. Steed's integration means that the audience is no longer united with our two Avengers against the world, but rather asked to redirect attention towards the often unclear workings of an entire organisation. The change in form creates a change in character: the slightly irascible, often insubordinate character of John Steed is forced into position where he's at the whim of his eccentric superior, his hands tied by protocol.

As the only character to appear in all six seasons of *The Avengers*, Steed always formed the steady, energetic centre of the show. By Season 6, however, he appears to have lost much of the intensity and charisma usually associated with his character. There are whole episodes where he fails to make a joke or even crack a smile; often, as in *Legacy of Death*, playing straight man to increasingly bizarre and eccentric characters. His apparent humourlessness in some episodes is further heightened by sudden violence that has him slamming people against walls, and threatening to crush villains' hands with car bonnets. Steed's character undergoes a powerful shift from the gentlemanly, erudite figure of the Emma Peel era, regressing to the ruthless agent of the Cathy Gale period. Yet even in those murky early years, Steed's humour remains tantamount to his charm, his energy and aestheticism a contrast to his ruthlessness. That vitality has been sapped from Season 6, and Steed is reduced to playing the straight man in his own show. Shorn of the joy of its main character, *The Avengers* ceases to be fun.

What goes up must surely come down. Season 6 of *The Avengers* aspires to some of the heights of its predecessors and, through confusion of tone, script, and characterisation, never quite achieves what it sets out to. The season could not have been saved or cured by a single change, but seems to represent a slow gutting of what made *The Avengers* powerful and ground-breaking to begin with. The hero becomes a humourless straight man, the heroine a cloying damsel, the pastiche a hollow simulacrum of *Avengerland*. While there are moments of brightness in the morass, while some episodes are as elegant and 'Avengerish' as anything a passionate fan could ask for, they are too few and too fleeting to leave a lasting impression. At the end of the series, Season 6 turned *The Avengers* anti-clockwise: in exactly the wrong direction.

© Lauren Humphries-Brooks

1. This is in contrast to Emma Peel who ridicules overtly complex psychobabble by translating it into 'normal' language, as in *Room Without A View*.
2. I think that even an ardent fan of Season 6 – such as myself – would find it hard to argue with this suggestion.
3. It is a sexual stereotype which is refreshingly reversed in *The Hidden Tiger* when Emma comes to the rescue of a bound Steed. Lauren's comments here raise important questions about the mis/use of all the female co-leads in the series.
4. Linda Thorson has said as much herself, unhappy with the way in which Mother often relegates her character from the 'front line': "Mother was an embellishment. It seemed to me that he was there because there was a loss of confidence in the partnership between the man and the woman."(Cited in *The Avengers: A Celebration*, p. 129.)

AFTERWORD

If one were to plot the trajectory of *The Avengers*' evolution, with outrageous sci-fi and fantasy elements measured against time, it would ascend gradually before ultimately peaking with the colour Emma Peel episodes. Encompassing everything from mind-swapping devices to shrinking rays, murderous house cats to electrically-charged men, Season 5 followed in the grand tradition set by the previous season's cybernauts, psychics, and man-eating plants from space. Indeed, *The Avengers* utilised sci-fi and fantasy elements throughout much of its run, resulting in the series' trademark 'out-there' plots. And yet, by 1967, the show's increasingly fantastical bent was viewed as undesirable by the powers-that-be. Convinced that the series would benefit from a more realistic approach, producers Albert Fennell and Brian Clemens were let go, replaced by John Bryce, the producer of the more down-to-earth Cathy Gale years. The change-over echoed similar shifts in the series' past, as Bryce had replaced Leonard White, the series' original producer, in Season 2. Bryce, in turn, had been replaced by Clemens and Fennell (and Julian Wintle) in Season 4. Despite his history with the series, Bryce's second *Avengers* production stint would be extremely brief.

We will never know exactly how Season 6 would have unfolded had Bryce's tenure not been so short-lived. There is only so much that can be gleaned from the episodes produced during his tenure, and even those do not appear in their original forms, having been either edited and intercut with new, Clemens-produced scenes (*Have Guns, Will Haggle* and *Invasion of the Earthmen*), or raided for spare parts (*Homicide and Old Lace*). Bryce himself has long since passed away, so an in-depth firsthand account of his vision for the Tara

King era is sadly out of reach, and production documentation can only reveal so much. But despite Bryce's unceremonious removal as producer after falling behind in production, and the reinstatement of Clemens and Fennell, Bryce managed to leave his mark on the series, both in the King era and what came after. Ironically, the fact that he had any influence at all is largely due to the reason he was let go. Had Clemens had the luxury of preparing for the new season at his convenience, he no doubt would have thrown out everything Bryce-related and started afresh. Yet, because new episodes were needed quickly, this was not possible, and Clemens was forced to work with what his short-lived predecessor had left behind. This meant that the three episodes Bryce had managed to complete before his departure would appear in Season 6 in one form or another, Clemens having no choice but to utilise them in order to get something 'in the can'. More importantly, Clemens was forced to retain both the actress Bryce had cast as the new *Avengers* girl, Linda Thorson, and the character she embodied, Tara King. [1]

Tara's occupational status signalled a new direction for the series. For the first time in the show's history, Steed was partnered with a fellow spy, 'Agent 69', rather than another in the long line of 'talented amateurs' who had formed his partners up to that point. Casting both leads as professional spies allowed for a greater emphasis on the organisation behind Steed (sometimes called The Ministry or The Department, among other things, though never identified in any formal capacity). This, in turn, resulted in more espionage-based plots surrounding the Ministry's internal operations and attempts to penetrate its security. The emphasis on spies and spying inevitably led to a greater focus on betrayal and loss, putting Steed in the position of dealing with either fallen or treacherous colleagues, themes that would feature prominently in *The New Avengers*. It also allowed for plenty of appearances by

Steed and Tara's fellow agents, who took an increasingly active role in the proceedings, and produced memorable one-off characters, such as second-in-command Father, and Steed's fellow agent Lady Diana Forbes-Blakeney, whose positions within the department at large lent them a semi-official status among the series' leads. Most notably, the ministerial emphasis led to the introduction of a pair of recurring characters in the form of wheelchair-bound boss Mother, and his silent assistant, Rhonda. These aspects were a marked departure from the Emma Peel years, in which Steed ostensibly reported to no one, and fellow agents' roles were mainly confined to turning up dead in order to move the plot along. And yet, in many ways, the series was actually cycling back to its early years, namely the Keel and Gale seasons, in which Steed had any number of irascible bosses, including One-Ten, One-Twelve, Five, and Charles, some of them sharing Mother's tendency of popping up in the oddest places. Indeed, taken as a whole, the Emma Peel seasons, which placed little emphasis on Steed's employers, are the series' anomaly, and characters such as Mother are more in the 'classic' *Avengers* tradition of old.

Season 6 drew on the show's past in other ways as well. In spite of the management's insistence that the show get 'back to reality', Season 6 featured its fair share of out-there storylines, from near-sentient computers and killer black boxes, to mind transfers and invisibility formulas, all of which would have been equally at home in the Peel era. And yet, the aforementioned emphasis on espionage, the stealing of secrets, and the Ministry's internal workings was a throwback to the mood, themes, and plots of the series' earliest seasons, when Cathy Gale and David Keel fought more grounded threats. The Tara King season, therefore, has a foot in both camps, featuring Gale and Keelesque realism and spy drama, and Peel era fantasy and science fiction, a similar position to that later adopted by *The New Avengers*. [2] The season also (unintentionally) acknowledged its past through the casting of Canadian Linda Thorson, whose nationality echoed that of the series' 'creator', Sydney Newman. Even the appearance of Emma Peel in *The Forget-Me-Not*, though largely included for transition purposes, is a case of the series drawing on, and referencing, its own (recent) past to a degree it never had before, another trend that would be picked up by *The New Avengers*. Therefore, the series, at this point in its lifecycle, was still moving forward, but, in classic *Avengers* tradition, it was doing so in its own unique way, sometimes by cycling back to its roots.

Thematically, this particular era of the series also bore a strong predilection for psychological torture/manipulation and body horror. On the psychological side, cases of characters' minds and/or perceptions being somehow manipulated or interfered with appear in *The Forget-Me-Not, Split!, My Wildest Dream, Super Secret Cypher Snatch, False Witness, The Interrogators, Love All, Stay Tuned, Pandora,* and *Requiem*. Bodily interference is featured in *You'll Catch Your Death, They Keep Killing Steed*, and, most viscerally, *Take-Over*, which revolves around the surgical implantation of bombs in characters' necks. Even *Whoever Shot Poor George Oblique Stroke XR40?* echoes this focus on the physical with its electronic 'surgery' scenes, and Mother and Father's respective physical disabilities are spotlighted through the use of elaborate and creative sets. These elements had featured somewhat in previous seasons, but never to such an extent, and it lends the season a particularly disturbing, visceral quality all its own, unique from the Emma Peel era's surreal fantasyland or the underlying grittiness of the Gale and Keel years.

Character-wise, the season used Tara King as a means by which to play with the concept of the *'Avengers* girl'. Moulded partly by Thorson herself (she even got to choose her character's name, a first amongst the series' leads), Tara was conceived to be more stereotypically 'feminine' than her predecessors. Cathy Gale had been set with the task of convincing audiences that a female lead could be every bit as capable, both physically and intellectually, as her male counterpart, and as such was bestowed with the most overtly 'masculine' characteristics of the three main original series *Avengers* women. Honor Blackman was even instructed to 'toughen up' her portrayal after her first episode, and the series' scriptwriters wrote her as they would a male lead. Cathy's trailblazing allowed for her successor, Emma Peel, to regain some of her femininity in dress, demeanour, and skill-set, while losing none of her credibility in other, traditionally male-dominated subject areas, such as science and mathematics. Tara was an attempt by the minds behind the series to push the formula one step further and have a traditionally 'feminine' *Avengers* girl, an inexperienced, trainee agent who was younger than either of her predecessors, and who Thorson elected to play as in love with Steed. This inevitably shifted the dynamic between the leads, departing from the often-antagonistic relationship between Steed and Cathy, and the effortless synchronicity between Steed and Emma, to the outright adoring and paternal relationship between Steed and Tara, while still retaining the 'are they/aren't they?' ambiguous quality that served as one of the series' key ingredients.

It can be argued that Tara's love for Steed was often played too heavily, and, coupled with her status as a trainee, this put her character at more of a disadvantage in the partnership than was the case for her predecessors. Indeed, Tara's character is at her best away from Steed, a first for a series which traditionally shone brightest when its leads shared the screen. As a result, episodes and scenes that allowed Tara to fly solo gave the character room to breathe that was often lacking in the Steed/Tara scenes. To this end, it was, ironically, advantageous for her character that the leads were often split up in order to speed up filming for the sake of production deadlines, in much the same way that the series' first three 'shot as live' seasons often alternated scenes between leads in order to lighten the burden on the actors. [3] However, Tara's characterisation was also hindered by the fact that she was not an invention of Brian Clemens. Because he did not create her, there is a distinct sense that he was somewhat unsure of how to write her, and, as a result, was unable to provide any guidance regarding her character to the rest of the show's writers. The result was a noticeable unevenness in her characterisation, resulting in her appearing extremely capable in one episode or scene, and at a loss in the next. [4]

Despite these difficulties, Tara's character also built on the legacy of her predecessors. The widowed Mrs. Gale and Mrs. Peel were created as such for propriety's sake, assuring the audience that they 'knew what it was all about', and making it socially acceptable for them to spend their time in the company of Steed. Tara was originally envisioned as 'Mrs. King' until Linda Thorson put her foot down, arguing that it made more sense for a single woman to accompany Steed than a married one, and aligning her marital status with the series' earliest female leads, the unattached Carol Wilson and Venus Smith, in the process. This breakaway from social niceties would liberate Tara's successor in *The New Avengers*, Purdey, to the extent that she could be single, keep the company of her two male colleagues, *and* have a romantic past, including an ex-fiancé. Tara's inexperience as an agent meant that her fight scenes gained an improvisational, spontaneous aesthetic, a scrappiness and creativity made possible because she was not portrayed as a dedicated student of martial arts, as Emma and Cathy had been. And despite their initial uncertainty, the writers did eventually manage to gain a handle on her character, with the result that Tara gradually matured and grew in confidence and competence as the series went on. There is a marked difference between the character introduced in *The Forget-Me-Not*, and the one who appears toward the season's end in *Who Was That Man I Saw You With?*, both in her capabilities as an agent, and in her ability to hold her own with Steed. This makes Tara the first of Steed's partners to noticeably grow and evolve throughout her tenure. [5]

Season 6 was decidedly uneven in some respects, largely due to its less-than-ideal production circumstances. But, in a roundabout way, the problems behind-the-scenes, coupled with Bryce's legacy, allowed it to adhere to the all-important *Avengers* rule of moving in new directions, while at the same time drawing on the show's past. [6] It would have been interesting to see how another Tara season, *sans* the behind-the-scenes drama, and starring a more confident Thorson backed by scripts tailored to showcase her character's full potential, would have unfolded. Sadly, that unrealised Season 7 is as intangible as the Bryce-helmed Season 6, but Tara's legacy would live on, in a fashion, in the series' next iteration, *The New Avengers*.

© JZ Ferguson

1. While *Bowler Hats and Kinky Boots* suggests that the American ABC network had the final say in the casting of Linda Thorson, there is little doubt that incoming producer John Bryce was a factor in the choice.
2. I think that this is a key point. Many people's 'problem' with the Tara King season stems from the disconcerting mix of

storylines. However, this seems to me to be a fascinating strength of the 'final' season, in which audience expectation is constantly challenged.
3. The nature of 'live' videotape recording also often required the leads to appear in separate scenes, allowing the other time to change or prepare for his/her next scene.
4. We could go a step further here by observing that Brian Clemens did not like or want Thorson/King in the show, a fact that he has admitted on numerous occasions.
5. These observations offer a fascinating counter-argument to Lauren Humphries-Brooks' essay (and Sunday Swift's in the previous volume, *Mrs. Peel, We're Needed*) once again demonstrating how split opinion is on this final season of the original series.
6. This also reflects the constant element of serendipity which coloured *The Avengers*' fascinatingly uneven, non-linear evolution/history. Serendipity – and champagne – would play a major role in the relaunch of the show as *The New Avengers*, just a few years later.

CONTRIBUTORS

Darren Burch became a fan of *The Avengers* through the 1980s Channel 4 repeats. He lives in East London. His interests include cult 1960s TV, swimming, running, composing music, graphic design, and photography. He is currently a youth worker and caretaker of a church. He has contributed chapters on *The Curious Case of the Countless Clues*, *My Wildest Dream* and *Homicide and Old Lace*.

Richard Cogzell lives in Birmingham, England. He is a self-employed hairdresser and chiropodist. His main interest is amateur dramatics. He won a best actor award in 2013. His all-time favourite role was Richard Hannay in *The 39 Steps* in 2012. He also loves reading, and would like to get a novel or a play of his own published one day. He has contributed the chapters on *Game* and *Stay Tuned*.

Sam Denham is a professional writer who first encountered *The Avengers* through the pages of a 1960s Corgi toys catalogue, and when he was allowed to stay up late enough caught the tail end of the Tara King series on TV. The arrival of *The New Avengers* piqued his interest in seeing more of the original, and with the Scala cinema and Channel 4 screenings of the early 1980s the "wonderfully written and stylishly visualised world of *Avengerland* was opened up" to him. Since then he has helped others revisit the 'real' world of *The Avengers* through his contributions to the *Avengerland* locations guides and websites, and is never happier than when "tootling through the leafy lanes of its quintessentially English landscape". He has contributed chapters on *You'll Catch Your Death* and *False Witness*.

J.Z. Ferguson is interested in all aspects of British and Canadian popular culture, but has a particular love for television. She resides in her native Canada, where she studies an eclectic array of subjects. She has contributed the Afterword, in addition to the chapters on *They Keep Killing Steed* and *Who Was That Man I Saw You With?*

Bernard Ginez lives in the south of Paris. He is one of the webmasters of *Le Monde des Avengers*, the French website dedicated to *The Avengers*. He enjoys science fiction and fantasy television series, particularly *The Avengers* and *Doctor Who*. He has contributed a chapter on *Homicide and Old Lace*.

Margaret J Gordon MD is a practising psychiatrist in Northern California where she lives with her family. "I grew up watching the Emma Peel era with my dad, simply for the entertainment value. She was a young girl's role model. I never realised the full psychological power of these episodes until I sat down and analysed them. There are megalomaniacs and phallic symbols at every turn." Her other passions include jazz piano, her family and a terrier dog called Purdey. She has contributed chapters on *Legacy of Death* and *Take-Over*.

Frank Hui is a molecular biologist in Austin, Texas. His interests include comic books and photography. He has been a fan of *The Avengers* since the early 1970s. For six years he curated the film and programming schedule for the Austin Gay and Lesbian International Film Festival. He has contributed chapters on *Look – (stop me if you've heard this one) But There Were These Two Fellers...*, *The Morning After* and *Take Me To Your Leader*.

Lauren Humphries-Brooks is a writer and media journalist. She holds a Master's degree in Cinema Studies from New York University, and in Creative Writing from the University of Edinburgh. She regularly contributes to film and pop culture websites, and has written extensively on Classical Hollywood, British horror films, and the sci-fi, fantasy, and horror genres. She has contributed a chapter on Tara King's character.

Piers Johnson was born in England but has spent almost his entire life in Australia. He holds degrees in History and Computing Science and lives in Sydney with his wife and three children where he builds websites. His *Mrs Peel, We're Needed!* site has been constantly updated since 1993. He has contributed the chapters on *The Invasion of the Earthmen*, *Wish You Were Here* and *Requiem*.

Matthew Lee is a card-carrying Anglophile with a voracious appetite for and passionate appreciation of British television and film. Matthew believes the work of art that is *The Avengers* to be ITV's best and most enduring output. "A televisual rose and gun which combines beauty and danger with the finest fashions, females and fiends, the series has always been a little left of a foreign field that is forever England – and therein lies its culture-defining brilliance". He has contributed chapters on *Whoever Shot Poor George Oblique XR40?*, *The Rotters*, *Legacy of Death*, *The Interrogators* and *Bizarre*, in addition to the Foreword.

Rodney Marshall is a teacher and writer in Suffolk, UK and Poitou-Charentes, France. His main passions are Ian Rankin's *Rebus*, *The Avengers* and Chamois Niortais FC. He has written a number of books about *The Avengers* as well as editing *The Avengers on film* series. He has contributed chapters on *Noon Doomsday*, *Super Secret Cypher Snatch*, *Killer*, *Love All*, *False Witness* and *Pandora*.

Dan O'Shea, after spending 35 years in the corporate world, has retired along with his wife to live on a ranch in Arkansas, USA, and raises Arabian horses. He first saw an *Avengers* episode (*Murdersville*) when he was in college and has been hooked on *The Avengers* ever since. He has contributed the chapters on *The Forget-Me-Knot* and *Have Guns – Will Haggle*.

Mark Saunders is a 50-something civil servant from the Isle of Wight, but his heart is in television and film appreciation. He enjoys seeking out, watching, and occasionally writing about original and well-made British and American programmes and films from all eras. He's also a voracious reader, particularly of detective novels and graphic novels, enjoys electronic music, and dabbles in fiction writing, song writing, singing, and drawing. His favourite television show is probably *Doctor Who* in the 1970s, but *The Avengers* comes a close second. He has contributed chapters on *Split!* and *Get-A-Way!*

Frank Shailes was impressed enough by *The Avengers* to join a government Ministry soon after the show was repeated on the UK's new Channel 4. Sadly, Frank got nowhere near Steed's department, although he did enjoy hanging about derelict research centres, and just being around old derelicts generally. He started watching *The Avengers* because he loved *The Prisoner* and "it seemed just as fun, stylish, wacky and intelligent." The Cathy Gale era is his favourite vintage and especially Cathy's avante-garde hats and biting sarcasm. He has contributed the chapters on *All Done With Mirrors* and *Thingumajig*.

Sunday Swift is a PhD student at Lancaster University, UK. Her area of research focuses on masculinity and Dandyism in contemporary British and American television. Additional areas of research include: Fashion, Popular culture, Television of Britain and American from 1960-1990, Irish Gothic literature, Cinema, and Contemporary Gothic television. She has contributed the chapter on *Fog*.

QUOTATIONS GLOSSARY

A quotations glossary has been added to each volume of *The Avengers on film* at the request of many of our readers. Some of the contributors in *Anticlockwise* draw heavily on citations from the episodes' written dialogue. Others don't. Either approach is fine. However, much of the enjoyment of *The Avengers* stems from the written dialogue, be it witty, diabolical, ideological, philosophical, daringly countercultural or simply bizarre.

This glossary offers some of the (spoken) highlights from each and every episode of Season 6. It is by no means exhaustive and the selection of citations is obviously highly subjective.

I have included some dialogue which was cut from the final filmed versions.

Like *Anticlockwise* itself, this section will have been a success if it has you journeying/returning to the episodes themselves. After all, to paraphrase Shakespeare and *Coca Cola*, the episode is 'the (real) thing'.

Rodney Marshall

THE FORGET-ME-KNOT

Steed: (introducing Mortimer to Mrs. Peel) Sean Mortimer.
Sean: How do you do?
Steed: No, you're Sean Mortimer, this is Mrs. Peel.
Sean: Oh, then who are you?
Steed: John Steed.
Emma: And who is he?
Steed: Don't you start.
Emma: I mean, what does he do?

Emma: (re. Mortimer) Missing, on all cylinders.

Steed: (re. Tara staring at him) My feeding time is one-thirty.

Tara: Your Achilles heel.
Steed: Rubber-soled shoes?
Tara: The opposite sex.

Mother: Don't quote the regulations to me, I made them!

Filson: (re. Steed) Even the biggest idols can have feet of clay.

Mortimer: This is really strange.
Emma: Certainly a coincidence...that we both seem to be suffering from amnesia.
Mortimer: What's amnesia?
Emma: Loss of memory.
Mortimer: Ah...who's lost their memory?
Emma: We have.
Mortimer: Sorry. I'd forgotten.

Mortimer: At least we know, you're Steed...and I'm Peel...Where do we go from here?
Emma: Not far, I'm afraid. The door's locked.

Tara: (re. Steed's 'guilt') You assume too much, Simon – you really do.

Steed: See you're using the single-handed death grip. Ooh!
Tara: It's recommended.
Steed: Your Judo master teach you how to counter it?
Tara: No.
Steed: Highly recommended.

Burton: The drug – it works, erases the memory.
Steed: Only temporarily.
Burton: Well, it varies from person to person…Meanwhile, a bullet erases the memory completely.

Emma: (re. Mr. Peel turning up in the Amazonian jungle) It's corny.
Steed: Ridiculous.

Emma: Always keep your bowler on in times of stress. And watch out for diabolical masterminds.

Emma: He likes his tea stirred anticlockwise.

INVASION OF THE EARTHMEN

Steed: You should always try, wherever possible, to toss your opponent through the nearest window – double glazed preferably. It's more effective and much more spectacular.

Steed: (re. Alpha Academy) Deserted, isn't it?
Tara: It's like the other side of the moon.

Steed: I hate locked rooms...the war, you know.

Brett: There is little future in today's world for a soldier.

Brett: Today's youngsters are tomorrow's people.

Tara: I really saw an inflated astronaut that looked like Humpty Dumpty.

Brett: There is the future, Miss King. The new worlds of space... hanging like ripe plums in the sky, waiting for the first men who have the courage to snatch them. Earth, over-populated, under-fed, its wealth sucked dry.

Student: The Brigadier says everybody's got a secret fear. In that tunnel you come face-to-face with that fear.

Steed: Miss King, have I ever let you down?
Tara: There's always a first time.
Steed: Telling the truth can be very destructive to a relationship.

THE CURIOUS CASE OF THE COUNTLESS CLUES

Dawson: What's happened? Has there been an accident?
Earle: No, sir – a murder.
Dawson: A murder? But who's been murdered?
Earle: You, sir.

Sir Arthur: I see you walked through the park this morning. Your shoes carry a film of pale blue dust peculiar to that area...Deduction, Steed. Deduction.
Steed: I see you've changed your secretary [pulling a blonde hair from Doyle's coat]. The last one was brunette. Seduction, Sir Arthur?

Steed: I thought everything had a price.
Flanders: Oh that's a fallacy. What price freedom? Honour? Reputation?

Earle: Crime, these days, rarely pays. The scientific evidence soon seeks out the criminal. So I have turned a drawback into a virtue. I have made you a murderer.

Earle: (re. 'mechanic' Stanley) He's not very good at repairs, but excellent at alibis.

Earle: I only do business with men of taste. They have so much more to offer.

Steed: I wouldn't like you to choke to death on a cheap cigar. I'll give you just enough air to stay alive and tell me who's behind all this...Three breaths, that's enough, now talk.

Earle: A *crime passionnel*. It will make an interesting variation.

SPLIT!

Tara: Clearly the handwriting of a strong/weak, happy/sad, anxious/carefree man.

Swindin: The personality of the writer has completely changed. It's…it's fantastic…remarkable…a mind of great cunning. A brutal, extrovert man. A man who would stop at nothing to achieve his ends. A man to whom cruelty means pleasure.

Constantine: I don't like it. When Steed gets this close.

Constantine: (re. Kartovski) He was always one for a pretty woman. His appetite was remarkable. Voracious. And he could be cruel. So cruel.

Constantine: I kept him alive.
Petra: You call that alive?
Constantine: Well his brain still lives.

Constantine: Relax, Miss King, and let his mind flood into yours.

Rooke: Steed, pick up the gun and kill me…
Steed: Kill you old chap? I'd rather cure you.

GET-A-WAY!

Steed: To Paul Ryder and George Neville. We trained together, we fought together and I hope we shall remain together for many years to come.
Neville: Oh dear, it's all gone solemn. Positively sepulchral.

James: He disappeared right here...I told you – the whole thing's impossible.
Steed: But it happened, Colonel.

Steed: How do you occupy yourself?
Ezdorf: I think...I ruminate. I plan.

Lubin: I wanted you to see me before I killed you.

Tara: You don't believe in invisible men do you?
Steed: Only when I can't see them.

Tara: I'll check at the Ministry.
Steed: And I'll check at the monastery.

James: Chains and manacles. If we resort to that sort of thing we might as well –
Steed: Join the other side.

Ezdorf: I do admire you. Incisive, thorough, relentless. A worthy adversary. Equally matched. We are very alike you and I. Identical.
Steed: No!
Ezdorf: What's the difference? We are both dedicated to our country. We are both prepared to die for it. You have killed – I have killed.
Steed: There is a difference. I kill when I have to. You, because you like it.

Peters: (re. chameleon) It's something to do with the chromaphores in their skin. They merge with the background...Nature's camouflage...You'd never know he was there.

Magnus: A pigmented plastoid. More concentrated and spontaneous than the cells of that humble but remarkable little lizard. You just pour it on and one assumes the texture and colour of the background.

Ezdorf: It's like a riddle. I was trained never to turn my back on an enemy. Because to turn my back put me at my most vulnerable. But – if I turn my back now – I am at my most invulnerable. Ha! Ha!

HAVE GUNS – WILL HAGGLE

Tara: They bounced in.
Steed: And blasted their way out.
Tara: After they got what they wanted there was no need for subtlety.

Spencer: (ballistics expert) I cannot abide loud, sharp noises.

Spencer: Well, it's passed all fifty-two tests, positive. I think one can safely hazard that this was fired from an F.F.70.
Tara: Safely hazard?
Spencer: Well, one mustn't commit oneself.
Tara: Official procedure.
Spencer: Yes, precisely.

Steed: You had to endure fifty-two approved tests.
Tara: Fifty-three. After I left Ballistics, someone attacked me. They tried to get the bullet back.
Steed: And tenaciously you held on through thick and thin.

Steed: (to Nsonga re. *Small Game for Big Hunters* music) I see you're playing our tune.

Steed: The President's a little worried about the *coup d'état* season creeping up on him.

Crayford: You've got to make it look good, like last time – a violent attack.

Steed: Loyalty, among other virtues, was something they impressed upon me at Eton.

Adriana: Like the man who sells vacuum cleaners shows them at work, cleaning carpets...We sell weapons. And there is only one way to display them.

Adriana: (re. her brother, Conrad) The creature has yet to be born that he cannot kill with a single bullet. He prides himself on it.

Steed: During training the record for opening handcuffs was thirty-two seconds.
Tara: Well, you'll have to break it.

LOOK – (STOP ME IF YOU'VE HEARD THIS ONE) BUT THERE WERE THESE TWO FELLERS...

Steed: In the event of war where would the Government go?
Tara. The moon?
Steed: Underground.

Steed: It doesn't make sense. Gigantic footprints. Magical bunches of flowers. Red ping pong balls.

Tara: May I come in?
Marcus: *Come in?*
Tara: Yes...
Marcus: It's most unusual.
Tara: You *are* a public office.

Marcus: You see before you twenty-two years of patient brushwork ...every clown's face in Britain, registered and copyrighted, by being painted on an egg...large size.

Maxie: I don't think Marcus saw the yoke.

Steed: I'm not in the entertainment business.
Marler: Oh, television.

Marler: Theatres and music halls close. Vaudeville Variety dies...
Steed: Times change.

Dessington: We bought...a whole chain of Vaudeville theatres. Thirty or forty of them, all due for demolition. Huh! As you know, Vaudeville's dead.
Steed: Looks as if Vaudeville may have just decided to fight back.

Tara: Oh Officer, thank goodness you're here. You see there were these two men...

Fiery Frederick: You'll go down in history my girl. The very first woman to be burnt in half. Oh I know plenty who have been sawn in two...but burnt, never.

MY WILDEST DREAM

Jaeger: Fear and hatred – they are one…like a sore that festers …swells up into unbearable tension. We must relieve these tensions, Gibbons…these aggressions…live them out.

Chilcott: The voice in the night – do you never tire of it?...all this fun and games, this cloak and dagger stuff with Steed. What's so special about Steed anyway?

Jaeger: You'd like to kill him – to be rid of him. Well you can – you must. The taboos, the restrictions of society prevent you. But there are no restrictions here – no taboos.

Steed: Seriously suspecting…
Tara: As we usually do…

Jaeger: Excellent, Mr. Slater. Kill, destroy and erase. I particularly like erase.

Slater: You're not in my dream – go away.

Reece: You killed him…Murder. Cold blooded murder…
Slater: A dream. I dreamed it…
Reece: A reality, Slater.
Slater: No. No.
Reece: A nasty reality.

Steed: I think it's time I consulted my aggresso-therapist.

Steed: (to Nurse Owen) What a nice voice you have – soothing. I bet you have a nice telephone manner too.

Steed: I keep thinking I'm a horse. Must be something to do with my name. Well it distresses my friends terribly. I'm given to cantering across the quiet room of my club.

Jaeger: You use the word 'dabble' like a sword. Like an offensive weapon.

Jaeger: Your eyes are sceptical.
Steed: I'll keep them half-closed.

Jaeger: Your ancestors were killers – hunters of men.
Steed: I had a great aunt on my mother's side – ruthless with a knitting needle!
Jaeger: I am talking of a million years ago. A mere [clicks his finger], in evolutionary terms, primeval man.
Steed: Oh him!
Jaeger: He still lurks in us all, Mr. Steed. His appetites. His instincts. But modern society inhibits them. I channel, I release these inhibitions.

Jaeger: I am talking of killing in *fantasy*. That is my technique. I seek out a man's secret enemy and allow him to kill that enemy, here, in this room, many times. A catharsis, a release of all repressions and hatreds. A man lives out his dream, his wildest dream...harmlessly.

Steed: The insatiable craving, the perpetual desire, the uncontrollable urge – to lay my hands on a bottle of champagne, is for a very very different reason.
Tara: Dare I ask?
Steed: Ah – because – I happen to like it.

WHOEVER SHOT POOR GEORGE OBLIQUE STROKE XR40?

Ardmore: Murder – cold blooded murder. Poor George never had a chance.
Tara: Was it – he – working on any special project?

Baines: I designed it myself. The purity of the right angle. Not a curve anywhere. Why to have curves in my place would be sacrilege.
Tara: In that case perhaps I'd better...?
Baines: No, no...The furnishings. I don't like right angled girls. Although I don't mind girls with the right angle.

Ardmore: A shot disabled him, but from the moment it was fired – George could compute the range, velocity, mass kinetic energy and impact ratio...
Tara: Only one thing he couldn't do really.
Ardmore: What's that?
Tara: Duck.

Steed: How's George?
Tara: Oh, hanging on. The last thing he computed was two plus two equals five.
Steed: I'd always suspected that.

Ardmore: (re. 'Fred') Mark Three. George's ancestor as it were, but of course by comparison with George – a half-witted, empty-headed fool. A moron.

Tara: There's someone else here, someone hiding behind a locked door.
Steed: The master mind.

Anaesthetist: What did you hit him with?
Steed: With a great deal of venom.

Tara: Ah, my prince, on his fiery steed.
Steed: No, I'm an asbestos-clad Steed. An uninflammable, unfiery Steed.

Steed: I asked him [George] to give me the recipe for the most deliciously potent cocktail in the world.
Tara: And he gave you the answer?
Steed: He hiccupped it up in four seconds flat.

YOU'LL CATCH YOUR DEATH

Camrose: All clear.
Farrar: Are you sure?
Camrose: Can you afford to pay my fees and question my diagnosis?

Steed: I told you this was a mystery tour. We've got to solve the mystery.

Mother: A disease that chooses its victims too carefully for my liking. Find the antidote before it spreads.
Steed: But first of all find the disease.

Tara: I see. I go out and protect the whole medical profession, while you stay at home and have a cosy paper chase.

Tara: It seems there's nothing deadlier than the mail.

Maidwell: What would a Nursing Academy want with ten thousand envelopes?

Steed: My foundation is dedicated to the service of the sick.
Matron: I see. Buying your way to Heaven?
Steed: Hmm. With the meek inheriting the earth, it's the only place left.

Steed: If one's born with a silver spoon in one's mouth, one must see that it feeds as many people as possible.

Steed: I don't share your knack of unconcern.
Mother: Practical.
Steed: Eh?
Mother: I'm being practical. Fill your mind with anxieties about Tara, and you'll be thinking below par...and reducing your chances of finding her.

Butler: Curiosity, sir, was responsible for the demise of the cat.
Steed: Not to worry. I have eight lives left.
Butler: My advice would be, sir, not to throw them away too easily.

Dexter: If you want to play games little lady, we must give you a copy of the rules.

Steed: Death by post. Simple!

Preece: (re. Steed) He'll have found the envelope – sniffed it –
Dexter: And snuffed it.

Glover: The oldest motive, the oldest cliché – they...they 'knew too much'.

ALL DONE WITH MIRRORS

Seligman: Watney – I know how it's done – mirrors – all done with mirrors.

Mother: You don't think she can do it?
Steed: ...she's female...and she's vulnerable.

Tara: A Colonel in a lighthouse?
Barlow: Yes, odd isn't it? The Colonel comes from a family of soldiers, yet at heart he always wanted to be...
Tara: A sailor...How far is it?
Barlow: Oh, about a year. The Colonel's little joke. There are three hundred and sixty five of these stairs. He says it takes about a year to climb them.

Fake Withers: The great, grand rolling ocean. And ships. Ships under sail, under way, heading for exotic locations. Oh no, Miss King, you won't find me looking at land.

Tara: I must say a year passes more quickly on the way down.

Steed: (re. Tara 'falling' from cliff edge) Now what are the chances?
Mother: Chances? If she survived the fall, if she missed the rocks, if she wasn't swept out to sea, I'd say her chances were quite good.

Tara: Don't worry, I won't haunt you. If you promise to take me out to dinner tonight.
Steed: Disembodied and still got an appetite.

Steed: Table for one and one ethereal voice!

SUPER SECRET CYPER SNATCH

Betty: What kind of day has it been?
Masters (Guard): Oh, the usual Monday, Miss...routine and boring.

Mother: (re. MI12) Terrible preoccupation with gimmicks and gadgets...No gadget will ever take the place of a man.
Steed: Or woman.

Tara: Astonishing that Mr. Jarret should have all these marvellous gadgets and still disappear.

Ferret: Impossible. Webster had a triple star clearance. He can't lie.

Lather: At Classy Glass the world is our window.

Lather: (re. Cypher HQ) Double glazed with moulded frame...urgh – ghastly!...All that grey concrete – quite soul destroying.

Tara: I suppose it could be a perfectly harmless company?
Steed: With a very lethal line in ladders.

Maskin: Tomorrow is yesterday again.

Maskin: Scare off any unwelcome visitors...unless Steed shows his face.
Davis: And then?
Maskin: Put a bullet in it.

Voice Over: It has just begun to rain. Otherwise, it is a perfectly normal, perfectly ordinary day.

Lather: You see, that's the beauty of hypnotics. People only see what you want them to see.

GAME

Steed: Snakes and ladders! No note.
Tara: Someone's playing a game with you.

Tara: This in the Jigsaw Centre?
Manager: The centre of the jigsaw universe.
Tara: And you're the manager?
Manager: The Master.

Bristow: If you win the game, you will walk from here a free man. If you lose, your pills remain where they are. With the resultant loss of your life.

Wishforth-Brown: (re. tea) Even in times of war one must observe the formalities.

Bristow: Do we shape our destinies – or does destiny shape us?

Manager: Mr. Bristow – the Games King.

Bristow: The others played for their lives – well, you in your profession, your life is cheap – you set no store by it. But Miss King, let's hope her life means a little more to you.

Bristow: I devised the game myself. It's not particularly complex, but it calls upon all the qualities required of a secret agent: courage, strategy, a certain degree of animal cunning and, of course, embodied in the game is that traditional element of all spy sagas, the damsel in distress.

FALSE WITNESS

Steed: Trouble in Botswana?
Mother: Trouble in the abdomen. Too many oysters.

Mother: The Department's losing agents and I'm losing sleep.

Mother: Forewarned is forearmed.
Tara: Not against a knife in the back.

Melville: (re. Steed's punch) What did you do that for?
Steed: For services not rendered.

Sykes: (in milk vat room) Worried about lack of vitamins?
Tara: Desperately. I'm just wasting away.
Sykes: Then we must bring the roses back to your cheeks, mustn't we?

Tara: This is very unimportant.
Sir Joseph: Well, don't bother me now then, I'm rather busy.
Tara: I don't want to warn you.
Sir Joseph: I beg your pardon?
Tara: Whatever you do, don't be careful.

Steed: Do you take milk in your coffee?
Melville: Yes, usually.
Steed: In future, take it black.

Sykes: Butter wouldn't melt in your mouth, Miss King. Or would it? ...Put her in the butter machine.

NOON DOOMSDAY

Mother: I absolutely abhor noise – and what I like about you is your complete noiselessness. A rare quality in a woman.

Tara: (re. Department S) The approach is the tiniest bit unconventional.

Steed: What's more vulnerable than a wounded agent?
Tara: Two wounded agents?

Steed: I don't think there is a collective noun for us. How about a lurking of secret agents?
Tara: A skulking?
Steed: A contentment.
Tara: Agents aren't particularly contented.
Steed: Mmm. This one is.

Hyde: (re. sundial) Two minutes slow.

Farrington: A bullet's very accurate. But noisy.

Grant: What time is it? Well?
Farrington: Not yet.

Mother: It's a pleasure working with a colleague who has such a versatile cellar...Jolly good fellow Steed, and absolute paragon of – I wonder if he buys it all on expenses!

Farrington: My goodness, you do get edgy, don't you?
Grant: You don't, I suppose?
Farrington: I *did*. First dozen or so times. But it's just a job of work, sometimes a little messy I'll agree – but not too arduous, and remarkably well paid.

Farrington (re. Tara): It's only a girl.

Grant: Turn around. I don't like to see the eyes.

Steed: (re. nursing home) And I came here for a rest.

LEGACY OF DEATH

Sidney: I didn't travel four thousand miles to meet up with a dead man! How dare he die before we had a chance to kill him? I won't allow it.

Steed: I thought you didn't like parties?
Tara: No I don't really. That's why I'm trying to get them all in in one evening.

Ho Lung: Me not buying.
Tara: Me not selling.

Oppenheimer: What symptoms did he exhibit before he collapsed?
Steed: Don't the bullet holes in his coat give you the tiniest clue?

Sidney: Violence is no use. Subtlety is what is needed. Subtlety.
Humbert: But after we've been subtle – then can I kill him?

Steed: Can I get you a drink?
Humbert: Nothing thank you. I may have to operate later.
Steed: Are you a surgeon?
Humbert: It's just a hobby with me.

Sidney: That worthless trinket was once the property of my Aunt Amelia – rest her soul.
Steed: She's dead?
Sidney: I hope so, sir; she's been buried some years.

Steed: Bodies. Dagger. Tara.

Steed: Inferior type of assassin.
King: Just don't make them like they used to.
Steed: It's the age of the amateur.

King: Where are we going?
Steed: Where indeed! Philosophers have asked that question for a thousand years. Quo Vadis? Whither goest thou? Man's eternal search for his destiny. You may well ask, 'Where are we going?'
King: Where *are* we going?
Steed: Turn left, next lights.

King: I think we're being followed.
Steed: By whom?
King: Just about everybody.

Von Orlack: We have ways of finding out.

Sidney: A monstrous pearl. Black as night and spawned up by some gigantic mollusc before time began. The largest – the most priceless pearl on Earth.

THEY KEEP KILLING STEED

Mother: I must say I'm looking forward to going under the water. It'll be very quiet down there.

Baron: (to Tara) It was a privilege being married to you.
Steed: These holiday romances. They never last.

Steed: Gentlemen, I use the word loosely, I have a shrewd suspicion that there's dirty work afoot.
Arcos: Yes. Yes. We intend to infiltrate the Peace Conference.
Steed: With a forged pass?
Arcos: No – with a forged face.

Steed: Instant plastic surgery.

Steed: Dedicated idealist, or altruistic opportunist?
Zerson: Do what?

Zerson: He hit me.
Arcos: Huh. He shows wisdom.

Arcos: The British are all the same, you treat war like as if it were a game.
Steed: I didn't know we were at war.
Arcos: Your kind and my kind should always be at war.

Mother: Nice of you to drop in my dear.

Mother: Straight down stream and turn left at the salmon nets.

Arcos: I see you rely a great deal upon your knight.
Steed: I like his nobility. The unfettered free-lance of the board.
Arcos: You can tell a man's character from the way he plays chess.
Steed: I couldn't agree more. You seem to rely heavily on your pawns.

Steed: You don't like losing do you?
Arcos: It's a bad habit.

Smythe: Any other Steeds must be shot on sight.

Baron : (re. multiple Steeds) Look! The woods are full of them.

WISH YOU WERE HERE

Tara: (reading postcard) "Having a wonderful time – place is absolutely captivating – wish you were here."

Mother: (to Nephew Basil) I'm not your Uncle, I'm your Mother.

Mother: It's a simple case. A man with the mentality of a child of seven could handle it.
Steed: On that basis, Basil qualifies.

Tara: As a damsel in distress, I have a feeling that a Knight in shining armour on his trusty Steed will come and rescue us any moment.

Tara: I'm so glad you're here. But I wish you hadn't come.

Basil: It's not like a prison. No locked doors, iron bars, warders.

Kendrick: Your whole operation depends upon normality. Discretely hold a man prisoner here amongst a crowd of bona fide guests.

Steed: Do you by any chance have a room for a weary but successful viper hunter?

KILLER

Mother: This cadaver was discovered in rather odd circumstances.
Steed: How odd?
Mother: In a graveyard.
Steed: There's nothing very odd about that.
Mother: But this one was wrapped in plastic and tied with ribbons.
Steed: Now that is very interesting.

Steed: How did he die?
Clarke: In alphabetical order, he was clubbed, poisoned, shot, spiked, stabbed, strangled and suffocated. And his ear drums are damaged.
Steed: His neck's broken as well.

Clarke: The most baffling thing about it is that he looks so...
Steed: Tidy?
Clarke: The body appears to have been washed, sterilised, dry-cleaned.
Steed: Packaged.
Clarke: Quite. Even the bullet holes in his jacket have been invisibly mended.

Steed: How did you get in?
Forbes: Agent's manual, section three, paragraph four. Always go in through a skylight.

Merridon: One million pounds he cost me.
Steed: To mass produce murder.
Merridon: To decimate your intelligence services, Steed. The perfect killer.

Steed: The trouble with computers is that they have no loyalty. They'll take orders from anybody.

THE ROTTERS

Mother: Come on, Rhonda! Pump! Pump! I'm taking on a starboard list!

Carter: We don't deal in secrets in this department, we plant trees. When they grow up, we cut them down.
Steed: What a full rich life you must lead.

Kenneth: I detest imitations. I loathe anything inferior. You look rather inferior to me, old man.

Kenneth: I do despise the working classes. They're so, so…
George: Working class?
Kenneth: Quite!

Palmer: He's a bad lot, Sawbow. No principles. Bit of a rotter.

Kenneth: Lovely old place, isn't it?
George: Mmm. Charming. Adore the countryside. Have you ever strangled anyone old chap?
Kenneth: Strangled. No, no, I can't say I have. Trees are awfully nice at this time of year, aren't they? Don't you think?
George: Mmm. Awfully nice. Just a hint of autumn in the leaves. I wonder what it's like.
Kenneth: What?
George: Strangling.
Kenneth: Strangling. Rather unpleasant I should imagine. Not a method a gentleman would use.
George: Oh quite, quite. Awfully vulgar. Mmmmmm. Country air, jolly invigorating.
Kenneth: Yes – it makes one glad to be alive.
George: Mmmm. Shall we do it now?
Kenneth: I don't think so, no. Just get a good look at the geography and come back tonight. It's always better in the dark.
George: Much better. More sort of – dramatic.

Pym: Dry...dry...
Tara: Do you want water?
Pym: No thank you. Dry rot.

Steed: Well, *is* he in prison?
Tara: He's in the antique business.
Steed: Stealing them?
Tara: No, restoring them.
Steed: What, to their rightful owners?

Sawbow: I'd like to check up on your firm before we do any business. There's a lot of very shady people in this game.
Steed: You astonish me!

Forsyth: Have you seen what they did to my mother's piano?
Steed: Seen what they did? I was under it!

George: (re. killing females) There are certain ethics, standards of behaviour, certain actions which a gentleman would never consider.

Wainwright: Consider a world without wood, Miss King. My dry rot will make the nuclear bomb, the greatest earthquake, the mightiest volcano seem as insignificant as a teardrop in Niagara.

THE INTERROGATORS

Mannering: They all talk. Eventually.
Caspar: You'll get nothing from me. Nothing.
Mannering: On the contrary, Lieutenant. We shall get everything we want from you. Everything.

Norton: Hand-rolled, custom-made, mixture of Virginia and Turkish, with a preponderance of oriental herbs. Smoked by a right-handed male of medium build. Of course, that's only in the nature of a wild guess at this stage.

Mannering: Which do you think is worse, Minnow, the sound or not knowing when it will begin again? You become your own torturer really.

Mother (re. exotic cigarette stub): I think you'd better watch your step – anyone who smokes such a revolting mixture must be evil incarnate.

Mannering: You watch others, we watch you.
Tara: Big Brother.
Mannering: Well we had hoped our interest was slightly more paternal.

Steed: You must admit it's clever.
Mother: Turn our own secret bureaucracy into a weapon.
Steed: Tie us up with our own red tape. It's very simple.
Mother: Persuade our agents that the course is genuine, get their full co-operation and interrogate them for as long as they like.
Steed: Until they talk.

Steed: Follow that pigeon!

THE MORNING AFTER

Tara: (re. Merlin) A double agent.
Steed: Quadruple would be nearer the mark.

Merlin: Do you think the world's ended and they forgot to tell us?

Hearn: Firing party into line! Take aim! Fire!

Hearn: I'm the judge. The sentence is death!

Merlin: I'm your prisoner, right?
Steed: Right.
Merlin: So I'm your responsibility, right?
Steed: Right.
Merlin: So it's your duty to take care of me, right?
Steed: Wrong.
Merlin: What? Well what about the rules?
Steed: You know that there are no rules in this game, Merlin.

Merlin: A man murdered in cold blood without even a trial? Why didn't they just arrest him?

Hearn: We're not taking a bomb apart. We're putting it together.
Jenny: Building a bomb?
Steed: It makes a twisted kind of sense. They declare the area clear, people move back in again.
Hearn: And then we make our demand: "Pay up, or else!"

Hearn: (re. brigadier) He's been told he's going to be replaced. Made redundant by a computer...Kicked out of the service to make room for a machine.

LOVE ALL

Martha: I'm interested in everything about you, especially your secrets.

Steed: Three shots. Very civil. You even shoot people in triplicate.

Steed: Intimidation.
Mother: Blackmail.
Tara: Infatuation.

Mother: Whoever heard of a respectable gentleman like Sir Rodney losing his head over a woman? I have never heard anything so ridiculous in all my life.

Mother: (re. Sir Rodney) Jumped through a window – twenty feet from the ground. Now what on earth would make a middle aged civil servant do a stupid thing like that?
Steed: Desperation?
Tara: Love?

Bellchamber: (re. his brother) He's away at the moment in Provence, crushing Lily –
Tara: Really, I'm surprised she doesn't object.
Bellchamber: Crushing lilies for Lily of the Valley, Madam.

Tara: Is – mm – 'Reckless Abandon' a popular brand?
Bellchamber: Among the wealthy and the discerning, Madam. It's – mm – priced a little high for most pockets.

Mother: This wretched affair's taking on a pattern and I don't like the picture.

Steed: On a cold winter's night, I like nothing more than curling up in front of the fire with Rosemary Z Glade.

Thelma: (re. Rosemary the computer) Every romantic situation in the world is built into her memory circuits. The keys activate the situations.
Steed: Moonlight kisses. Wife hears rumours. Girl meets wife. Wife sues girl. Wife leaves husband. Husband leaves wife. Girl returns ring. Boy gives flowers. Ah! Fascinating!

Tara: I love you.
Bromfield: Who doesn't?

Bromfield: It's been scientifically proven that love is the most potent emotion in the universe…The man or woman in the thrall of love is as easily manipulated as soft putty.

Steed: I know love is meant to be blind, but this is ridiculous.

TAKE ME TO YOUR LEADER

Captain Andrews: The man at the top.
Tara: Mr. Big.
Andrews: The master mind.
Tara: The arch-villain.

Steed: (re. cheap London hotel) It has a sort of faded gentility. It's probably full of lovely old ladies in lavender lace who sit sipping tea and remembering.
Tara: Remembering what?
Steed: Whatever it is old ladies remember.

Sally: Aren't we going to weight him down with cement and toss him in the river?

Mother: I think I make a very good number one suspect.

Cavell: It's the eyes. I don't like looking at the eyes when I do it.

Steed: That's a sad epitaph for a musician. He died flat.

STAY TUNED

Steed: You can't just lose three weeks.

Dr. Meitner: An emotional stress. Perhaps mental strain. Then of course there's the classic reason so beloved of fiction writers – the blow on the head.

Meitner: Do you remember last night?
Steed: Huh! I remember perfectly. I went to bed and woke up yesterday morning.

Proctor: A post hypnotic suggestion. It's part of Steed's conditioning. He was told I do not exist. My image has been hypnotised from his mind. He can't see me.

Wilks: His mind…it's been conditioned to perform one single act. Until that act is done, there's no escape. Every time he tries to break out of the mental cell we've created, we simply start the cycle over again.

Kreer's voice: When you next hear the word Bacchus, you will kill Mother. Kill Mother.

Steed: Every time I try to remember, I find that it is yesterday again.

Mother: If we can't trust you, who can we trust?

FOG

Knife Grinder: Fine steel this, Sir...Like a surgeon's scalpel.

Haller: Has a steam pipe broken or something?

Steed: Eh? Oh, that's fog...we still lead the world in that department.

Steed: If the Gaslight Ghoul was still riding around he would be – oh I'd say a hundred and fifty years old by now.

Mother: The Gaslight Ghoul Club. A society of harmless eccentrics.

Travers: Come in and I'll show you the nasty things in our wood shed.

Travers: Victorian Scalpel. They don't make them like that anymore.
Steed: I should hope not.
Travers: Can you imagine that in the wrong hands? Clean, quick and efficient.

Travers: What were you looking for?
Steed: A wolf – in wolf's clothing.

Dr. Armstrong: Lock up when you go will you? And don't forget to turn the gas off, and the fog.

Steed: I must get you a doctor.
Armstrong: I am a doctor – I'll be all right. But you can send me an undertaker.

WHO WAS THAT MAN I SAW YOU WITH?

Tara: We're not playing war games. This is deadly serious.

Fairfax: Yes Mother. No Mother. Of course Mother. Goodbye Mother.
Tara: Took the news well I see.

Fairfax: You'll have to take action.
Mother: Don't tell me what I have to do boy! I was making life and death decisions when the only choice in life you had to make was whether to eat your baby cereal or spit it out!

Dangerfield: You know, most people's feet are so ugly. Mine are so elegant.

Tara: I've never been under house arrest before. What are the rules?
Phillipson: You just carry on as normal, except that if you attempt to escape I will shoot you.

Tara: The best bit of framing since the Mona Lisa.

Steed: (toasting at the champagne fountain) To Tara King, of whom I never suspected funny business for one moment.
Tara: Never?
Steed: Well, almost never.

PANDORA

Rupert: People call it 'ragtime'.
Henry: I think it's excessively vulgar.
Rupert: Oh come on, Henry, we must move with the times.

Mother: This is utterly unprecedented, Steed. Sending for me, dragging me down from my Headquarters, well it's like – it's like –
Steed: Like a cuckoo leaving the nest.

Henry: The whole thing is mad; you're mad.

Steed: It's hard to forget eh, to kick over the traces – once it's in your blood – old agents never die.

Juniper: All those modern resources you've got nowadays, still can't find her, eh?

Henry: Women given the vote? What would they do with it? You'll be suggesting women in Government next.

Rupert: The year is nineteen hundred and fifteen.

Tara: I'm to be married?
Rupert: The happiest day of your life.

THINGUMAJIG

Professor Truman: May I ask you something? What caused this?
Tara: Well that's what I want you to tell me.
Truman: Oh!

Steed: At least its activities are confined underground at the moment – I only hope it stays that way.

Truman: Atishoo. Atishoo. Atishoo.
Tara: Bless you. Bless you. Bless you.

Kruger: (re. axe head) I imagine this might have taken human life. A savage weapon from a savage past.
Teddy: Err – well – yeah – well it – it comes from a much more – err – barbarous period.
Kruger: No more barbarous than now...the stone axe has become a gun or a bomb. Man has ever sought the perfect method of destroying man.

Grant: Curiosity killed the cat.
Steed: It led to the invention of anaesthetics, the aeroplane, the wheel, electricity.

Truman: Would you care for a pinch, Miss King?
Tara: Of snuff?
Truman: Oh at my age it's the only kind of pinching in which I can indulge.

Steed: (to vicar) You baptise and bury them, and I'll try and see that the interval between the two is as long as possible.

HOMICIDE AND OLD LACE

Harriet: We thought you'd have five fingers of old red-eye.
Mother: What?
Georgina: We read all the spy books you know. 'Five fingers of old red-eye'. It's the conventional thing.

Harriet: (re. the Great-Great Britain Crime) How did it start? With a killing, eh?

Mother: This time our agent was able to contact Headquarters with a message before he was gunned down.
Harriet: Convenient.

Steed: Interpol helps the police against the criminals. Intercrime helps the criminals against the police.

Mother: Now look here Aunts, this is my story and if I wish to make Tara King sky-blue pink, I will!

Mother: We had a lucky break.
Harriet: Ah, I was waiting for one of those.

Dunbar: Mr. Steed. You should be dead.

Mother: (re. Tara) Determined to grit her teeth, keep a stiff upper lip, keep her back to the wall and charge fearlessly forward...
Harriet: That's anatomically impossible!

Mother: An impasse was reached.
Georgina: What's an impasse?
Mother: It is...
Harriet: When they run out of plot!

Steed: Give the signal – 'Operation Britannia' – put all your art eggs in one basket – Colonel Corf's vaults – and then...

Dunbar: Anaesthetics. Tranquillisers. Hacksaw. Nylon Rope...Before going on a mission, each man would be issued with one of these survival kits...Phrase book in fifteen languages.
Osaka: (reading) 'I am on the run from the police. Kindly direct me to a suitable hideout'.

Harriet: Miss Christie and Mr. Erle Stanley Gardner never leave such loopholes.

Mother: I have run out...
Harriet: ...of ideas
Mother: ...of *breath*.

Harriet: It all ended happily ever after.
Mother: Naturally.
Harriet: But they *always* end like that.
Georgina: Couldn't we have a *downbeat* ending for once?

REQUIEM

Steed: Why don't you make yourself comfortable? Take off your nose!

Major Firth: Mother is dead.

Tara: Steed's childhood is simply littered with grand and stately houses.

Steed: The British can't lose the Battle of Trafalgar!
Miranda: Sorry, but I think they have.

Miranda: What do you think the chances are?
Steed: Depends on your knight.
Miranda: No, I meant about me.

Tara: Doctor! Come to congratulate me on my miraculous recovery?
Wells: I think you are about to have a relapse.

Mother: What a fantastic story! Dastardly plan. Fiendish!

TAKE-OVER

Steed: I'm going to the heart of the country, shooting, fishing, fine wine, good food, away from it all.

Grenville: Nothing compares with an English log fire for keeping out the chill of February.

Grenville: Circe works very hard at being a 'character', don't you, Circe my dear?

Bill: We haven't met, have we?
Grenville: No, never.
Laura: But you said…
Grenville: No, no, my dear – *you* said…

Grenville: Up until now everything has been civilised and quite delightful. Don't spoil it.

Sexton: It's awful coffee. It's not fresh. You'd think that people who lived in a house like this could at least afford fresh coffee.

Grenville: I can't bear raised voices. And hysteria in a man is very unbecoming.

Circe: I'm going to tell on you. What will you give me if I don't?

Sexton: February is an awful month for table setting. No garden flowers.

Grenville: You have a fine ear, Mr. Steed. I hope you hang on to it.

Circe: I spend all my money on new noses.
Steed: Well, everyone should have a hobby.

Circe: You ought to leave here, Mr. Steed. Fenton doesn't like you at all.

Grenville: (re. hunting trip) A hundred guineas for the first kill of the day.

Grenville: Do stay away from the marshy ground, won't you. You could get trapped in the mud and disappear.
Sexton: Without a trace.

Grenville: May the best man win.
Steed: Thank you. I intend to.
Grenville: Goodbye Mr. Steed.

Circe: When I was little I used to get the most awful pains in my head. I used to think how nice it would be if I could cut a little hole in the temple and take the hurting part out. That's why Fenton and I are so much alike. If anything hurts him or gets in his way, he just removes it.

Circe: It's nice to be nearly a genius when you're as pretty as I am.

Steed: I should have stayed in town. That's the problem with the country – nothing ever happens.

BIZARRE

Cordell: Did she fall or was she pushed?

Helen: A coffin. A dead man. A dead man in a coffin! A dead man who wasn't dead.

Happychap: Happychap.
Steed: Well, moderately.

Happychap: Really Mr. Steed, this morbid curiosity is verging on an obsession. If it's digging you're interested in, why not take up gardening?

Happychap: People like to feel a certain permanence about burial.

Happychap: But this is awful – simply awful! There's no body left!
Steed: The Great Grave Robbery.

Shaw: You don't actually have to get off the coach. We provide written summaries of every memorable experience you might have had in each city – so that you can impress your friends.

Mother: There's no night guard at Happy Meadows?
Steed: No. Well, why should there be? There's no reason to believe that the inhabitants are going anywhere!

Mother: It's an open and shut case. Open the grave. Shut the grave.

Steed: They say you can't buy your way to Paradise, but I aim to try.

Master: If you were dead, the world would not pursue you any further.

Master: Death is only the beginning, Mr. Steed.

Master: You won't live to regret it, I promise you.
Steed: I sincerely hope I do!

Mother: They'll be back. You can depend on it. They're unchaperoned up there!

SEASON 6 PRODUCTION ORDER

October 1967-March 1969

The Invasion of the Earthmen

The Curious Case of the Countless Clues

The Forget-Me-Knot

Split!

Get- A-Way!

Have Guns – Will Haggle

Look – (stop me if you've heard this one) But There Were These Two Fellers...

My Wildest Dream

Whoever Shot Poor George Oblique Stroke XR40?

All Done With Mirrors

You'll Catch Your Death

Super Secret Cypher Snatch

Game

False Witness

Noon Doomsday

Legacy of Death

PRODUCTION ORDER (continued)

October 1967-March 1969

They Keep Killing Steed

Wish You Were Here

Killer

The Rotters

The Interrogators

The Morning After

Love All

Take Me To Your Leader

Stay Tuned

Fog

Who Was That Man I Saw You With?

Pandora

Thingumajig

Homicide and Old Lace

Requiem

Take-Over

Bizarre

BIBLIOGRAPHY OF WORKS CONSULTED

The Avengers: Digitally Restored Special Edition: The Complete Series 2 (Optimum Classic/Studio Canal, 2010)

The Avengers: Digitally Restored Special Edition: The Complete Series 3 (Optimum Classic/Studio Canal, 2010)

The Avengers: Digitally Restored Special Edition: The Complete Series 4 (Optimum Classic/Studio Canal, 2010)

The Avengers: Digitally Restored Special Edition: The Complete Series 5 (Optimum Classic/Studio Canal, 2010)

The Avengers: Digitally Restored Special Edition: The Complete Series 6 (Optimum Classic/Studio Canal, 2010)

The Avengers: A Celebration (Marcus Hearn, Titan Books/Studio Canal, 2010)

Subversive Champagne: Beyond Genre in The Avengers: the Emma Peel Era (Rodney Marshall, Amazon, 2013)

Adventure & Comic Strip: Exploring Tara King's The Avengers (Rodney Marshall, Amazon, 2013)

Bright Horizons: The Monochrome World of Emma Peel: The Avengers on film Volume 1 (Amazon, 2014)

Mrs. Peel, We're Needed: The Technicolor World of Emma Peel: The Avengers on film Volume 2 (Amazon, 2014)

The Strange Case of the Missing Episodes: The Lost Stories of The Avengers Series 1 (Hidden Tiger, 2013)

Bowler Hats and Kinky Boots: The Unofficial and Unauthorised Guide to The Avengers (Michael Richardson, Telos, 2014)

The Avengers Forever! (David K Smith, copyright 1996-2008)
theavengers.tv/forever

Le Monde des Avengers (*theavengers.fr*)

Mrs. Peel – We're Needed! The Avengers 1961-1977 (Piers Johnson)
dissolute.com.au/the-avengers-tv-series/

Delightful, diabolical debate with fellow *Avengers* can be found at:
avengersfanforum.s2.bizhat.com

Any questions, feedback or criticism about this book can be directed to me at:
rodneymarshall628@btinternet.com

AVENGERLAND REGAINED

Reassessing *The New Avengers*:
The Avengers on film: Volume 4

edited by Rodney Marshall and JZ Ferguson

The Avengers was a unique, genre-defying television series which blurred the traditional boundaries between 'light entertainment' and disturbing drama. It was a product of the constantly-evolving 1960s yet retains a timeless charm.

The creation of *The New Avengers*, in 1976, saw John Steed re-emerge, alongside two younger co-leads: sophisticated action girl Purdey and Gambit, a 'hard man' with a soft centre. The cultural context had changed – including the technology, music, fashions, cars, fighting styles and television drama itself – but *Avengerland* was able to re-establish itself. Nazi invaders, a third wave of cybernauts, Hitchcockian killer birds, a sleeping city, giant rat, a deadly health spa, a skyscraper with a destructive mind…The 1970s series is, paradoxically, both NEW yet also part of the rich, innovative AVENGERS history.

Avengerland Regained draws on the knowledge of a broad range of experts and fans as it explores the final vintage of *The Avengers*.

"*The Avengers* challenged audiences to enjoy art beyond the ordinary." (Matthew Lee)

Published: May 2015

Printed in Great Britain
by Amazon.co.uk, Ltd.,
Marston Gate.